SECOND EDITION

CRUISES

Selecting, Selling, and Booking

Juls Zvoncheck, CTC

REGENTS / PRENTICE HALL
Englewood Cliffs, New Jersey 07632

Library of Congress Cataloging-in-Publication Data

Zvoncheck, Juls.
    Cruises : selecting, selling, and booking / Juls Zvoncheck.—2nd ed.
        p.   cm.
    Includes index.
    ISBN 0–13–192691–8
    1. Ocean travel.   2. Cruise ships.   I. Title.
G550.Z86   1993
910.4′5—dc20   93–7594
                                                                 CIP

Acquisitions editor: Robin Baliszewski
Production supervision: Inkwell Publishing Services
Prepress buyer: Ilene Sanford
Manufacturing buyer: Edward O'Dougherty

 © 1993, 1988 by Regents / Prentice-Hall, Inc.
A Division of Simon & Schuster
Englewood Cliffs, New Jersey 07632

Printed in the United States of America

10   9   8   7   6   5   4   3   2   1

ISBN 0-13-192691-8

Prentice-Hall International (UK) Limited, *London*
Prentice-Hall of Australia Pty. Limited, *Sydney*
Prentice-Hall Canada, Inc., *Toronto*
Prentice-Hall Hispanoamericana, S.A., *Mexico*
Prentice-Hall of India Private Limited, *New Delhi*
Prentice-Hall of Japan, Inc., *Tokyo*
Prentice-Hall of Southeast Asia Pte. Ltd., *Singapore*
Editoria Prentice-Hall do Brasil, Ltda., *Rio de Janeiro*

To

Holland America Line

*For pioneering travel agency sales staff education and
training programs, and cruise sales development and
promotion, via seminars-at-sea and ashore.*

CONTENTS

PREFACE

The cruise industry is still very much in a state of development and growth.

Each year, new cruise companies, ships of innovative design and size, and distinctive itineraries and exotic destinations are added to the expanding cruise sales inventories.

In principle, all cruise lines are alike; in practice, however, they are different. Standardization is not a cruise industry trademark. Each company has its own distinctive cruise product and programs, as well as reservations policies and practices.

Therefore, in-depth familiarity with the cruise industry in general, and with individual cruise lines in particular, is very necessary to be able to select, sell, and book the proper cruises for clients.

Ordinarily, a cruise sales agent is self-educated. Formal cruise education and training are not readily available. Too few cruise lines, if any, conduct educational/training seminars to enlighten sales agency personnel about the fundamentals of their operation.

The cruise industry itself is not in a position to provide a fully comprehensive training program. CLIA (Cruise Lines International Association), the lines' collective body, must be tactful with its own seminar curriculum to avoid offending any of its members. Therefore, its coverage of cruise product, programs, and practices is restricted.

An opportunity to attain a comprehensive familiarity with cruises and other sources of information is provided herein.

A look back is made to the early days of cruising and how the combining of shipboard traditions with modern concepts has made today's cruise a delight for both the vacationer and travel agent.

Chapter 2 contains a detailed description of the cruise product and the types of cruises being operated.

The anatomy of a cruise ship, support services, and fact sheets are described in Chapter 3.

Chapter 4 offers an insight into the types of staterooms, ratesheets, and deckplans.

Background information regarding the cruise market, booking inducements, cruise features, and selling techniques is furnished in Chapter 5.

Chapter 6 indicates supplemental sources of information and cruise familiarization trip opportunities.

And, finally, making the reservation, initial deposit, final payment, deducting the agent's commission, and the client's shipboard arrangements are covered in Chapter 7.

Additional graphic information is contained in the six appendices.

ACKNOWLEDGMENTS

The publisher and author gratefully acknowledge the following for materials reproduced in this text:

Carnival Cruise Lines—Festivale on page 55, and *Ecstasy* on page 71.

Celebrity Cruises—Zenith on page vii.

Clipper Cruise Line—Yorktown Clipper on page 15 and *Nantucket Clipper* on page 21.

Cunard Line—Sagafjord on page v and *Queen Elizabeth 2* on page 39.

Diamond Cruise Line—Radisson Diamond on page 16.

*Holland America Line—*Front cover and *Noordam* on page 1.

Norwegian Cruise Line—Southward on page 165.

Princess Cruises—Regal Princess on page 7 and *Star Princess* on page 47.

Royal Caribbean Cruise Line—Monarch of the Seas on page 10 and *Song of Norway* on page 69.

Windstar Cruises—Wind Song on page 31.

CHAPTER 1

The Cruise Industry
Yesterday, Today, and Tomorrow

A Look Backward

During the late nineteenth and early twentieth centuries, seventeen million European immigrants entered the United States through Ellis Island, a small island in New York Harbor, now transformed into a special immigration museum. This restoration and the celebration of the Statue of Liberty's Centennial reminded many Americans that their ancestors left their homes in distant lands and travelled by sea to the United States of America in search of freedom and a better life.

Many first- and second-generation Americans can recount the all but unbelievable tales about their grandparents', or parents', journey across the Atlantic. The men, women, and children who made those voyages were part of one of the most exciting and impressive periods in American history. For sheer drama, it compares very favorably with the arrival of the first colonists to American shores in the 1600s. In magnitude, it is overwhelming.

As more and more ships were built, they became larger, more comfortable, and even luxurious. These unique transatlantic liners were divided into three distinct classes—First Class, Cabin Class, and Tourist Class—thereby accommodating passengers of every socioeconomic level.

The section of the ship which carried hordes of poor immigrants was called steerage. We have often seen this dark and crowded space depicted

in films and illustrations. Steerage, by the way, received its name from its location in the area of the ship containing the steering apparatus. Confined to the holds or cargo compartments, steerage passengers did not have access to deck space for recreation or fresh air. Their accommodations were limited to a fenced-in area of cattle-like corrals or open areas marked with chalklines to indicate the amount of space allocated to each passenger. In reality, there were no sleeping quarters, as such, and no privacy whatsoever. Sanitation facilities did not exist. Such were the conditions and circumstances under which masses of immigrants travelled across the sea. Perhaps some of your ancestors travelled in steerage and recall their shipboard experiences with a measure of disbelief, but as a price worth paying to come to live in America.

Steerage-type conditions and accommodations existed until World War II. During this era, every European country with access to the sea had its own shipline operation to the United States. The officers and crew were of one nationality, engendering a sense of tremendous national pride in their ship and service. Sad to relate, however, few of the shiplines of this era remain.

Even our own United States Lines ceased operations a long time ago. Its superliner, the *United States*, set the speed record for crossing the North Atlantic—approximately three-and-one-half days. American Export Line used to sail her proud ships, *Constitution* and *Independence*, between New York and Italy. These ships, under their original names, are still in service for American Hawaii Cruises. Grace Line had a fleet of excellent ships, all painted white, featuring the luxurious 300-passenger *Santa Paula* and *Santa Rosa*, plus a number of smaller "Santas." Grace Line operated between New York and South America.

A contemporary operator in the same category of class and service, as well as destination, was Moore-McCormack Line. Its vessels were the *Argentina* and *Brazil*, both of which are still in service, under new names and ownership. On the West Coast, Matson Line, with the *Lurline, Mariposa,* and *Monterey,* served Hawaii, while American President Line operated a worldwide passenger service. Canada lost its national passenger service when the Canadian Pacific Line discontinued operations. The line's modern vessels, *Empress of Canada* and *Empress of England,* are kept in service by new owners.

It is surprising that most of the famous European steamship companies from the prosperous days of transatlantic travel no longer exist. For example, the truly fabulous French Line, with its fleet of legendary ships, such as the *Liberté, Normandie, Ile de France,* and the *France* (now the *Norway*), plus others, could not compete successfully in the new cruise age. Germany's Norddeutscher Lloyd operated two of the most popular ships, *Bremen* and *Europa.* In its heyday, the highly respected Swedish-American Line had such renowned ships as the *Gripsholm, Kungsholm,* and *Stockholm.* These quality vessels are still operational elsewhere. Italy had its Italian Line and such famous ships as the *Leonardo da Vinci, Michelangelo,* and *Raffaello* serving North America. The Greek Line featured the *Queen Anna Maria* and the *Olympia.* And Japan had its far-ranging Mitsui Line.

The port of New York was the hub of ship travel. There was so much ship activity in the port of New York that *The New York Times* had a special page devoted exclusively to shipping news. Liners remained in port for several days before making the return voyage. There was no rush for quick turnarounds, as there are today. Embarkations and debarkations were newsworthy events, with many famous people travelling to or from Europe.

The First Cruises

Beginning in the very late 1930s, an effort was made by some steamship companies to operate a few cruises, but the travelling public's reception to them was lukewarm. With the onset of World War II, cruises remained dormant. In the 1950s, immediately after World War II, there was a tremendous demand for transatlantic transportation. Families on both sides of the Atlantic wanted to be reunited and immigration continued apace, both to the United States and Canada. However, it was not until the second half of the 1950s that a substantial number of cruises out of New York were scheduled on a regular basis. Until that time, regular cruise programs were operated primarily out of Miami to the Bahamas and West Indies.

On May 3, 1951, Furness-Withy became the first shipline to operate a permanent weekly cruise program, from New York to Bermuda, with the ships *Queen of Bermuda* and *Ocean Monarch.* A notable feature of these ships was that all the staterooms were equipped with private bath and toilet facilities. Another exclusive cruise operation was begun by Incres Line, for whom Home Lines acted as general sales agents. It operated a weekly cruise from New York to the Bahamas with a ship named *Nassau.* Eventually, Home Lines committed itself fully to operating weekly cruises to Bermuda and the Bahamas.

The early cruises out of New York invariably were operated during the transatlantic off-season, the winter months; the cruise season began at

Christmas and lasted into March. The two- and three-week Christmas cruise and the heart-of-winter February departures highlighted the season. These cruises were studies in high fashion and social excitement, and prominent business people and professionals made up the passenger lists. Cruises departed late at night, anywhere from 10:00 P.M. until midnight, and this gave them an aura of excitement and romance. Embarkation became a gala event and was marked by elegance and high spirits as passengers and friends seeing them off arrived in a happy, festive mood. Women came aboard dressed in full-length fur coats and gowns and sparkling jewelry. It was a veritable high fashion show. Newspaper reporters and photographers also were on hand to record and report on the rich and the famous. Sunday editions carried the photos and stories. A cruise experience was becoming a definite vacation attraction, even though the season generally was limited to the winter months.

New, modern passenger transportation ships entered service in 1957, featuring comfort and convenience. Cabin Class was virtually eliminated: Tourist Class staterooms were upgraded extensively, and each stateroom included private facilities, thereby making them acceptable for cruising.

Among the leaders was Holland America Line with the new *Statendam*. Although this was built as a Tourist Class vessel in 1957, the quality of her accommodations was ideally suited for cruises. Then, in 1959, came the *Rotterdam*, a larger ship with both First and Tourist Classes. Passengers could go from one class to the other by way of a unique, circular stairway. Home Lines was not far behind with their *Oceanic*, which began full-time cruise service in 1965.

In the early days of cruising, some clients were so affluent they would send their private interior decorators to the ship beforehand to arrange their staterooms to their own design and comfort. Some passengers would even supply their own steaks, orange juice, and water, or pillows, mattresses, and blankets! Instead of suitcases or trunks, large stand-up wardrobe containers were delivered to the ship a day or two before departure. The contents were unpacked, wrinkle-free, and placed in the wardrobe closets and dresser drawers. On sailing day, passengers simply walked on board knowing everything would be ready for them.

The cruise ship provided the ultimate in amenities, service, and cuisine, as well as total individual attention. Shoes could be placed outside the cabin door in the evening and would be perfectly shined by morning. At night, the passengers' sleepwear was neatly laid out on the bed and the bedcover turned down. This is still done on luxury ships today. Traditionally, staterooms were serviced by a steward *and* a stewardess, so that there was a great degree of intimacy in the services rendered; on today's ships, either a steward or stewardess is assigned to each cabin.

Into the Jet Age

The North Atlantic was the last ocean to be conquered by air. Distance, unreliable weather, and strong prevailing westerly winds made passenger air travel impossible until reliable, long-range aircraft could be built. On May 20, 1939, Pan American Airways' *Yankee Clipper* made the first transatlantic flight, carrying seventeen passengers and the U.S. mail. However, it was not until October 26, 1958 that Pan American inaugurated regularly scheduled transatlantic passenger service.

By 1960, eleven other airlines had started jet service. As a result, the demand for ship transportation dwindled dramatically. Travelling by ship to or from Europe took six or seven days. By jet, the trip took six or seven hours. The knockout blow came on January 22, 1970, when the 747 Jumbo Jet made its first flight from New York to London, carrying the unbelievable total of five hundred passengers! Once the jet airplane was used regularly for transatlantic passenger service, most shiplines were forced to abandon passenger transportation services and enter the cruise field.

During the next fifteen years many of the passenger steamship companies could not make a successful transition to full-time cruising. Some ships were unable to provide sufficient cabins with facilities, essential for attracting cruise clients. Some claimed the American market was not yet sufficiently developed to respond to such year-round vacation attractions. Operating costs were a major factor also. Since cruising was a first-class-only type of operation, a higher quality of cuisine, service, and entertainment had to be provided. To do so, additional crew members were required to furnish and sustain such high standards.

From that remarkable and romantic generation of North Atlantic passenger steamship companies and early cruise operators, only Cunard Line, Cunard/Norwegian American Line, and Holland America Line remain today. However, many vessels of that era are still operated under different names or by new owners in all parts of the world. Some of them have been completely refitted, from the hull out, while others have undergone drastic renovations to improve their attractiveness. But, as the new generation of modern cruise ships enters service, the older vessels are slowly disappearing from the cruise scene.

Today's Cruise—An American Vacation Phenomenon

The modern cruise vacation concept is barely a generation old, but it is already showing great maturity. Only in the last twenty-five years has cruising begun to develop into a unique, all-inclusive vacation alternative. In the process, many obstacles had to be overcome; some of them still exist.

The early cruise markets were located mainly in the larger metropolitan areas in the Northeast. Most cruise passengers came from Boston, New York, Philadelphia, Baltimore, and Washington, D.C. For them, the port of New York was readily accessible by automobile or train. The lack of convenient transportation made it difficult for people from secondary and distant metropolitan market areas to participate. As a result, people residing outside the Northeast corridor were unfamiliar with the potential of cruising.

In the late 1950s and early 1960s, only a few travel agencies existed. Those that did handled ethnic immigration business almost exclusively. Travel agents were not involved in the pleasure travel business. They did no vacation sales development or promotion whatsoever.

The speed and relative economy of jet travel forced the cruise companies to reevaluate their operations. It was no longer economically viable for them to maintain a seasonal operation, serving the social elite; instead they had to make cruises attractive to the average vacationer. This was not

Regal Princess—70,000 tons/1,590 passengers.

an easy task. Many old-line shipowners clung to their traditionally high standards on board ship in order to continue to outperform their competitors. They were reluctant to compromise their reputations for excellence. To them, that would have been a backward step. They faced a dilemma, to say the least.

A major part of that dilemma was educating the public. The potential new cruiser was generally skeptical about a shipboard vacation. Seasickness, rough seas (hurricanes, particularly), restricted living quarters, the Bermuda Triangle, fear of boredom, memories of World War II servicemen who were transported in overcrowded ships or who served in the U.S. Navy, the stories about immigrant travel—all were sources of sales resistance that had to be overcome. Even some of the positive aspects of shipboard life disillusioned and discouraged would-be cruisers. For some, the formality aboard ship was frightening; others were put off by the thought of meeting and associating with sophisticated "big-city folk."

Today, however, there is a tremendous awareness of cruising among the entire American public, due in large part to the popular television series, *Love Boat*, based on shipboard life. Cruise operators have not yet fully capitalized on this vast potential. The marketing process continues to develop rather slowly. The advent of new cruise companies and the introduction of new ships is placing the cruise vacation concept into proper perspective. Great strides have been made to qualify and quantify the cruise as an experience to be enjoyed by everyone. A cruise can now stand on its own merit, without being compared to other vacation alternatives, as in the past. Today's cruise is indeed a vacation phenomenon. It is available, affordable, and accessible. Most importantly, it can be a totally pleasurable and gratifying personal experience.

Itinerary choices are varied and numerous; some popular ones are offered by a number of cruise lines simultaneously. Cruises range in length from six hours to over one hundred days and depart from at least 34 American and Canadian cities, plus 14 Caribbean islands, as well as Mexico. Free air passage, or a small air add-on charge, make accessibility to all the port cities readily feasible. Locally, bus service might be provided directly to and from the pier. Upon arrival at the port city air terminal, meet-and-greet service is provided to escort passengers and their baggage directly to the ship and vice versa. Actually, the travel agent can arrange door-to-door service.

The quality of services, facilities, programs, and activities on board is enough to satisfy the most reluctant, or demanding, of clients. Passengers are catered to every hour of the day in one way or another. Personal attention, courtesy, and graciousness are shown each passenger, at all times, no matter what fare was paid.

The average American has been influenced by the fast pace of today's living standards—television with its instantaneousness, VCRs, packaged and/or fast-food service, and so on—and in the process readily accepts informality as a relative norm. On a cruise, however, the graciousness of shipboard life can be a unique and contrasting experience.

Informal wearing apparel is acceptable on almost all ships during daytime hours. Evenings, a jacket and tie or just a jacket is in order on some ships. On others, sports shirts for men and slacks for women are permitted at all times. On a seven-day cruise, two evenings ordinarily will be devoted to optional formal dress, that is, dinner jacket or tuxedo, or a jacket and tie. The average American has few opportunities to dress formally and a cruise can fulfill the desire to do so. Casino gambling, dancing to Big Band sounds (even a big-name band itself) and disco, together with sophisticated professional entertainment, closed-circuit color television, and movies all help to make a cruise vacation very satisfying.

Calls at ports are made during daylight hours, allowing passengers to go sightseeing and shopping or to pursue other activities ashore. Tour arrangements can be made on board at a nominal cost. On major cruises, tour reservations are made at the time of booking. For cruise passengers who wish to play tennis or golf or who want to enjoy the local beaches, arrangements often can be made on board ship.

Whether it is a cruise to Nowhere, to Bermuda or the Bahamas, up the Saguenay and St. Lawrence Rivers, to New England, through the inland waterways of the United States and Canada, to the Caribbean Islands, to Central and South America, down the Amazon and Orinoco Rivers, to Mexico, Alaska, Hawaii, Tahiti, even the Arctic and Antarctic regions, or— the grandest cruise of all—around the world, there is a destination to satisfy every vacationer. People from every walk of life—cosmopolites and sub-urbanites, exurbanites and ruralists—are represented on cruise passenger lists. The increasing popularity and appreciation of the cruise vacation concept, the product and programs, plus the convenience, make the cruise vacation an American phenomenon.

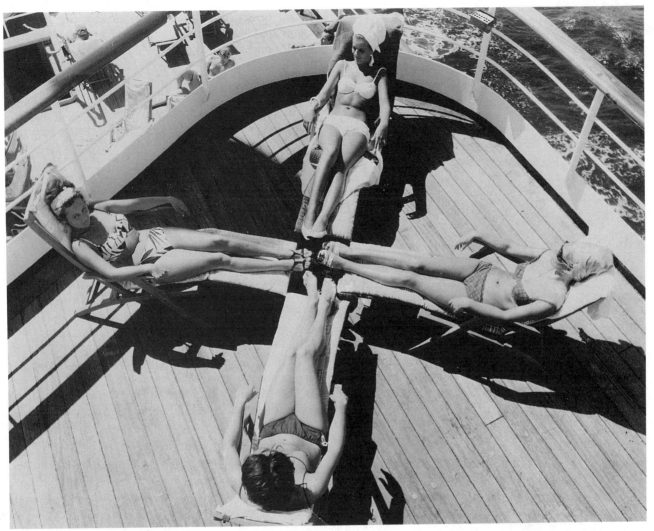

Basking in the sun and enjoying light conversation with friends in a totally relaxing atmosphere.

Combining Cruise Traditions with Modern Concepts

The lure of a cruise vacation once was based on the traditional degree of formality aboard a ship. Cruising has now entered a new era in which former cruise standards have been joined and/or replaced by new product and destination concepts. The cruise industry suffered from a "cruise-is-a-cruise" type of marketing syndrome, even though all cruise lines' total products were not necessarily equal. With the development of several individually identifiable concepts, such as recreation, adventure and theme cruises, among others, cruise selection has now reached a "cross-over" point.

The current fleet of popular cruise ships numbers about 165. These include some holdovers from the transatlantic era, the fast-growing generation of modern vessels, both in the luxury and conventional cruise classes, and a new category of recreational and adventure/explorer ships.

Most of these ships operate principally in North American waters, but an increasing number of them are being stationed in other parts of the world.

Still ranking at the top are:

Cunard Line's *Queen Elizabeth 2, Sagafjord,* and *Vistafjord.*

Royal Viking Line's *Royal Viking Sun* and *Royal Viking Queen.*

The *Crown Princess, Regal Princess,* and *Star Princess* of Princess Cruises.

The *Crown Odyssey, Royal Odyssey,* and *Golden Odyssey* of Royal Cruise Line.

The *Nieuw Amsterdam, Noordam,* and *Rotterdam* of Holland America Line.

From time to time, these lines operate cruises throughout the world. Other luxury ships include Royal Caribbean Cruise Line's superliners *Majesty of the Seas, Monarch of the Seas,* and *Sovereign of the Seas.* These established companies have now been joined by deluxe cruise operators such as Crown Cruise Line, Crystal Cruises, Diamond Cruises, Renaissance Cruises, Seabourn Cruise Line, and Seaquest Cruises.

The most amazing success story is Carnival Cruise Lines. Adopting a "Fun Ship" philosophy and designing their ships to accommodate the wishes of the recreation-minded vacationers, Carnival has led the industry in marketing the modern cruise experience.

Some lines operate year-round programs to the same destinations, while others alternate operations seasonally in various geographic areas.

Many of the older luxury vessels, including the *Queen Elizabeth 2,* have been renovated and refitted, making them virtually new ships, to meet

Royal Caribbean Cruise Line's *Monarch of the Seas.*

Monarch of the Seas Fun Facts.

Royal Caribbean Cruise Line's newest ship, *Monarch of the Seas*, is 880 feet long, measures approximately 75,000 tons, and can carry a maximum of 2,766 passengers. But how big is big?

* *Monarch* contains 14,000 tons of steel (twice that of the Eiffel Tower and 70 times that of the Statue of Liberty).
* Over 800 miles of electrical cable run through *Monarch*, which is almost enough to stretch from Miami to *Monarch*'s homeport of San Juan.
* In addition, *Monarch* contains over 40 miles of piping, 4 miles of corridors, 20,000 electrical fixtures, 2,000 telephones, and over 150,000 square feet of open decks (the size of 50 tennis courts).
* The 2.1 million square feet of steel that were used in *Monarch*'s construction is the same area as 42 football fields.
* There are more than 16,000 square feet of galley area.
* *Monarch*'s 710,000 square feet of interior space is equal to five times the interior space of RCCL's six-story headquarters buildings in Miami.
* *Monarch* has a total volume of more than 7.5 million cubic feet, which is over three and a half times as large as the huge silver geodesic sphere at Disney's EPCOT Center in Florida.
* Four Pielstick main engines generate 29,700 horsepower (the power of 432 Honda Civics).
* Auxiliary engines generate more than 13 million watts of power, which is enough electrical power to supply the needs of a town of 10,000.
* Two 1,500-horsepower bow thrusters equal 272 riding lawn mowers (a line of mowers a quarter of a mile long).
* The desalinization equipment is capable of producing 700 tons of potable water daily or enough for one adult to take 11,255 showers. That's a shower a day for more than 30 years.
* The *Monarch*'s ice machines are capable of producing 18.5 tons of ice daily, or enough to cool over a half million drinks a day.
* *Monarch of the Seas* is more than 170 feet high, the same height as the Statue of Liberty.

competitive standards. Others underwent lesser renovations. Often, public lounges were enlarged or added to accommodate more passengers. Cabins were modernized and new ones added wherever possible. Age and size can reflect the types of facilities and staterooms on board. Certain areas on some of the older ships could not be altered—the size of staterooms, for example, or public deck space.

These luxury ships pride themselves on offering fine amenities, such as Rosenthal china, crystal glassware, crisp linens, and sterling silver utensils. They often have the most skilled chefs—frequently members of the Confrères de la Cháine des Rotisseurs, the by-invitation-only society of renowned world chefs. They also retain the eight-course dinner and the

Windjammer Barefoot Cruise *Yankee Clipper*.

flamboyance that goes with the preparation of exciting dishes, such as crepes suzette, at tableside.

The traditional graciousness and elegance of cruising are being diminished somewhat by the new generation of ships that provide a practical, resort-type facility and emphasize recreation and informality. Though few in number, some leading companies are creating, developing, and expanding the cruise market with this new recreational concept of cruising.

Physically, cruise ships are making great strides both in size and design. On the outside, the appearance of the luxury-type ships has not greatly altered; for example, open deck space for sitting and walking is still amply available. But new ships, built to provide short-cruise service, are maximizing the use of space internally, and they are receiving instant acceptance. These ships are losing the traditional outward appearance, with totally solid sides, squared aft decks and steel-enclosed forward sections. Even the traditional term *steamship* will soon be passé, as more and more ships become propelled with regular engines. Thrusters have eliminated the need for tugboats, as ships can dock and depart easily. Virtually gone is the use of the term *flagship*, to designate the main vessel of the fleet. Also, *Commodore* is rarely, if ever, used to identify the senior captain or commander of the flagship. The titles *Chief Steward* and *Chief Purser* are

The "Ain't Misbehavin'" disco aboard Royal Caribbean's *Monarch of the Seas*, will use computer programming, fiber optics, curtains of revolving light, and glowing light columns to create spectacular audio/visual effects.

beginning to disappear, as well. Funnel colors and logos, which used to be familiar identifying symbols, in time will be used again.

Many innovative design concepts are being used by all new vessels. For example, showroom (nightclub) lounges now have seating capacities for up to 1,000 guests. The traditional luxury ships have a more sophisti-

The dramatic five-deck "Centrum" aboard Royal Caribbean Cruise Line's *Monarch of the Seas* features glass elevators, balconied walls, sweeping bronze staircases, a luminous mirrored ceiling, and splashing fountains.

cated entertainment program than the new resort ships, which feature exciting Las Vegas-type presentations. Casinos are becoming steadily larger, some now capable of accommodating 400 players. Dining rooms are now two-tiered and include booths, a deviation from tradition. The disco also is a major facility, accommodating literally hundreds of passengers. This is in sharp contrast to the small rooms set aside on the older ships for this purpose. On the other hand, the very large theater is a more modest, although still quite ample, size. Some ships have a permanent pizza parlor, snack bar, or ice cream parlor.

All new ships have larger, dramatic observatory-type lounges, some with as much as a 270-degree panoramic view of the sea. Royal Caribbean Cruise Lines' *Sovereign of the Seas* features a five-story, center-ship lobby atrium, with twin, glass-walled elevators, fountains, large plants, and other attractions.

Everything on board is now computerized. From signing for a drink at the bar to a purchase in the gift shop—every transaction is automatically recorded and charged to the passenger's shipboard account.

Going beyond the shipboard product, some cruise lines call at their own islands for recreational purposes; others operate their own resort hotels. One line is developing a major resort for the exclusive use of its passengers; it will include individual beaches for beginner, intermediate, and advance snorkelers. Permanently stationed 250-passenger boats (called tenders) will operate between the ships anchored offshore and the resort. Still another tender will have a stern-mounted, waterline sports deck and a large glass bottom for viewing coral formations. Old cruise traditions have met their rival modern counterparts—they will prove to be compatible.

The Future of Cruising

Today's cruise ships vary in size from 100 tons to 75,000 tons, and can accommodate from 64 to 2,766 passengers. Table 1-1 shows a breakdown of the number of ships in each category, according to size.

TABLE 1-1
Cruise ships according to size.

Tonnage	Number of Ships*	Average Passenger Capacity
70,000–75,000	10	2,150
60,000–70,000	2	1,660
50,000–60,000	6	1,310
40,000–50,000	14	1,369
30,000–40,000	16	1,062
20,000–30,000	25	811
10,000–20,000	31	566
1,000–10,000	30	147
Under 1,000	16	82

*Does not include daytime-only cruises.

In the late 1980s, a new type of cruise ship began operating in the inland waterways of the American Far West, Midwest, East Coast, and

The *Yorktown Clipper*'s small size and maneuverability allow her to take passengers to seldom-visited areas along Florida's Gulf Coast where big cruise ships cannot go.
Photo Courtesy Clipper Cruise Line

Canada, as well as among the remote islands of the West Indies. Special exploration- and expedition-type attractions, including ecocruises, along with the traditional panoramic and historic routes, are included in the itineraries. American Canadian/Caribbean Line, Clipper Cruise Line, and Special Expeditions are prominent operators.

These yacht-like vessels offer first-class accommodations and service, some in the deluxe luxury category. Having a shallow draft, they can navigate the remotest of waterways. These ships remain in sight of land at all times, docking overnight at downtown marinas, instead of commercial piers. Excluded from this group are the steamboat-type vessels plying the Mississippi River.

Another exclusive category of small luxury cruise ships is operated by Cunard Sea Goddess, Club Med, Renaissance Cruises, and Windstar Sail Cruises. They provide the ultimate in comfort, convenience, service, and cuisine, as well as destinations.

For example, the *Seabourn Pride* has a fold-out water sports marina extending directly from the stern of these ships, providing the opportunity for sailboarding and snorkelling, as well as ski-boating and motor boats for certified divers. Seabourn's vessels have still another unique feature: an underwater viewing room, made possible by two thick plates of glass in the outer hull where high-powered lights are focused to enhance the view and attract sea creatures. This room accommodates 16 viewers at a time. Guests can also tune in to such activity via closed-circuit television in each suite.

These vessels are scheduled seasonally in such diverse areas as Alaska, Western Europe and the Mediterranean, Japan, East Asia, the Caribbean, and Polynesia.

The SSC *Radisson Diamond*—a revolutionary new cruise ship design.

Windstar Sail Cruises developed a still different type of cruise ship, combining sails with modern engines for propulsion, and was followed by Club Med and Star Clippers. Tall Ship Adventures has restored one of the few remaining authentic tall ships, as did Windjammer Barefoot Cruises.

No sooner did the sailing ships make their appearance than another cruise ship design was introduced. The SSC *Radisson Diamond* is being hailed as the most innovative cruise ship concept of the twenty-first century. It is the largest twin-hull ship ever built: 19,000 tons and 354-passenger capacity. The letters "SSC" stand for *semi-submersible craft*. Its propulsion machinery is housed in submerged hulls beneath the water line. This vessel and its sister ships will be marketed to the most upscale segment of the cruise market.

In 1992, the 13 newest entries into cruise service ranged in size from 3,025 tons to 73,941 tons and from 180- to 2,354-passenger capacities. They included:

	Tonnage	Passenger Capacity
Majesty of the Seas, Royal Caribbean Cruise Line	73,941	2,354
Statendam, Holland America Line	55,000	1,256
CostaClassica, Costa Cruise Lines	50,000	1,300
Zenith, Celebrity Cruises	47,500	1,374
Dreamworld, Norwegian Cruise Line	41,000	1,246
Royal Majesty, Majesty Cruises	32,400	1,056
CostaAllegra, Costa Cruise Lines	30,000	800
Crown Jewel, Crown Cruise Line	20,000	820
Radisson Diamond, Diamond Cruises	19,000	354
Royal Viking Queen, Royal Viking Line	10,000	212
Club Med II, Club Med	10,000	386
Renaissance VIII, Renaissance Cruises	4,500	114
Star Clipper, Star Clippers	3,025	180

Nine new ships will enter cruise service in 1993/1994:

	Tonnage	Passenger Capacity
Sensation, Carnival Cruise Lines	70,000	2,600
Fascination, Carnival Cruise Lines	70,000	2,600
Maasdam, Holland America Line	55,000	1,266
Ryndam, Holland America Line	55,000	1,266
CostaRomantica, Costa Cruise Line	50,000	1,300
Windward, Norwegian Cruise Line	41,000	1,246
Crown Dynasty, Crown Cruise Line	20,000	820
Radisson Ruby, Diamond Cruises	19,000	354
Radisson Sapphire, Diamond Cruises	19,000	354

The major ports of embarkation for Pacific cruises include:

Acapulco, Mexico	San Diego, Cal.
Honolulu, Hawaii	San Francisco, Cal.
Los Angeles, Cal.	San Jose, Costa Rica, Central America
Papeete, Tahiti	Vancouver, British Columbia
Portland, Oreg.	

Along the Mississippi/Ohio/Cumberland/Tennessee Rivers, the ports are:

Chattanooga, Tenn.	Nashville, Tenn.
Cincinnati, Oh.	New Orleans, La.
Memphis, Tenn.	Pittsburgh, Penn.
Minneapolis/St. Paul, Minn.	St. Louis, Miss.

In the Northeast Quadrant, passengers can embark at:

Baltimore, Md.	Norfolk, Va.
Boston, Mass.	Philadelphia, Penn.
Charleston, S.C.	Portland, Mn.
Charlottetown, Prince Edward Island (Canada)	Quebec City, Quebec
Montreal, Quebec	Warren, R.I.
New York, N.Y.	Washington, D.C.

In the Southeast Quadrant:

Charleston, S.C.	Palm Beach, Fla.
Fort Lauderdale, Fla.	Port Canaveral, Fla.
Jacksonville, Fla.	Port Everglades, Fla.
Miami, Fla.	Tampa, Fla.

In the Caribbean area:

Antigua, BWI	Manaus, Brazil
Aruba, NA	Montego Bay, Jamaica
Belize, Central America	Nassau, Bahamas
Bridgetown, Barbados	San Juan, PR
Freeport, Bahamas	St. Maarten, WI
Fort-de-France, Martinique	St. Thomas, USVI
Grenada, BWI	Tortola, BVI
Guadeloupe, FWI	

Appendix A lists the various cruise lines, their addresses, phone numbers, fleets, ports of embarkation, lengths of cruises, and destination areas. This listing helps associate ship names with their cruise lines, as well as the ports of call involved.

REVIEW QUESTIONS

1. What circumstance prompted the rapid growth and development of ship travel?

   _____

   _____

2. What was steerage? Describe it.

   _____

   _____

   _____

3. When was the first effort made to operate cruises? The second?

   _____

4. What shipline operated the first full-time cruise program? To where?

   _____   _____

5. Why and at what time of year were cruises initially operated out of New York?

   _____

   _____

6. When did new, modern passenger ships begin to enter cruise service? What significant improvements did they possess?

   _____

   _____

   _____

   _____

7. What effect did the onset of the jet airplane have on ship travel?

   _____

   _____

   _____

8. Why was the North Atlantic the last ocean to be conquered by air?

   _____

   _____

9. a. What significant event took place on January 22, 1970?

   _____

   b. What effect did that event have on the steamship companies?

   _____

   _____

10. What new cruise concept is being developed alongside the traditional?

    _____

    _____

    _____

11. Name some of the significant interior design changes in new ships.

_____

_____

12. Define the terms "flagship" and "Commodore."

_____

_____

13. What are some cruise lines offering beyond the shipboard cruise product?

_____

_____

14. How long has the modern cruise era been in existence?

_____

15. Where were the original cruise markets mainly located? Why?

_____

_____

16. Describe the travel agencies of the 1950s and 1960s.

_____

_____

17. Why did cruise operators have to compromise their original shipboard standards to entice more passengers?

_____

_____

18. Initially, cruising encountered sales resistance. Why, and how was it overcome?

_____

_____

_____

19. Describe the dress codes allowed on board cruise ships.

_____

_____

20. At what time of year are most cruise ships operating in the Caribbean?

_____

21. What are the popular seasons for each of the following destinations?

Bermuda: _____ Alaska: _____

New England/Canada: _____ Mexico: _____

22. When do major (interocean) cruises depart the United States? Why?

_____

_____

CHAPTER 2

Living, Dining, and Having Fun on Board

The Cruise Product

The cruise product contains all the ingredients for a fulfilling vacation experience: transportation (air and sea), living accommodations, all meals, personalized service, entertainment (formal and informal), ports of call, and such facilities as a gymnasium, game room, lounges, disco, swimming pool, deck chairs, and library/writing room.

Accommodations

Living quarters on a ship are called staterooms, cabins, or just rooms. Officially, *stateroom* is a term used exclusively to denote a room on a ship. *Cabin* is a nautical term, perhaps derived from the French *cabine*, meaning a small room on a ship for the private use of one or more persons, distinguishing it from accommodations used by the crew and steerage occupants.

All cruise ships provide staterooms for single, double, triple, and quadruple occupancy. In most cases, staterooms are equipped with twin beds. Third and fourth persons are accommodated in upper (Pullman) berths. In very rare instances, a fifth person might be berthed in a cabin; if so, it will be on a folding cot. Occasionally double, queen-size, and Murphy beds will be available. Another exception: two ships provide a "three-on-the-floor" sleeping arrangement; that is, a king-size bed and convertible sofa bed.

In general, there are at least seven types of staterooms available, but all ships do not provide each of them. There is no standardization of descriptive names, either, although several lines do use the same terms to describe their own rate categories. For example, some lines use the term "suite" to indicate their top-rated stateroom and "deluxe" to describe their next four rate categories. Another line uses "deluxe" for its top three rate categories.

It is very important, therefore, to become familiar with the various types of staterooms, in order to avoid any possible confusion that would result from using one line's descriptive term when discussing another line. (We will examine stateroom selection in detail in Chapter 4.)

Staterooms range from luxury split-level suites and/or penthouse suites to economy cabins, consisting of a lower bed and upper berth. Applicable rates vary, of course, depending on the size and location of the stateroom. Please note: *No matter what rate is paid, each and every passenger equally enjoys the use of ALL the ship's facilities, entertainment, meals, and so on.*

Basically, all staterooms have such standard facilities as clothes closets (one per passenger), a dresser, make-up or vanity table, bathtub and/or shower, washstand, and toilet. Rooms are air-conditioned, with individual thermostatic controls. Every cabin is equipped with a telephone for ship-board communication. Ship-to-shore calls direct from the stateroom are possible on some ships; on others, such calls are made from a phone booth located near the Radio Room.

More and more shiplines are placing color television sets for closed-circuit viewing in each stateroom. Programming includes daily news shows, movies, ship information, daily activities notes, shore excursion details, taped sporting events, and the ship's own live entertainment shows. Music channels, including stereo, are provided.

Meals

Breakfast, lunch, and dinner are served on a regular, scheduled basis in the main dining room. Some ships have two dining rooms of equal standards. Meals are served at two sittings (called seatings) on all major cruise ships, except for Royal Viking's *Sea*, *Star*, and *Sky*, and the *Sagafjord* and *Vistafjord*, which can accommodate all passengers at one sitting. Tables for two, four, six, and eight are available. (More information on dining room arrangements appears in Chapters 3 and 7.)

Additionally, a Lido Restaurant is operated on some ships for casual breakfast/brunch and lunch. Where a Lido Restaurant is not available, the brunch and buffets are available in a lounge area or on deck. An early bird breakfast is served around 6:00 or 6:30 A.M. A continental breakfast, usually consisting of juice, coffee, and Danish, can be enjoyed in the stateroom upon request. This service varies with each line. Brunch is served to late risers through midmorning and a midafternoon snack is provided as well.

The popular midnight buffet is offered nightly and is a tradition on most lines. On cruises of seven days or longer, a special show buffet also is staged one night, usually the day of the Captain's Gala Dinner. Time is

Royal Cruise Lines

provided for picture taking, and passengers should be encouraged to take along their cameras. Words cannot describe the chefs' artistry or the food displays.

In between meals, pizza, hot dogs, hamburgers, etc., are served at various times, at a snack bar, pizzeria, or on deck. Passengers can make their own sundaes, as well, and, if desired, there is always room service to provide a bowl of fruit, cheese and crackers, or a complete dinner, if requested.

All of this dining and snacking is part and parcel of the cruise ticket. There is no extra charge for any of it! In fact, Table 2-1 could be a most effective sales tool.

TABLE 2-1
Comprehensive comparison of inclusive costs and features.

Resort Hotel vs. Cruise

Features	Nassau Resort	Cruise
Airfare	Yes	Yes
Airport Transfers	Yes/No	Yes
Room	Yes	Yes
Meals:		
Continental Breakfast	Extra	Yes
Breakfast	Yes	Yes
Brunch	Extra	Yes
Lunch	Extra	Yes
Dinner	Yes	Yes
Midnight Buffet (nightly)	No	Yes
Post-Midnight Show Snack	No	Yes
Snack Bar	Extra	Yes
Pizza Restaurant	Extra	Yes
Ice Cream Parlor	Extra	Yes
Room (food) Service	Extra	Yes
Service Charges:		
Gratuities	n/a	5% App.
Service on Meals	15%	n/a
Maid Service	Extra	n/a
Government Room Tax	6%	n/a
Energy Surcharge	Extra	n/a
Port Tax	n/a	Prepaid

For five-plus star service, the dining room aboard the *Vistafjord* offers fine dining, along with an ocean view.

⫸ APPETIZERS ⫷

Stuffed Mushrooms   **Plantation Pasta**

⫸ SOUPS ⫷

Andouille Sausage Gumbo

Green Split Pea Soup

⫸ SALADS ⫷

Marinated Tomato Mozzarella with Fresh Basil Vinaigrette and Fresh Dijon

♥ Steamboat Salad

⫸ ENTREES ⫷

Prime Rib with Yorkshire Pudding   **Chicken Dijon**

Seasoned, roasted prime rib of beef   *Skinless, boneless breast of chicken*
served in its own natural juices.   *in a dijon mustard sauce.*

Veal California   **♥ Baked Snapper**

Sautéed veal cutlet baked with tomato,   *Filet of snapper baked and served*
avocado, monterey jack cheese and   *with lemon-lime butter.*
served over a port wine sauce.

⫸ SUGGESTED WINES ⫷

Glen Ellen White Zinfandel   **Robert Mondavi Chardonnay**

Fresh, fruity and soft on the palate   *A dry crisp wine with a long finish.*
with a light sweet finish.

⫸ DESSERTS ⫷

Peach Cobbler   **Black Forest Cake**

Cheese Cake with Fruit Topping

♥ Seasonal Fresh Fruit

♥Sherbets and Assorted Ice Creams

⫸ BEVERAGES ⫷

Freshly Brewed Coffee   **Freshly Brewed Decaffeinated Coffee**

Iced and Hot Tea

Milk   **Soft Drinks**

♥ The chef has prepared this recipe for the "HEARTSMART" steamboater.

The evening menu of Delta Queen Steamboat Co.'s *Mississippi Queen*.

Entertainment

Entertainment provided on board a cruise ship is of the highest standard. It ranges from intimate piano music to Las Vegas-type revues or Broadway musicals. Famous entertainers perform in concert. Variety shows consist of professional singers, comedians, magicians, and specialty acts. Big Bands provide dance music as well as nostalgia. Additional dance music is found in all the lounges and a DJ holds down the fort in the disco. Movies are shown regularly in the theater, on closed-circuit television, or on large-screen sets in some lounges.

From time to time, cruise lines enhance their cruises by injecting special themes into their regular programs to entice passengers to their shiplines. With or without special themes, there are always countless organized activities offered in which passengers can participate or simply observe and be amused. In essence, each day is full and every evening is like a night on the town!

Shipboard Activities

Every morning, upon waking, passengers will find a copy of the day's shipboard program of activities and events. There is something scheduled for every hour of the day. Below is a comprehensive list of typical activities selected from the daily programs of several cruise lines:

Anniversary Parties. Whatever excuse there might be for an anniversary celebration, there will be a party.

Astrology and Horoscope Sessions.

Bingo! It is usually played for cash and/or gift prizes, some of major proportions.

Bridge. Lectures and instruction sessions are given by a bona fide bridge expert. There are duplicate and rubber matches and tournament play.

Captain's Gala Dinner. Usually held the next to the last day of the cruise. It is a formal and fantastic event.

Captain's Gala Welcome-Aboard Party. Normally held the second night out so passengers can meet the Captain and his staff. Drinks are "on the house," of course.

Country Fair. It is amazing how much flair can be brought to a country fair on board ship. A real treat!

Dancing. There is music for all types of dancing, and for every age group. Also, free group lessons: ballroom, Latin, disco, and other types of dancing. Private lessons also are available, for a fee.

Demonstrations. Included among the many offerings are flower arranging, hairdressing, ice sculpting, vegetable carving, etc.

Exercise Classes. Classes include aerobics, disco, Nautilus equipment, weight-training, yoga, jogging, walk-a-thon, walk-a-mile, and so on.

Fashion Shows. They are staged by the ship's boutique, and, while in port, by local shops.

Royal Cruise Lines

Fun Events. These include a passengers' Olympics, masquerade party, madhatter's party, jousting over the swimming pool, a male nightgown contest, a beer drinking contest. Passengers should be encouraged to bring along their own paraphernalia and costumes for participating in either or both events. Otherwise, materials are provided on board.

Games. Various types of board games are provided: backgammon, cribbage and domino tournaments, chess, checkers, mah-jongg, table tennis, shuffleboard, paddle tennis, and more.

Golf. A Golf Pro gives free group lessons. Private instruction is available, for a fee. A golf platform is available to practice driving balls into a net. Also a golf driving contest is held on the aft end of the ship. Some vessels even have a miniature golf course. Arrangements for golfing at the ports of call are possible, particularly aboard luxury vessels, and are made by the Golf Pro.

Grandma's Braggin' Party. For grandmothers only—an opportunity to boast and compare notes with their contemporaries.

Honeymooners' Party. A private affair for all the newlyweds on board.

Lectures. Professionals in the fields of business, banking, government, investments, history, geography, astronomy, space, politics, the arts, etc. are brought aboard to enlighten and educate passengers (mostly on longer, luxury cruises).

Service Clubs. A collective, informal meeting is conducted, presided over by the Cruise Director.

Singles Get-Together. An opportunity for single passengers to meet and have an enjoyable time.

Sing-Along. A spontaneous and informal gathering around a piano in one of the out-of-the-way lounges. An opportunity to sing the night away.

Talent Show (Passengers'). It is amazing how much good talent can be found among the passengers. Auditions are held to qualify.

Tours Aboard Ship. A tour of the Bridge is scheduled aboard just about every ship; a Galley tour is available only on certain vessels.

Trapshooting. This unique activity, for which there is a nominal charge, is conducted while the ship is at sea.

Travelogs. Lectures and films are shown on local and worldwide ports of call.

Ukulele Lessons. These are conducted aboard ships of American Hawaii Cruises, of course.

Video Games, Speed Reading Lessons, and **Handwriting Analysis.** These are among the wide variety of other activities to be found aboard ship.

The Cruise Staff

At the center of all the shipboard entertainment and activities is the Cruise Staff. The Cruise Director and his/her assistants coordinate all the programs on board. The Cruise Director on some ships might also be a professional performer, as well as serving as the Master of Ceremonies at all the major functions.

The Cruise Host/Hostess serves as a liaison between the passengers and ship's staff, and performs such other specific duties as called for in the day's program, such as serving as the official greeter at the formal welcome-aboard party and introducing passengers personally to the ship's captain and staff.

Cruise staff duties include conducting the various fun-and-games activities on deck and around the pool, plus Bingo, tournaments, and the like. Those with specialized skills offer instruction in dancing, card games, aerobics and use of gym equipment, computers, arts and crafts. The Cruise Staff's daily work schedule is a formidable one, encompassing a 20-hour day, from early morning to late night.

Types of Cruises

There is no popular, let alone official, classification of cruises, as yet. Perhaps that is because of the relative newness of the cruise vacation concept, coupled with the wide variety of cruise ships. However, most cruises fall into the following categories.

The Classic (Traditional) Cruise

The term *classic cruise* is based on the traditional concept of standards aboard large ocean-going ships of the past, which feature a marked degree of formality, epicurean dining, personalized service, and other forms of living in a grand style. Such paragons of shipboard life are still provided by certain cruise lines, among which are Crystal Cruises (*Crystal Harmony*), Cunard Line (*Queen Elizabeth 2, Sagafjord,* and *Vistafjord*), Holland America Line (*Rotterdam, Nieuw Amsterdam, Noordam,* and *Westerdam*), Princess Cruises (*Crown Princess, Regal Princess, Star Princess, Sky Princess,* and *Royal Princess*), Royal Cruise Line (*Crown Odyssey, Golden Odyssey,* and *Royal Odyssey*) and Royal Viking Line (*Royal Viking Queen* and *Royal Viking Sun*). Other luxury cruise operators (Seabourn Cruise Line, Sea Goddess, and Windstar Cruises) are described under "Special (Niche) Cruises."

These cruise lines and vessels have a genuine reputation for elegance and graciousness. The atmosphere aboard their ships is refined and formal, socially and culturally enriching, and esthetically satisfying. Accommodations are spacious and unusually comfortable. Also, the number of passengers is limited, so that the crew can provide the utmost in personal services. As a result, the per-diem cost is higher-than-average.

The clientele is generally sophisticated, professional, and primarily business-oriented. Their average age is over 55, and they are inclined to plan every aspect of the cruise. These passengers are greatly interested in the ports of call, which are often varied and exotic. Ordinarily, cruise lengths are two weeks and longer. Some of these ships operate worldwide cruises, as well as in such diverse areas as the North Cape, the Mediterranean, and the Far East.

Because passengers usually wish to familiarize themselves with destinations, scholars and lecturers are aboard to provide in-depth information about the historical and natural aspects of the places visited. Tours are also available and must be purchased prior to sailing. These clients usually are experienced travelers, who know precisely what accommodations they want, and only require the travel agent to arrange their specific needs.

The Deluxe Cruise

The *deluxe cruise* connotation applies to the same cruise lines operating classic (traditional) cruises. One difference is that the vessels will accommodate their full passenger capacity. These cruises retain a relative degree of formality and are ideal for those clients who cannot avail themselves of the longer classic cruise. At the same time, they include the fun-and-games aspects of modern cruising. For those reasons, deluxe cruises are quite attractive to the 45-and-up age group. Furthermore, they are more readily accessible, sailing primarily from various U.S. ports and affordable because of their shorter duration. Itineraries of up to two weeks are normally scheduled.

The Standard Cruise

For want of a better term, *standard* can best describe the category of cruises that contains all the basic ingredients of cruising and that has mass appeal. These cruises are "standard" because their regular three-, four-, and seven-day schedules are operated year-round. Ambience on board is easygoing, though not necessarily formal. Entertainment is fast-paced and flamboyant, and activities are such that passengers can become involved if they so desire. Public rooms are unusually spacious and varied.

Marketwise, these cruises have mass appeal, and so this segment of the cruise industry is the fastest-growing. Most of the newest and largest ships are included: Celebrity Cruises (*Horizon*, *Meridian*, and *Zenith*), Costa Cruise Lines (*CostaAllegra*, *CostaClassica*), Norwegian Cruise Line (*Dreamward*, *Norway*, *Seaward*, and *Windward*), Royal Caribbean Cruise Line (*Majesty of the Seas*, *Monarch of the Seas*, and *Sovereign of the Seas*).

In the forefront of this type of cruise operation is Carnival Cruise Lines, the largest cruise line in the world, whose fleet includes some of the largest and most innovative vessels afloat, like the *Ecstasy*, *Fantasy*, *Fascination*, and *Sensation*, advertised as the Fun Ships. Carnival Cruise Lines has made cruising universally popular. The marketing and promotion of their exciting shipboard ambience has developed a whole new generation of cruisers.

Special (Niche) Cruises

Niche is the term adopted by the cruise-selling industry to identify the category of out of the ordinary cruises. Their uniqueness lies in diverse types of vessels, shipboard standards, special facilities and accommodations, destinations and itineraries, special themes, and the like. (See Table 2-2.)

Sailing ships, for example, are a niche product that are increasing in number. They provide a shipboard ambience ranging from the totally informal—aboard Windjammer Barefoot Cruises, Star Clippers, and Tall Ship Adventures, where passengers can voluntarily participate in sailing and ship-handling—to Club Med and the luxury standards of Windstar Cruises.

The yacht-like ships of American Canadian/Caribbean Line, Clipper Cruise Line, and Special Expeditions offer a first-class product and feature

Windstar Cruises' 440-foot cruise ships feature the latest in high-tech, computerized sailing. Each of the four-masted ships—*Wind Star*, *Wind Song*, and *Wind Spirit*—can unfurl sails in less than two minutes.

distinctive itineraries. Sea Goddess and Seabourn Cruise Line provide the ultimate in luxury service and accommodation in the niche category.

Premier Cruise Line's Big Red Boats (*Starship Atlantic*, *Starship Oceanic*, and *Starship Majestic*) certainly occupy a special niche with their close relationship with Disneyworld.

Delta Steamboat Company's paddle-wheeled river boats, *Delta Queen* and *Mississippi Queen*, operate on the Mississippi/Cumberland/Ohio/Tennessee Rivers.

TABLE 2-2
Niche cruise ships.

	Tonnage	Passenger Capacity
Radisson Diamond, Diamond Cruises	19,000	354
Radisson Ruby, Diamond Cruises	19,000	354
Radisson Sapphire, Diamond Cruises	19,000	354
Universe, World Explorer Cruises	18,000	550
Golden Odyssey, Royal Cruise Line	10,500	460
Club Med I, II, Club Med	10,000	386
Royal Viking Queen, Royal Viking Line	10,000	323
Seabourn Spirit, Seabourn Cruise Line	10,000	204
Seabourn Pride, Seabourn Cruise Line	10,000	204
Song of Flower, Seven Seas Cruises	8,282	172
Frontier Spirit, Seaquest Cruises	6,700	164
Stella Oceanis, Sun Line	6,000	300
Wind Star, Windstar Cruises	5,350	148
Wind Song, Windstar Cruises	5,350	148
Wind Spirit, Windstar Cruises	5,350	148
Renaissance I, II, III, IV, Renaissance Cruises	4,500	100
Renaissance V, VI, VII, VIII, Renaissance Cruises	4,500	114
Sea Goddess I, Cunard Sea Goddess	4,250	116
Sea Goddess II, Cunard Sea Goddess	4,250	116
Stella Maris, Sun Line	4,000	180
Sea Cloud, Special Expeditions	3,530	70
Mississippi Queen, Delta Queen Steamboat Co.	3,364	436
World Discoverer, Clipper Cruise Line	3,153	138
Caledonian Star, Seaquest Cruises	3,095	135
Star Flyer, Star Clippers	3,025	180
Star Clipper, Star Clippers	3,025	180
Aquanaut Ambassador, Aquanaut Cruise Line	2,573	200
Society Explorer, Society Expeditions	2,500	98
Polaris, Special Expeditions	2,214	84
Delta Queen, Delta Queen Steamboat Co.	1,650	180
Aquanaut Holiday, Aquanaut Cruise Line	815	80
Melanesian Discoverer, Special Expeditions	130	92
Sea Lion, Special Expeditions	99.7	70
Sea Bird, Special Expeditions	99.7	70
Yorktown Clipper, Clipper Cruise Line	99.5	138
Nantucket Clipper, Clipper Cruise Line	99.5	102
New Shoreham II, American Canadian/Caribbean Line	98	72
Caribbean Prince, American Canadian/Caribbean Line	90	80
Polynesia, Windjammer Barefoot Cruises	n/a	126
Amazing Grace, Windjammer Barefoot Cruises	n/a	96
Fantome, Windjammer Barefoot Cruises	n/a	84
Flying Cloud, Windjammer Barefoot Cruises	n/a	78
Mandalay, Windjammer Barefoot Cruises	n/a	72
Yankee Clipper, Windjammer Barefoot Cruises	n/a	65
Sir Francis Drake, Tall Ships Adventures	n/a	34

Diamond Cruises' *Radisson Diamond* and its sister-ships are the largest ships in the niche class and are committed exclusively to corporate business meetings and incentive sales groups. Royal Cruise Line's *Golden Odyssey* and *Royal Viking Queen* cater to the rich and sophisticated traveler.

A popular feature of a niche cruise can be its itinerary for adventure, exploration, ecology, or destination. Available are trips down the Amazon and Orinoco Rivers, Antarctica, United States intracoastal waterways, as well as to intimate ports and coves in the Virgin Islands and the Mediterranean, and to other places that are inaccessible to regular cruise ships. Other niche cruises feature cultural programs, such as music, art, culinary, the likes of which are not readily available aboard other cruise ships.

Theme Cruises

To enhance the attractiveness of certain off-season departures, a popular theme is added and specially promoted. The idea is to develop additional bookings among patrons of such specific themes.

Nostalgia plays a big part in convincing such would-be cruisers to come aboard. One of the more successful enticements is the presence on board of a big-name band, such as the Glenn Miller or Tommy and Jimmy Dorsey bands.

Other popular themes are classical music (featuring renowned opera and concert singers and instrumentalists), Broadway revues, food (gourmet, diet, wine, etc.), sports celebrities, and the like.

There is a potential client for each and every type of cruise. A salesperson's overriding commandment should be: Product can and should be sold first, regardless of price. Price will take care of itself.

Comparing Cruises

A comparison of sample menus in Appendix B reflects some obvious differences in the quality of the cruise. For example, the higher a cruise is rated, the more sophisticated is its menu.

The classic cruise readily provides individual requests for entrees not included in the printed menu. Such an alternative is less available or nonexistent on other vessels.

Dinner menus in the appendix vary among the likes of the ultraluxurious *Seabourn Pride*, The Queen's and Princess Grills aboard the *QE2*, Holland America Line, Premier Cruise Lines, and Carnival Cruise Lines. The nationality of a ship—such as Italian, French, English, or Greek—can have a significant influence on its cuisine.

Typical daily programs of shipboard activities are illustrated in Appendix C. Each program encompasses almost an 18-hour day and has something to offer every passenger. Even while a ship is in port, an abbreviated program is scheduled.

Name _____ Date _____

REVIEW QUESTIONS

1. Define the cruise product.

   _____

   _____

   _____

   _____

2. How many passengers can be accommodated in the various state-rooms?

   _____

3. Indicate the types of beds available.

   _____

   _____

4. What sleep accommodations are found in economy cabins?

   _____

5. List the standard facilities in a typical stateroom.

   _____

   _____

   _____

6. Name the ships featuring a one-sitting dining room policy.

   _____

7. Besides mealtimes, what eating opportunities are available?

   _____

   _____

   _____

   _____

8. What special eating delight is available after the Captain's Gala Dinner? Describe its features.

   _____

   _____

9. What item(s) in the Comparison of Inclusive Costs and Features should be called to a potential cruise client's attention?

   _____

   _____

10. What types of entertainment are provided on board a cruise?

_____

_____

_____

_____

_____

_____

11. Describe the cruise staff and some of their functions.

_____

_____

_____

_____

_____

_____

12. Describe the classic (traditional) cruise.

_____

_____

_____

13. Name the cruise lines that operate classic cruises.

_____

_____

_____

14. Describe the typical classic cruise passenger.

_____

_____

15. What is the main difference between a classic and deluxe cruise?

_____

_____

_____

16. Why does the standard cruise enjoy popular appeal?

_____

_____

_____

_____

Name ______________________________ Date ______________

17. List some of the newest ships (excluding Carnival Cruise Lines') in the standard cruise category.

____

____

____

____

18. Which cruise line revolutionized the cruise vacation concept? How?

____

____

____

____

____

19. What are special (niche) cruises?

____

____

____

20. What are some significant structural differences among niche ships?

____

____

____

21. Which niche cruise lines provide the ultimate in luxury service?

____

____

22. What is a theme cruise?

____

____

____

CHAPTER 3

The Anatomy of a Cruise Ship

Common Cruise Ship Terms

The definitions of the following terms will help you understand the physical features of a cruise ship.

Aft. Near or towards the stern or back end of the ship.

Berth. A bed in a stateroom.

Bridge. Located on an elevated deck, forward, facing the sea, from which the vessel is navigated and its operation monitored.

Draft. The distance from the waterline to the lowest point of the ship underwater.

Engine Types. Most people are curious about the meaning of the letters appearing before a ship's name. The following is a list of the most popular ones:

MS—Motor Ship
MV—Motor Vessel
RMS—Royal Mail Ship
SS—Steamship

SSC—Semi-Submersible Craft

TS—Twin Screw

TSS—Turbine Steamship

Forward. The bow or front end of the ship.

Gangway. The passageway or ramp used for embarking and debarking ship.

Gross Registered Tonnage. The cubical capacity of a vessel, divided by 100. GRT has nothing whatsoever to do with the actual weight of a ship.

Knot. A measure of speed, not distance. It is a unit of speed equal to one nautical mile per hour or about 1.15 statute miles (6,076 feet). Although no resource indicates the origin of the word knot, it might have been an abbreviated phonetic derivation from the term "nautical" mile.

Portside. Facing forward, the left side of the ship. The term originated in the seventeenth century, when ships of that era had their only loading facility on the left side, next to the port. The term was readily accepted because of its contrast in sound to the word Starboard.

Ship's Registry. In years past, ships were registered in the country where the parent company and home port were located. Since almost all of the shiplines operating in the United States are foreign-owned and without a national home port, such registry is now made in various other countries, generally chosen for financial (tax) purposes.

However, all ships must conform to international standards for shipboard safety. Ships operating out of United States ports must comply with local state and federal health regulations, as well.

Space Ratio. The GRT (gross registered tonnage) divided by the number of passengers indicates the amount of cubic space per passenger.

Stabilizers. Fins extending from both sides of a ship underwater to steady (stabilize) ship motion.

Starboard. The right side of the ship, facing forward. The term dates back to the days when a steering-board was found on the right side of a vessel; and, as time went by, the pronunciation of steering-board became corrupted into today's accepted Starboard.

Tender. A small enclosed vessel used to transport passengers from the ship to and from shore, while the ship is at anchor offshore.

Touring the Cruise Ship

A cruise ship is a virtual floating resort hotel. In fact, a cruise ship provides more guest services, activities, and entertainment than any resort hotel. However, the traditional shipboard operations are giving way to the modern hotel management concept. For example, many ships now have a *Hotel Manager* on board to supervise passenger operations.

Although there is some similarity in land and sea hotel operations, some terms used to describe facilities aboard ship differ from those ashore.

For example, the Chief Purser's Office really functions as the Front Desk. On some ships, there now is a Front Desk per se, where the usual passenger business is transacted, such as the payment of shipboard charges. Here, safety deposit boxes are available, usually free of charge. Special shipboard arrangements can be made at the Front Desk, such as arranging a cocktail party, gift wine orders, anniversary celebration arrangements, etc. Open 24 hours a day, the Front Desk is also the ship's information center.

Also, a ship has *decks*, not floors. On nine out of ten vessels, decks have specific names, rather than identifying numbers or letters.

The Decks

Perhaps the only "standard" deck names are the self-explanatory Bridge, Boat, Promenade, Sports, and Sun Decks, which are used on about 50 percent of the ships. Of 65 deck plans checked, an assortment of 120 different deck names was found. Main Deck appeared most frequently— 32 times. Surprisingly, Riviera and Upper Decks were next, 16 times each.

In discussing a ship's layout with a potential customer, remember, there are no standard names for specific deck types. For example, on one ship Promenade Deck might have an open-air or an enclosed walking area, or both, stretching completely around the entire ship. On another ship, Promenade Deck might be public rooms only, taking up the full width of the vessel.

Bridge Deck. This is the nerve-center of the ship, where the Captain and his staff perform their respective duties. A master control panel monitors every function and condition relating to the ship's operation, such as electricity, water supply, air conditioning, status of the safety doors, etc. The Captain's and Officers' quarters are located on Bridge Deck.

Boat Deck. It is so-called because the ship's lifeboats are located here. Lifeboats may be of any design or size and must be carried on the decks of all ships. By law, their combined capacity must be sufficient to accommodate all people on board, passengers and crew alike. Each lifeboat must have a watertight compartment in the bow and stern, equipped with life preservers, emergency radio and signal flares, search flashlights, drinking water, food, etc. Today's lifeboats are self-propelled.

Sports and Sun Decks. Located on the topmost levels of the ship, these decks are used for activities such as paddle tennis, shuffleboard, trapshooting, halfcourt basketball, and the like as well as for sun bathing. Deck chairs are available on all ships, mostly free of charge and are often set aside for privacy while sun bathing. Chair reservations may be made for a special fee. A miniature golf facility is found on some ships.

Promenade Deck. This used to be one of the most popular features on a ship for casual strolling and deck chair relaxation. On many ships, Promenade Deck is that in name only. Walking and jogging are done on the so-called Boat or Sun Deck. On the traditional Promenade Deck, a passenger could circumambulate the ship without hindrance and measure the distance covered over the course of the entire trip in the process.

Royal Cruise Lines

Norwegian Carribbean Lines

The Dining Room

The dining room is a focal point on any cruise ship. It sets the tone for elegance and deep personal satisfaction. The attention shown the individual passenger is at the maximum while dining. The atmosphere is always one of warmth and beauty. The table settings, flowers, friendliness of the stewards, and the menu choices combine to make dining a memorable experience.

Since there is no limit on how many courses a passenger can order, no one leaves the dining room feeling shortchanged. (This is in sharp contrast to dining policies at almost all resort hotels.) It is also one of the reasons some passengers humorously complain about eating aboard ship.

The Lounges

Each ship has its own variety of lounges, depending on its size. The Main Lounge, often named just that, is the largest public room on the ship. It is the setting, therefore, for such happenings as the Captain's Gala Welcome-Aboard Party, professional entertainment, and continuous dancing to Big Band sounds and Soft Rock music.

On the newest of ships, there is a difference between the Main Lounge and Nightclub, perhaps because the latter has a theater-type layout similar

The center for entertainment aboard Royal Caribbean Cruise Line's *Monarch of the Seas* is the bilevel "Sound of Music" show lounge. It features the first-ever "video wall" at sea, 50 screens on two motorized movable banks.

to that found in resort hotel. And the disco is now a major facility, with all the exciting lighting effects and embellishments popular in such rooms.

A number of other lounges might be included to allow small musical combos to perform in a more subdued setting. Still other very intimate lounges—such as an observatory-type, with a pianist or folk singer—might be featured. But, these observatory-type lounges are giving way on newer ships to a major public room, with a dramatic panoramic view of the sea.

Bars

Every ship has a number of bars. The traditional Ocean Bar, for example, is ideal for leisurely conversation, with no distractions. Other bars are conveniently located throughout the ship and are often near the pool or an upper deck, isolated from the crowds (these are usually discovered by just a few and become a special gathering place for small groups of friends). Bar prices on board ships are far more reasonable than shoreside prices.

The Theater

Every large cruise ship except for one or two of the newest, has a theater (sometimes called the Cinema). Modern-day ship designers appear to be divided on the subject of the theater. Some still include it; others do not, perhaps because of the availability of closed-circuit color television sets in each stateroom and the huge nightclub lounge, which precludes the need for a separate theater. Some of the newest ships have all three facilities.

Theater seating capacities average between 230 and 330 on most ships, including the newest and largest ones. In sharp contrast, however, the largest shipboard theater is on the *Rotterdam*, with 620 seats. The two largest ships afloat today, the *Norway* and *Queen Elizabeth 2*, have theaters seating 541 and 530, respectively. All three theaters have an orchestra and balcony.

Current-run movies are shown, together with classic films, travelogs, etc. Concert-type performances, as well as stage productions, may be presented in the ship's theater. The theater is also ideal for business and convention meetings. Religious services might be held here, as well as in other public rooms.

Meeting Rooms

While meeting rooms are available on most ships, their relative sizes are modest. In recognition of the need for such facilities, new ships have increased their ability to handle business meetings. In the next generation of ships (the ultralarge ones), there will be greater emphasis on catering to business meetings and convention groups.

Audiovisual equipment and all the other incidental necessities for conducting meetings are available on board.

Shops

The *boutique* is stocked with the usual array of designer clothing and accessories, both formal and informal. Cameras, binoculars, watches, jewelry, figurines, crystal, perfumes, etc., can be found in the *gift shop*. Toiletries, notions, film, cigarettes, etc., can be purchased in the *drugstore*.

Every ship has a *photo gallery* of one type or another. Photos taken by the ship's photographer during the course of the cruise are on display and available for purchase.

Recreation Rooms

Gymnasium. More and more, state-of-the-art exercise equipment is being provided on board cruise ships: rowing machines, bicycles, free and pulley weights, motorized jog-o-matic machines, the multi-purpose "Big Mac" stretching machines, etc. A qualified Exercise Director is on hand to supervise their use. Free lectures are given and a structured fitness program is arranged.

Whirlpool baths and sauna are also commonplace. A masseur/masseuse is available by appointment. A fee is charged for their services.

Every ship has one or more swimming pools, outdoor and/or indoor, plus a children's wading pool. Traditionally, such pools are located at the aft end of the ship. Now, however, the new ships are placing them on an upper deck, midship, with a Magradome-type cover.

Card Room. This room has four to eight tables for convenient card games.

Casino. Free instruction is provided to beginners and inexperienced players for all games in the casino such as blackjack, craps, roulette, slot machines, wheel of fortune, etc.

Children's Playroom. Featured here are a puppet theater, arts and crafts, and games.

Computer Center. This center is found mostly on the luxury-type ships. Free instruction and hands-on practice are provided for passengers who are interested in learning to use a computer system. The Computer Center is open all day. An assortment of games, plus such things as a flight simulator that teaches one how to fly a small aircraft, are included. Also available is the Video Game Room. Business programs, word processing programs, and spread sheets for business and accounting application also are available.

Library and Reading/Writing Room. A fair selection of hardcover and paperback books and a variety of national magazines and other periodicals are available for loan. Comfortable chairs and writing desks are provided in these secluded corners of the ship.

Service Facilities

Hospital. A physician and nurse(s) are available every day. There is a nominal charge for medical services.

Beauty Salon/Barber Shop. This service is available by appointment, and a nominal fee is charged.

Launderette and Ironing Room. Facilities, complete with washing machine and dryer, plus steam iron and ironing board, are available for individual use, free of charge.

Cruise Ship Support Services

Hotel Department

The care and comfort of passengers is the prime responsibility of the Hotel Department. Since a cruise ship is a veritable floating hotel, it requires special types of support services. The Hotel Department is responsible for the food, drink, bedding, passenger activities, and entertainment, plus all the incidental personal services necessary to ensure the well-being of every passenger. Food purchases, preparation, and service are the most important functions of the Hotel Department. Dining is one of the highlights of shipboard life, so fresh food must be secured as much as possible from local port sources, especially on long cruises. Otherwise, frozen foods are used.

The Hotel Department hires the chefs, specialty cooks and bakers, as well as the entire kitchen staff. It also is responsible for hiring top-notch dining-room personnel and training them in the line's own traditional standards of courtesy and efficiency.

Lounge and deck stewards and bartenders are part of the Hotel service team as are the room stewards/stewardesses, whose reputation for fast and efficient service borders on the fantastic. They, too, require special training.

The tradition of one-nationality officers and crew is changing, although it is highly desirable, because it tends to foster better morale and pride. Since most cruise lines employ foreign nationals, crew members are literally year-round staff. Home leave becomes an emotional event, particularly for the many youngsters who have completed their first tour of duty. The Hotel Department management is, of course, most sensitive to this situation.

Besides the professional training given these crew members, the Hotel Department also arranges for their personal development and improvement. For example, English language courses, as well as vocational subjects, are provided.

Entertainers, on the other hand, are hired on a short-term basis. Famous performers usually are hired for one trip only. Other forms of entertainment, such as movies, games, computer center equipment and supplies, and so on, are the responsibility of the Hotel Department.

Arrangements for business meetings on board, as well as catering to special groups, are handled by the Hotel. Special dietary, medical, or other personal needs are arranged through this department.

Fleet Department

The ship's operational personnel are administered by the Fleet Department. This includes the ship's officers, engine and deck crew, radio operators, etc. The prime responsibility of the Fleet Department is the maintenance of the ships, from painting the deck rail and hull to maintaining the satellite equipment. Since a ship must remain in constant service to be profitable, the process of painting and incidental redecorating is an ongoing process.

The Fleet Department makes all the arrangements for the handling of the vessels at the respective ports of call, including the berthing, refueling, and restocking of supplies. Also, they arrange for the periodic dry-

Star Princess—63,500 tons/1,470 passengers.

docking of each ship. At certain intervals, a ship must be taken out of the water completely for a total exterior inspection. This is the time when major renovation or replacement needs are completed. Since this is costly and time-consuming, more and more underwater inspections are being done while the ship remains in service.

Sanitation Department

Until recently, the United States Public Health Service conducted regular and systematic inspections aboard ships, to protect the health of cruise passengers and crew. Due to budget cuts, this service is no longer provided routinely.

Some cruise lines have Sanitation Departments of their own. Health and Sanitation Officers are fully qualified individuals who received either a Bachelor of Science or Master's degree in public health or environmental sanitation from leading universities in the United States. They supervise conditions surrounding food preparation areas, inspect kitchens between mealtimes, test drinking water, and check on the personal cleanliness of kitchen personnel. They report directly to the ship's captain.

The Fleet and Marine Hotel Departments are based at the company's headquarters, while the Sanitation Department is on board ship.

Ships' Capacities

Low Density. When a ship of specific tonnage carries fewer passengers than another ship of the same size, it is said to have *low density*. Usually, the low density ship has larger staterooms on average and more public rooms, and will be in the luxury class. (See Table 3-1.)

TABLE 3-1
Ocean-going cruise ships by gross registered tonnage.

Ship/Company	Tonnage	Passenger Capacity
Norway, Norwegian Caribbean Line	75,000	2,044
Majesty of the Seas, Royal Caribbean Cruise Line	73,941	2,354
Monarch of the Seas, Royal Caribbean Cruise Line	73,941	2,354
Sovereign of the Seas, Royal Caribbean Cruise Line	73,192	2,282
Ecstasy, Carnival Cruise Lines	70,367	2,044
Fantasy, Carnival Cruise Lines	70,367	2,044
Sensation, Carnival Cruise Lines	70,000	2,600
Fascination, Carnival Cruise Lines	70,000	2,600
Crown Princess, Princess Cruises	70,000	1,590
Regal Princess, Princess Cruises	70,000	1,590
Queen Elizabeth 2, Cunard Line	67,139	1,850
Star Princess, Princess Cruises	63,500	1,470
Statendam, Holland America Line	55,000	1,256
Ryndam, Holland America Line	55,000	1,256
Maasdam, Holland America Line	55,000	1,256
Westerdam, Holland America Line	53,872	1,494
CostaClassica, Costa Cruise Lines	50,000	1,300

(Continued)

TABLE 3-1 (*Continued*)

Ship/Company	Tonnage	Passenger Capacity
CostaRomantica, Costa Cruise Lines	50,000	1,300
Crystal Harmony, Crystal Cruises	49,400	960
Nordic Princess, Royal Caribbean Cruise Line	48,563	1,610
Zenith, Celebrity Cruises	47,500	1,374
Celebration, Carnival Cruise Lines	47,262	1,486
Jubilee, Carnival Cruise Lines	47,262	1,486
Horizon, Celebrity Cruises	46,811	1,354
Holiday, Carnival Cruise Lines	46,052	1,452
Sky Princess, Princess Cruises	46,000	1,200
Royal Princess, Princess Cruises	45,000	1,200
Seaward, Norwegian Cruise Line	42,000	1,534
Dreamward, Norwegian Cruise Line	41,000	1,246
Windward, Norwegian Cruise Line	41,000	1,246
Viking Serenade, Royal Caribbean Cruise Line	40,132	1,514
Starship Oceanic, Premier Cruise Lines	40,000	1,500
Rotterdam, Holland America Line	38,645	1,075
Festivale, Carnival Cruise Lines	38,175	1,146
Song of America, Royal Caribbean Cruise Line	37,584	1,390
Tropicale, Carnival Cruise Lines	36,674	1,022
Starship Atlantic, Premier Cruise Lines	36,500	1,600
Royal Viking Sun, Royal Viking Line	36,000	740
Crown Odyssey, Royal Cruise Line	34,250	1,052
Nieuw Amsterdam, Holland America Line	33,930	1,214
Noordam, Holland America Line	33,930	1,214
Royal Majesty, Majesty Cruises	32,400	1,056
CostaRiviera, Costa Cruise Lines	31,500	974
Meridian, Celebrity Cruises	30,440	1,106
Constitution, American Hawaii Cruises	30,000	798
Independence, American Hawaii Cruises	30,000	798
CostaAllegra, Costa Cruise Lines	30,000	800
Westward, Norwegian Cruise Line	28,000	828
Royal Odyssey, Royal Cruise Line	28,000	765
Sunward, Norwegian Cruise Line	28,000	790
Carnivale, Carnival Cruise Lines	27,250	950
Mardi Gras, Carnival Cruise Lines	27,250	906
Britanis, Fantasy Cruises	26,000	922
Sagafjord, Cunard Line	25,147	589
CostaMarina, Costa Cruise Lines	25,000	770
Fair Princess, Princess Cruises	25,000	890
Vistafjord, Cunard Line	24,492	736
Regent Star, Regency Cruises	24,294	950
Regent Sun, Regency Cruises	24,000	836
Crown Seawind, Seawind Cruises	24,000	656
Enchanted Seas, Commodore Cruise Line	23,500	736
Enchanted Isle, Commodore Cruise Line	23,395	731
Nordic Prince, Royal Caribbean Cruise Line	23,200	1,012
Song of Norway, Royal Caribbean Cruise Line	23,005	1,022

(*Continued*)

TABLE 3-1   *(Continued)*

Ship/Company	Tonnage	Passenger Capacity
Caribe I, Commodore Cruise Line	23,000	875
Regent Sea, Regency Cruises	22,000	729
Sea Breeze, Dolphin Cruise Line	21,000	840
CarlaCosta, Costa Cruise Lines	20,000	734
Crown Jewel, Crown Cruise Line	20,000	820
Crown Dynasty, Crown Cruise Line	20,000	820
Ocean Breeze, Dolphin Cruise Line	20,000	756
Amerikanis, Fantasy Cruises	20,000	619
Sun Viking, Royal Caribbean Cruise Line	18,556	726
Stella Solaris, Sun Line	18,000	620
Starship Majestic, Premier Cruise Lines	17,750	950
Cunard Countess, Cunard Line	17,593	800
Cunard Princess, Cunard Line	17,586	750
Daphne, Costa Cruise Lines	17,000	422
Southward, Norwegian Cruise Line	16,607	752
Skyward, Norwegian Cruise Line	16,254	730
Starward, Norwegian Cruise Line	16,107	758
Crown Monarch, Crown Cruise Line	15,270	550
Mermoz, Paquet French Lines	13,691	680
Dolphin IV, Dolphin Cruise Line	13,000	588
Royal Pacifica, Starlite Cruises	13,000	600
Ocean Pearl, Ocean/Pearl Cruise Lines	12,475	480
Ocean Princess, Ocean/Pearl Cruise Lines	12,200	460
Golden Odyssey, Royal Cruise Line	10,500	460

Royal Cruise Line's dazzling 1,000-passenger *Crown Odyssey* features state-of-the-art design and distinctive amenities befitting its "royal" heritage. The luxury liner's worldwide itineraries include cruises in Europe and Scandinavia, Hawaii, the Mexican Riviera, Panama Canal, and South America, as well as transatlantic cruises.

High Density. A vessel with a relatively higher passenger capacity compared to others of its size is considered to be of high density. Usually, it has more, but smaller, staterooms. It is extremely important to know which vessels fit into each category. Some clients might not be happy with smaller-than-average staterooms, no matter what ship is involved. The following list reveals these ratios.

Cruise Ship Fact Sheets

Fact sheets on each of the cruise ships are contained in Appendix D, in alphabetical order and somewhat condensed form. Included are such details as:

- A ship's former name, if applicable.
- When it was built and/or refurbished.
- Its tonnage, length and width, speed, capacity, crew size and nationality, number of decks and state rooms.

The sample fact sheet of Carnival Cruise Lines' *Ecstasy* in Table 3-2 indicates every conceivable statistic and feature regarding the vessel.

These fact sheets are available from a cruise line's Public Relations Department, upon request.

TABLE 3-2
Fact sheet for the superliner *Ecstasy* of Carnival Cruise Lines.

Approximate cost:	$275 million
Shipyard:	Masa-Yards
	Helsinki, Finland
Delivery Date:	April 1991
Country of registry:	Liberia
Speed:	21.0 knots
Approximate crew size:	920
Nationality of crew:	
Officers	Italian
Hotel staff	International
Cruise staff	International
Size/capacity:	
Gross registered tonnage	70,367
Length	855 feet
Beam	105 feet
Beam at pooldecks	118 feet
Maximum draft	25 feet, 9 inches
Total passenger capacity (including uppers)	2,594
Normal cruise capacity (basis 2)	2,040
Passenger decks:	10
Space ratio	34

(Continued)

TABLE 3-2 *(Continued)*

Accommodations:

Outside suites*	28
Outside demisuites*	26
Outside twins*	564
Inside twins*	383
Inside upper & lowers	19
Total:	1020

Public rooms & capacities

Name	*Capacity*
Blue Sapphire Lounge (main)	1,300 +
Wind Star Dining Room (forward)	650
Wind Song Dining Room (aft)	658
Chinatown	109
Stripes Discotheque	230 +
The Rolls Royce Cafe	58
City Lights Boulevard	230
Society Bar	92
Starlight Lounge (aft)	541
The Neon Bar	92
The Explorer's Club	43
Panorama Bar & Grill	722
Crystal Palace Casino	450
Spa, Health Club & Beauty Salon	12,000 sq. ft.

Facilities		*Equipment*
Fully equipped	Photo gallery	Stabilizers
Spa & health club	Shuffleboard	Bow thrusters (3)
Full casino	Teen club	Stern thrusters (3)
Dining rooms (2)	Skeet shooting	Twin rudders
Barbershop	Swimming pools	(individually controlled)
Bars & lounges (10)	(outside—3)	Diesel electric
Beauty shop	Tour office	Propulsion system
Boutique	Closed-circuit TV	6 medium-speed engines
Drug store	Jogging track	Developing approximately
Duty-free shops	Six whirlpools	50,000 hp
Elevators (14)	VCR rentals	
Infirmary	Children's playroom	

*All convert to king size beds and include whirlpool bathtub and queen size beds; all cabins feature closed-circuit TV, stereo, telephone, and 110 A.C. current.

REVIEW QUESTIONS

1. What are the traditional shipboard terms for

   front desk? _____   floors? _____

2. What is the Bridge Deck?

   _____

   _____

3. What is a ship's total lifeboat capacity?

   _____

4. What is the largest public room on board any ship?

   _____

5. Describe the Promenade Deck.

   _____

   _____

6. Name some of the various lounges on board.

   _____

   _____

7. What is the average capacity of a ship's theater?

   _____

8. Which ships have the largest theaters?

   _____

   _____

9. Describe a ship's gymnasium.

   _____

   _____

10. What is the policy regarding deck chairs?

    _____

    _____

11. What are the main functions of the Hotel Department?

    _____

    _____

    _____

12. What programs do cruise lines provide foreign crew members for their
    personal betterment?

    _____

    _____

13. What advantage does a one-nationality crew provide?

_____

_____

14. Why must a ship remain in constant service?

_____

_____

15. Explain low density: _____

_____

High density: _____

_____

16. Define the following terms:

Gross registered tonnage _____

Per diem _____

Tender _____

Ship's registry _____

Use Appendix D to answer the following questions.

17. What is the passenger capacity of the _Sagafjord_? _____

How many cabins does the ship contain? _____

18. What is the gross registered tonnage of Seawind Cruises' _Seawind Crown_?

_____

19. How many staterooms does Carnival Cruise Lines' _Celebration_ have?

Outside staterooms: _____

Inside staterooms: _____

20. In what country is Celebrity Cruises' _Horizon_ registered?

_____

21. What is the former name of Norwegian Cruise Line's _Norway_?

_____

CHAPTER 4

Selecting Staterooms

Types of Staterooms

This chapter examines some of the differences among the various types of staterooms. It is important to remember that stateroom terminology varies with each shipline. For example, a top-rated stateroom on one ship might have the same descriptive name as the third-rated stateroom on another ship. The best staterooms are located on upper decks and midship, to minimize motion. Photographs and/or cut-out drawings of the respective types of staterooms usually are shown on deck plans to provide a clearer perspective.

Grand Deluxe Suite. There is only one such accommodation available anywhere. It is aboard the *Norway*, having a living room, private dining room, double bedroom, vanity consoles, two full baths, TV, and refrigerator.

Luxury Split-Level Suite. Only two of these suites are available, and they are on the *Queen Elizabeth 2*. They consist of a living room, two bedrooms, vanity consoles, bathroom with tub and shower, private verandah, TV, and refrigerator.

Penthouse, Apartment, or Luxury Duplex Suites. This type of stateroom can have most, if not all, of the following: a large, open living room (some with an additional sofa bed), walk-in closet, separate bedroom with two

A deluxe twin stateroom aboard Premier Cruise Line's *Starship Homeric*.

lower beds, vanity, TV, refrigerator, bathroom with tub and shower, whirl-pool bathtub, and a private balcony with patio furniture.

Deluxe Suites. A composite deluxe suite can have a living room or living room area, double bedroom, two lower beds, wardrobe room, bathroom with tub and shower, whirlpool, TV, and refrigerator.

Suites. Consist of a bedroom with two lower beds, large sitting room area, bathtub and shower, and TV.

Large Outside/Inside Double Rooms. Normally, these staterooms are booked on the basis of two-in-a-room since they have two lower beds, bathtub and/or shower, and TV. However, a high percentage of these cabins are capable of accommodating three, four, and even five people. One or two upper (Pullman) berths are available; plus, in just a few instances, a fifth person can be accommodated on a sofa bed or cot bed.

Economy Outside/Inside Rooms. These rooms have a lower bed and upper (Pullman) berth and shower. Some are minimum-rated, depending on location, and in some cases they are listed for single occupancy.

Beds consist of queen-size, double-bed, regular twin-size, sofa bed, and upper (Pullman) berth.

Ratesheets and Deck Plans

Ratesheets

It is standard practice for rate categories to be color-coded, to relate to the similarly color-coded staterooms in the deck plan. Some ratesheets merely indicate the types of staterooms, with applicable rates. Others go a step further and indicate the facilities in the cabins and the name of the deck location. Still other ratesheets contain all the foregoing, plus the individual room numbers.

The rates shown always are per-person, double occupancy. Third and fourth berth rates are indicated on the bottom line of the ratesheet. Single occupancy rates are explained separately, not always as part of the ratesheet, but in the General Information part of the brochure. They can range from 150 percent to 200 percent of the per-person rate.

In most instances, the rates shown will include air arrangements. When air transportation is not involved, the ratesheet will indicate the credit applicable so as to arrive at the cruise-only fare. Where airfares are not included in the published rate schedule, a separate section of the brochure will show the necessary air add-ons from various cities. Air reservations are made by the cruise company.

Also shown at the bottom of the ratesheet are the required port taxes.

Deck Plans

As with ratesheets, each cruise line adopts its own version of deck plans. Whatever the types, both must be used in combination, of course. Sizewise, deck plans range from condensed one-page versions to triple page pull-outs (*QE2*).

Some deck plans will indicate stateroom numbers only, with descriptive details shown separately or in the ratesheet.

The SS *Rotterdam*'s deck plan is a good example (see Figure 4-1). The partial deck plan shows the stateroom number and symbols signifying the facilities in each cabin, plus such incidental information as connecting rooms.

FIGURE 4-1

Deck Plans ss Rotterdam

NAVIGATION DECK

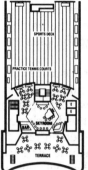

SUN DECK
ROOMS 1-25

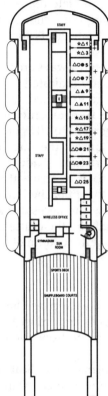

BOAT DECK
ROOMS 31-65

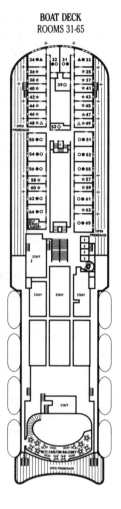

- ● Bath with overhead shower
- ■ Sofa bed
- ⊙ Single (one lower bed)
- ◇ Double (one lower, one Pullman)
- ▲ Double (two lowers)
- ☆ Double bed
- ◆ Economy Triple (two lowers, one Pullman suitable for children under 12)
- ○ Triple (two lowers, one Pullman)
- □ Quad (two lowers, two Pullmans)
- ◨ Quad (two lowers, one Pullman, one sofa bed)
- ★ Quad (three lowers, one Pullman)
- △ Partially obstructed view
- + Connecting rooms with doorway between cabins
- ⊞ Connecting rooms with common hallway between cabins

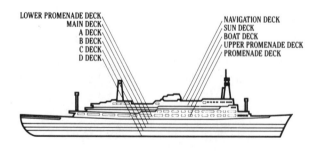

LOWER PROMENADE DECK
MAIN DECK
A DECK
B DECK
C DECK
D DECK

NAVIGATION DECK
SUN DECK
BOAT DECK
UPPER PROMENADE DECK
PROMENADE DECK

FIGURE 4-1 (*Continued*)

UPPER PROMENADE DECK

PROMENADE DECK

LOWER PROMENADE DECK
ROOMS 100-271

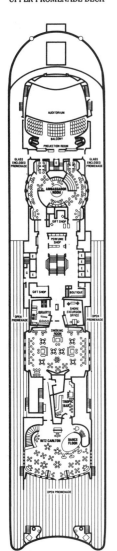

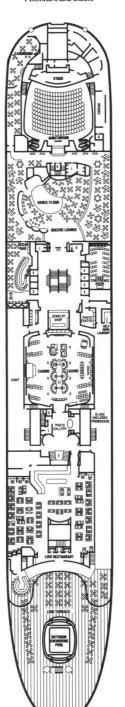

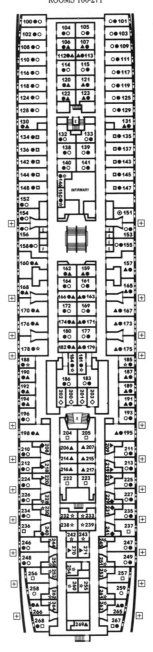

Name _____ Date _____

REVIEW QUESTIONS

1. There is only one grand deluxe suite in the entire cruise fleet. What ship is it on?

   _____

2. Name the only ship with luxury split-level suites. How many does it have?

   _____   _____

3. List the five categories with the largest number of staterooms, in order of quality.

   _____   _____   _____

   _____   _____

4. What advantage does a midship-located stateroom have?

   _____

5. What is the maximum number of passengers per stateroom?

   _____

6. What category includes minimum-rated staterooms? Why?

   _____

   _____

7. List the types of beds available aboard ship.

   _____   _____   _____

   _____   _____   _____

8. How are ratesheets set up for ready reference and stateroom identification?

   _____

   _____

   _____

9. How can ratesheets differ from one cruise line to another?

   _____

   _____

10. Are the rates shown per-cabin or per-person? Describe the rates fully.

   _____

   _____

11. Is air transportation normally included in most cruise rates? If not, where can the air add-on rates be found?

   _____

   _____

12. Who arranges the air transportation and issues the tickets?

_____

13. Describe the significant aspects of a deck plan.

_____

_____

_____

_____

Name ____________________ Date ____________________

STUDENT EXERCISE: SS *ROTTERDAM* DECK PLAN IDENTIFYING STATEROOM FACILITIES

Identify the facilities available in each of the following staterooms (all rooms have bath and shower)(see Figure 4-1).

Cabin No. 53

Cabin No. 148

Cabin No. 191

Cabin No. 178

Cabin No. 229

Cabin No. 48

Cabin No. 143

Cabin No. 15

Name _____   Date _____

STUDENT EXERCISE: CABIN SELECTION AND IDENTIFICATION

Princess Cruise Lines' *Fair Princess*
7-day cruise departing June 6th

Locate the following staterooms in the deck plans on pages 66–67, and give details (per-person):

	Category	Room No.	Deck	Tariff Rate
Outside suite		Capri		
Minisuite		11		
Outside double w/twin beds		C-198		
Outside 2 beds		B-159		
Inside 2 beds		A-163		
Outside single		A-198		
Inside single		C-190		
Minimum-rated		B-178		
Third and fourth person in stateroom (adult/child)				
Port charges				

STATEROOM DIAGRAMS

SUITE (CATEGORY A)
Private bedroom with double beds. Capri and Portofino suites have twin beds. Sitting area for entertaining. TV. Refrigerator. Bath with tub and shower.

MINI-SUITE (CATEGORY B)
Private bedroom with sitting room area for entertaining. TV. Extra-large wardrobe closets.

OUTSIDE OR INSIDE DOUBLE (CATEGORIES CC, C, DD, D, E, FF, F, GG, HH, H, I, J, K, L & M)
Two lower beds with two upper berths. Extra-large wardrobe closets.

OUTSIDE OR INSIDE SINGLE/DOUBLE (CATEGORIES G, N & P)
Typical lower-priced stateroom. One lower bed. One upper berth. Extra-large wardrobe closets.

FAIR PRINCESS & DAWN PRINCESS

890 passengers. 25,000 gross tons. 608 feet in length. Three swimming pools. Pizzeria. Casino. Gym. Beauty salon. Spacious staterooms, most with upper berths. Liberian registered.

Cruisetour Upgrade Supplement	Stateroom Category	ACCOMMODATIONS	7-DAY CRUISE-ONLY FARES				
			Budget May 16, 23, Sept 19	Low May 30, Sept 12	Economy June 6, Sept 5	Value June 13, Aug 29	Peak June 20-Aug 22
COLUMN A			COLUMN 1	COLUMN 2	COLUMN 3	COLUMN 4	COLUMN 5
$2,210	A	Outside suite. BAJA	$3,209	$3,309	$3,409	$3,509	$3,609
$1,650	B	Outside mini-suite. BAJA	$2,649	$2,749	$2,849	$2,949	$3,049
$1,150	CC	Outside—two lower beds. BAJA	$2,149	$2,249	$2,349	$2,449	$2,549
$1,100	C	Outside—two lower beds. CARIBE	$2,099	$2,199	$2,299	$2,399	$2,499
$1,050	DD	Outside—two lower beds. ALOHA, CARIBE, DOLPHIN	$2,049	$2,149	$2,249	$2,349	$2,449
$1,000	D	Outside—two lower beds. DOLPHIN	$1,999	$2,099	$2,199	$2,299	$2,399
$ 950	E	Outside—two lower beds. DOLPHIN, EMERALD	$1,949	$2,049	$2,149	$2,249	$2,349
$ 900	FF	Outside—two lower beds. EMERALD	$1,899	$1,999	$2,099	$2,199	$2,299
$ 800	F	Outside—two lower beds (views obstructed). ALOHA, BAJA	$1,799	$1,899	$1,999	$2,099	$2,199
$ 700	GG	Outside—two lower beds. FIESTA	$1,699	$1,799	$1,899	$1,999	$2,099
$ 400	G	Outside—one lower bed and one upper berth. ALOHA, CARIBE, DOLPHIN, EMERALD	$1,399	$1,499	$1,599	$1,699	$1,799
$ 550	HH	Inside—two lower beds. ALOHA, BAJA	$1,549	$1,649	$1,749	$1,849	$1,949
$ 500	H	Inside—two lower beds. CARIBE	$1,499	$1,599	$1,699	$1,799	$1,899
$ 450	I	Inside—two lower beds. DOLPHIN	$1,449	$1,549	$1,649	$1,749	$1,849
$ 350	J	Inside—two lower beds. EMERALD	$1,349	$1,449	$1,549	$1,649	$1,749
$ 300	K	Inside—two lower beds. FIESTA	$1,299	$1,399	$1,499	$1,599	$1,699
$ 250	L	Inside—two lower beds. GALA	$1,249	$1,349	$1,449	$1,549	$1,649
$ 200	M	Inside—two lower beds. GALA	$1,199	$1,299	$1,399	$1,499	$1,599
$ 100	N	Inside—one lower bed and one upper berth. ALOHA, BAJA, CARIBE, DOLPHIN	$1,099	$1,199	$1,299	$1,399	$1,499
Base	P	Inside—one lower bed and one upper berth. BAJA, CARIBE, DOLPHIN, EMERALD, FIESTA, GALA	$ 999	$1,099	$1,199	$1,299	$1,399
		3rd/4th person in stateroom (adult/child)	$ 500	$ 550	$ 600	$ 650	$ 700
		Port Charges	$ 119	$ 119	$ 119	$ 119	$ 119

Cruisetour Supplements (Column A) Cruisetour prices, including a *Fair* or *Dawn Princess* cruise, are per person, U.S. dollars, and based on shared P category inside staterooms. Superior accommodations are available at the supplementary per person rates listed above. Add supplement to base prices listed on cruisetour itinerary.

Cruise Fares (Columns 1-5) All fares are per person, U.S. dollars, based on double occupancy.

Single Occupancy Fares (Cruise only) For categories A and B: 200% of full tariff. Categories CC-P: 140% of full tariff (not eligible for Early Booking Discount).

NOTE: Single supplement and 3rd/4th person fares do not apply to cruisetour passengers. Pricing available upon request.

42

Deck plans inside. See pages 45-46. ➡

FAIR PRINCESS
& DAWN PRINCESS
DECK PLANS

All staterooms (excluding suites, mini-suites and categories K, N, & P) have two upper berths.

Distances listed are from the bow or stern to the nearest stateroom.

FORWARD

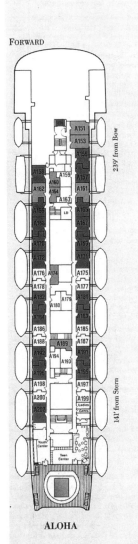

ALOHA

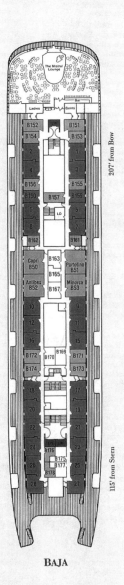

BAJA

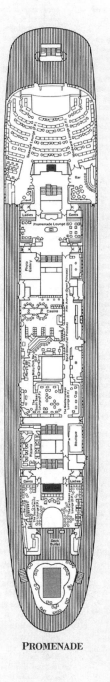

PROMENADE

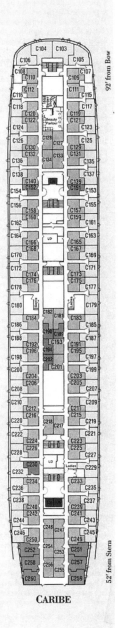

CARIBE

45

CHAPTER 5

Reaching the Cruise Market

The Cruise Market

The public's awareness of a cruise vacation has increased so dramatically in recent years that the potential market is immeasurable. The cruise industry itself reports that only upwards of 4 percent of the national population has ever taken a cruise. Its immediate annual goal is to top the 4 million mark. In terms of possible cruise sales, the total market is said to be over 38 million, based on the industry's own socioeconomic surveys.

One of the nice things about that tremendous undeveloped market is the absence of such a term as a "cruise-type" person. In other words, there is no restriction or limitation as to who might possibly take a cruise vacation. Everybody is a potential client!

There is no truth to the adage that a cruise is for older people only. Age, however, does affect the type of cruise selected. For example, on a world cruise, the passengers' average age is 67. At the other end of the spectrum, among seven-day summer cruise passengers, two out of three are under 55. Of these, more than 50 percent will be first-timers. As to marital status, passengers are more likely to be married compared to the national average. Longer cruises are characterized by a disproportionate number of widows and otherwise "unattached" individuals. However, young marrieds and singles are developing into an ever-increasing cruise market. There was a time when young singles shied away from a cruise vacation. Not anymore.

People who travel on longer cruises usually are at the top of the economic spectrum, while the average income is relatively lower for passengers on shorter cruises. Educationally, more than 50 percent of cruise passengers will have had some college education, as compared to the national average of 35 percent. Cruise passengers come from every walk of life, from every section of the country, and from every type of community—urban, suburban, small town, and rural.

In view of the current awareness of cruising, it is vitally important for the travel (cruise) sales agent to be able to furnish a potential client with all the information possible. Past surveys have shown that a cruise vacation is not necessarily presold by a cruise line's advertising. The same surveys indicate that a majority of first-time cruise vacationers have been influenced by word-of-mouth, with family members and friends being the most effective motivators.

Passengers on longer cruises definitely are experienced travelers. Sometimes they will take a short cruise on a ship to make certain it will meet their standards.

Repeat cruise customers do not need any convincing, but simply require the agent's expertise and knowledge about still other ships, other lines, and possibly new programs. Repeaters will have made two to three cruises within the past five years.

A significant factor in identifying and selling the potential market is the amount of vacation time a person has. In recent surveys, the smallest percentage of passengers had only two weeks; almost 40 percent had three or four weeks; and, the rest had five or more weeks. In all, a large percentage of the passengers had more than two weeks of vacation and divide their vacations into two or more periods. As a result, they represent off-season potential as well.

A dramatically increasing segment of our national population is known as the "senior" or "adult" market. These people are receptive to traveling, since they have the time and the means. Under normal circumstances, when peak season rates are at their highest and do not fluctuate, these price-conscious travelers are receptive to off-season offerings, when rates are seasonally lower. Of course, the present state of the national economy and its effect on cruise demand, together with the over-supply of staterooms, have made cruise prices attractive year-round.

More than 95 percent of all cruise reservations are made by travel agencies. That is no reason for a cruise sales agent to sit back and wait for a potential cruise client to walk into the agency. Cruise sales agents should make use of their cruise expertise by giving informal presentations to family groups, local clubs, and organizations, to enlighten them about a cruise vacation.

Booking Inducements

When the demand for cruise accommodations is slow, cruise lines will offer special inducements to attract customers.

In the normal course of events, third and fourth persons occupying a stateroom with two full-fares would pay an incredibly low fare (not

Carnival Cruise Lines' new SuperLiner *Ecstasy* began service June 2, 1991, on an alternating schedule of seven-day cruises to the Eastern and Western Caribbean from Miami.

including free air, however). On the basis of cruise-only, four people can sail for less than three full fares. This is an ideal situation for family groups or friends.

Discounted fares are available. However, these are not normally advertised inducements since cruise lines have a rule not to advertise any rates lower than their established minimum rates. Such rate information is made known to travel agencies via the line's telemarketing service, newsletter, or the line's Field Sales Representative. Therefore, it behooves the cruise sales agent to remain updated as to the availability of discounted fares.

Early reservations and deposit payments can earn a handsome rebate from some lines. This is more prevalent on longer cruises. Alternatively, repeat passengers' booking early might receive the exclusive benefit of utilizing this year's passage fare for next year's cruise. A new trend in inducements is the giving of material gifts, both to first-timers and repeaters, based on the type of accommodations purchased. Still another inducement, although not a common practice, is a free cruise to a client who has taken five or ten previously.

Group Sales

Cruise lines try to encourage multiple (group) bookings by offering the special incentive of an override commission to the travel agency, and, to the group leader or escort, one free ticket for every fifteen full-fare passengers booked on the same sailing. Group sales incentives can vary depending on the competitive climate at the time. On a nonaffinity (general) group booking promotion, that free (sixteenth) passage can be sold and the proceeds retained by the travel agency, thereby deriving an extra 6⅔ percent profit. Or the value can be divided among the entire group, thereby reducing each group member's fare proportionately. Other possibilities can be the group's wish to use that money to arrange transportation to/from the airport or pier, cocktail parties on board, or other extras.

Multiple bookings can be developed among affinity groups, such as fraternal, civic, and church organizations, plus business meetings and sales incentive groups, for which specially discounted fares and inducements possibly can be negotiated with a cruise line.

Cruise Salesmanship

There have been a number of best-selling books on the subjects of selling and salesmanship, written by successful salespeople or sales executives. No one has yet been able to define the subjects in a comprehensive and objective manner: in theory, yes; hypothetically, yes; but practically, no! Thus, these authors can only speak for themselves, of their own individual experiences. Some salespeople are successful because they are perseverent and hard working. Some practice self-discipline and self-denial. Others make it with education and training. Still others use inventiveness and innovation—that is, devising practical ways and means to satisfy a client's immediate need, knowing how to take advantage of opportunity. What was effective and successful for them might not necessarily work for others.

Every industry, every product, requires its own special brand of salesmanship. While "born" salespeople often feel they can sell anything, to sell well one must *know the product*. Selling travel/leisure is a most difficult task because an intangible product is to be sold. A cruise vacation is not something stocked on the travel agency's shelf. What is to be sold is personal service to a client who needs help in fulfilling a pleasant human need.

Defining salesmanship is always difficult, but is particularly so in the case of selling a cruise vacation. Perhaps this definition applies: Salesmanship is an instinctive action taken in response to a given sales situation or opportunity. In other words, the travel sales agent is totally confident that he or she can cope with whatever sales opportunity might arise. A successful salesperson must have complete self-confidence.

How does salesmanship work in practice? When a client enters the travel agency, communication must be established immediately. It can be done in two ways: either subtly or indirectly, by eye-contact and a smile, which conveys a cordial hint of welcome, or directly, through a personal greeting and conversation. A good appearance also helps. Neatness and good grooming on the part of the travel sales agent always make a good first impression on the client.

It is quite possible that first-time cruise clients enter a travel agency feeling sheepish, nervous, or downright unsure of themselves. Sheepish because they are afraid of embarrassing themselves by not knowing exactly what might be involved in booking a cruise. Nervous because they are considering a rather large expenditure and are a bit apprehensive about booking that initial cruise. And unsure because they are somewhat unfamiliar with the details involved. Since a cruise vacation is a very personal

Breakfast in the privacy of one's cabin is an example of the many luxuries
to be enjoyed on a cruise.

matter, potential clients should be greeted warmly, with a smile and an
expression of sincere welcome. In selling a cruise vacation, as with any
major sale, honesty and sincerity are important assets, to which clients will
respond favorably.

When potential cruise clients visit an agency, it may be assumed that
they are inclined to make a purchase. They will have some preconceived
notion, right or wrong, about a particular cruise line or vessel, or about
cruising in general, from their discussions with friends and relatives. They
will have some understanding of the cruise vacation concept.

The principal task of the cruise sales agent is to enumerate the reasons
for choosing a cruise: the dream, the excitement, and the practicality, with
the emphasis on affordability, that the entire cruise costs can be budgeted
before leaving home. Market surveys show that relaxation, visiting ports
easily, general comfort and convenience, and all-inclusivity are the prime
factors in buying a cruise.

As the clients study the cruise brochure given them, from time to
time they should be reminded of incidental cruise features, such as enter-

tainment, personal services (diet, medical, religious), depending on the age of the clients. They must be reassured there is no need for doubt or worry about life aboard ship.

Potential clients should be shown that a cruise is not beyond their realm, financially or socially. Some would-be cruise passengers feel a cruise might be too sophisticated for them. However, when it is explained that there is a choice about evening attire, for example, that worry is removed. Not many people own formal wear and are reluctant to rent, let alone purchase it, for the cruise. This is not to say that formality should be downplayed altogether. Some clients just might welcome the opportunity. If so, they should be encouraged to take along formal clothes.

Whether or not clients know what they want, or merely ask a general question about a cruise vacation, a scenario must be set that will lead them through a description of the cruise concept. Since clients know how much they can afford, at an early opportunity state the minimum and maximum rates that apply to, say, a seven-day cruise. Specific rates can be discussed later. Remember: Product can and should be sold regardless of price. Prices vary and are competitive.

To keep the client's interest alive, give them a copy of a competitive cruise line's brochure for comparison. Having two brochures to compare gives the clients time to assimilate the information already given them, and at the same time it makes them feel less pressured to make an immediate decision.

As the clients pore over the brochures, qualify each cruise product in a casual, informative manner, again without a hint of pressure but with incidental bits of information highlighting cruise features. One effective sales technique is to try verbally to place the clients on board the ship. Describe in very personal terms just what they will be doing and enjoying. Keep the sales talk on a very personal level.

At some point in the discussion, the clients in their own minds will make a decision, in principle, as to which cruise would provide them with the greatest pleasure and value for their money. However, it is quite possible they will not make it known and will indicate only that the cruise concept is attractive to them. The clients should be reassured that, no matter which rate category they select, they will still enjoy every amenity and feature on the ship. At that moment, a phone call should be made to the cruise line's reservations department to ascertain the availability of staterooms and advise the clients, accordingly.

By so doing, the clients have a definite idea of choice and cost. They are now in a position to state their preference. It is advisable to try to consummate the booking immediately by asking for a fully refundable deposit, or by arranging an option date for acceptance of a specific stateroom. The clients can decide then and there to leave a deposit or to make their decision in a day or two.

Cruise Features

A cruise is a unique, personally rewarding, and memorable vacation experience, leaving a lasting impression. The high standards of cuisine, service, entertainment, and accommodations often surpass expectations, and the total experience is extremely gratifying. Every moment of every day contains something of interest, to enjoy and participate in. No untold or unfavorable surprises crop up on board to burden the passenger. In fact, quite the opposite is true.

Relaxation

It is not surprising that relaxation is the most popular reason for cruising. The entire atmosphere on a ship is relaxed. Passengers follow a full but unhurried schedule, having nothing else to do but to enjoy everything around them, easily and conveniently.

Relaxation can be a positive or negative selling point. Some clients think shipboard life will be inactive and boring. To them, that is what the term "relaxation" connotes. What is true—and what should be stressed—is that cruising provides a relaxed atmosphere, free from the usual everyday distractions and intrusions. But it is far from boring.

Passengers can derive much pleasure from dining, dancing, making new friends and acquaintances, being entertained nightly, participating in a wide variety of activities, gambling, and sightseeing at the ports of call.

In the past, a cruise was even prescribed by doctors as therapy for patients recuperating from an illness or who are under heavy stress. No doubt, it can have a therapeutic effect on those who work at a fast pace. A few days without stress can be quite rejuvenating indeed.

Ports of Call

At most ports of call, cruise ships dock directly at piers located conveniently to the downtown areas. Passengers can walk freely on and off the ship. Normally, the vessels remain in port during daytime hours, or for as long as there might be something of interest for the passengers to enjoy.

If a vessel is too large to dock alongside, it will anchor offshore, as near as possible to the island, and passengers are transported ashore in tenders. In most instances, such trips take only a few minutes.

The number of ports of call in an itinerary is an excellent sales feature, and clients should be apprised of the various attractions. Such a presentation is made on board prior to arrival at the port of call. Tour arrangements can be made on board ship. Of course, shopping is a popular shore exercise.

Once aboard, passengers will be required to complete cruise questionnaire forms for Immigration and Customs purposes upon return to the home port.

On the day before arrival at the home port, room stewards help passengers prepare for debarkation. Tags bearing a code letter or number are affixed to the baggage for identification. Baggage is to be packed and placed outside the stateroom door for pickup by the ship's personnel. It will be unloaded immediately upon docking. Passengers should retain an overnight bag and carry their own small bags, especially those containing valuables.

Passengers may remain on board for up to two hours after arrival while they are being cleared through Immigration and Customs and baggage is being put ashore. Upon clearance, passengers can locate their personal luggage on the pier under the code number or letter assigned to them and move on for Customs inspection.

Comfort

As for comfort, at every opportunity the cruise passenger is accorded total individual attention. Room and dining stewards extend gracious and courteous service, as do lounge and deck personnel. Passengers are made to feel they are the most important people on board. This is one of the more memorable aspects of a cruise experience.

All-Inclusivity

The fact that a cruise is an all-inclusive package—transportation, room, meals, entertainment, ports of call, everything—is most attractive to a curious, uncertain potential cruise customer. First-time cruise vacationers will also be reassured by knowing they can budget their funds accurately. Any possible additional expenditures are known beforehand, and they are minimal, even optional.

Such extra expenditures could include bar bills and dinner wine, laundry and pressing, hair stylist, medical, gambling, shopping and tours ashore.

Actually, passengers can get along for an entire cruise without cash. They can sign for just about every aforementioned shipboard service and purchase. A charge account is automatically established for every passenger and a computerized printout of all charges is furnished to the passengers at the end of the cruise for their information and payment.

Payment of shipboard charges can be made at the Front Desk (Purser's Office) by traveler's checks (highly recommended for safety reasons), credit card, or, of course, cash. Some lines will accept personal checks in a limited amount. Credit card users can enjoy the convenience of having the voucher delivered to their stateroom for signature, thereby avoiding the need to stand in line at the Front Desk.

Tipping

The only additional obligatory expenditure on board is tipping, which can be calculated in advance and budgeted for. Some cruise lines include tipping in the cruise price.

The payment of gratuities (tipping) is always at the discretion of the individual passenger. However, many lines will indicate suggested tipping amounts in their cruise brochure. For example, a suggested tip for each cabin steward and dining room steward is $2.50 per day, per passenger, and for the assisting bus-boy, $1.25 per day, per person.

Gratuities can best be paid to dining room personnel at dinner time on the evening prior to the ship's return to the home port, and to the cabin steward at some point during the course of the same evening. Bar and deck stewards are tipped in an ongoing manner. For convenience sake, some lines provide a plain envelope for tip payment.

Should passengers have doubt about tipping, inquiry can be made at the Front Desk for discreet suggestions.

A no-tipping policy exists on just a few lines. Such gratuities are included in the passage fare. Passengers can still offer gratuities voluntarily for *exceptional* or *outstanding* service, of course, but no solicitation of same by the ship's staff will be tolerated by the cruise company.

On extended cruises, gratuities are paid periodically, either weekly or fortnightly.

Ashore, porters are available to cart baggage from the Customs area to street level for ongoing transportation. They are to be tipped for their services, usually per bag.

Meals

One of the more popular attractions for cruising is dining. Not only can meals on board ship be described in lavish terms, but also as a virtual around-the-clock experience. Starting with the Early Bird Continental breakfast on deck or in the cabin, through the regularly scheduled dining room mealtimes, brunch and midafternoon snacks on deck, hot and cold hors d'oeuvres during cocktail hour, a free pizza restaurant (on some ships), snack and ice cream bars, together with the traditional midnight buffet and postmidnight show snacks, there are about 20 hours worth of eating time. This is not to mention the around-the-clock room service. Remember, all of this is included in the cruise fare.

Dining on board is sheer delight. The quality and choice of entrees are impressive (selections vary with each ship, of course). And the service, simply put, is exciting, yet gracious. There is an elegance to which everyone immediately relates. Very few resorts provide comparable standards.

Entertainment

Entertainment aboard ship is more than ample. A full day of scheduled events is the norm. Daytime activities include deck sports, games, swimming, dance lessons, aerobic exercise classes, bingo, jogging, gym equip-

The right wine recommended by a knowledgeable sommelier adds just the right touch to dinner.

Royal Caribbean Cruise Lines

ment, computer game rooms, bridge, free movies in the theater or on closed-circuit television in the stateroom, plus passenger participation events. During the evenings, there is professional entertainment of the highest quality, from Broadway musicals, Las Vegas-type revues, variety shows, to the greatest names in entertainment—plus a postmidnight show. Of course, every cruise line cannot provide the same variety of programming due to available shipboard facilities, but none can be faulted or criticized for their own quality or quantity of entertainment.

One of the most popular activities on board is dancing—lots of it. Big Bands, intimate combos, rock, and disco are all to be found. Dancing is to be enjoyed by young and old alike, each generation having its own type of music.

The Casino. While enticing to some clients, the casino is not always a selling feature to others. Therefore, its presence and popularity need not be overstated in the selling process. Its mere presence on board will serve as its own lure, even to the uninitiated.

Activity and entertainment-wise, a ship is "alive" into the wee hours of the morning.

A Rewarding Experience

For many people, a cruise vacation can be a dream trip, even a once-in-a-lifetime experience. Many people acknowledge how much they would like to go on a cruise, someday, because in their mind's eye they fantasize about what it might be like and how much they would enjoy it. This is often one of the prime motivations for taking a cruise vacation. The thought of the personal attention received on board is overwhelming. It certainly is warm and human, a people-to-people event.

To remove any apprehensions clients might have, every bit of preliminary information must be given to them. For example, many clients will be pleased to learn that religious services are conducted on board. Each cruise line has its own policy regarding chaplains.

A doctor-and-nurse team aboard, plus hospital facilities, is reassuring to those clients who may have some sort of ongoing ailment. Special medication can be brought aboard and stored in the infirmary for later use. Handicapped passengers are made readily comfortable with special facilities and provisions being made for them. Special diet requirements can be fulfilled.

First-time cruise passengers are bound to ask about seasickness, and they deserve an answer. Most ships are equipped with stabilizers to minimize motion in the event the seas are rough. This feature is especially important where long distance ocean transit is involved. However, on cruises to the Caribbean, especially from Florida ports, the distances between ports of call are relatively short, thereby minimizing the possibility of motion sickness. If it is any consolation, ship movements are made during the night.

A number of effective preventive medications and devices are available on board or can be secured at local pharmacies. If motion sickness is a major concern, clients should be advised to ask their own doctor to prescribe the medication. An effective cure for some can be a dip in the pool, which helps one to regain equilibrium.

The inexperienced cruise client might ask about weather, particularly the possibility of a hurricane. Normally, the weather in the Caribbean, for example, is sunny and hot. Hurricanes can occur, infrequently and seasonally August through October. If one should appear, it is limited to a relatively small area and does not necessarily affect the entire cruising area. When the weather and/or the seas become extremely difficult, ships pull into port or skirt around the storm area. There is never any danger to the cruise passengers.

Meeting people on board is a pleasant experience. On a ship, people are brought together under the best of circumstances, in the best frame of mind. There are many opportunities to create friendships and acquaintanceships with tablemates in the dining room, on deck, or in the lounges. It is not unusual for passengers to make friendships that last beyond the cruise.

Total Value

When all the tangible aspects of a cruise vacation are put together, the cruise passage fare is more than reasonable. Adding the intangibles, the total value is incalculable. What price can be placed on complete personal satisfaction, the pleasures enjoyed, and the memories made?

Every potential client can be convinced to take a cruise vacation. Product can and must be sold first, regardless of price. Price will take care of itself!

REVIEW QUESTIONS

1. What percentage of Americans are said to have ever cruised?

   _____

2. Is there such a thing as a "cruise-type" person? Why?

   _____

3. How does the age factor affect potential cruise markets?

   _____

   _____

4. What/who is the prime motivation for first-time cruisers?

   _____

5. What percentage of cruise bookings is made through travel agencies?

   _____

6. How many potential cruise prospects are there, based on the cruise industry's own estimates?

   _____

7. Many Americans are not yet aware of cruising. Do you agree? Why?

   _____

   _____

8. Why is selling travel a difficult task?

   _____

9. What traits are required of a salesperson dealing with a client?

   _____

   _____

10. What intangibles make a cruise vacation attractive?

    _____

    _____

11. Could relaxation be a negative selling point to a potential client? Why?

    _____

12. Can all ships dock alongside all ports? If not, how are passengers brought ashore?

    _____

13. What is the usual time for embarkation?

    _____

14. What are some embarkation procedures?

_____

_____

15. What are some embarkation procedures followed at the port city airport?

_____

_____

16. After embarkation, what questionnaire forms may passengers be asked to complete?

_____

17. What are some debarkation procedures regarding baggage?

_____

_____

_____

_____

_____

18. What is meant by "all-inclusivity?"

_____

_____

19. What out-of-pocket expenditures might be necessary aboard ship?

_____

_____

20. Do you agree that very few resort hotels provide the same atmosphere, standards, and entertainment as aboard a cruise ship? Describe the differences.

_____

_____

_____

_____

21. What advantage does a resort hotel have over a cruise ship?

_____

_____

22. How would you explain the dress code aboard ship?

_____

_____

CHAPTER 6

Reading the Cruise Line's Descriptive Brochure

Information Sources

The most important source of sales information is the descriptive brochures distributed by each cruise company. One of these is reproduced in Appendix F.

Cruise Brochures

No matter how large or small cruise lines' brochures might be, they all have a standard format, covering four important aspects.

1. The initial pages describe the *product*—the attractiveness of shipboard dining, service, and entertainment.

2. The second section is devoted to the *program*—schedules and itineraries, with detailed descriptions of the ports of call.

3. The final one-third of the brochure contains *booking information*—rate-sheets and deck plans, with photographs and/or cut-out drawings of the various types of staterooms, and general information. The General Information section contains the line's official reservation policies, port locations, embarkation hours, cancellation fee schedules, meal hours, disclaimers, etc. This information is vital to the cruise sales agent, who must advise clients accordingly.

Since it is an inconvenience for a cruise sales agent to keep track of all the brochures available, and because there is no collective source of up-to-date booking information, a three-ring binder is a handy way to store this information for quick reference. Put together the ratesheets, deck plans, and general information pages of each cruise line, and file them alphabetically in the binder. Similarly, additional information about special rates, incentives, and cruise themes can be included. Since all cruise brochures are a standard size, the pages will fit easily. The binder can be kept current as new information is received.

Trade Publications

The three most popular travel trade publications are distributed twice a week, and each has a different format. These are:

Travel Agent
   825 Seventh Avenue
   New York, NY 10019

Travel Trade
   15 West 44th Street
   New York, NY 10036

Travel Weekly
   500 Plaza Drive
   Secaucus, NJ 07094

Cruise supplements are published monthly: *Cruise Advisor* (*Travel Agent*), *Cruise Trade* (*Travel Trade*), and *Cruise Guide* (*Travel Weekly*). They contain a wealth of general and detailed information and should be kept as reference material.

A fourth publication is issued by The Travel Magazines Division of the Official Airlines Guides, 1775 Broadway, New York, NY 10019, on a regional basis. *TravelAge East*, *TravelAge Midwest*, and *TravelAge West* are furnished without charge to full-time travel agency sales personnel upon written request. They feature local industry news, calendar of events, sales information, and special supplements.

There are additional advantages to subscribing to these publications. For one, an advance copy of a cruise line's newest brochure is sometimes included; also, the publications are involved in the sponsorship of national cruise seminars.

Cruise Lines International Association (CLIA)

The Cruise Lines International Association is comprised of approximately 35 cruise lines. It has no industry regulatory powers, its main purpose being marketing and cruise sales training.

Travel agencies can enjoy such benefits by joining CLIA. Membership allows agencies to receive CLIA's *Cruise Manual*, *Agent's Reference Manual*, and a *Cruise Night Planning Guide*. Year-round schedules of local seminars are conducted throughout the country for sales staff personnel and owners/managers, highlighted by several national seminars in various port cities throughout the year, which include ship inspections.

Institute of Certified Travel Agents

ICTA is a national educational organization that sponsors local seminars leading to accreditation as a Certified Travel Counselor (CTC). The broad curricula provide opportunities to develop a higher degree of professionalism in the travel industry.

The OAG (Overseas Airline Guide) Cruise and Shipline Guide—Worldwide Edition

The OAG Guide provides clear, concise information on shipline companies and reservation offices, ship profiles, port terminal diagrams, cruise listings and itineraries, and passenger/freighter service. It contains a world of information to help the travel agent sell cruises. It is divided into three sections: (1) reference and information pages, (2) port-to-port and ferry schedules, and (3) cruise destinations of popular ships.

Reference and Information

First Section. This presents information about ships and shipline companies, passenger ship terminal maps, and sea route maps. Shiplines are listed alphabetically, with addresses, telephone numbers, and related information. The "Shipline Personnel Directory" is a listing of some of the shipline companies, their addresses, and executive personnel.

"Ship Profiles" is very important to travel agents because it alphabetically lists information about ships in service. Categories of information include ship name, tonnage, operator, year commissioned, year rebuilt or refurbished, nationality of crews, hotel staff number, country of registry, ship's former name, passenger capacity, cruise or regular passenger capacity. It also contains such details as those about air-conditioning, stabilizers, and accessibility for handicapped passengers. (See Figure 6-1.)

Passenger Ship Terminals. Diagrams of international passenger ship terminals are included and can be helpful to those passengers who drive to the docks. See the Miami Terminal in Figure 6-2. The top illustration shows the location of the Port of Miami and its proximity to the airport. The illustration below shows parking facilities and the location of piers. Passengers may park their cars in the parking area closest to the pier of their departure.

For passengers using taxi or limousine services, average rates are indicated. Also shown is the amount of traveling time passengers should allow from the airport to the ship terminal.

Port to Port

Because many European countries are bordered by water, it is more convenient and less expensive, generally, to travel by sea. The sea routes in *The OAG Cruise and Shipline Guide* show port cities where services are available. (See Figure 6-3.) Ships carrying passengers only are indicated by a broken dash. Ferries carrying both passengers and automobiles are shown by a solid line. Seasonal routes are marked by a dotted line. The illustration shows sea routes across the North Sea. Clients traveling from England to

FIGURE 6-1

SHIP PROFILES

Ship	Ton-nage	Operator	Commis-sioned	Year Rebuilt/ Refurbished	Nationality of Crew	Hotel Staff Number	Registry	Former Name	Passenger Capacity	Air Cond.	Stab.	Handi-capped Access
Botnia Express	4,152	Vaasaferries	1972	...	Finnish	96	Finland	Diana	1,320	a		
Bowen Queen	1,476	British Columbia Ferry Corporation	1965	...	Canadian	6	Canada	....	394			
Brakzand	140	Wagenborg Passagiers Diensten	1967	1985	Dutch	7	Netherlands	Pr. Willem IV	1,000			
Bremerhaven	916	Weserfaehre GMBH	1954	...	German	...	Germany	....	500			
Brightlingsea	51	Orwell & Harwich Navigation Co.	...	...	British	...	U.K.	....	168			
Britanis	26,000	Fantasy Cruises	1931	1986	Greek	550	Panama	Monterey	1,100	a		
Britannia	1,160	KD German Rhine Line	1969	...	German/Swiss	54	Germany	....	208	a		
Brittania	226	Vedettes Armoricaines	1976	...	French	2	France	....	340			
Bruernish	69	Caledonian MacBrayne	1973	...	British	...	U.K.	....	164			
Bucanero	2,400	Galapagos Center	1952	1977	Ecuadorian	60	Ecuador	St. Ninian	90	a	s	
Bugel-Eussa	130	Service Maritime Carteret-Jersey	...	...	French	...	France	....	220		s	
Caledonia	1,156	Caledonian MacBrayne	1966	...	British	...	U.K.	Stena Baltica	650			
Caledonian Star	3,095	SeaQuest Cruises Ltd.	1985	1991	European/International	55	Bahamas	North Star	130	a	s	
Camelie	69	Navigazione Lago Maggiore	1974	...	Italian	...	Italy	....	80			
Camille-Marcoux	6,122	Societe des Traversiers du Quebec	1974	...	Canadian	15	Canada	....	600		s	
Camoscio	157	Navigazione Lago Maggiore	1973	...	Italian	...	Italy	....	280			
Canadian Empress	463	St. Lawrence Cruise Lines Inc.	1981	...	Canadian	11	Canada	....	66	a		
Canberra	45,000	P&O Cruises	1961	1988	British/Goanese	800	U.K.	....	1,641	a	s	
Canna	69	Caledonian MacBrayne	1975	...	British	...	U.K.	....	50			
Cape Henlopen	2,152	Cape May-Lewes Ferry	1981	...	U.S.	10	U.S.	New Del	800			
Cape May	2,119	Cape May-Lewes Ferry	1985	...	U.S.	10	U.S.	....	800			
Capriolo	157	Navigazione Lago Maggiore	1974	...	Italian	...	Italy	....	280			
Capt. Shepler	100	Shepler's Mackinac Island Ferry	1986	1986	U.S.	3	U.S.	....	265		s	
Caribbean Prince	89	American Canadian Caribbean Line	1983	1989	U.S.	17	U.S.	....	80	a		
Caribe I	23,000	Commodore Cruise Line	1953	1988	International	349	Panama	Olympia	874	a	s	
Caribou	22,294	Marine Atlantic	1986	...	Canadian	84	Canada	....	1,200	a	s	
Cariddi	3,122	Italian State Railways	...	1932	Italian	...	Italy	....	1,800	a		
Carnivale	27,250	Carnival Cruise Lines	1956	1990	Italian/International	350	Panama	Empress of Britain	950	a	s	h
Carola	1,626	Scandinavian Ferry Lines	1964	...	Swedish	...	Sweden	....	703		s	
Catherine Legardeur	1,348	Societe des Traversiers du Quebec	1985	...	Canadian	12	Canada	....	400			
Cathlamet	1,772	Washington State Ferries	1981	...	U.S.	...	U.S.	....	1,200			
Celebration	48,000	Carnival Cruise Lines	1987	...	Italian/International	...	Liberia	....	1,486	a	s	h
Cerbiatto	158	Navigazione Lago Maggiore	1973	...	Italian	...	Italy	....	280			
Challenger	71	Neuman Boat Line	1947	...	U.S.	3	U.S.	....	250			
Champlain	440	Lake Champlain Transportation Co.	1930	...	U.S.	7	U.S.	City of Hampton	329			
Chelan	1	Washington State Ferries	1981	...	U.S.	...	U.S.	....	1,200			
Chi-Cheemaun	6,991	Ontario Northland Marine Services	1974	...	Canadian	75	Canada	....	600	a	s	
Cinderella	44,000	Viking Line	1989	...	Finnish/Swedish	...	...	....	2,500	a	s	
Citta di Piombino	496	Navarma Lines	1964	...	Italian	11	Italy	....	406			
City of Myconos	5,000	Cycladic Cruises	1956	1980	Greek/International	125	Greece	St. Marlo	318	a	s	
City of Rhodos	8,000	Cycladic Cruises	1966	1981	Greek/International	220	Greece	....	508	a	s	
Cierzo	3,367	Compania Trasmediterranea	1979	...	Spanish	24	....	....		a		
Ciudad De Algeciras	3,717	Compania Trasmediterranea	1980	...	Spanish	39	....	Bahia DeCadiz	1,300		s	
Ciudad De Alicante	2,442	Compania Trasmediterranea	1979	...	Spanish	27	....	Roll-Man	12		s	
Ciudad De Badajoz	7,419	Compania Trasmediterranea	1979	...	Spanish	64	....	....	1,300		s	
Ciudad De Cadiz	2,442	Compania Trasmediterranea	1980	...	Spanish	27	....	Roll-All	12		s	
Ciudad De Cauta	2,753	Compania Trasmediterranea	1975	...	Spanish	32	....	Monte Contes	750		s	
Ciudad de Compostela	7,263	Compania Trasmediterranea	1967	...	Spanish	81	Spain	....	1,000		s	
Ciudad De La Laguna	4,212	Compania Trasmediterranea	1967	...	Spanish	54	....	Botnia	1,042		s	
Ciudad De Palma	7,393	Compania Trasmediterranea	1967	...	Spanish	64	....	Canguro Cabo San Jorge	1,300		s	
Ciudad De Salamanca	7,054	Compania Trasmediterranea	1982	...	Spanish	64	....	....	1,300		s	
Ciudad De Sevilla	7,113	Compania Trasmediterranea	1980	...	Spanish	64	....	....	1,300		s	
Ciudad De Valencia	7,054	Compania Trasmediterranea	1984	...	Spanish	64	....	....	1,300		s	
Ciudad De Zaragoza	2,753	Compania Trasmediterranea	1976	...	Spanish	36	....	Monte Corona	750		s	
Clara Schumann	...	KD Elbe River Cruises	...	1991	European	29	Germany	....	128	a		
Claymore	1,631	Caledonian MacBrayne Co.	1978	...	British	...	....	....	500			
Club Med I	14,000	Club Med Sales, Inc.	1990	...	International	...	French West Indies	....	425	a		
Clytus	30	Orkney Islands Shipping Co.	1944	1970	British	2	U.K.	....	46	a		
Coho	5,315	Black Ball Transport	1959	...	U.S.	...	U.S.	....	1,000	a		
Coll	69	Caledonian MacBrayne	1974	...	British	...	U.K.	....	50			
Colonia Del Sacramento	129	Belt S.A./Alimar	1971	1980	Uruguayan	7	Uruguay	Condor 3	127	a	s	
Columba	1,420	Caledonian MacBrayne	1964	...	British	...	U.K.	....	870		s	
Columbia	3,946	Alaska Marine Hwy.	1974	...	U.S.	66	U.S.	....	675	a		
Columbus Caravelle	7,500	Transocean Cruise Lines	1990	...	Ukranian/Russian	120	Bahamas	....	330	a	s	
Commuter	82	Neuman Boat Line	1960	...	U.S.	2	U.S.	....	150			
Cone Johnson	797	Texas State Dept. of Public Trans.	1950	1977	U.S.	6	U.S.	....	500		s	
Constitution	30,090	American Hawaii Cruises	1951	1991	U.S.	320	U.S.	Oceanic Constitution	798	a	s	
Coral Star	231	Coral Bay Cruises	1986	1990	U.S./Jamaican	7	U.K.	Global Star	18	a	s	
Corbiere	4,371	British Channel Island Ferries	1970	1982	British	70	Bahamas	Benodet	800	a		
Coregone	213	La Traverse Du Lac Temiscouata	1976	...	Canadian	...	Canada	....	99			
Cornemuse	74	Vedettes Armoricaines	1965	1975	French	1	France	....	160			
Cornouailles	3,382	Brittany Ferries	1977	1980	French	55	France	....	500	a		
Corse	12,676	Societe Natl. Maritime Corse Medit.	1983	...	French	110	France	....	2,262	a		
Corsica Serena II	4,800	Corsica Ferries	...	...	Italian	60	Panama	....	1,400	a	s	
Corsica Vival	4,650	Corsica Ferries	1969	1980	Italian	55	Panama	Innisfallen	1,200	a	s	
Corvo (Jetfoil)	305	Far East Hydrofoil Co.	1975	...	Hong Kong	12	Hong Kong	Kamehameha	268	a		
Costa Classica	50,000	Costa Cruise Lines	1991	...	Italian/International	750	Italy	....	1,300	a	s	h
Costa Marina	25,000	Costa Cruise Lines	1990	...	Italian/International	385	Italy	Italia	770	a	s	
Costa Riviera	31,500	Costa Cruise Lines	1962	1988	Italian/International	500	Italy	Marconi	984	a	s	
Cowes Castle	911	Red Funnel Ferries	1965	1975	British	9	U.K.	....				
Crown Jewel	20,000	Crown Cruise Line	...	...		320	Bahamas	....	820	a	s	
Crown Monarch	15,270	Crown Cruise Line	1990	...	Filipino	200	Panama	....	556	a	s	
Crown Odyssey	34,250	Royal Cruise Line	1988	...	Greek	470	Bahamas	....	1,052	a	s	h
Crown Princess	70,000	Princess Cruises	1990	...	Italian	696	Italy	....	1,590	a	s	
Crystal Harmony	49,000	Crystal Cruises	1989	...	International	505	Bahamas	....	960	a	s	
Cunard Countess	17,593	Cunard	1976	1986	British/International	350	U.K.	....	956	a	s	
Cunard Princess	17,495	Cunard	1977	1985	British/International	350	Bahamas	Cunard Conquest	962	a	s	
Daino	156	Navigazione Lago Maggiore	1974	...	Italian	...	Italy	....	280			
Daldean	99	Blue Water Ferry	1951	...	Canadian	7	Canada	....	125			
Dalmacija	5,650	Jadrolinija	1965	1987	Yugoslavian	115	Yugoslavia	Rijeka	314	a	s	
Dana Anglia	14,399	Scandinavian Seaways	1978	...	British/Scandinavian	140	Denmark	....	1,372	a	s	
Danae	17,000	Costa Cruise Lines	1956	1984	Italian/International	250	Liberia	Port of Sydney	420	a	s	
Danmark	6,352	DSB Ferry Service	1968	...	Danish	...	Denmark	....	1,500			
Danube Princess	444	Peter Deilmann Reederei	1983	...	....	75	Germany	....	215	a		
Daphne	17,000	Costa Cruise Lines	1955	1988	Italian/International	250	Liberia	Port of Melbourne	420	a	s	
Darnia	3,455	Sealink British Ferries	1977	1986	British	43	British	....	412	a	s	
Daunia	823	Adriatica Line	1965	...	Italian	...	Italy	....	500	a	s	
Davik	151	Fylkesbaatane I Sogn og Fjordane	...	...	Norwegian	...	Norway	....	150			
Dawn Princess	24,700	Princess Cruises	1958	1989	Italian	430	Liberia	Fairwind/Sylvania	890	a	s	
Delaware	2,139	Cape May-Lewes Ferry	1974	...	U.S.	10	U.S.	....	800			
Delfino	225	Navigazione Lago Maggiore	1950	1978	Italian	...	Italy	....	400			

PASSENGER SHIP TERMINAL INFORMATION

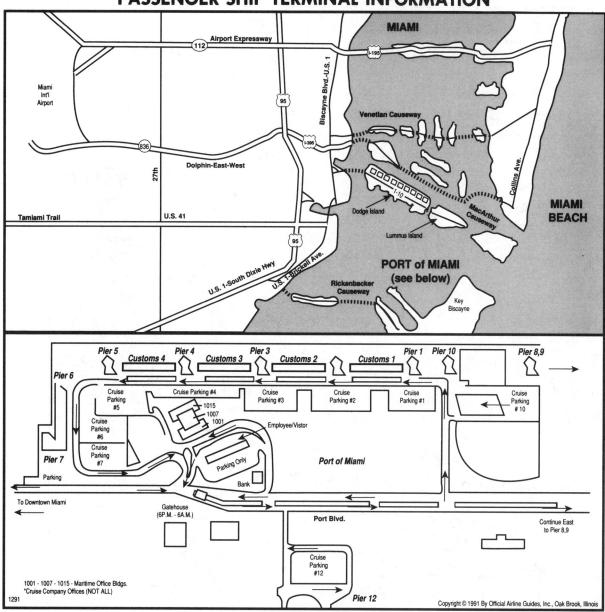

MIAMI

Port Area:

Located in Biscayne Bay just off downtown Miami.

Transportation To Cruise Pier:

Taxi:

From Miami International Airport, $14.00 per person. From Miami Beach, $8.00 to $27.00.

Cars:

Drive onto the port from Biscayne Blvd. at Northeast 5th Street, across a bridge into port area. Color coded signs direct driver to his ship.

Limousine:

From Miami International Airport, $5.50 per person. From Hollywood and Ft. Lauderdale, $11.50 per person.

Parking:

Park-and-lock, secured parking lots directly adjacent to each departure lounge, $6.00 a day.

Piers:

Pier	
Pier 1	*Britanis*
Pier 1 & 2	*Norway*
Pier 2	*Sunward II*
Pier 3	*Dolphin IV*
	Seabreeze
Pier 4	*Nordic Prince*
Pier 5	*Nordic Empress*
	Song of America
	Sovereign of the Seas
Pier 6	*Seascape*
Pier 8	*Holiday*
Pier 9	*Celebration*
	Ecstasy
	Fantasy
Pier 10	*Caribe I*
	Seaward
Pier 12	*Club Med 1*
Gantry Deck	*Americana*

Sea Routes — NORTH SEA

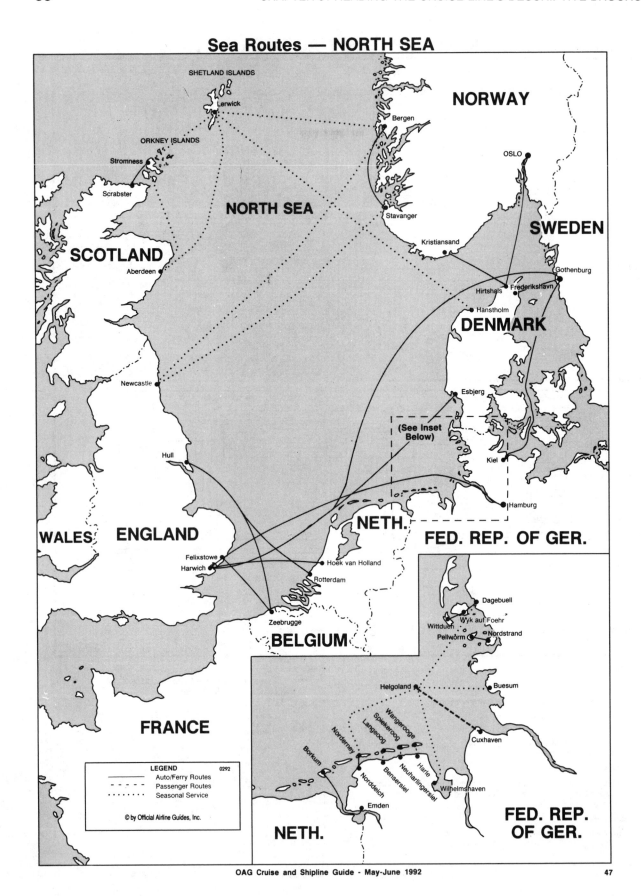

the European continent must consult the Channel Crossing Map because each sea route covers a specific area.

The Guide maps also include Scandinavia, the Western and Eastern Mediterranean Sea, the Adriatic Sea, the Greek islands, and a map showing ports of call visited by ships sailing the Caribbean.

Reference and Information

The sample alphabetical listing of ships in *The OAG*'s "Cruise Destination" section includes the name of the cruise line, port of embarkation, destination, and the length of the cruise. In Figure 6-4, the *Tropicale*, operated by Carnival Cruise Lines, is in service year-round, departing San Juan every Saturday on seven-day cruises to the Caribbean.

Cruise Listings. Follow the cruise listing illustration in Figure 6-5 as you read this explanation. In the section of cruise listings, destination areas are shown in large type and in alphabetical order. In this illustration, the destination is the Caribbean. The originating ports are shown in horizontal alphabetical order.

The next section shows the originating ports listed vertically, in alphabetical order. Listed under each port are the ships departing from it, the date of departure, the itinerary, and related information. Each cruise listing is separated by a solid line. A broken line, or dashed line, separates the regular cruise sailings from the occasional departures.

Regular sailings are presented in order of the earliest departure date. If the dates are the same, the shortest cruise is listed first. If the lengths of the cruises are identical, the shortest cruise is listed first. If cruise lengths are identical, they are listed alphabetically by ship's name.

In the example, *Crown Princess* is the first ship listed. It departs Port Everglades on Saturdays from January 11 through April 18 on seven-day cruises. The remarks section shows that lower rates are available for sailings on January 11 and from April 4, as compared to the regular rates shown.

Since *The OAG Cruise and Shipline Guide* uses the 24-hour clock, the departure and arrival times are listed in that format. The sail and return column in the illustration shows that the *Crown Princess* sails from Port Everglades, Florida, at 1700 hours (5:00 P.M.) and ends at Port Everglades, Florida, at 0800 hours (8:00 A.M.), seven days later. Her itinerary includes Nassau, San Juan, St. Thomas, and the Private Out Island. The cost range is $1,350 to $2,845.

Port-to-Port and Ferry Schedules

This is a listing of ship and ferry services for passengers and automobiles. Note with care that these services operate on irregular schedules.

The listing in Figure 6-6 uses a numerical coding system to indicate the days of the week, known as *frequency codes*:

1—Monday

2—Tuesday

3—Wednesday

4—Thursday

FIGURE 6-4

CRUISE DESTINATIONS OF POPULAR SHIPS
(Alphabetically by Ship Name)

RENAISSANCE III - Renaissance Cruises
Until Oct. 17 Barcelona/Civitavecchia/Venice/Piraeus/ Monte Carlo to Mediterranean (7-11*)

RENAISSANCE IV - Renaissance Cruises
Until Oct. 26 Venice/Piraeus/Monte Carlo/ Civitavecchia/Istanbul to Mediterranean (7)

RENAISSANCE VI - Renaissance Cruises
Until Oct. 24 Barcelona/Monte Carlo/Venice/ Civitavecchia/Piraeus/Istanbul to Iberia/Mediterranean (7-8*)

RENAISSANCE VII - Renaissance Cruises
Until Jun. 20 Piraeus/Istanbul/Venice/Civitavecchia/Monte Carlo/ Barcelona to Mediterranean/Iberia (7)
Jun. 27 - Aug. 29 La Rochelle/Copenhagen/Stockholm/Edinburgh to North Sea/Baltic/Norway (7)
Sep. 5 - Oct. 17 La Rochelle/Barcelona/Monte Carlo/Venice/ Civitavecchia to Iberia/Mediterranean (7)
Nov. 10 - Mar. 14, *1993*, Rio de Janerio/Puerto Montt/ Ushuaia to South America (10-24*)

RENAISSANCE VIII - Renaissance Cruises
Until May 30 Monte Carlo/Civitavecchia/Venice/Barcelona to Mediterranean/Iberia (7)
Jun. 6 - Aug. 22 La Rochelle/Copenhagen/Stockholm/Trondheim to North Sea/Baltic/Norway (7)
Aug. 29 - Oct. 31 La Rochelle/Barcelona/Civitavecchia/Venice/ Monte Carlo/Piraeus to Iberia/Mediterranean (7-8*)

ROTTERDAM - Holland America Line
May 17 - Sep. 20 Vancouver/Seward to Alaska (7)
Sep. 27 Vancouver to Hawaii (19)
Dec. 16 Norfolk to Caribbean (19)
Jan. 4, *1993*, New York Around the World (99)

ROYAL MAJESTY - Majesty Cruise Line
Sep. 18 - Sep. 3, *1993*, Miami to Bahamas every Mon. (4), every Fri. (3)

ROYAL ODYSSEY - Royal Cruise Line Ltd.
May 1 Los Angeles to Mexico (9)
May 10 - Aug. 6 Los Angeles/San Francisco/Vancouver/Whittier to Alaska (7-12*)
Aug. 18 & Nov. 20 San Francisco/Acapulco to Mexico (7)
Aug. 25 & Nov. 9 Acapulco/San Juan Transcanal (10,11)
Sep. 4 & Oct. 28 San Juan/New York to Atlantic Coast (12)
Sep. 16 - Oct. 14 New York/Montreal to Maritime Provinces (7-14*)
Nov. 27 Ensenada to Hawaii (16)
Dec. 13/22 Los Angeles to Mexico (9,12)

ROYAL PRINCESS - Princess Cruises
May 1 Barcelona to Mediterranean (12)
May 15 Southampton to North Sea (12)
Jun. 27 - Aug. 19 London to Baltic (12)
Aug. 31 London Transatlantic to New York (8)
Sep. 8 - Oct. 8 New York/Montreal to Maritime Provinces (10)

ROYAL VIKING QUEEN - Royal Viking Line
May 11 - Jun. 6 Seville/Venice/Monte Carlo to Mediterranean (11-14*)
Jun. 17 Lisbon to North Sea (10)
Jun. 27 - Jul. 25 London/Copenhagen to Norway/Baltic (14)
Aug. 8 Copenhagen to British Isles (14)
Aug. 22 & Sep. 5 London/Monte Carlo to Mediterranean (14)
Sep. 19 Istanbul to Black Sea (10)
Sep. 29 & Oct. 9 Piraeus/Venice to Mediterranean (10)

ROYAL VIKING SUN - Royal Viking Line
May 14 - Jul. 9 Civitavecchia/Copenhagen/London to North Sea/ Baltic/Norway/Iberia (14)
Aug. 10/24 Barcelona/London to North Sea/British Isles (14,16)
Sep. 9 - Oct. 3 Montreal/New York to Maritime Provinces (10-14*)
Oct. 13 Montreal to Atlantic Coast (14)
Oct. 27 Port Everglades to South America (50)
Dec. 16 Port Everglades Transcanal to San Francisco (21)

SAGAFJORD - Cunard/NAC
May 3 Port Everglades to Bermuda (12)
May 15 Port Everglades Transcanal to Los Angeles (14)
May 29 Los Angeles to Mexico (10)
Jun. 8 & Sep. 3 Los Angeles/Vancouver to Pacific Coast (3)
Jun. 11 - Aug. 24 Vancouver/Anchorage to Alaska (10-11*)
Sep. 6 Los Angeles Transcanal to Port Everglades (14)
Sep. 20 Port Everglades to Maritime Provinces (13)
Oct. 3 Montreal to Atlantic Coast (14)
Oct. 15 Port Everglades to Bermuda (10)
Oct. 25 Port Everglades to Caribbean (14)
Nov. 8 Port Everglades to Amazon (14)
Nov. 22 - Dec. 20 Manaus/Port Everglades to Caribbean (14-16*)

SEABOURN PRIDE - Seabourn Cruise Line
Until Aug. 26 Bordeaux/London/Copenhagen to North Sea/ Baltic/Norway (13-14*)
Sep. 9 London Transatlantic to New York (10)
Sep. 19 & Oct. 3 New York to Maritime Provinces (14)

SEABOURN SPIRIT - Seabourn Cruise Line
Until Sep. 21 Nice/Istanbul/Venice/Barcelona/Piraeus to Mediterranean/Black Sea (14)

SEABREEZE - Dolphin Cruise Line
Year-round Miami to Caribbean every Sun. (7)

SEA GODDESS I - Cunard Sea Goddess
May 2/9 Civitavecchia/Monte Carlo to Mediterranean (7,8)
May 23 - Aug. 29 Monte Carlo/London/Copenhagen/Stockholm to British Isles/Baltic/Norway (7-11*)
Sep. 8 - Oct. 21 London/Monte Carlo/Venice/Piraeus to Mediterranean (7-11*)
Oct. 31 Malaga to Iberia (5)
Nov. 5 Funchal Transatlantic to St. Thomas (9)
Nov. 14 - Mar. 27, *1993*, St. Thomas/Barbados to Caribbean (7-11*)

SEA GODDESS II - Cunard Sea Goddess
Jun. 6 - Oct. 17 Civitavecchia/Venice/Piraeus/Monte Carlo/ Istanbul to Mediterranean/Black Sea/Aegean Sea (7-12*)
Nov. 1 Haifa to Indian Ocean (14)
Nov. 15/28 Bombay/Singapore to Asia (13,10)
Dec. 8 - Jan. 5, *1993*, Bali/Cairns to South Pacific (14)
Jan. 19 - Apr. 10 Bali/Singapore/Bangkok to Asia (10-13*)
Apr. 23 Bombay to Indian Ocean (13)

SEA PRINCESS - P & O Cruises
Until Nov. 2 Southampton to Iberia/Mediterranean (10-25*)
Jun. 7/20 & Aug. 14 Southampton to Baltic/Norway (13-16*)
Nov. 14 & Dec. 16 Southampton to Caribbean (31,24)
Jan. 11, *1993*, Southampton Around the World (91)

SEAWARD - Norwegian Cruise Line
Year-round Miami to Caribbean every Sun. (7)

SEAWIND CROWN - Seawind Cruise Line
Year-round Aruba to Caribbean every Sun. (7)

SKY PRINCESS - Princess Cruises
May 5 Port Everglades Transcanal to San Francisco (16)
May 21 - Sep. 18 San Francisco to Alaska (10)
Nov. 3 - Dec. 23 Port Everglades to Caribbean (10)

SKYWARD - Norwegian Cruise Line
Year-round San Juan to Caribbean every Sat. (7)

SONG OF AMERICA - Royal Caribbean Cruises
May 9 - Dec. 26 Acapulco/Los Angeles to Mexico every Sat. (7)

SONG OF FLOWER - Seven Seas Cruise Line
Jun. 21 - Sep. 7 Vancouver/Whittier to Alaska (7)
Oct. 21 - Dec. 22 Tokyo/Hong Kong/Singapore/Bali/Cairns to Asia/South Pacific (7-13*)

SONG OF NORWAY - Royal Caribbean Cruises
May 4/16 Barcelona/Venice to Mediterranean (12)
May 28 - Sep. 1 Barcelona/Amsterdam to North Sea/Baltic/Iberia (12)
Sep. 13 - Nov. 23 Barcelona/Venice/Santa Cruz to Mediterranean /Iberia (11-12*)
Dec. 19 San Juan Transcanal to St. Thomas (14)
Jan. 2, *1993*, San Juan/Recife/Buenos Aires to South America (9-11*)
Feb. 22 Recife to Caribbean (9)
Mar. 3/14 San Juan/Acapulco Transcanal (10,11)
Mar. 24 San Juan to Iberia (10)

SOUTHWARD - Norwegian Cruise Line
Year-round Los Angeles to Mexico every Mon. (4), every Fri. (3)

SOVEREIGN OF THE SEAS - Royal Caribbean Cruises
Year-round Miami to Caribbean every Sat. (7)

STAR PRINCESS - Princess Cruises
May 8 - Oct. 23 Barcelona/Venice/Piraeus/Southampton to Mediterranean/Black Sea (12-14*)
Nov. 4 Barcelona to Caribbean (12)
Nov. 21 - Dec. 26 San Juan to Caribbean every Sat. (7)

STARWARD - Norwegian Cruise Line
Year-round San Juan to Caribbean every Sun. (7)

STELLA MARIS - Sun Line
May 1/15 Piraeus to Aegean Sea (7)
May 22 Piraeus to Aegean Sea (6)
May 30 - Aug. 29 Venice/Nice to Adriatic every Sat. (7)
Sep. 7 Piraeus to Aegean Sea (4)
Sep. 11 - Oct. 23 Piraeus to Aegean Sea every Fri. (7)

STELLA OCEANIS - Sun Line
Until Oct. 30 Piraeus to Aegean Sea every Mon. (4), every Fri. (3)

STELLA SOLARIS - Sun Line Cruises
Until Oct. 26 Piraeus to Aegean Sea/Mediterranean every Mon. (7)

SUN VIKING - Royal Caribbean Cruises
May 2/9 Los Angeles to Mexico (7)
May 16 Los Angeles to Pacific Coast (8)
May 24 - Sep. 13 Vancouver to Alaska every Sun. (7)
Sep. 20/27 Vancouver/Los Angeles to Pacific Coast/Mexico (7)
Oct. 4 - Oct. 24 Acapulco/San Juan Transcanal (10-14*)
Nov. 7 - Mar. 27, *1993*, San Juan to Caribbean every Sat. (7)

SUNWARD II - Norwegian Cruise Line
Year-round Miami to Bahamas every Fri. (3), every Mon. (4)

TRITON - Epirotiki Lines
Until Oct. 30 Piraeus to Mediterranean every Fri. (7)

TROPICALE - Carnival Cruise Lines
Year-round San Juan to Caribbean every Sat. (7)

UNIVERSE - World Explorer Cruises
May 17 - Aug. 23 Vancouver to Alaska (14)

VIKING SERENADE - Royal Caribbean Cruises
Year-round Los Angeles to Mexico every Mon. (4), every Fri. (3)

VISTAFJORD - Cunard/NAC
May 3 Venice to Black Sea (13)
May 16 Genoa to British Isles (6)
Jun. 1 - Jul. 15 Amsterdam/Hamburg to Baltic/Norway/Iberia (8-15*)
Aug. 10/20 Barcelona/Venice to Mediterranean/Aegean Sea (10)
Aug. 30 - Oct. 4 Barcelona/Venice/Genoa to Black Sea/ Mediterranean (10-14*)
Oct. 17/24 Genoa/Barcelona to Iberia (7,14)
Nov. 21 Naples to Caribbean (15)
Dec. 6/20 Port Everglades/Los Angeles Transcanal (14,16)
Jan. 5/16, *1993*, Port Everglades to Caribbean (11,13)
Jan. 29 Port Everglades to South America (22)
Feb. 20 - Apr. 3 Rio de Janerio/Port Everglades to Caribbean (14)
Apr. 17 Port Everglades to Iberia (13)

WESTERDAM - Holland America Line
May 2 Port Everglades Transcanal to Vancouver (21)
May 23 - Sep. 19 Vancouver to Alaska every Sat. (7)
Oct. 5 Vancouver Transcanal to Port Everglades (19)
Dec. 19/26 Port Everglades to Caribbean (7)

WESTWARD - Norwegian Cruise Line
Until Oct. 3 New York to Bermuda every Sat. (7)
Oct. 10 New York to Caribbean (7)
Oct. 17 San Juan Transcanal to Acapulco (7)
Oct. 24 - Dec. 26 Acapulco/Los Angeles to Mexico every Sat. (7)

WORLD RENAISSANCE - Epirotiki Lines
Jul. 25 - Sep. 5 Nice to Mediterranean (14)

ZENITH - Celebrity Cruises
Until Dec. 26 Port Everglades to Caribbean every Sat. (7)

FIGURE 6-5

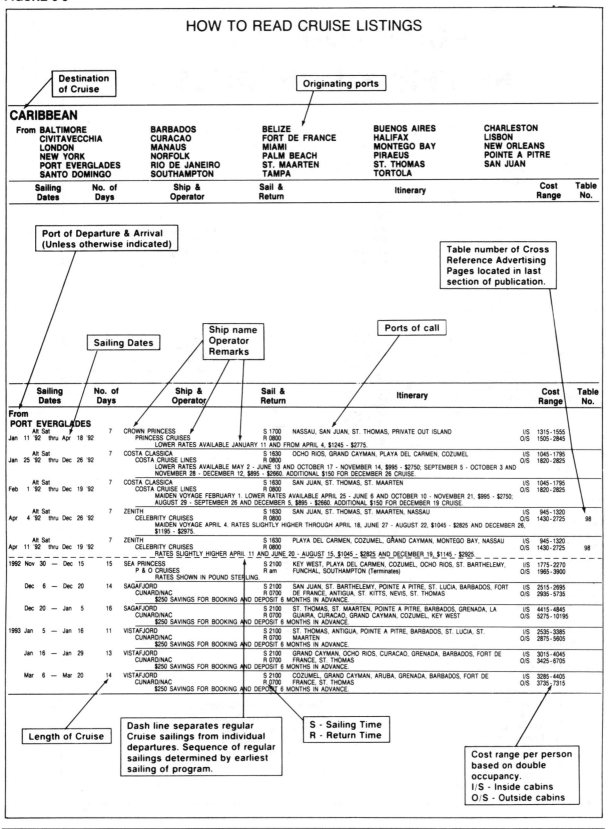

FIGURE 6-6

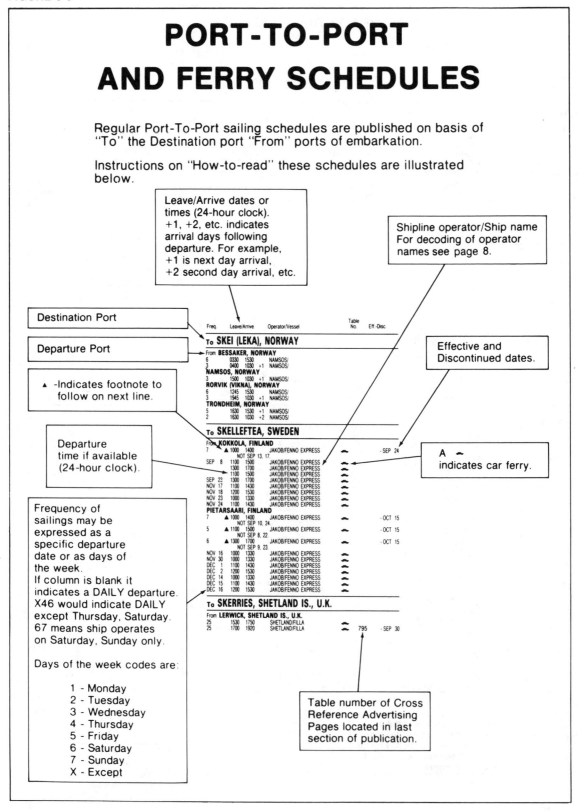

PORT-TO-PORT
AND FERRY SCHEDULES

Regular Port-To-Port sailing schedules are published on basis of "To" the Destination port "From" ports of embarkation.

Instructions on "How-to-read" these schedules are illustrated below.

Leave/Arrive dates or times (24-hour clock). +1, +2, etc. indicates arrival days following departure. For example, +1 is next day arrival, +2 second day arrival, etc.

Shipline operator/Ship name For decoding of operator names see page 8.

Destination Port

Departure Port

▲ -Indicates footnote to follow on next line.

Departure time if available (24-hour clock).

Frequency of sailings may be expressed as a specific departure date or as days of the week. If column is blank it indicates a DAILY departure. X46 would indicate DAILY except Thursday, Saturday. 67 means ship operates on Saturday, Sunday only.

Days of the week codes are:

    1 - Monday
    2 - Tuesday
    3 - Wednesday
    4 - Thursday
    5 - Friday
    6 - Saturday
    7 - Sunday
    X - Except

Effective and Discontinued dates.

A ⌒ indicates car ferry.

Table number of Cross Reference Advertising Pages located in last section of publication.

5—Friday

6—Saturday

7—Sunday

X—Except

The destination port is always listed alphabetically and in the largest type print found in this section. It is bordered by two solid lines. Both the port city and country are shown within these lines. Under the destination port is an alphabetical listing of the departure ports. All information pertaining to a single sailing is shown on one line. For example, the destination port is Skei (Leka), Norway. The *Namsos* departs Bessaker, Norway, on Saturday, at 0330 hours, arriving Skei at 1350 hours. The car symbol indicates that automobiles are accommodated. The last column shows the effective and discontinued dates of service. In the case of the *Namsos*, the blank space means the service is daily, year-round.

Freighter/Passenger Listings. Many freighters have a limited number of passenger cabins, usually accommodating 12 passengers. If a ship carries more than 12 passengers, a doctor must be on board. Freighter travel provides an interesting means of transportation for clients without time constraints. It is leisurely and restful, with the possibility of calling at interesting, even remote, ports. Ports of call and trip lengths can be changed even during the course of a voyage, predicated on freight requirements, be they coastal, intercontinental, or around-the-world. Accommodations and food are quite adequate. Social activities are minimal.

In this section of *The OAG Guide*, as shown in Figure 6-7, departures are shown in large type, followed by destination, shipline, and sailing frequency. Next are the ports of departure, the length of the voyage, and the cost. Last is the listing of the ports of call. For example, the destination is Africa. The shipline is Lykes Bros. The ship sails two or three times monthly from Galveston, Houston, and New Orleans. The full cruise is 60/70 days, and the roundtrip fare is $4,300. Ports of call are Dakar, Monrovia, Abidjan, Tema, Douala, Cabinda, Cape Town, Port Elizabeth, East London, Durban, Maputo, Beira, Dar-es-Salaam, and Mombasa.

Cruise Line Organization

Each cruise company has its own version of a sales and marketing structure, depending on its corporate size. For example, the larger lines have senior vice presidents while smaller ones have regular vice presidents. There are similar variations on other positions, as well. Whatever the case, all lines still have the same sales and marketing functions to perform.

Vice President—Sales. This individual has the overall responsibility, among other duties, for:

■ Developing and implementing policies for general sales, ship charters, group sales, incentive sales, and business meetings.

■ The reservations department, travel agency sales, and sales seminars.

■ Training and direction of field sales representatives.

■ Rate- and commission-setting policies.

FIGURE 6-7

FREIGHTER/PASSENGER SERVICE

From U.S. GULF PORTS

To Africa (South & East)
Lykes Bros. Two/Three Times Monthly.
  From Last U.S. Gulf Port

Full Cruise (60-70)	$4300
Dakar	—
Monrovia	—
Abidjan	—
Tema	—
Douala	—
Cabinda	—
Cape Town	—
Port Elizabeth	—
East London	—
Durban	—
Maputo	—
Beira	—
Dar-es-Salaam	—
Mombasa	—

To Mediterranean
Lykes Bros. Three/Four Times Monthly.
  From Last U.S. Gulf Port

Full Cruise (35-50)	$3400
Morocco	—
Algeria	—
Tunisia	—
Italy	—
Egypt	—
Israel	—

To North Europe
Lykes Bros. Two/Three Times Monthly.
  From New Orleans

Cruise One Way Only (12-13)	$1500
Antwerp	—
Bremerhaven	—
Felixstowe	—
Le Havre	—
Galveston	—

To Orient/Pacific
Lykes Bros. Twice Monthly.
  From Last U.S. Gulf Port

Full Cruise (60-80)	$4500
Yokohama	—
Nagoya	—
Kobe	—
Busan	—
Keelung	—
Manila	—
Shanghai	—
(Alternate Itinerary):	
Manila	—
Singapore	—
Hong Kong	—
Jakarta	—

To South America
Ivaran Lines. Monthly.
  From Houston

Full Cruise (50-53)	$6000
All Ports in Brazil	—
Uruguay/Argentina	—

Lykes Bros. Once Monthly.
  From Last U.S. Gulf Port

Full Cruise (30-40)	$3500
Cartagena	—
Barranquilla	—
Balboa	—
Guayaquil	—
San Antonio	—
Valparaiso	—
Matarani	—
Callao	—
Buenaventura	—

From U.S. WEST COAST PORTS

To Around the World
Egon Oldendorff (Freighter World Cruises).
  From Long Beach

Full Cruise (84)	$6190-$7960
Oakland	—
Japan	—
Korea	—
Taiwan	—
Hong Kong	—
Singapore	—
Antwerp	—
Rotterdam	—
Felixstowe	—
Bremerhaven	—
New York	—
Norfolk	—
Savannah	—
Long Beach	—

To Around the World
Hanseatic Marine (Freighter World Cruises).
  From Long Beach

Full Cruise (84)	$7960
Oakland	—
Yokohama	—
Osaka	—
Pusan	—
Kaohsiung	—
Hong Kong	—
Singapore	—
Antwerp	—
Rotterdam	—
Felixstowe	—
Bremerhaven	—
New York	—
Norfolk	—
Savannah	—
Long Beach	—

To Around the World
Laeisz Line (Freighter World Cruises).
  From Long Beach

Full Cruise (84)	$8400-$8850
Oakland	—
Yokohama	—
Osaka	—
Pusan	—
Kaohsiung	—
Hong Kong	—
Singapore	—
Antwerp	—
Rotterdam	—
Felixstowe	—
Bremerhaven	—
New York	—
Norfolk	—
Savannah	—

To Around the World
Projex (Freighter World Cruises).
  From Long Beach

Full Cruise (84)	$7960
Oakland	—
Yokohama	—
Osaka	—
Pusan	—
Kaohsiung	—
Hong Kong	—
Singapore	—
Antwerp	—
Rotterdam	—
Felixstowe	—
Bremerhaven	—
New York	—
Norfolk	—
Savannah	—

To Australia
Columbus Line (Freighter World Cruises).
Six Sailings Annually.
  From Los Angeles

Full Cruise (42-45)	$5150-7900
Sydney	—
Melbourne	—
Auckland	—
Wellington	—
Noumea	—
Suva	—
Seattle	—

To Canada
Containerships Reederei (Freighter World Cruises).
  From Long Beach

Full Cruise (10-11)	$1150-$1375
Oakland	—
Seattle	—
Vancouver	—
Long Beach	—

To Europe
Containerships Reederei (Freighter World Cruises). Monthly.
  From Seattle

Full Cruise (46)	$4375-$5000
Vancouver	—
Oakland	—
Long Beach	—
Bremerhaven	—
LeHavre	—
Long Beach	—

To Orient
Chilean Line (Freighter World Cruises).
  From Long Beach/Honolulu

Full Cruise (50-55)	$5500-$5950
Yokohama	—
Nagoya	—
Kobe	—
Pusan	—
Keelung	—
Kaohsiung	—
Hong Kong	—
Honolulu	—

To Orient
Egon Oldendorff (Freighter World Cruises).
  From Savannah

Full Cruise (115)	$8750
Philadelphia	—
Tampa	—
Kushiro	—
Ishinomaki	—
Kashima	—
Hososhima	—
Nagoya	—
Kobe	—
Yokohama	—
Savannah	—

To Orient/South America
Marcon Line (Freighter World Cruises).
  From San Francisco

Full Cruise (120)	$9477-$12000
Japan	—
Korea	—
Taiwan	—
Hong Kong	—
Singapore	—
Mauritius	—
South Africa	—
Argentina	—
Uruguay	—
Brazil	—
South Africa	—
Sri Lanka	—
Singapore	—
Hong Kong	—
Taiwan	—
Korea	—
Japan	—
San Francisco	—

To South America
Chilean Line (Freighter World Cruises).
  From Long Beach/Honolulu

Full Cruise (45)	$3750-$4050
Guayaquil	—
Callao	—
Arica	—
Iquique	—
Antofagasta	—
Valparaiso	—
Long Beach/Honolulu	—

Vice President—Reservations. Other titles for this position might be Manager or Director of Reservations. The main responsibility is to maximize bookings. Equally important is maintaining the computerized reservation system at the highest level of efficiency, as well as overseeing inventory control and reservations staff training and direction.

Manager—Individual Sales. This manager supervises the reservations staff in the booking of individual passengers, and provides guidance and direction.

Manager—Group Sales. This individual analyzes group requests and allocates space accordingly, while monitoring the progress of such group promotions and coordinates all the related details.

Manager—Inventory Control. This is a very important internal activity. The manager is responsible for keeping management fully posted as to the number of staterooms sold (according to rate categories), the space allocated, and the staterooms that remain unsold, so that immediate decisions can be made to improve bookings, if necessary.

Manager—Administration. In addition to supervising the issuance of all booking documents and information, the administration manager oversees the operation of the Air Reservations and Shore Excursion divisions. A cruise line is a major buyer of airline tickets to cover the air transportation included in the cruise air/sea package. The development, pricing, and operation of sightseeing tours at the respective ports of call are important functions of this department as well.

Director—Field Sales. The Director's major responsibility is to provide guidance and direction to the field sales representatives and to sustain a working relationship with travel agencies. Since more than 95 percent of all cruise bookings are made by travel agencies, it is vital that travel agency owners/managers and staff are given every opportunity and all the assistance they need to succeed.

Field Sales Representatives. The official title can be Regional Sales Manager, Regional Sales Director, District Sales Manager, Account Executive, or (the original) Field Sales Representative.

"Sales reps" are paid to assist owners/managers in the development and promotion of cruise sales, as well as to educate and train agency staff members in company-related matters. To a marked degree, a field sales rep can (and should) be utilized as the travel agency's own cruise expert.

Since visitations from sales reps might be infrequent, it is in the travel agency's interest to contact the reps for special assistance and active support.

Vice President—Marketing. This VP develops and implements the company's marketing strategies in advertising, public relations, and brochure and promotional item production.

The Advertising Department, besides the normal development and placement of advertisements, can provide travel agencies with ad slicks for an agency's own advertising program, as well as blank flyers and shell folders. (See Figure 6-8.)

Public Relations activities are being placed in the hands of outside firms for the issuance of press releases, ship photographs, and other in-

FIGURE 6-8

THE BAHAMAS
CITY TOUR & ARDASTRA GARDENS

By Taxi
Duration: approximately 3 hours   Price $19.00
Departure: 9:15 a.m.

After a 1-1/2 hour historic city tour, you will arrive at Ardastra Gardens — set in almost five acres of the most beautiful creation of tropical plants, animals and birds from all over the world. By following a set of clearly marked arrows you can conduct yourself on a fascinating and leisurely tour of the exotic flora.

Then sit back and be treated to the world-famous marching Flamingo Show, featured in National Geographic Magazine and TV's "That's Incredible." These World-Famous Flamingos of the Ardastra Gardens first performed in the 1950's and have been seen by thousands of people from all over the globe. Be sure to bring your camera and plenty of film to capture this remarkable and unusually humorous display by these beautiful and exotic tropical pink birds as they march in drill formation. Return to the SeaBreeze after the performance.

PUERTO RICO
OLD AND NEW SAN JUAN

Duration: approximately 2-1/2 hours   Price $14.00
Departure: On arrival

Depart from the pier via air conditioned buses and drive through the Old City of San Juan, where History and Architecture are felt in the air everywhere.

Visit the massive ancient fortress and the great stone walls that have protected the Capital since the "Conquistadores" built it in the 16th Century.

The order of highlights may vary, but will include a visit to El Morro Fortress, which guards the entrance to San Juan Harbor, San Jose, the second oldest church in the hemisphere, the famous Cristo Chapel and the Governor's Mansion.

Continue onto El Condado, a section of the New San Juan, and drive through Isla Verde, where there will be a stop for photographs.

The tour will bring you back to the pier.

If you prefer to stay in Old San Juan you may do so, and return to the ship at your expense.

EL YUNQUE RAIN FOREST

Duration: approximately 4 hours   Price $24.00
Departure: On arrival

Depart from the pier on air conditioned buses to enjoy the 28,000 acre EL YUNQUE rain forest.

El Yunque, named after the good spirit "YUQUIYU" is in the Luquillo Mountain Range. The rain forest is verdant with feathery ferns, thick rope-like vines, white tuberoses and ginger, miniature orchids, and about 240 different species of trees. During the year more than 100 billion gallons of rainwater fall on the forest. The highest peak in the forest is 3,532 feet, named El Toro.

The rare Puerto Rican parrot also finds his home in El Yunque, along with millions of tiny (about one inch in length) frogs known as "coquis."

After departing from the rain forest the tour will continue to one of the Island's best and most popular beaches, Luquillo, with its crescent shape and adorned with coconut palm trees, where you will have opportunity for picture taking or a short stroll admiring the pristine waters.

The tour ends at the pier.

FLAMENCO FESTIVAL

Duration of Show: approximately 1 hour   Price $34.00
Departure: To be advised on the ship

Directly from Spain, to the chords of guitar strings and castanets, Marcelo Productions and the El San Juan Hotel & Casino with great pleasure bring you Carmen Motta's International Spanish Ballet.

Carmen Motta's Ballet has stormed many International stages such as South America and Europe; including their own native Spain, bringing audiences to their feet with olés and euphoria.

All the grace and magical charm of the Andalucian-born flamenco transported to your feet at the Club Tropicoro.

Come, lose yourself in all the mystery and enchantment. Feel your blood race with passion and excitement. You just might come out shouting... OLÉ!

Tour includes:
• Round trip ground transportation to and from the ship
• Admission to the Tropicoro Night Club
• Two drinks

U.S. VIRGIN ISLANDS
ST. JOHN

ISLAND TOUR

Duration: approximately 2 hours   Price $14.00
Departure: On arrival

The tour consists of a scenic drive around the beautiful island of St. John, with stops at such overlooks as Cruz Bay, Maho Bay, Whistling Cay (with great down-island view of the British Virgin Islands), Coral Bay, the first settlement on St. John and Caneel Bay overlooking the Rockefeller Plantation.

Also included is a 15 to 20 minute stop at Annaberg ruins which was the 1st working sugar plantation on St. John. A guided tour of the ruins as well as a brochure is included in the visit.

The tour ends at Cruz Bay from where you will board the tender returning to St. Thomas to join the SS SeaBreeze.

BEACH TOUR

Duration: approximately 3 hours   Price $21.00
Departure: On arrival

By safari bus you will drive from the National Park Dock, past sights such as Laurence Rockefeller's Caneel Bay Plantation, and lovely Hawksnest Beach, arriving at Trunk Bay to enjoy two hours of swimming or sunbathing.
Rum punch and fruit punch included.
On the beach are changing rooms/rest rooms, and fresh water showers. The tour will end at Cruz Bay from where you will board tender returning to St. Thomas to join the SS SeaBreeze.

formation. The in-house PR department develops promotional items, such as descriptive brochures, posters, and visual aids. The latter includes 16-mm films and, now more commonly videocassettes, featuring individual ships or the line in general. Also, educational and sales training videocassettes are being made available by some lines. No doubt, others will follow suit.

Cruise Familiarization. Cruise familiarization trips are available to cruise sales agents, either free of charge or at a reduced rate.

From time to time, cruise lines have familiarization cruises and will accommodate sales agents on a complimentary basis. Since such seminars at sea are not necessarily advertised, the cruise line's Field Sales Representative should be advised of one's personal interest. On the other hand, reduced rates are available throughout the year, as space is available. An official letter from the travel agency's owner/manager is required. The same rate is extended to an agent's spouse.

Many cruise lines conduct local seminars at breakfast, luncheon, or evening functions, at which their upcoming cruise programs are featured. Attendance is not necessarily restricted, although an RSVP is expected.

The cruise line's films and videocassettes can be borrowed, although the cassettes are also available for purchase, which is recommended, since they can be used as a sales tool as well.

Cruise information can be derived from local travel associations, by socializing with one's peers. Experiences can be exchanged, and ideas and knowledge shared. Guest speakers and destination presentations are always featured.

Name _____ Date _____

REVIEW QUESTIONS

1. What is the most important cruise sales tool?

   _____

2. What are the three basic aspects of a cruise brochure?

   _____

   _____

   _____

3. Why is the General Information page so important?

   _____

   _____

   _____

   _____

   _____

4. Since a comprehensive cruise sales manual is not readily available, what can be done to develop one?

   _____

   _____

   _____

   _____

5. What are the advantages to subscribing to travel industry publications?

   _____

   _____

   _____

6. What is CLIA? What are its basic functions?

   _____

   _____

   _____

   _____

7. What are some of the titles given to cruise sales representatives?

   _____

   _____

8. Of what value to a travel agency is a line's Field Sales Representative?

   _____

   _____

9. How can a cruise line's marketing department be of help to a travel agency?

Advertising division: _____

_____

Public relations division: _____

_____

10. What materials are available for educational and promotional purposes?

_____

_____

_____

_____

11. How does one get to experience a familiarization cruise?

_____

_____

_____

_____

_____

OAG EXERCICES

Answer these questions using the samples from *The OAG Worldwide Cruise and Shipline Guide* reproduced in this chapter.

1. Indicate the details for each of the following ships:

Name of Ship	Tonnage	Year Commissioned	Crew Nationality	Registry	Passenger Capacity
Crown Princess					
Caribe I					
Club Med I					
Crystal Harmony					
Celebration					

2. What was the previous name of the following vessels?

Britanis   _____

Carnivale   _____

Costa Riviera   _____

Dawn Princess   _____

3. In the Port of Miami, what ships dock at the following piers:

Pier 1 _____   Pier 5 _____

_____   _____

Pier 3 _____   Pier 9 _____

_____   _____

Pier 4 _____

_____

4. From which port in England would a passenger leave for:

Zeebrugge, Belgium? _____

Hamburg, Germany? _____

5. What ship sails from Southampton, England, on cruises year-round?

_____

6. According to the Cruise Listings page, what ships were scheduled to make their maiden voyages?

_____   _____

7. What ships provide a special fare inducement?

_____

_____

How much is it? _____

Under what conditions is it available? _____

_____

8. What passenger/freighter shipline sails from U.S. Gulf Ports to Africa (South and East)?

_____

What is the length of the cruise?

_____

What is the cruise fare?

_____

9. What is the name of the ferry operating between Lerwick and Skerries, Shetland Islands, U.K., departing September 30?

_____   Departing: _____ hours   Arriving: _____ hours

CHAPTER 7

Working with the Cruise Lines

Reservation Procedures

All cruise lines have toll-free nationwide or in-state 800 and local telephone numbers, as well as FAX machines, to handle reservations. As of 1992, only one cruise line had an automated system.

Cruise lines' Reservations Departments located on the eastern seaboard are open late (8:00 P.M. Eastern Time) to accommodate Midwest and Far West travel agencies; conversely, those on the West Coast open early (6:00 A.M. Pacific Time) to service Eastern travel agencies. From time to time, some cruise lines open their Reservations Departments on weekends.

Preliminary Preparation

A cruise reservation can be made quickly with a bit of preliminary preparation. It is most important to collect all the pertinent information before contacting a cruise line's Reservations Department, to avoid time-consuming and unnecessary talk when booking the reservation. Proper communication, in the presence of the client, reflects favorably on the agent's professionalism.

The following information should be immediately at hand when booking a cruise reservation:

1. The name of the ship and the sailing date.
2. If it is an air-sea (fly-cruise) package, the name and location of the local airport.
3. Definite parameters as to the client's price range or budget.
4. Type and location of desired stateroom.
5. Full names of the clients.
6. Special requirements, if needed (for example, help for a handicapped client).

Space and Wait-Lists

Based on this information, the cruise line's reservationist can inform you of the availability of the stateroom, its rate, room number, deck location, and the facilities provided in the room. He or she can then offer you and your clients a stateroom for acceptance.

If the desired type of stateroom is not immediately available, the reservationist might suggest that the request be placed on the ship's wait-list, in case such a stateroom becomes available. This wait-list remains active only for a short period of time, so it is sometimes best to contact the cruise line from time to time to try to initiate the booking anew.

Some cruise lines have a *guaranteed* wait-list, based upon payment of a good-faith deposit of, say $200 or $250. This assures the applicant of continued consideration for the desired type of space and also protects the client against any increase in fares. If space becomes available, the good-faith deposit is automatically credited toward the normal deposit requirements, or final payment. A full refund of the deposit is made in the event

FIGURE 7-1
Booking confirmation.

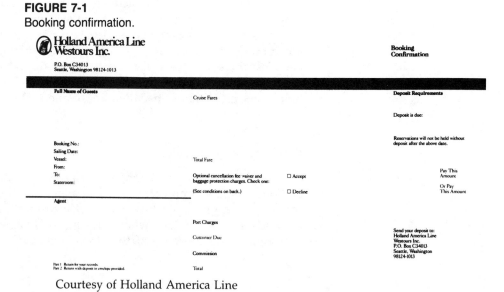

Courtesy of Holland America Line

no space becomes available. Once you have made the reservation, the cruise line sends a booking confirmation, often called an invoice. It contains information such as booking number, sailing date, name of vessel, port sailing from, port cruising to, stateroom, deposit requirements, and the date the deposit is due. The booking confirmation form is shown in Figure 7-1. This is the procedure that Holland America follows, but procedures may vary depending on the policy of each cruise line.

Guarantees

From time to time, a cruise line may offer guaranteed accommodations at the rate requested. In other words, the cruise line is stating the client will definitely be booked. The normal deposit is remitted. In the event a stateroom is not available in the rate category requested and guaranteed, the cruise line will upgrade the reservation and assign a stateroom in a higher-rated category, at no extra charge! Generally this is done when a particular category is not selling well. For example, the demand is strong for category A which is less expensive than category B, the next category, for which the demand is very weak. The cruise line will guarantee your reservation for category A, and when it becomes overbooked, they will move you up to category B. In this fashion, they've filled the space that otherwise would have remained unsold.

Automation

Completely automated cruise reservations system are becoming a reality. The first such system to be instituted is CruiseMatch 2000, by Royal Caribbean Cruise Line (RCCL), which is a model for industry systems to follow. (See Figure 7-2.)

CruiseMatch 2000:

- Offers real-time, direct access to Royal Caribbean Cruise Line's full inventory, including specific cabin number, cabin category availability and pricing, and a deck plan.
- Allows agents to enter passenger-specific information.
- Provides instant confirmation and agency-specific pricing.
- Provides information and booking capability for pre- and postcruise land packages and promotional fares in effect at the time of booking.
- Ensures confidentiality via a unique security program.
- Continues to provide an alternative booking system for traditional telephone reservations.
- Provides total assistance via CruiseMatch 2000 Help Desk.

System Partners: Sabre, System One, and Worldspan.

Facsimile Service: Agents can request booking information and receive confirmation via facsimile machine. Fax service is provided by all cruise lines, from instantaneous to regular confirmation of space. RCCL's is called CruiseFax.

CruiseFlex: Another innovation of RCCL, CruiseFlex can handle a travel agent's special client requests or problems, such as air/sea arrangements or documentation, including verification of flights, correcting flight information and names, locating missing documents, clarifying how and when

FIGURE 7-2

Royal Caribbean Cruises Ltd.'s CruiseMatch 2000, the first and only direct access, availability, and booking system for cruises.

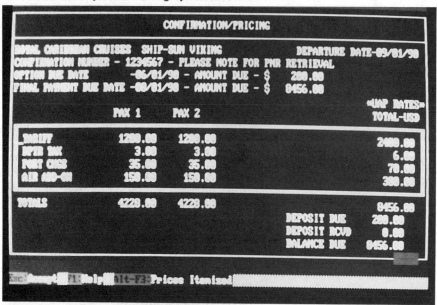

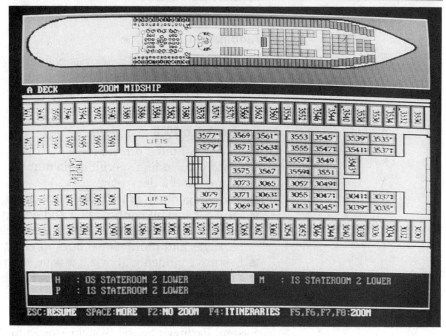

documents will be mailed, extending pre- and postcruise stays, and providing airline upgrades.

Personal Computers: RCCL has developed a PC version for cruise-only agencies.

Cruise Databases: General cruise information software is being developed by a number of concerns.

Acceptance of Space

At the time the stateroom is offered to the travel agent, the reservationist stipulates a specific Option Date for Acceptance, usually a week to ten days later. Shortly thereafter, the cruise line provides the agent with a computerized printout confirming the reservation, the applicable fare, port taxes, possible air add-on, the amount of deposit required, and the option expiration date (of course). A reminder about possible cancellation penalties is included.

Baggage

There is no limit to the amount of personal luggage that can be taken on board most vessels (there are some exceptions). However, airline restrictions on baggage amounts should be considered.

All baggage is subject to possible search. Film should not be packed except in special protective bags; it is best to carry it on board. Valuables also should be carried on board. They can be placed in safety deposit boxes at the Front Desk, if desired.

Baggage insurance against loss or damage is not necessarily provided by the cruise line. Some companies have very limited coverage and others none at all. It is very important to refer to the general information page of the line's brochure to ascertain its baggage loss/damage liability. In general, passengers should secure appropriate baggage insurance coverage through their travel agent. Some cruise lines may provide complimentary luggage tags as shown in Figure 7-3.

FIGURE 7-3
A complimentary luggage tag.

Courtesy of Holland America Line

Cancellation Fees Waiver

Some passengers may wish to protect themselves should they have to cancel their plans. Such cruise passengers may purchase a Cruise Fees Waiver policy from many of the lines. The decision to do so *must* be made when the deposit is remitted. It cannot be done at another time, and it is nonrefundable. The coverage costs approximately $50. (See Figure 7-4.)

When the passenger pays the nonrefundable Cancellation Fees Waiver and Baggage Protection, no cancellation charges or penalties will be assessed, provided the cruise line involved receives a written or telephone notice at least 24 hours prior to departure or as otherwise indicated by the respective cruise line. Should a cancellation be made within 24 hours of departure, the normal charges and penalties apply.

Each cruise line has its own policy regarding cancellations. The general information page of every cruise brochure indicates the specific schedule of penalties which can be applied against late cancellation. It could be a flat sum or a percentage of the fare paid.

In practice, however, most lines do not assess a penalty if written notice is received by a certain date, e.g., 45 to 60 days prior to departure date. However, some lines impose a small administrative charge.

Assessed penalty charges for early cancellation might be retained by some cruise lines as a credit (only) towards the purchase of another cruise within a year, with some possible restrictions.

FIGURE 7-4
Cancellation fees waiver.

Cancellation Fees Waiver And Baggage Protection

Cancellation Fees Waiver Conditions
Payment of the NON-REFUNDABLE CANCELLATION FEES WAIVER (to be made at the time of your deposit) protects you (the passenger) against the following cancellation charges:

If Cruise/Tour Cancelled By Passenger	Cancellation Fee/Charge
More than 60 days prior to scheduled departure	No Charge
Within 60 to 30 days prior to scheduled departure	$100 per person
Within 29 to 15 days prior to scheduled departure	50% of gross fare
14 days or thereafter prior to scheduled departure	75% of gross fare
Non-appearance (without prior written notice) at time of scheduled departure	100% of gross fare

In addition, the protection enables the passenger to cancel for any reason whatsoever, at the sole discretion of the passenger, so long as written notice is actually received by Holland America Line-Westours Inc. at its office located at 300 Elliott Avenue West, Seattle, WA 98119, at least twenty-four (24) hours prior to the vessel's scheduled departure date at port of embarkation, or, in the event of a fly/cruise package, written notice to be received at least twenty-four (24) hours prior to the departure of the airline flight.

REFUNDS: Submit all claims for cancellation refunds (which are to be accompanied by passenger's cruise and/or tour vouchers) to: Reservations Control, Holland America Line-Westours Inc., 300 Elliott Avenue West, Seattle, Washington 98119. Refunds will be processed on the basis of net payment(s) received by Holland America Line-Westours Inc. (excluding the NON-REFUNDABLE "waiver" fee.)

HL61784

Courtesy of Holland America Line

Payment of Deposit

Upon receipt of the deposit check, the cruise line sends a second confirmation printout, called a deposit receipt, acknowledging receipt of payment, reconfirming the arrangements made, and providing a reminder of the date the balance is due. Holland America Line's deposit receipt is shown in Figure 7-5. The deposit check *must* be received by the cruise line prior to the expiration of the option date. Otherwise, the reservation could be cancelled automatically (computers can be that efficient).

FIGURE 7-5
Payment of deposit receipt.

Holland America Line
Westours Inc.

P.O. Box C34013
Seattle, Washington 98124-013

Deposit Receipt

Party No.   Guests   Cabin No.

Booking No.:   Gross Sales:

Ship: Commission:

Sailing: Previous
                                             Payments:

Sailing Date:

Total Passengers:

                                             Total Paid:

Agent

                                             Remaining Due:

                                             Final payment must be received
                                             at least 60 days before sailing.

Part 1 Please Retain for your Records
Part 2 Return this portion with remittance in the envelope provided

Courtesy of Holland America Line

Together with the deposit receipt, the cruise line will send a Special Services Request Form, which is to be completed and submitted to the cruise line with the final payment.

Most lines will accept major credit cards. In general, certain administrative procedures must be followed:

1. Authorization from the credit card company must be obtained.
2. The cruise line must be advised and the appropriate forms sent to it.
3. Within a reasonable time after receipt of such forms for final payment, the commission is automatically forwarded by the cruise line to the travel agency.

Once your clients have submitted their deposit, tell them about the documents they will need when returning to U.S. shores. They will be required to show proof of citizenship. A birth certificate (or certified copy), a current or recently expired passport, a voter's registration card, or a U.S. Naturalization Certificate will be sufficient. Resident aliens will need an Alien Resident Card. For other aliens, a valid passport and valid U.S. Re-Entry Permit is required. Other requirements may apply. The cruise line will advise accordingly.

On longer cruises, the U.S. Immigration Service recommends that a passenger's passport be valid for at least six months beyond the cruise completion date.

Passengers must also complete a Customs Declaration Form, indicating what purchases, if any, were made during the cruise. United States residents are allowed up to $1,200 in retail purchases, including five liters of liquor, per adult, if the cruise called at St. Thomas, USVI. Of that total amount, up to $600 in retail purchases, including one liter of liquor, may be made at other ports. Excluding the call at St. Thomas, U.S. residents are allowed up to $600 in retail purchases, including two liters of liquor per adult, depending on the port of purchase. Since some restrictions might apply, detailed information will be provided aboard ship.

Any applicable duty payments are to be made to Customs before passengers will be permitted to leave the pier.

Final Payment

Final payment is made anywhere from 30 to 45 to 60 days prior to the sailing date, depending on the cruise line's policy.

The applicable commission is deducted from the final (balance) payment. When a credit card is used, commission payment will be forthcoming from the cruise line within a reasonable time. Each line has its own policy for such commission payment.

Upon receipt of final payment, the cruise line issues all the necessary documents, including the cruise passage ticket, round-trip airline tickets, transfer coupons for service between the airport and the ship, baggage tags and labels, plus whatever informational pamphlets might apply.

Special Services Request Form

When remitting final payment, a Special Services Request Form must be returned. It covers the personal arrangements required on board, which include the following:

Dining Room Reservations. Ascertain your clients' preference for their dinner hour. First sitting usually is at 6:15 or 6:30 P.M., and the second sitting at 8:15 or 8:30 P.M. Each has its advantage. In the main, however, the choice is usually based on personal habit. The second sitting provides ample time

FIGURE 7-6a
Dining room and gift order request.

Holland America Line

300 Elliott Avenue West, Seattle, WA 98119
Attn: Ship Services

Dining Room and
Gift Order Request

Passenger(s):

Booking No:
Sailing Date:
Vessel:
From:
To:
Stateroom:

Agent

Important: Return top three copies with payment to address above. Retain bottom copy for your records.

Dining Room Seating Request
PLEASE NOTE: This is a request only. Actual confirmation will be advised onboard. While it is not possible to accommodate every request, our staff will do their best to assign dining fairly on a FIRST COME, FIRST SERVE BASIS.

Sitting: 1st ☐ 2nd ☐ Table Size: ☐ 2 ☐ 4 ☐ 6 Smoking: ☐ Yes ☐ No Age Preference: ☐ 60/70 ☐ 40/50 ☐ 20/30

Dinner is served in two sittings at 6:15 p.m. and 8:15 p.m. (Alaska, 30 minutes earlier). Breakfast and lunch are normally served in an open sitting 8-9:30 a.m. and 12:15-1:30 p.m. respectively. These hours may be altered during voyage when arrival and departure times make this necessary.

Please Seat With: Mr/Mrs ______ Cabin ______
Mr/Mrs ______ Cabin ______
Mr/Mrs ______ Cabin ______

Special Requests: ☐ Kosher ☐ Salt Free ☐ Diabetic ☐ Birthday ______ ☐ Anniversary ______
☐ Other ______ Please specify Mr or Mrs: ☐ Mr ☐ Mrs

GIFT ORDER (See list and policy on back)

Item No.	Quantity	Size	$ Amount

SHIPBOARD CREDIT ______
May be used for shore excursions, shop purchases, bar credits, massage, photos and beauty shop.

Total Remittance ($ U.S.) $ ______

GIFT MESSAGE

To: ______

From: ______

Serve: ☐ At Embarkation ☐ At Leisure ☐ Cruise: Day ___

Courtesy of Holland America Line

FIGURE 7-6b
Cocktail party request information.

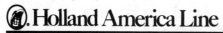 **Holland America Line**

**Cocktail Party
Request Information**

Honor your clients with a festive event they'll never forget—a cocktail party on board one of Holland America's elegant cruise ships!

Prelunch/Predinner Cocktail Party

- Minimum 10 passenger charge
- 45 minute Open Bar, premium liquor
- Invitations
- Hot hors d'oeuvres
- Music

Price: $ 12.00 per person
Addition of cold hors d'oeuvres: $ 3.00 per person
For each additional 15 minutes: $ 3.00 per person

Nonalcohol Party

- Minimum 10 passenger charge
- Fruit punch/soft drinks/mineral waters
- Invitations
- Hot hors d'oeuvres
- Music

Price: $ 6.00 per person

You may request: an area, date and time. Please be aware that this request will not be confirmed prior to sailing. All confirmations will be made by the ship's Beverage Manager. Once on board, we encourage tour conductors to meet with the Beverage Manager to reconfirm requested cocktail party details.

Payment: Full Payment in U.S. funds only must be received in Ship Services no later than 2 weeks prior to sailing. Please make your checks payable to: Holland America Line Westours Inc. You may also charge your cocktail party to your escort's onboard account, payable at the end of the voyage by cash, personal check, traveler's check, VISA, American Express or MasterCard. Should you have further questions or concerns regarding Cocktail Parties, please call the following Ship Services number:

1-800-541-1576 (U.S. and Canada)

Prices are subject to change. Current prices effective as of 9/92.

Cocktail Party Request Form

Group/Booking # _____   No. of Passengers _____

Sail Date _____   Ship_____

Group Name/Agency _____   Agent's Name _____

Agent's Phone # _____   Escort Name & Cabin # _____

Prelunch $12.00pp ☐   **Predinner $12.00pp** ☐   **Nonalcohol $6.00pp** ☐

Requested Date   _____   Invitations to Read _____
Requested Time   _____   _____
Requested Room   _____   _____

☐   Charge to Escort's **Onboard Account.**
☐   Enclosed agency check. Prepaid amount enclosed **$**_____ (U.S. funds)

Please tear off the top white copy and send to the following address: Holland America Line Westours
Attn: Ship Services
300 Elliott Avenue West
Seattle, WA 98119

White–Ship Services   **Yellow–Travel Agent**

Courtesy of Holland America Line

for preparing for dinner and having cocktails with friends beforehand. The first sitting allows more time for after-dinner events. The same first and second sitting arrangements apply to breakfast and lunch in the dining room, as well.

Whenever and wherever possible, a request for dining room reservations should be made when the final payment is made. Although re-

FIGURE 7-6c
Special requirements information.

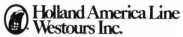

SPECIAL REQUIREMENTS INFORMATION

Dear Guest:

Holland America Line-Westours, Inc. will not discriminate against persons on the basis of disability. We seek, to the extent feasible, to accommodate the needs of all passengers so they are able to enjoy our ships and other facilities. In limited situations where an individual with a disability would be unable to satisfy certain specified safety and other criteria, even when provided with appropriate auxiliary aids and services, we will not permit the person to travel unless he or she is able to make alternative arrangements that would enable him or her to meet such criteria. The following information is necessary so that we are fully aware of any special medical, physical or other requirements you may have:

Your Name: _____ Booking No.: _____

Your Telephone: ( ) _____ - _____ (home) ( ) _____ - _____ (office)

Alaska Passengers Only: Are you taking a Cruise or CruiseTour?

Cruise Only ____   CruiseTour ____

First Day of Cruise or CruiseTour: _____ , 199___

Ship: _____ Cabin Number (if known): _____

Describe any special medical, physical or other requirements you have:

_____

_____

Will you have a service animal with you? Yes ____ No ____

Although Holland America Line-Westours, Inc. does not require that you be accompanied by an attendant who is willing and able to provide you with assistance, the presence of an attendant may enable you to meet the safety and other criteria necessary for travel. Are you being accompanied by an attendant? Yes ____ No ____

SPECIAL NOTE: It would be most helpful for you to carry with you a copy of your medical records (e.g., EKG, medication list, allergies, telephone number for your personal physician) should medical care be required during your travel. You may also want to discuss supplemental travel medical insurance with your travel agent.

Thank you for your assistance in helping us make your travel as enjoyable and beneficial as possible.

✉ ✉ ✉ ✉ ✉ ✉ ✉ ✉ ✉ ✉ ✉ ✉ ✉ ✉ ✉ ✉ ✉ ✉ ✉ ✉

TRAVEL AGENTS: Please deliver this form to your passengers upon receipt so they may complete it and return to:
Holland America Line-Westours, Inc.
300 Elliott Ave. W., Seattle, WA 98119 (USA)
Attn: Medical Department
FAX: (206) 283-2687 • (206) 281-7110

White - Medical Department   Yellow - Ship Services   Pink - Ship Physician

Courtesy of Holland America Line

quests for a particular sitting or table size are not necessarily guaranteed, every effort is made to oblige.

On most ships, the dining room reservation card is in the passenger's stateroom upon embarkation. In some instances, table assignments are confirmed to the passengers on the pier, at the embarkation check-in desk. On still others, passengers have to stand in line on board ship to make table reservations themselves, which can be inconvenient and annoying. Passengers should be told of the dining room reservation procedures when they book the cruise.

Size of Table. On most ships, tables are available to accommodate two, four, six, and possibly eight people.

First-time cruisers, particularly, might wish to be seated at a large table. This will give them an opportunity to meet several people. Chances are they will be compatible with at least one person assigned to the same table.

Smoking and Nonsmoking Sections. For the comfort and convenience of all passengers, sections of the dining room are set aside for nonsmokers.

Special Dietary Needs. Should your clients have special dietary requirements (for example, salt-free, low-calorie, diabetic, dietetic, etc.; kosher food, to some degree, can be provided), cruise lines will make every effort to accommodate them. Contact the cruise line directly to find out what is available.

It is customary to request special dietary arrangements when final payment is made. Some lines suggest they be submitted at least two to four weeks prior to departure. Tell your clients to reconfirm their dietary arrangements with the maître d'hôtel after embarkation.

Wine Orders and/or Bar Credits. The list of wines, champagnes, and other alcoholic beverages available on board, and their respective prices, are indicated on the Special Services Request Form. The travel agent can and should provide this service to the purchaser.

When a bottle of champagne or wine is ordered as a gift, the recipient will be presented with an appropriate gift card containing the personal message and name of the sender. This is done at the dinner table, and can be scheduled for any night desired.

A bar credit can be arranged as a gift for the passengers. A gift order in a prescribed amount can be credited to the client's shipboard account. Such credit will be applied when the clients close out their account at the end of the voyage.

Should a client not use up the total amount of the champagne/wine order and/or bar credit, the balance will be refunded.

Bon Voyage Parties. Arrangements for a bon voyage party must be made and paid in full at least two weeks prior to the sailing date, depending on the cruise line's individual policy. Such parties can be held in the passenger's stateroom or in a reserved section of the public lounge. Some cruise lines impose a minimum charge for the use of public room space which covers the food and refreshments provided by the line. Liquor, ice, setups, mixers, snacks, and canapés normally can be ordered. A choice of liquor brands might not be possible, however, due to Customs restrictions in some ports.

In view of the tight security measures being taken these days, some cruise lines do not permit any visitors whatsoever on board during embarkation hours.

Where visitors are permitted on board, two visitor passes are included in the document packet sent to the passenger. The travel agent may request additional passes from the cruise line.

Bon Voyage Gifts. In addition, arrangements can be made to purchase such gifts as a basket of fruit, flowers, box of candy, or a tray of canapés in the stateroom at embarkation time. Many agents order such gifts as goodwill gestures.

Beauty Shop. First-time cruisers might well wish to make such appointments during the course of the cruise. Once aboard ship, they will be able to anticipate their personal needs better. They should have no problem doing so.

Experienced cruisers, however, might make their appointments beforehand. They are well aware of shipboard activities and events and know how to plan accordingly. Payment for beauty shop services is made on board.

Massages. Requests for massage appointments can be made prior to sailing date. Payment for the service is made on board.

Commission Structure

The basic commission paid by cruise lines is 10 percent of the total air-and-cruise fare package. Port taxes are not commissionable. A supplemental (override) commission might be applicable if your agency is a member of a consortium and the cruise line involved is one of their preferred suppliers. Also, an override commission is offered as an incentive to individual travel agencies to promote a multiple (group) booking on a particular departure date. In fact, this is a most attractive inducement. You may also earn a free ticket for every 15 full fare individuals booked, which amounts to another 7 percent profit. These are the normal perks offered for special promotions. Others may be negotiated or offered.

Air-Sea (Fly-Cruise) Programs

In the case of an air-sea (fly-cruise) arrangement, clients must fly to the port city on the flight designated by the cruise line. The initial airline reservations and ticket issuance is handled by the cruise line. In most instances, cruise lines provide their own "meet-and-greet" services for their clients arriving at the port city air terminal. A transfer service to/from the ship is provided. A transfer coupon is furnished by the cruise line for this convenient service.

For the return flight, however, clients may have the option to travel independently, if they so desire. They may wish to remain in the port city area for local sightseeing, etc. It is imperative that the travel agent double check with the cruise line regarding any possible limitations or restrictions that might apply on such return air tickets. Any change in the return flight arrangement must be handled by the travel agent.

REVIEW QUESTIONS

1. What communications facilities are used to make cruise reservations?

   _____

   _____

2. What preliminary information should be at hand before contacting the
   cruise reservations department?

   _____   _____

   _____   _____

   _____   _____

3. What is a wait-list?

   _____

   _____

4. Explain a guarantee.

   _____

   _____

   _____

   _____

5. List the features of CruiseMatch 2000.

   _____

   _____

   _____

   _____

   _____

   _____

6. How much time is allowed for acceptance of space?

   _____

   _____

7. What guideline should be used in advising clients about baggage?

   _____

   _____

8. When must the Cancellation Fee Waiver and Baggage Insurance be
   purchased?

   _____

9. What protection does the Cancellation Fee Waiver provide?

_____

_____

_____

_____

10. Where can the precise information relating to cancellations be found?

_____

11. What action is undertaken by the cruise line upon receipt of a deposit payment?

_____

_____

_____

_____

12. What procedures must be followed in the use of a credit card for cruise reservation payment?

_____

_____

13. When is the commission paid when using a credit card?

_____

_____

14. What documents constitute proof of citizenship for returning cruise passengers?

_____

_____

_____

_____

_____

15. On longer cruises, what recommendation does the Immigration Service make regarding passports?

_____

_____

16. What official documents must be completed on board ship?

_____

_____

17. What amount of duty-free purchases is permitted?

_____

_____

_____

_____

Name ______________________ Date ______________

18. When is final payment due?

19. What booking commission is paid to the travel agency?

20. How is the regular commission paid on each reservation?

21. What is the Special Services Request Form? When must it be submitted?

Name _____ Date _____

RESERVATIONS EXERCISE

Using the brochure in Appendix F, complete the following reservation form, based on the preliminary information (Cabin 343) provided, and answer the questions that follow:

SAMPLE CRUISE SALE/RESERVATION INFORMATION FORM

Date: _____ File Ref. _____

Name of Passenger(s): Mr. and Mrs. Joshua L. Summers

Address: 1707 Shoreham Drive, Chicago, IL 60666

Home Phone No. (____)_____ Bus. (____)_____

Reservation Requirements

Shipline: HOLLAND AMERICA LINE   **Vessel**: _____

Name of Cruise: European Capitals Cruise

Length of Cruise: _____ **Departure Date**: _____

Port of Embarkation: _____ **Debarkation**: _____

Rate Category Desired: _____ **Rate**: _____

Stateroom Required: Single ☐   Double ☐   Triple ☐   Other ☐   Outside Cabin ☐   Inside ☐

Local Airport: _____ Return Trip Airport: _____

Precruise Package: LONDON

Postcruise Package: ROME

Dining Room Reservations: First Seating (   )   Second Seating (   )

Table for Two (   )   Table for Four (   )   Table for Eight (   )

Special Requirements: _____

_____

_____

Reservation Information

Cruise Line Res. Phone No. 1-800-_____

_____

Vessel: _____ Sailing Date: _____

Cabin No. **343** Deck: _____

Rate (per person): $_____

Early Booking Rebate $ _____
(Per Person)

Applicable Rate (pp) $ _____ Cruise Fare: $ _____ *

Air Add-on (pp): $ _____ _____ *

Tours (pp): Precruise $ _____   _____*

Postcruise $ _____   _____*

Port Taxes (pp) $ _____   _____

Cancellation Fee $ _____   _____
Waiver (pp)

                                        Grand Total: $ _____

Initial Deposit (pp) $ _____   Less Deposit: $ _____

                                        Balance: $ _____

                                    Less Commission: $ _____

                                        Balance Due: $ _____

Option Date For Acceptance: _____

Final Payment Due: _____
        *Commissionable at 10%.

1. Describe the stateroom in the foregoing reservation.

   _____

   _____

2. How soon after a reservation is made must the deposit be paid?

   _____   Final payment? _____

3. What immigration rules apply? _____

   _____

   _____

4. What protection does the Cancellation Fees Waiver provide?

   _____

   _____

5. Describe HAL's cancellation policy. _____

   _____

   _____

6. When does shipboard embarkation take place? _____

   _____

7. What are the mealtimes on board ship?

   Breakfast: _____   Lunch: _____   Dinner: _____

8. What items are not included in the cruise fare? _____

   _____

120

9. When and how can shipboard expenses and purchases be paid?

_____

_____

10. What should passengers do about their valuables (jewelry, cameras, etc.)?

_____

11. What liability does HAL assume regarding a passenger's baggage?

_____

_____

12. How are medical needs handled on board ship? _____

_____

Cruise Line Reservation Information

AMERICAN CANADIAN/CARIBBEAN LINE   1-800-556-7450
461 Water Street
Warren, RI 02885

Fleet: *Caribbean Prince* 80 passengers 90 GRT
       New Shoreham II 72   98
       Mayan Prince   90   99

Port(s) of Embarkation: Warren, RI, St. Thomas, Nassau, Belize City, CA

Cruise Length(s): 12 days

Destination Area(s): Caribbean, Canada, Bahamas, Central America

---

AMERICAN HAWAII CRUISES   Individual: 1-800-765-7000
550 Kearney Street   Groups: 1-800-765-5555
San Francisco, CA 94108

Fleet: *Constitution* 798 passengers 30,090 GRT
       Independence 798   30,090

Port(s) of Embarkation: Honolulu

Cruise Length(s): 7 days

Destination Area(s): Hawaiian Islands

AQUANAUT CRUISE LINE   Reservation Numbers:
241 E. Commercial Blvd.   1-800-327-8223
Fort Lauderdale, FL 33334   1-800-432-8894 (FL)

Fleet: *Aquanaut Ambassador* 200 passengers   2,573 GRT
      Aquanaut Holiday   80   815
      Aquanaut Explorer   40   309

Port(s) of Embarkation: Tortola

Cruise Length(s): 7 days

Destination Area(s): British Virgin Islands

CARNIVAL CRUISE LINES   Individual: 1-800-327-1800
3655 N.W. 87th Avenue   Groups: 1-800-327-5782
Miami, FL 33178-2428   1-800-641-6410 (FL)

Fleet: *Sensation*   2,600 passengers   70,000 GRT
      Fascination   2,600   70,000
      Ecstasy   2,044   70,367
      Fantasy   2,044   70,367
      Celebration   1,486   47,262
      Jubilee   1,486   47,262
      Holiday   1,452   46,052
      Festivale   1,146   38,175
      Tropicale   1,022   36,674
      Carnivale   950   27,250
      Mardi Gras   906   27,250

Port(s) of Embarkation: Miami, Port Canaveral, San Juan, Los Angeles

Cruise Length(s): 3, 4, and 7 days

Destination Area(s): Caribbean, Bahamas, Mexican Riviera

CELEBRITY CRUISES   Individual: 1-800-437-3111
5200 Blue Lagoon Drive   Groups: 1-800-437-4111
Miami, FL 33126

Fleet: *Zenith*   1,374 passengers   47,500 GRT
      Horizon   1,354   46,811
      Meridian 1,106   30,440

Port(s) of Embarkation: San Juan, Fort Lauderdale, New York

Cruise Length(s): 7, 10, and 11 days

Destination Area(s): Caribbean, Bermuda

CLIPPER CRUISE LINE   1-800-325-0010
7711 Bonhomme Avenue
St. Louis, MO 63105

Fleet: *World Discoverer* 138 passengers   3,153 GRT
      Yorktown Clipper   138   99.5
      Nantucket Clipper 102   99.5
      Society Explorer   98   2,500

Port(s) of Embarkation: Portland, OR; Vancouver; Juneau; Prince Rupert; Kodiak; Panama City; San Jose, Costa Rica; LaPaz, Peru; New Orleans; Ft. Lauderdale; Manaus; Rio de Janeiro; Grenada; Caracas; St. Thomas; Curacao; St. Maarten; Jacksonville; Palm Beach; Charleston; Norfolk; Washington, D.C.; Baltimore; New York; Boston; Charlottetown, PEI; Rochester, N.Y.; Quebec

Cruise Length(s): 7, 8, 11, 12, 14, 15, 17, and 23 days

Destination Area(s): Alaska/British Columbia, Coastal Mexico, Central America, East Coast South America, Florida Gulf Coast, Mississippi Delta, Virgin Islands, Amazon/Orinoco Rivers, Intracoastal Waterways, Chesapeake Bay, St. Lawrence River

---

CLUB MED   1-800-CLUB-MED
40 West 57th Street
New York, NY 10019

Fleet: *Club Med I*   386 passengers   10,000 GRT
     Club Med II 386   10,000

Port(s) of Embarkation: Fort-de-France, Toulon

Cruise Length(s): 7, 14, and 21 days

Destination Area(s): Caribbean, Mediterranean

COMMODORE CRUISE LINE   Individual: 1-800-237-5361
800 Douglas Road, Suite 700   Groups: 1-800-538-1000
Coral Gables, FL 33134

Fleet: *Caribe I*   875 passengers   23,000 GRT
    Enchanted Seas 736   23,500
    Enchanted Isle 731   23,395

Port(s) of Embarkation: New Orleans, San Diego

Cruise Length(s): 7 days

Destination Area(s): Caribbean, Mexican Riviera

COSTA CRUISE LINES   Individual: 1-800-462-6782
80 S.W. 8th Street   Groups: 1-800-862-6782
Miami, FL 33130-3097

Fleet: *CostaClassica* 1,300 passengers   50,000 GRT
    CostaRiviera   974   31,500
    CostaAllegra   800   30,000

Port(s) of Embarkation: Vancouver, San Juan, LaGuaira, Valparaiso, Buenos Aires, Manaus, Genoa

Cruise Length(s): 16, 17, 18, 20, and 95 days

Destination Area(s): Alaska, Trans-Canal, Caribbean, South America, Mediterranean, Africa

CROWN CRUISE LINE   Individual: 1-800-237-5361
800 Douglas Road   Groups: 1-800-538-1000
Coral Gables, FL 33134   1-800-237-5671 (FL)

Fleet: *Crown Jewel*   820 passengers   20,000 GRT
       Crown Dynasty 820   20,000
       Crown Monarch 550   15,270

Port(s) of Embarkation: Palm Beach, Fla., New York, Montreal

Cruise Length(s): 7, 14, 21, and 22 days

Destination Area(s): Eastern and Western Caribbean, Trans-Canal, Canada, New England

---

CRYSTAL CRUISES   Individual: 1-800-446-6645
2121 Avenue of the Stars   Groups: 1-800-446-6620
Los Angeles, CA 90067

Fleet: *Crystal Harmony* 960 passengers   49,400 GRT

Port(s) of Embarkation: Los Angeles, San Juan, Fort Lauderdale, Acapulco, New York, Montreal, San Francisco

Cruise Length(s): 10, 12, 13, 15, 16, 17, and 23 days

Destination Area(s): Mexican Riviera, Alaska, New England/Canada, Trans-Canal, Western and Northern Europe, Mediterranean

---

CUNARD LINE   1-800-5-CUNARD
555 Fifth Avenue
New York, NY 10017

Fleet: *Queen Elizabeth 2* 1,850 passengers   67,139 GRT
       Vistafjord   736   24,492
       Sagafjord   589   25,147
       Cunard Countess   800   17,593
       Cunard Princess   750   17,586

Port(s) of Embarkation: New York, Southampton, Fort Lauderdale, Los Angeles, Rio de Janeiro, Amsterdam, Hamburg, Barcelona, Valletta, Malaga, Venice, Genoa, Naples, Piraeus, Athens, Haifa

Cruise Length(s): 5, 7, 8, 10, 11, 14, 15, 16, and 100 days

Destination Area(s): Around the World, Transatlantic, Caribbean, Trans-Canal, Mediterranean, Black Sea, South Pacific

---

CUNARD SEA GODDESS   1-800-458-9000
555 Fifth Avenue
New York, NY 10017

Fleet: *Sea Goddess I* 116 passengers   4,250 GRT
       Sea Goddess II 116   4,250

Port(s) of Embarkation: St. Thomas, Barbados, London, Copenhagen, Stockholm, Madeira, Barcelona, Monte Carlo, Venice, Civitavecchia, Valletta, Piraeus, Istanbul, Singapore, Bali, Cairns, Phuket

Cruise Length(s): 7, 8, 9, 10, 11, 12, and 14 days

Destination Area(s): Caribbean, Riviera, Mediterranean, Greek Islands, Northern Europe, Baltic/North Cape, Indonesia/Malaysia, Great Barrier Reef, Thailand

---

DELTA QUEEN STEAMBOAT CO.   1-800-458-6789
Robin Street Wharf   1-800-543-7637
New Orleans, LA 70130-1890

Fleet: *Mississippi Queen* 436 passengers   3,364 GRT
      Delta Queen   176   589

Port(s) of Embarkation: New Orleans, St. Louis, Nashville, Memphis, Chattanooga, Minneapolis/St. Paul, Cincinnati, Pittsburgh

Cruise Length(s): 2, 3, 4, 5, 6, 7, and 11 days

Destination Area(s): Mississippi, Ohio, and Cumberland Rivers

---

DIAMOND CRUISES   1-800-333-3333
2875 N.E. 191st Street
No. Miami Beach, FL 33180

Fleet: *Radisson Diamond* 354 passengers   19,000 GRT
      Radisson Ruby   354   19,000
      Radisson Sapphire 354   19,000

Port(s) of Embarkation: San Juan, Nice, Civitavecchia

Cruise Length(s): 4, 5, and 7 days

Destination Area(s): Caribbean, Mediterranean

DISCOVERY CRUISES   1-800-937-4477
1850 Eller Drive
Fort Lauderdale, FL 33316

Fleet: *Discovery I*   1,300 passengers   12,224 GRT

Port(s) of Embarkation: Port Everglades, Fort Lauderdale

Cruise Length(s): 1 day

Destination Area(s): Freeport

DOLPHIN CRUISE LINE   1-800-222-1003
901 South America Way
Miami, FL 33132

Fleet: *Sea Breeze*   840 passengers   21,000 GRT
      Dolphin IV 588   13,007
      Ocean Breeze 756   20,000

Port(s) of Embarkation: Miami, Aruba

Cruise Length(s): 3, 4, and 7 days

Destination Area(s): Western and Southern Caribbean, Panama Canal

EPIROTIKI LINES   1-800-221-2470
551 Fifth Avenue   (212) 599-1750
New York, NY 10017

Fleet: *Pegasus*   686 passengers   14,000 GRT
       Orpheus   304   6,000
       World Renaissance 536   12,500
       Odysseus   452   12,000
       Jason   278   5,500
       Argonaut   166   4,500
       Neptune   194   4,000
       Triton   706   14,100
       Pallas Athena   746   19,900

Port(s) of Embarkation: Martinique, Manaus, Nice, Genoa, Venice, Piraeus,
        Crete, Rhodes

Cruise Length(s): 1, 2, 3, 4, 7, 12, 14, and 21 days

Destination Area(s): Caribbean, Amazon River, Mediterranean, Greek Is-
        lands

FANTASY CRUISES   Individual: 1-800-423-2100
5200 Blue Lagoon Drive   Groups: 1-800-445-0048
Miami, FL 33126

Fleet: *Britanis*   922 passengers   26,000 GRT
       Amerikanis 619   20,000

Port(s) of Embarkation: Miami, San Juan, Ft. Lauderdale, New York

Cruise Length(s): 2, 5, and 7 days

Destination Area(s): Mexico, Caribbean, Nassau, Bermuda

HOLLAND AMERICA LINE   Individual: 1-800-426-0327
300 Elliott Avenue West   (U.S. & Canada)
Seattle, WA 98119   (206) 281-1997 (Local)
                           Groups: 1-800-426-0329
                                         (U.S. & Canada)
                                         (206) 281-1997 (Local)

Fleet: *Statendam*   1,256 passengers   55,000 GRT
       Ryndam   1,256   55,000
       Maasdam   1,256   55,000
       Westerdam   1,494   53,872
       Nieuw Amsterdam   1,214   33,930
       Noordam   1,214   33,930
       Rotterdam   1,075   38,645

Port(s) of Embarkation: Vancouver, Los Angeles, Tampa, Fort Lauderdale,
        Norfolk, New York, Rio-de-Janeiro

Cruise Length(s): 2, 7, 10, 11, 12, 14, and 99 days

Destination Area(s): Alaska, Around-the-World, Caribbean, Trans-Canal,
        Orient, Bermuda, Hawaii

MAJESTY CRUISES	Individual:	1-800-222-1003
PO Box 019514	Groups:	1-800-222-1003
Miami, FL 33132-2062		

Fleet: *Royal Majesty* 1,056 passengers   32,400 GRT

Port(s) of Embarkation: Miami

Cruise Length(s): 3 and 4 days

Destination Area(s): Key West, Nassau, Royale Isle

NORWEGIAN CRUISE LINE	Individual:	1-800-327-7030
Two Alhambra Plaza		(U.S. & Canada)
Coral Gables, FL 33134		(305) 445-1195
		(Dade Co.)
		(305) 728-8101
		(Broward Co.)
	Groups:	1-800-327-7936
		(U.S. & Canada)
		(305) 445-1195
		(Dade Co.)
		(305) 728-8104
		(Broward Co.)

Fleet:	*Norway*	2,044 passengers	75,000 GRT
	Seaward	1,534	42,000
	Dreamward	1,246	41,000
	Windward	1,246	41,000
	Westward	829	28,000
	Sunward	790	28,000
	Starward	758	16,107
	Southward	752	16,607
	Skyward	730	16,254

Port(s) of Embarkation: Los Angeles, Acapulco, San Juan, New York

Cruise Length(s): 3, 4, and 7 days

Destination Area(s): California, Mexico, Caribbean, Bahamas, Bermuda

OCEAN/PEARL CRUISE LINES	Individual:	1-800-556-8850
1510 S.E. 17th Street	Groups:	1-800-426-3588
Fort Lauderdale, FL 33316		

| Fleet: | *Ocean Princess* | 460 passengers | 12,200 GRT |
| | *Ocean Pearl* | 480 | 12,475 |

Port(s) of Embarkation: Miami, Buenos Aires, Punta Arenas, Guayaquil, San Juan, Manaus, Nice, Venice, Le Havre, Plymouth, Copenhagen, Bombay, Singapore, Bangkok, Sydney, Hong Kong, Beijing, Pusan, Manila, Mombasa

Cruise Length(s): 11, 13, 14, 15, 17, 18, 19, 20, 21, 22, 23, 24, 25, 26, and 27 days

Destination Area(s): South America, Amazon River, Mediterranean, Western Europe, British Isles, Scandinavia/Russia, Asia, Australia

PAQUET FRENCH LINES   1-800-999-0555
1510 S.E. 17th Street
Fort Lauderdale, FL 33316

Fleet: *Mermoz* 680 passengers   13,691 GRT

Port(s) of Embarkation: Marseille, Acapulco, San Juan, Fort Lauderdale, Guadeloupe

Cruise Length(s): 7, 14, and 21 days

Destination Area(s): Mediterranean, California/Mexican Riviera, Caribbean, Galapagos/Trans-Canal, South America

---

PREMIER CRUISE LINES   Individual: 1-800-327-3113
400 Challenger Road   Groups: 1-800-327-9703
Cape Canaveral, FL 32920

Fleet: *Starship Atlantic* 1,600 passengers   36,500 GRT
       Starship Oceanic 1,500   40,000
       Starship Majestic 950   17,750

Port(s) of Embarkation: Port Canaveral

Cruise Length(s): 3 and 4 days

Destination Area(s): Bahamas

PRINCE OF FUNDY CRUISES   1-800-341-7540
PO Box 4216, Station A
Portland, ME 04101

Fleet: *Scotia Prince* 1,054 passengers   11,968 GRT

Port(s) of Embarkation: Portland, Me.

Cruise Length(s): 1-day (11 hours)

Destination Area(s): Nova Scotia

PRINCESS CRUISES   Individual: 1-800-421-0522
10100 Santa Monica Boulevard   Groups: 1-800-421-1700
Los Angeles, CA 90067

Fleet: *Crown Princess* 1,590 passengers   70,000 GRT
       Regal Princess 1,590   70,000
       Star Princess 1,470   63,500
       Sky Princess 1,200   46,000
       Royal Princess 1,200   45,000
       Fair Princess 890   25,000
       Island Princess 610   20,000
       Dawn Princess
       Pacific Princess

Port(s) of Embarkation: Vancouver, Los Angeles, San Diego, Acapulco, Fort Lauderdale, San Juan, Manaus, New York, Montreal, London, Barcelona, Venice, Athens, Sydney, Auckland, Singapore, Hong Kong, Papeete, Honolulu

Cruise Length(s): 6, 7, 8, 9, 10, 11, 12, 14, 16, and 17 days

Destination Area(s): Alaska, Mexico, Trans-Canal, Caribbean, South America, Amazon River, New England/Canada, Scandinavia/Russia, Mediterranean/Black Sea, Orient, South Pacific, Hawaii

---

REGENCY CRUISES   Individual: 1-800-388-5500
260 Madison Avenue   Groups: 1-800-388-6600
New York, NY 10016   (212) 972-4499 (NY)

Fleet: *Regent Star* 950 passengers   24,294 GRT
      Regent Sun 836   24,000
      Regent Sea 729   22,000

Port(s) of Embarkation: Montego Bay, San Juan, Tampa, New York, Montreal, Vancouver, Anchorage, Los Angeles, San Diego, Honolulu

Cruise Length(s): 7, 10, 11, 14, and 15 days

Destination Area(s): Caribbean, New England/Canada, Alaska, Hawaii, Trans-Canal

---

RENAISSANCE CRUISES   1-800-525-5350
1800 Eller Drive, PO Box 350307   (305) 463-0982 (FL)
Fort Lauderdale, FL 33335

Fleet: *Renaissance I, II, III, IV*   100 passengers   4,500 GRT
      Renaissance V, VI, VII, VIII 114   4,500

Port(s) of Embarkation: Safaga, Egypt; Athens; Istanbul; Venice; Rome; Las Palmas; Barcelona; La Rochelle; Trondheim; Copenhagen; Edinburgh; Stockholm; Antigua; Mombasa; Mahe, Seychelles

Cruise Length(s): 7, 8, 11, 14, and 21 days

Destination Area(s): Caribbean, South America, Africa, Baltic, Mediterranean

---

ROYAL CARIBBEAN CRUISE LINE   1-800-327-6700
1050 Caribbean Way   1-800-245-7225 (Canada)
Miami, FL 33132   1-800-432-6559 (FL)
                                         (305) 379-4731 (Dade Co.)
                            Groups: 1-800-327-2055
                                         1-800-245-7225 (Canada)
                                         1-800-432-3568 (FL)
                                         (305) 374-7432 (Dade Co.)

Fleet: *Majesty of the Seas* 2,354 passengers   73,941 GRT
      Monarch of the Seas 2,354   73,941
      Sovereign of the Seas 2,282   73,192
      Nordic Empress 1,610   48,563
      Viking Serenade 1,514   40,132
      Song of America 1,390   37,584
      Nordic Prince 1,012   23,200
      Song of Norway 1,022   23,005
      Sun Viking 726   18,556

Port(s) of Embarkation: Vancouver, Los Angeles, Acapulco, Miami, San Juan, New York, Barcelona, Amsterdam, Venice, Tenerife

Cruise Length(s): 3, 4, 6, 7, 8, 9, 10, 11, 12, 13, 14, and 15 days

Destination Area(s): Alaska, Mexico, Trans-Canal, Caribbean, Bermuda, Bahamas, South America, Canary Islands, Mediterranean, Scandinavia/Russia, Transatlantic, Far East

---

ROYAL CRUISE LINE   1-800-227-4534
One Maritime Plaza   1-800-792-2992 (CA)
San Francisco, CA 94111   (415) 788-0610
                                                  (SF Bay Area)

Fleet: *Crown Odyssey* 1,052 passengers   34,250 GRT
     Royal Odyssey   765   28,000
     Golden Odyssey   460   10,500

Port(s) of Embarkation: Vancouver, San Francisco, Los Angeles, San Diego, Aruba, Bridgetown, San Juan, New York, Montreal, Barcelona, Lisbon, Nice, Bombay, Mombasa, Sydney, Auckland, Singapore, Hong Kong, Honolulu

Cruise Length(s): 7, 8, 9, 10, 11, 12, 13, 14, 16, 19, 20, 21, 27, 45, and 61 days

Destination Area(s): Alaska, Mexican Riviera, South America, Canary Islands, Mediterranean, Africa, Asia, Australia, South Pacific

---

ROYAL VIKING LINE   Individual: 1-800-422-8000
95 Merrick Way   Groups: 1-800-423-1834
Coral Gables, FL 33134

Fleet: *Royal Viking Sun*   740 passengers   36,000 GRT
     Royal Viking Queen 212   10,000

Port(s) of Embarkation: San Francisco, Fort Lauderdale, New York, Montreal, London, Dublin, Copenhagen, Stockholm, Barcelona, Seville, Monte Carlo, Venice, Athens, Istanbul, Santiago, Buenos Aires

Cruise Length(s): 7, 10, 14, 16, 21, 23, 26, 48, 71, and 74 days

Destination Area(s): Trans-Canal, Around South America, New England/Canada, Scandinavia/Russia, Western Europe, Mediterranean, Asia, Australia, Hawaii

---

SEABOURN CRUISE LINE   1-800-351-9595
55 Francisco Street   (U.S. & Canada)
San Francisco, CA 94113

Fleet: *Seabourn Spirit* 204 passengers   10,000 GRT
     Seabourn Pride 204   10,000

Port(s) of Embarkation: Singapore, Bangkok, Lisbon, London, Copenhagen, Aruba, Barbados, Manaus, Boston

Cruise Length(s): 7, 11, 12, and 14 days

Destination Area(s): Southeast Asia, Northern Europe, Mediterranean, Caribbean, Amazon River, New England/Canada

SEAESCAPE CRUISES   Individual: 1-800-327-7400
8751 W. Broward Boulevard   Groups: 1-800-327-2005
Plantation, FL 33324   1-800-432-0900 (FL)

Fleet: *Scandinavian Dawn* 1,180 passengers   22,000 GRT

Port(s) of Embarkation: Fort Lauderdale

Cruise Length(s): 1 day

Destination Area(s): Freeport

SEAQUEST CRUISES   1-800-223-5688
600 Corporate Drive
Fort Lauderdale, FL 33334

Fleet: *Frontier Spirit*   164 passengers   6,700 GRT
       Caledonian Star 135   3,095

Port(s) of Embarkation: Antigua, Barbados, Manaus, New York, Hamburg, Amsterdam, Oslo, Copenhagen, Nome, Pusan, Hong Kong, Singapore, Sydney, Auckland, Hobart

Cruise Length(s): 10, 11, 15, 16, and 18 days

Destination Area(s): South America; Amazon/Orinoco Rivers; British Isles; Baltic Sea; North Cape; Greenland/Iceland; Northwest Passage; Soviet Far East; China; Vietnam; Indonesia; Great Barrier Reef, Australia; New Zealand; Antarctica

SEAWIND CRUISES   1-800-258-8006
1750 Coral Way   (305) 285-9494 (FL)
Miami, FL 33145

Fleet: *Seawind Crown* 656 passengers   24,000 GRT

Port(s) of Embarkation: Aruba

Cruise Length(s): 7 days

Destination Area(s): Caribbean

SEVEN SEAS CRUISES   1-800-661-5541
2300-555 W. Hastings St.   (305) 682-1706 (FL)
Vancouver, BC V6B 4N5

Fleet: *Song of Flower* 172 passengers   8,282 GRT

Port(s) of Embarkation: Vancouver, Juneau, Singapore, Phuket, Penang

Cruise Length(s): 7 days

Destination Area(s): Alaska, East Asia, Japan, China

SPECIAL EXPEDITIONS   1-800-762-0003
720 Fifth Avenue
New York, NY 10019

Fleet: *Sea Cloud*   70 passengers   3,530 GRT
       Polaris   84   2,214
       Sea Lion   70   99.7
       Sea Bird   70   99.7
       Melanesian Discoverer 92   130

Port(s) of Embarkation: Vancouver; Portland, OR; San Francisco; Belize, CA; Antigua

Cruise Length(s): 4, 7, 8, 11, 12, and 14 days

Destination Area(s): Alaska, Columbia/Snake Rivers, Sacramento Delta, Mexico, Central America, Caribbean, Amazon and Orinoco Rivers

---

STAR CLIPPERS   1-800-442-0551
4101 Salzedo Avenue
Coral Gables, FL 33146

Fleet: *Star Flyer*   180 passengers   3,025 GRT
        Star Clipper 180   3,025

Port(s) of Embarkation: St. Maarten, Nice

Cruise Length(s): 14 days

Destination Area(s): Caribbean, Mediterranean

STARLITE CRUISES   1-800-488-7827
1520 State Street
San Diego, CA 92101

Fleet: *Pacific Star*   1,050 passengers   13,000 GRT
        Rainbow   1,100
        Royal Pacifica 600   13,000
        Tropic Star   —   —

Port(s) of Embarkation: San Diego, Miami, Tampa

Cruise Length(s): 1, 2, and 5 days

Destination Area(s): Ensenada, Nassau

SUN LINE   1-800-872-6400
One Rockefeller Plaza   (212) 397-6400 (NY)
New York, NY 10020

Fleet: *Stella Solaris* 620 passengers   18,000 GRT
        Stella Oceanis 300   6,000
        Stella Maris   180   4,000

Port(s) of Embarkation: Piraeus, Venice, Nice, Fort Lauderdale, Galveston, Manaus, Buenos Aires

Cruise Length(s): 3, 4, 7, 14, and 17 days

Destination Area(s): Greek Islands, Turkey, Egypt, Israel, Caribbean, South America

---

TALL SHIPS ADVENTURES   1-800-662-0090
1010 South Joliet Street
Aurora, CO 80012

Fleet: *Sir Francis Drake* 34 passengers   450 DWT

Port(s) of Embarkation: St. Thomas

Cruise Length(s): 3, 4, and 7 days

Destination Area(s): U.S. and British Virgin Islands

WINDJAMMER BAREFOOT CRUISES   1-800-327-2601
PO Box 120
Miami, FL 33119

Fleet: *Fantome*   84 passengers
       Mandalay   72
       Polynesia   126
       Yankee Clipper   65
       Flying Cloud   78
       Amazing Grace   96

Port(s) of Embarkation: Antigua, Tortola, St. Maarten, Grenada, Freeport

Cruise Length(s): 6, 13, and 14 days

Destination Area(s): British Virgin Islands, West Indies, Grenadines

WINDSTAR CRUISES   1-800-258-7245
300 Elliott Avenue West
Seattle, WA 98119

Fleet: *Wind Star*   148 passengers   5,350 GRT
       Wind Song   148   5,350
       Wind Spirit 148   5,350

Port(s) of Embarkation: Nice, Madeira, Barbados, Antigua, Papeete

Cruise Length(s): 7, 9, 10, 11, 12, 13, 21, and 28 days

Destination Area(s): Mediterranean, Caribbean, French Polynesia

WORLD EXPLORER CRUISES   1-800-854-3835
555 Montgomery Street
San Francisco, CA 94111-2544

Fleet: *Universe* 550 passengers   18,000 GRT

Port(s) of Embarkation: Vancouver

Cruise Length(s): 14 days

Destination Area(s): Alaska

APPENDIX B

Cruise Line Menus

SEABOURN CRUISE LINE

CAPTAIN'S FAREWELL DINNER,
AT SEA, APRIL 22ND, 1991

CAPTAIN VALTER BERG
MASTER M/S SEABOURN PRIDE

Wines

1988, Chablis Grand Cru Le Clos, Jaboulet, A.C.	$ 52.00
1987, Opus One, Robert Mondavi, Napa Valley	$ 65.00

Chef De Cuisine
Johannes Bacher

Maitre D'
Harald Lange

APPETIZERS

Smoked Salmon Rolls with Cream Cheese and Cucumber
Ceviche of Sea Scallops
Pigeon Breast on a Bed of Tender Greens
Stuffed Potato in Beurre Blanc with Perigord Truffles

SOUPS

Sweet Pumpkin Soup
Clear Oxtail Soup with Old Sherry
Chilled Avocado Soup

SALAD

Warm Cabbage Salad and Crispy Bacon
Baby Mixed Greens, Tomato Vinaigrette

ENTREES

Grilled King Clip with Roasted Capers and Onion Confit
Butterfly of Cognac Flamed Macau Prawns
Veal Chop with Stuffed Morels
Spring Lamb "Wellington"
Noisettes of Venison in Chocolate Sauce,
Red Beet Mousseline and Cranberries

CHILLED SELECTED SEAFOOD PLATE

Commander's Fish Plate, Smoked Salmon, Jumbo Shrimps and Crabmeat

DESSERTS

Frozen Swan Lake a la Mode du Chef Patissier
Exotic Fruit Terrine, Apple - Mint Confit
Warm Bohmer Topfen Strudel, Vanilla Sauce
Freshly Made Fruit Sherbets and Frozen Yogurts
Ice Creams
Vanilla - Walnut - Peach Yogurt
Hot Chocolate Sauce - Hot Plum Sauce
Ice Pralines

ASSORTED INTERNATIONAL CHEESES
From the Cart

Princess Grill
Captain's Gala Dinner

22nd June 1991

CHEF'S SUGGESTION

RUSSIAN MALOSSOL CAVIAR
served with chopped Onion, Egg and Sour Cream

CREAM OF FRESH MUSHROOM SOUP

THE TRADITIONAL LOBSTER THERMIDOR
Fresh Lobster in Fine Wine Sauce, served with Sherry, Mornay Glace and Saffron Rice

CAESAR SALAD

LIME SORBET

ROAST AMERICAN PRIME RIB BEEF
*served "Au Jus" with French Green Beans, Carrot Sticks and Baked Potato
with Sour Cream and Chives*

THE FLAMBEE TROLLEY
Flamed Peaches with Raspberry Sauce and Vanilla Ice Cream

Coffee or Tea
Petit Fours

THE GOLDEN DOOR SUGGESTION

CHILLED VICHYSSOISE

POACHED CHICKEN BREAST
with Vegetables

FRESH STRAWBERRIES

The Wine Steward Recommends...

Veuve Clicquot Ponsardin	*Puligny-Montrachet*	*Chateau Lynch-Bages*
Veuve Clicquot, Brut	*Jean Lefort*	*5éme Cru Classé, Pauillac*
1982 &83 - $70.00	*1985 - $55.00*	*1976 - $65.00*

Executive Chef: Bernhard Stumpfel
Chef De Cuisine: Anthony Milton

MENU

HORS D'OEUVRES
RUSSIAN MALOSSOL CAVIAR
served with chopped Onion, Egg and Sour Cream

SMOKED SCOTTISH SALMON
with Horseradish Cream

MARINATED COCKTAIL OF FRESH BERRIES IN SEASON

SPAGHETTI CARBONARA
tossed with Onion, Ham and finished with a light Cream Sauce

SOUPS
Mock Turtle Soup with Cheese Sticks
Cream of fresh Mushroom Soup
Chilled Vichyssoise

SORBET
Lime Sorbet

ENTREES

COLD SPLIT MAINE LOBSTER "QUEEN ELIZABETH 2"
served with Sauce Cardinal, Asparagus tips, Vegetable Salad and Condiments
OR
THE TRADITIONAL LOBSTER THERMIDOR
Fresh Lobster in Fine Wine Sauce, served with Sherry, Mornay Glacé and Saffron Rice

ROAST AMERICAN PRIME RIB
served "Au Jus" with French Green Beans, Carrot Sticks and Baked Potato with Sour Cream and Chives

PORK MEDALLIONS SAUTEED IN BUTTER
*served on Bell Pepper strips with Mushrooms and Gorgenzola Cream, accompanied
by sautéed Vegetable Medley and Peaches, stuffed with mashed Sweet Potatoes*

BREAST OF CHICKEN "FORRESTIERE"
served on a bed of wild Mushrooms and Leek, accompanied with diced Potatoes, mixed baby Vegetables and Trfffle Sauce

SALAD
Caesar Salad a la Mode du Chef prepared by your Chef in the Dining Room
Or
Mixed Salad served with a dressing of your choice

DESSERTS
Steamed Vanilla Pudding with Amaretto Sauce
Japanese Chocolate Tree with Dark and White Chocolate Mousse and Mango Sauce
Fresh Strawberries with Vanilla Ice Cream and whipped Cream
Lime Sorbet
Ice- Creams: Vanilla, Pistachio and Rum & Raisin
Dessert Sauces: Orange, Chocolate Fudge and Vanilla

FLAMBEE TROLLEY
FLAMED PEACHES
with Raspberry Sauce and Vanilla Ice Cream, prepared in the Restaurant by your Restaurant Managers

CUNARD SERVES ONLY 100% COLUMBIAN COFFEE
Beverages
Ceylon and China Tea
Coffee, Decaffeinated or Regular
Hot Chocolate
Horlicks   Coffee Hag   Iced Tea   Iced Coffee
and we will be pleased to prepare for you an Espresso Coffee an Expresso Decaffeinated Coffee or a Capuccino

Queens Grill
Farewell Dinner

25th June 1991

CHEF'S SUGGESTION

PAPAYA AND AVOCADO SALAD
on a duet of Sauces

BEEF CONSOMME
with Meat Dumplings and Vegetables

SMOKED SALMON CREPE "FLORENTINE"
served on a light Cream Sauce

KIWI SORBET

BLACKENED SPICY GOUPER FILLET
garnished with a three Pepper Relish and Stirfried Greens

ROAST CAPON
with sautéed Onion and Bacon Cubes, served with Apple and Nut Stuffing, Giblet Gravy and Cranberries

CHOCOLATE PYRAMID
filled with Coffee Mousse on fresh Vanilla Sauce

Coffee or Tea
Petit Fours

THE GOLDEN DOOR SUGGESTION

Sliced Papaya

Roast Capon
with Baby Vegetables

Mixed Salad Bowl

The Wine Steward Recommends...

Bollinger & Co.	Chablis, Grand Cru, Blanchots	Chateau Ducru-Beaucaillou
Grand Année	Domaine Laroche	2éme Cru Classé
1982 - $70.00	1985 & 1987 - $70.00	St. Julien
		1978 - $90.00

Executive Chef: Bernhard Stumpfel
Chef De Cuisine: P. Freestone

MENU

HORS D'OEUVRES
PAPAYA AND AVOCADO SALAD *on a duet of Sauces*

WARM FRESH ASPARAGUS *served between Puff Pastry on Orange Butter Sauce*

FRESH SALMON *marinated in Fruit Juices, finished with diced Cucumber and Sour Cream*

SMOKED SALMON CREPE "FLORENTINE" *served on a light Cream Sauce*

SOUPS
Beef Consomme with Meat Dumplings, Vegetables and flavoured with Sherry
Cream of Asparagus with Croutons
Chilled Pinacolada Soup, flavoured with Meyers Rum

SORBET
Kiwi Sorbet

ENTREES
BLACKENED SPICY GROUPER FILLET
garnished with a three Pepper relish and stirfried Greens

ROAST CAPON
with sautéed Onion and Bacon Cubes, served with Apple and Nut Stuffing, Giblet Gravy and Cranberries

SIRLOIN STEAK NEW YORK CUT
served with Broccoli Rose, grilled Tomato, Sour Cream and Chives and Baked Potato

CUTLETS OF LAMB
coated with Dijon Mustard, Garlic and Herb Breadcrumbs, served with layered Ratatouille and Lamb Glaze

SALAD
Chinese Lettuce, topped with diced Onion, Croutons and Bacon Bits,
served with or without Vinaigrette dressing

DESSERTS
Kiwi Sorbet
Chocolate Pyramid filled with Coffee Mousse on fresh Vanilla Sauce
Orange Bavarois with Tangy Raspberry Sauce
Terrine of Pears, cooked in Red Wine and set in Jelly
Ice Creams: Vanilla, Mocca Almond Fudge and Pistachio
Dessert Sauces: Raspberry, Vanilla and Orange
A selection of International Cheeses from the trolley

CUNARD SERVES ONLY 100% COLUMBIAN COFFEE
Beverages
Ceylon and China Tea
Coffee, Decaffeinated or Regular
Hot Chocolate
Horlicks   Coffee Hag   Iced Tea   Iced Coffee
and we will be pleased to prepare for you an Espresso Coffee or Expresso Decaffeinated Coffee or a Capuccino

$$\mathscr{D} \quad I \quad \mathscr{N}$$

Appetizers and Salads

GARDEN RELISH TRAY

SAN FRANCISCO BAY SHRIMP COCKTAIL

BAKED EGGPLANT AND ONIONS
with Tomato Sauce
topped with Mozzarella Cheese

CORINTHIAN SALAD
of Shredded Carrots and Raisins
in our special Sauce

RUSSIAN SALAD WITH DICED HAM

Soups

CREAM OF CARROT SOUP
with Nutmeg
garnished with diced Carrots

DOUBLE CONSOMME CELESTINE

SOUP OF THE DAY
Fresh Vegetable Soup

♡

To Your Heart's Content

ARTICHOKE WITH BABY SCALLOPS
poached and surrounded with an array of shredded colorful Vegetables

Royal C.
Member of the Confrerie De
The World's Foremost an

N E R

Entrees

CHICKEN CASHEW
braised Chicken mixed with fresh Vegetables,
Cashews, and Water Chestnuts

FILET MIGNON
broiled as you like it! Béarnaise Sauce

PASTA
Linguine Napolitana with rich Clam Sauce

CROWN SCALLOPS
Scallops sauteed with Madeira Wine, Shallots and Cream Sauce
served with Rice

Garden Vegetables

ORIENTAL VEGETABLES

CHICHI BEANS PANCAKE

BAKED POTATO WITH SOUR CREAM, CHIVES AND BACON

Fresh Fruits and Cheeses

A SELECTION OF IMPORTED CHEESES AND SEASONAL FRESH FRUITS

Desserts

Indulge yourself with our
NOUGATINE CAKE   BAVAROIS MOCHA
RICE PUDDING WITH NUTMEG AND CINNAMON
STRAWBERRY ICE CREAM WITH MACEDONIA FRESH FRUIT TOPPING
SORBETS

FRESHLY BREWED COFFEE OR DECAFFEINATED COFFEE,
IMPORTED TEA, ICED TEA OR COFFEE,
MILK, HOT CHOCOLATE WITH WHIPPED CREAM

ruise Line
"La Chaine Des Rotisseurs"
Oldest Gourmet Society

HOLLAND AMERICA LINE
ms Nieuw Amsterdam

Captain Hans van Biljouw, Commander
Fekko J. Ebbens, Hotel Manager

WESTERN CARIBBEAN CRUISE

Sailing from Ocho Rios, Jamaica

Food Service Manager: Thomas Cairns
Executive Chef: Maximiliaan van Bergen
Maitre d'Hotel: Cees Schretzmeyer

Dutch Dinner

FOR YOUR AFTER DINNER PLEASURE:

Special Coffees, Chocolates, Espresso and Cappuccino
are available in the Explorers Lounge:
9:00 p.m. -12:00 midnight.

APPETIZERS

VOLENDAM SHRIMP COCKTAIL - this delicacy from the Dutch IJssel Lake is topped with a Dutch Cocktail Sauce, made of Tomato Ketchup, Cream and Brandy.

HUZAREN SALADE - this Dutch Salad consists of Veal, diced Apple, Pickles and chopped Onions.

MAATJES HERRING - North Sea Herring, garnished with chopped Onions.

FRESH FRUIT CUP- sections of seasonal Fruit topped with Orange Curacao or plain.

CRUDITES - fresh crisp Garden Vegetables with a Yoghurt -Dill Dip.

HOT APPETIZER

BARNEVELD PASTEITJE - a Patty Shell filled with Sweetbread, diced Chicken and Mushrooms in a Cream Sauce.

SOUPS

DUTCH VEGETABLE CONSOMME - a tasty Broth with crisp Vegetables, Vermicelli and Meatballs.

GREEN PEA SOUP - our special recipe: Green Peas, Broth, Bacon, Smoked Sausage, Celery, Onions and Leeks are combined to make this traditional Dutch Soup, accompanied with Bacon on Pumpernickle.

CHILLED TOMATO SOUP - a combination of sun ripened Tomatoes and Basil, finished with a touch of Dutch Genever.

SALADS

SALAD OF THE DAY:

MIXED WESTLAND SALAD - Boston Bibb Lettuce, chopped hard boiled Eggs, Tomato, Onions, Cucumber and Radishes tossed with an Oil and Vinegar Dressing.

FROM THE GARDEN:

ICEBERG - a wedge of Iceberg Lettuce with slices of Tomato and Cucumber.

TOSSED GREEN - with Alfalfa Sprouts, Baby Corn and shredded Carrots.

DRESSINGS : Italian, Blue Cheese, Raspberry Vinegar or Thousand Island.

LOW CALORIE DRESSINGS : Italian, Blue Cheese or Thousand Island.

ENTREES

FILLET OF DOVER SOLE MEUNIERE - pan-fried Dover Sole Fillets, served with Broccoli Florettes, Carrots, Parisienne Potatoes and browned Butter in Ramekin.

GRILLED TURBOT SCHEVENINGEN - Turbot Fillets, topped with Breadcrumbs, Lemon and melted Butter are grilled and served with a Mustard Sauce, parslied Baby Carrots, mashed Potatoes and a Fleuron.

TENDERLOIN STEAK THE DUTCH WAY- a pan-fried fillet of Beef served with a Tomato stuffed with Green Peas, Cauliflower Polognaise, Sauteed Mushrooms and home -fried Potatoes.

DUCKLING A L' ORANGE - a Biesbosch Duckling oven roasted served with an Orange Sauce, braised Red Cabbage, a half Bartlett Pear filled with Red Currant Jelly and Almondine Potato.
ALSO ON REQUEST WITH ANY ENTREE - a baked Idaho Potato with Sour Cream, Chives and fresh Bacon bits.

A TRADITIONAL COUNTRYSIDE DISH

HUTSPOT MET KLAPSTUK - a Hodge-Podge of Potatoes, Carrots and Onions, served with boiled Brisket of Beef.

A LIGHT AND HEALTHY ENTREE

Prepared in accordance with the American Heart Association, low in Cholesterol and Sodium
 VEGETARIAN PIE - made with fresh Vegetables. Approximately 250 calories.

IMPORTED CHEESE AND FRESH FRUIT

Our Dutch selection of Cheese from the Silvertray: Gouda, Edam, Kernheim, Leiden, with Dutch Rusks, Crackers, Pumpernickle or Crisp Bread.
Selection of fresh Fruits, Calimyrna Figs, Dates or Stemginger in Syrup.

DESSERTS

COUPE BOERENJONGENS - Vanilla Ice Cream topped with Raisins soaked in Dutch Brandy.
PARFAIT ROTHSCHILD - the perfect blend of Eggs, heavy Cream and crushed Almonds.
CHEVREUSE PUDDING - a fluffy Pudding with a Red Currant Sauce.
CHOCOLATE MOUSSE CAKE - a fluffy rich Chocolate Mousse served on a Chocolate Cookie Crust.
DUTCH APPLE PIE - with Raisins and Currants, served warm, with Vanilla Ice Cream.
CHOCOLATE ECLAIR - filled with a Custard Cream and dipped in Sweet Chocolate.
VANILLA BEAN, COFFEE or BURGUNDY CHERRY ICE CREAM, Whipped Cream and a crispy Wafer to complete.
THE PASTRY TRAY - an assortment of French Pastries.

THE LOW CALORIE SECTION

FRUIT JELLO.
PINEAPPLE SHERBET.
ORANGE WINE CAKE - 275 calories, prepared with sugar substitute.

BEVERAGES

Coffee, Tea, Herbal Teas, freshly brewed Decaffeinated Coffee or Milk.
Please ask your Dining Room Steward for our selection of Teas.

Antipasti

Antipasto alla Calabrese
Sliced peeled Tomatoes with Mozzarella Cheese, Basil and Virgin Olive Oil

Melone Con Prosciutto alla Veneziana
Refreshing sweet Melon Slices with Prosciutto Ham

Calamari al Pomodoro
Tender breaded Calamari rings, sauteed, served with Pomodoro Caper Sauce

Zuppe

Minestrone Con Pasta
Famous Italian Soup with a blend of Beans, Vegetables and Herbs

Linguine in Brodo
Light Double Beef Consomme' with Linguine Pasta,
served with crispy Cheese Sticks

Consomme' Freddo Con Pomodori e Celery
Chilled Consomme' with diced Tomato and Celery

Insalate

Insalada Primavera
Mixed Field Greens - An Italian Classic

Insalada Di Spinaci
Tender Leaf Spinach mixed with Fresh Basil and Bacon

Choice of Italian, Blue Cheese or Marco Polo Dressing

Pasta

Lasagna alla Lombarda
Semolina Lasagna Pasta with Chopped Beef, Vegetables and Cheese

Fettuccine al Frutta Di Mare
Served with a combination of Bay Scallops, Shrimp and Lobster Sauce

Carne & Pesci

Pesce Del Giorno
Fresh Catch of the Day

Ask Your Waiter for Today's Fresh Fish

Petto Di Pollo Alla Siciliana
Broiled Chicken Breast on a bed of chopped Tomatoes and fresh Herbs

Bistecca Di Manzo al Vino
Broiled Top Choice Sirloin Steak,
served with a classical Chianti Wine Sauce

Piccata Di Vitello alla Milanese
Veal Scallopini, dipped in Parmesan Egg Batter,
sauteed Golden Brown, served on a bed of Spaghetti

Legumi De Giorno

Fresh, seasonal Garden Vegetables are served with Entrees

BREAKFAST

MENU

EXPRESS BREAKFAST
Orange Juice   Scrambled Eggs   Crisp Bacon   Toast   Beverage

CHILLED JUICES
Grapefruit   Prune   Orange   Tomato   Apple
Apricot Nectar   Pineapple   V-8   Peach Nectar

FRUITS
Half Grapefruit   Sliced Bananas   Melon in Season
Orange Sections   Grapefruit Sections

STEWED FRUITS
Prunes   Baked Apple   Figs

DRY CEREALS
(Served with Fresh Milk)
Corn Flakes   Frosted Flakes   Special K
Rice Krispies   Puffed Rice   40% Bran Flakes
Sugar Pops   All Bran   Raisin Bran

HOT CEREALS
(Served with Fresh Milk)
Cream of Wheat   Oatmeal

FISH
Kippered Herring, Butter Sauce   Poached Finnan Haddie in Cream
Sliced Nova Scotia Salmon, Cream Cheese

EGGS
Boiled, Soft, Medium or Hard   Fried-Up, Over or Well Done
Scrambled   Eggs Benedict   Poached on Toast

OMELETTES
Plain   Ham   Cheese   Jelly   Minced Lox

FROM THE GRILL
(Served with Syrup or Honey)
Hickory Smoked Sliced Bacon   Sliced Breakfast Ham
French Toast   Corned Beef Hash
Old Fashioned Buttermilk Pancakes   Breakfast Link Sausages

BREADS AND PASTRIES
Assorted Rolls   Toast *(Upon request)*

JAMS AND JELLIES
Guava   Strawberry   Orange Marmalade   Grape   Honey

BEVERAGES
Brewed Coffee   Brewed Decaffeinated Coffee
Tea, Hot or Cold and a Selection of Herbal Teas
Milk   Skimmed Milk   Hot Chocolate

LUNCHEON

MENU

SLICED ASSORTED BREADS

JUICES

V-8   Pineapple

SOUPS

Cream of Spinach   Split Pea with Smoked Sausage

SALADS

† Bib Lettuce with Tomato and Cucumber
Sliced Tomatoes   Cottage Cheese

DRESSINGS

Oil and Vinegar   1000 Island

COLD LUNCHEON PLATE

† Fresh Spinach Salad with Mushrooms, Egg White,
Beets and Honey Lime Dressing

COLD SANDWICH

Deli Style Roast Beef on Hoagy Bun, Potato Salad

HOT SANDWICH

Jumbo Cheeseburger, French Fried Potatoes

ENTREES

Ravioli with Tomato and Basil Sauce

Shrimp Foo Yong
*(Omelette filled with a combination of shrimp,
Chinese cabbage and other vegetables)*

Grilled Pork Chops with Apple Rings

† Broiled Filet of Tuna, Cilantro Herb Margarine

VEGETABLES

Sauteed Yellow Squash and Tomato   Parsley Potato

DESSERTS

Cherry Pie, Whipped Cream   Peach Cobbler
Chocolate Eclair   † Sliced Melon

ICE CREAM

Vanilla   Chocolate   Strawberry   Butter Pecan

SHERBERT

Orange   Pineapple   Lime

BEVERAGES

Brewed Coffee   Brewed Decaffeinated Coffee
Tea, Hot or Cold and a Selection of Herbal Teas
Milk   Skimmed Milk   Hot Chocolate

† NAUTICA SPA FARE — Lower in calories, sodium, cholesterol and fat; diet salad
dressing available; dessert prepared with Sweet 'N Low or NutraSweet, no sugar

CAPTAIN'S GALA

DINNER

RELISH TRAY

Broccoli	Carrot Sticks	Black Olives

ASSORTED HOT ROLLS

JUICES

V8	Cranapple	Apricot Nectar

APPETIZERS

Louisiana Prawn Cocktail	Asparagus Vinaigrette
†Melon Balls	Fried Breaded Rumaki, Honey Mustard Sauce

SOUPS

Consomme Celestine
(Double beef broth with julienne of French pancakes)

Cream of Broccoli	Chilled Strawberry

SALADS

Caesar	†Hearts of Lettuce

DRESSINGS

Oil and Vinegar	Russian	Green Goddess

PASTA

Tortellini Carnivale *(Meat filled pasta rings
served with ham, mushrooms, and peas in cream sauce)*

SEAFOOD

Baked Filet of Scrod, Lemon Butter

ENTREES

Medallions of Pork Piccata *(Served with
prosciutto, artichoke hearts, mushrooms and tomato sauce)*

Surf and Turf *(Broiled petit filet of beef
and half Maine lobster, with butter sauce, oven baked)*

†Broiled Chicken Breast with Almonds and Raisins

VEGETABLES

Sugar Snap Peas	Country New Potatoes	Cauliflower Polonaise

Baked Idaho Potato with Sour Cream, Bacon Bits and Fresh Chives
(By Request)

DESSERTS

Baked Alaska	Black Forest Cake
Fruit Tranche	†Chocolate Swirl

ICE CREAM

Vanilla	Chocolate	Strawberry	Butter Pecan

SHERBERT

Orange	Pineapple	Lime

CHEESE

Port Salut	Brie	Gouda	Imported Swiss	Danish Bleu

BEVERAGES

Brewed Coffee	Brewed Decaffeinated Coffee

Tea, Hot or Cold and a Selection of Herbal Teas

Milk	Skimmed Milk	Hot Chocolate

After Dinner Mints

†NAUTICA SPA FARE — Lower in calories, sodium, cholesterol and fat; diet salad
dressing available; dessert prepared with Sweet 'N Low or NutraSweet, no sugar

DINNER

RELISH TRAY

Sweet Gherkins   Baby Corn   Radish Roses

ASSORTED HOT ROLLS

JUICES

Apple   Orange   Pineapple

APPETIZERS

Alaskan Smoked Salmon, Condiments   †Fresh Fruit Cocktail
Tennessee Ham Salad in Peach Half   Fried Oysters, Remoulade

SOUPS

Navy Bean Soup   Gazpacho Miami   Philadelphia Pepper Pot

SALADS

Mixed Greens, Asparagus Garnish   †Marinated Tomato and Cucumber

DRESSINGS

Oil and Vinegar   Blue Cheese   1000 Island

SEAFOOD

Seafood Newburg
(Prawns, scallops and lobster with sherry cream sauce over rice)
†Poached Filet of Salmon, Dill Margarine

ENTREES

Roast Tom Turkey, Dressing, Giblet Gravy, Whole Cranberry Sauce

Veal Oscar
*(Veal sauteed, topped with green asparagus, crab meat
and Bearnaise sauce)*

Roast Prime Rib of Beef, Au Jus

VEGETABLES

Peas and Mushrooms   Buttered Kernel Corn
Baked Idaho Potato with sour cream, bacon bits and chives

DESSERTS

Apple Pie   Boston Cream Pie   Chocolate Fudge Cake
Peach Meringue Glace, Raspberry Sauce   †Stuffed Baked Apple

ICE CREAM

Vanilla   Chocolate   Strawberry   Butter Pecan

SHERBERT

Orange   Pineapple   Lime

CHEESE

Port Salut   Brie   Gouda   Imported Swiss   Danish Bleu

BEVERAGES

Brewed Coffee   Brewed Decaffeinated Coffee
Tea, Hot or Cold and a Selection of Herbal Teas
Milk   Skimmed Milk   Hot Chocolate
After Dinner Mints

†NAUTICA SPA FARE — Lower in calories, sodium, cholesterol and fat; diet salad
dressing available; dessert prepared with Sweet 'N Low or NutraSweet, no sugar

AMERICAN NIGHT

FRENCH NIGHT

DINNER

RELISH TRAY
Radish Roses   Celery Sticks   Baby Corn

ASSORTED HOT ROLLS

JUICES
V8   Cranapple   Pear Nectar

APPETIZERS
Paté en Croute, Cranberry Sauce   Assorted Fruit Segments, Cointreau
† Cold Poached Salmon, Dill Cottage Cheese
Escargot *(Snails sauteed in garlic butter with Pernod)*

SOUPS
French Onion Soup   Chilled Shrimp Bisque   Cream of Asparagus

SALADS
† Tossed Greens, Watercress
Cabbage Slaw, Farmer Style
(Cole slaw with oil, vinegar and caraway seeds)

DRESSINGS
Oil and Vinegar   Blue Cheese   1000 Island

SEAFOOD
† Coquilles A La Nautica *(With fresh mushrooms and red pepper)*
Asparagus   Yellow Rice
Red Snapper Carnivale
(Filet of red snapper topped with cheese, shrimp and herbs)

ENTREES
Escalopes de Veau Calvados
(Sauteed veal with apples, mushrooms and apple brandy sauce)
Duck a La Orange
Entrecote Martinique
(Grilled New York steak served with pepper sauce)

VEGETABLES
Buttered Jumbo Green Asparagus   Stuffed Baked Potato
Mixed Vegetables
Baked Idaho Potato with Sour Cream, Bacon Bits and Fresh Chives
(By Request)

DESSERTS
Cheese Cake, Strawberry Sauce   Napoleon   Paris Breast
Crepe Fraises, Vanilla Sauce   † Lemon Cake

ICE CREAM
Vanilla   Chocolate   Strawberry   Butter Pecan

SHERBERT
Orange   Pineapple   Lime

CHEESE
Port Salut   Brie   Gouda   Imported Swiss   Danish Bleu

BEVERAGES
Brewed Coffee   Brewed Decaffeinated Coffee
Tea, Hot or Cold and a Selection of Herbal Teas
Milk   Skimmed Milk   Hot Chocolate
After Dinner Mints

†NAUTICA SPA FARE — Lower in calories, sodium, cholesterol and fat; diet salad
dressing available; dessert prepared with Sweet 'N Low or NutraSweet, no sugar

Columbia Restaurant
Luncheon

25th June 1991

GOLDEN DOOR SPA CUISINE
*Representing Today's Awareness of the Need for a
Healthy, Well Balanced Diet*

CHILLED MELON

CELERY CREAM SOUP
with Chives

EGG NOODLES
tossed with Garlic Button Mushrooms and topped with thin strips of crispy Chicken

SALAD BOWL
with your choice of dressing

The Wine Steward Recommends:

White	Red
Chardonay (callaway, Te Mecula) 1988	Volnay - Stanenos (Moillard) 1977
Chablis (Jean Claude Simmonnet) 1988/89	Gamay - Beaujolais (Buena Vista, Sonoma) 1989
White Zinfandel (Blush)(J. Pedroncelli, Sonoma)1989	Rioja (Domecg Domaine) 1983/85

A selection of non-alcoholic wines are available.

*Executive Chef: Bernhard Stumpfel
Chef De Cuisine: Josef Reitstatter*

MENU

APPETIZERS

Chilled Cranshaw Melon
Matjes Herring Scandinavian Style
Baby Shrimp Cocktail, served with a dressing of your choice

SOUPS

Beef Consommè with Vegetable Bisquit
Celery Cream Soup with Chives
Chilled Orange Soup with Tapioca

SALAD

Salad Bowl - Iceberg, Tomato and Oak Leaf, with Onion and Cucumber
Tossed Green Bean Salad
Served with dressing of your choice
Chef's Salad - Julienne of Turkey, Ham and Cheese, Tomatoes, Olives, hard boiled Eggs on Lettuce with your choice of
dressing

PASTA
CANNELONI BOLOGNAISE
Topped with Meat Sauce and gratinated with Parmesan Cheese

SORBET
Watermelon Sorbet

ENTREES
WIENER SCHNITZEL
Breaded Escalope of Veal, sautèed in Butter, served with Potato Salad, stewed Cranberry and Lemon wedge

PAN FRIED FILLET OF RED SNAPPER
with White Wine Veloute, chopped Tomatoes, Spring Onions and Parsley Potatoes

BARBEQUE PORK SPARE RIBS
Sreved with crisp Bacon, Coleslaw, medium spicy Sauce, Corn on the Cob and Western Potatoes

MARINATED CHICKEN SKEWER
served with Peanut Sauce, spring Onions on a bed of Vegetables fried Rice

DESSERTS
Biscuit Roulade "Swiss Style"
Iced Grand Marnier Souffle with Blackberry Sauce
Creme Caramel with whipped Cream
Watermelon Sorbet
Strawberry Cream Pie
Ice Creams: Vanilla Fudge, Butterscotch Praline and Burgundy Cherry
Dessert Sauces: Chocolate and Strawberry

CUNARD SERVES ONLY 100% COLUMBIAN COFFEE
Beverages
Ceylon and China Tea
Coffee, Decaffeinated or Regular
Hot Chocolate
Horlicks   Coffee Hag   Iced Tea   Iced Coffee
and we will be pleased to prepare for you an Espresso Coffee an Expresso Decaffeinated Coffee or a Capuccino

APPENDIX C

Cruise Line Shipboard Programs

DAILY PROGRAM
AT SEA
Scandinavian Capitals & Russia Cruise 96
Captain Stavros Dandouras, Master
Tonight's Suggested Dress: FORMAL
WEDNESDAY, JULY 10 1991
Sunrise: 04.54 hrs Sunset: 21.41 hrs
Kalimera ∘ Good Morning
CLOCKS WILL BE SET AHEAD ONE HOUR AT MIDNIGHT JULY 10/11

MEAL HOURS TODAY

6:30/7:30	Eye-Opener Coffee is served	Yacht Club, Deck 7
7:30/9:30	**BREAKFAST** is served - Main Seating	Seven Continents Restaurant
8:00/10:00	**BREAKFAST BUFFET**	Yacht Club, Deck 7
10:45/11:15	Morning Bouillon is served	Yacht Club, Deck 7
12:00	**LUNCHEON** is served - Main Seating	Seven Continents Restaurant
12:00/1:30	**LUNCHEON BUFFET** is served	Yacht Club, Deck 7
12:00/1:30	Soup, Salad and Sandwiches are served	Lido Lounge, Deck 8
12:00/1:30	Grilled specials are served (weather permitting)	Penthouse Grill, Deck 10
1:30	**LUNCHEON** is served - Late Seating	Seven Continents Restaurant
4:00/4:45	Afternoon Tea is served with Cakes and Cookies	Yacht Club, Deck 7
6:30	**WELCOME ABOARD DINNER** is served - Main Seating	Seven Continents Restaurant
8:45	**WELCOME ABOARD DINNER** is served - Late Seating	Seven Continents Restaurant
11:30/12:30	Late Evening Light Buffet is served	Yacht Club, Deck 7

OFFICE HOURS TODAY

8:30/3:30	The Purser's Office is open	Marina Deck, Deck 6
9:00/12:00	The Cruise Office is open	Marina Deck
2:00/6:00	The Cruise Office is open	Marina Deck
5:00/8:00	The Purser's Office is open	Marina Deck
10:00p/12:00a	The Purser's Office is open for Safety Deposit Boxes only	Marina Deck

FITNESS AFLOAT
with JANE MCMULLIN, our Fitness Director

8:00	LOW & LIVELY AEROBICS - Come & join the fun	Odyssey Show Lounge
8:30	TIGHT AND TONED - Floor work for all levels	Odyssey Show Lounge
10:00	SIT-N-BE-FIT - Great chair-ercises for all	Top of the Crown, Deck 11
11:00	WATER AEROBICS - Aerobics and endurance	Indoor Pool, Deck 1
11:30	AQUACISE Toning in the water	Indoor Pool, Deck 1
2:00	DO'S AND DON'TS OF STRETCHING	Gymnasium, Deck 1
3:00	AQUA FIT - Aerobics water walking and toning exercises	Indoor Pool, Deck 1
4:00	WONDERBANDS workout with rubber bands	Gymnasium, Deck 1

ACTIVITIES AND ENTERTAINMENT

8:00	CATHOLIC MASS - with Rev. Thomas F. McCormick	Coronet Theater, Deck 8
8:30	DAILY QUIZ first correct answers before noon wins the prize!	Cruise Office, Deck 6
9:00	GREEK II - Cruise Director Fernando teaches you more words	Lido Lounge, Deck 8
9:45	SPECIAL TALK: "Treasures of the Hermitage" including slides of St. Isaac's Cathedral. Join Mary Anne Whitney for a fascinating slide presentation. (To be repeated this afternoon at 4:00pm)	Coronet Theater, Deck 8
10:00		Odyssey Show Lounge

FASHION ON THE HIGH SEAS
A special showing of fashions from the Monte Carlo Court Boutique
you may have missed!! Come see the beautiful fashions we have in store for you!
The Staff and Entertainers will do the modeling!!

10:00	PING PONG Ladies's Singles with Duncan	Lido Deck 8, Aft
10:45	REGISTRATION for Navigational Bridge Visit: Meet Duncan in the	Lido Lounge, Deck 8
11:00	NAVIGATIONAL BRIDGE VISIT there will be others	Lido Lounge, Deck 8
11:00	EASY FRENCH I - Your Cruise Director Fernando helps you refresh your high school French!!	Lido Lounge, Deck 8
11:00	SPECIAL TALK: "New Technologies in Heart Care" Join Dr. Diethrich for this very informative talk.	Coronet Theater, Deck 8
11:15	PICTIONARY!! for all ages! Join Asst. Cruise Director Duncan & for fun, prizes too!!	Odyssey Show Lounge
11:30	TEENAGERS GET TOGETHER meet Hostess Ginger in the	Top of the Crown, Deck 11
11:30/12:30	Beautiful music from the harp with Patricia	Monte Carlo Court, Deck 7
12:00/1:00	Aperitif Melodies with Peggy at the ivories	Yacht Club, Deck 7
12:45	FILM: (2) RCL Promotional "The Mexican Riviera" & "Hawaii"	Coronet Theater, Deck 8
1:15	MOVIE: "HOME ALONE" Starring Macaulay Culkin & Joe Pesci Comedy, 103 min, PG	Coronet Theater, Deck 8
2:15	DUPLICATE & PARTY BRIDGE with Jean & Dorothy Bell	Card Room, Deck 8
2:15	TRIVIA!! - Join Fernando & Ginger for this fun game!!	Odyssey Show Lounge
2:30	SHUFFLEBOARD Men's Singles meet Duncan	Lido Deck, Deck 8 Aft
2:30	INFORMAL POKERS PLAYERS meet at the poker table in the	Lido Lounge, Deck 8
3:15	LUXURY LINERS OF THE PAST II - Fernando presents another slide show and talk on the luxury ships of the '20's, '30, & '40's, '50	Coronet Theater, Deck 8
3:30	INFORMAL BACKGAMMON Meet Asst. Cruise Director Duncan	Lido Lounge, Deck 8
4:00	$JACKPOT BINGO$ Join Fernando, Ginger, Theo & Yiannis for fun, laughs & cash prizes!! The KITTY is growing!	Odyssey Show Lounge
4:00	SPECIAL TALK: "Treasures of the Hermitage" including slides of St. Isaac's Cathedral. A repeat of Mary Anne Whitney's morning talk	Coronet Theater, Deck 8
4:00/4:45	Tea Time Melodies with Patricia	Yacht Club, Deck 7
4:45	Friends of Dr. Bob & Bill W meet each other	Yacht Club Cove, Deck 7

Royal Cruise Line

5:15	MOVIE: "HOME ALONE" Comedy, 103 min, PG	Coronet Theater, Deck 8
5:45/6:30	Annick & Anibal play your Latin favorites	Top of the Crown, Deck 11
5:45/6:30	Mellow Music with Peggy on the keyboards	Monte Carlo Court, Deck 7
5:45/6:30	Join the Malvisi Trio for a cocktail dance set	Yacht Club, Deck 7
5:45/6:30	CAPTAIN'S WELCOME ABOARD COCKTAIL PARTY	Odyssey Show Lounge
	Captain Dandouras cordially invites all guests of the MAIN SEATING	
	for cocktails. Music with the Odyssey Orchestra	
6:45/8:00	Patricia plays the harp for your listening pleasure	Monte Carlo Court, Deck 7
8:00/8:45	Annick & Anibal play your Latin favorites	Top of the Crown, Deck 11
8:00/8:45	Peggy on the keyboards for a mellow set	Monte Carlo Court, Deck 7
8:00/8:45	Join the Malvisi Trio for an international dance set	Yacht Club, Deck 7
8:00/8:45	CAPTAIN'S WELCOME ABOARD COCKTAIL PARTY	Odyssey Show Lounge
	Captain Dandouras cordially invites all guests of the LATE SEATING	
	for cocktails. Music with the Odyssey Orchestra	
8:15	VIDEO: "SOME LIKE IT HOT" Comedy, 121 min	Coronet Theater, Deck 8
9:00 & 10:45		Odyssey Show Lounge

SHOWTIME
with CENTER STAGE EIGHT
in
"DANCE, DANCE, DANCE"

9:45/11:00	Patricia at the harp with marvelous music	Monte Carlo Court, Deck 7
9:45/11:45	Dance to the music with Annick & Anibal	Top of the Crown, Deck 11
10:00/11:00		Casino Court, Deck 7

CASINO CHAMPAGNE PARTY
Complimentary champagne for all players. Come meet the casino staff,
and check out the casino special $15.00 in chips for only $10.00!!

10:15/1:00	The Malvisi Trio singing for your dancing pleasure	Yacht Club, Deck 7
10:30	MOVIE: "HOME ALONE" Comedy, 103 min, PG	Coronet Theater, Deck 8
11:00/12:15	Peggy plays a late night set for you to enjoy	Monte Carlo Court, Deck 7
11:45...	LATE NIGHT DANCING, DJ Jonathan spins with tunes	Top of the Crown, Deck 11

Kalinikta ○ Good Night

OPENING HOURS TODAY

BEAUTY SALON	8:00a - 7:00p
BOUTIQUE	Monte Carlo Court: 11:30a - 1:00p/3:00p - 6:00p
	Sundries Shop: 11:30a - 1:00p/3:00p - 6:00p
CASINO	Slots: 10:00a - Wee Hours
	Tables & Roulette: 2:00p - 6:00p / 8:30p - Wee Hours
HOSPITAL	9:00a - 11:00p / 6:30p - 7:30p (Dial 71 if in emergency)
LIBRARY	10:30a - 11:30p / 3:30p - 4:30p (for locked cases)
MASSAGE	8:00a - 7:00p
PHOTO SALES DESK	9:00a - 1:00p
RADIO OFFICE	OPEN AT SEA, CLOSED IN PORT (for telephones)
ROOM SERVICE	TEL. 71 - 24 HOURS A DAY
SAUNA	6:30a - 8:00p

HAVE YOUR PHOTOS TAKEN TONIGHT! Have your photo taken at the Captain's Welcome Aboard Cocktail parties! Also, tonight have your PORTRAIT taken. The photographers will be taking portraits in the Forum on Deck 6 from 5:15pm - 5:45pm and 7:30pm - 8:00pm. The portraits come mounted in a gilt edged folder at only $18.00.

MASTERCARD, VISA, AMERICAN EXPRESS: If you wish to use any of these credit cards to pay your end-of-cruise final account, please bring your card to the Purser's Office so that an imprint can be made. Just before the end of the cruise a copy of your final account and your receipt will be sent to your stateroom. Only accounts of $25 or greater will be charged. Please note that passengers who did NOT leave a credit card imprint will be required to come personally to the Purser's Office to settle their final account.

NOTE FROM THE PURSER'S - RUSSIAN STAMPS AND MAIL SERVICE: You may bring your letters and cards to the Purser's Office up until 1 hour before sailing. Although stamps won't be available until arrival, you may pay for your postage and the mail will be posted by the Purser's.

NOTE FROM THE DINING ROOM: The Wine Stewards will be available outside of the Dining Room to take orders for dinner wine selections this afternoon from 12:00pm - 1:45pm. Thank you.

IMPORTANT NOTICE REGARDING SMOKING: You are kindly requested to limit smoking material to cigarettes in designated areas of the dining room and some of the ship's lounges. Cigars and pipes may be used in the Top of the Crown (Bar area only) and on the open decks. Thank you for your cooperation.

GIFT ORDERS: Passengers who signed gift order forms for wines or champagne are kindly requested to redeem their bottles from the wine steward in the Seven Continents Restaurant before the end of the cruise. Thank You.

DUTY FREE LIQUOR AND TOBACCO: For your convenience you will find in your stateroom a duty free form for liquor and tobacco. Please fill it out and place your orders 3 days before the end of the cruise. Your shipboard account will be charged with the total value of your order. Your purchase will be delivered to your stateroom the last evening of the cruise. A reminder that once your order is placed, it is non-returnable.

MOSAIC FORMAL SEPARTES. New, from the House of Mosaic, formal separates to mix or match for any occasion. Choose from classic solids or express yourself vividly with unusual multi-colored prints in the following pieces: Culottes, camisoles, short sleeved blouses, jumpsuits, and jackets, ranging from $33 to $119. Or, pick up a two piece set for only $209!! These are the perfect travel companions, as they are completely uncrushable!!

ENJOY A BODY MASSAGE & SAUNA: Soothe your aches and pains away with a sauna and a body massage. Visit the spa on Deck 1 or call 77 for an appointment today.

LATE NIGHT THOUGHT
Man knows no greater thrill than to touch greatness or to be touched by it.
Sleep Well
Fernando de Oliveira - Executive Cruise Director

S/S Norway Cruise News

WELCOME ABOARD!

Saturday, February 29, 1992   **Sunset: 6:21pm**

MASTER
GEIR LOKOEN

STAFF CAPTAIN   **CHIEF ENGINEER**
Gulleik Svalastog   Steinar Hammervold
                          HOTEL DIRECTOR
                          Gunnar Mikkelsen
                                                        FOOD & BEVERAGE MGR
                                                              Guiseppe Marconi
                          CRUISE DIRECTOR
                          Charles Oski
                                                              CHIEF STEWARD
CRUISE STAFF   Ralph Lawson
J.B. L'Episcopo   Jim Polansky   David Steiner
Michelle Gayoski   David Hakala   Roberto Costa   **ITINERARY**
Laura Cobb   Craig Chamberlain   Sunday: At Sea
Ilona Alves   John Bolgrien   Monday: At Sea
Dawn Yoshida   Eric Bennedict   Tuesday: St. Maarten
Monica Steiner   Rob Beatty   Wednesday: St. John & St. Thomas
A.J Hayden   George Dunn   Thursday: At Sea
Annicken Julseth   Rob Lawracy   Friday: Pleasure Island
Cindy Hay   Lisa Linden
Michelle Buzzoni   Barbara Zarandy
Michelle Orfanos   Sally Evans

12:30pm	**EMBARKATION BEGINS**

1:00pm- 5:30pm	Beauty Salon & The "New" Roman Spa Hospitality Desk Information and appointments available, or call #44480. Int'l Deck Starboard Side

1:00pm-Midnight	The Information Desk is open. Cash Transactions may be carried out after 8:00pm. For Information, call #101 .... International Deck, Port Side
1:00pm-4:00pm	Welcome Aboard Snacks & Sandwiches .... Great Outdoor Restaurant, Int'l Deck Aft
1:00pm-7:00pm	Roman Spa is open for tours .... Dolphin Deck, Stairtower #3
1:00pm-3:30pm	Calypso Sailaway Music with our Calypso Band NEW WAVE..............Pool Deck Aft
1:30pm-4:00pm	Fitness Center Open House Only ....Fitness Center, Olympic Deck Aft
1:30pm-3:30pm	The S/S NORWAY TRIO plays for your listening pleasure.............. Club Internationale, Int'l Deck

1:30pm- 3:30pm	**Casino Hospitality Desk** Credit inquiries and Information on Casino Games. International Deck Portside

2:15pm & 3:15pm	**Sports Afloat** Orientation ....Fitness Center, Olympic Deck Aft

3:30pm	**U.S. Coast Guard Emergency Drill.** Please prepare for this drill by picking up your lifejacket from your cabin and reading the instructions on the back of your cabin door a few minutes **prior** to the **United States Coast Guard Emergency Lifeboat Drill.**

4:00pm	**U.S. COAST GUARD EMERGENCY BOAT DRILL**

All Passengers Are Required To Attend

If you have not already done so, please go to your cabin, pick up your lifejacket, then read the <u>**EMERGENCY INSTRUCTIONS**</u> on the back of your cabin door. Next, proceed to your lifeboat station. **Cruise Staff** will be on hand to assist you.

Stations 6-14, 20 & 22 (even numbers).....................................International Deck, Portside
Stations 5-13, 19 &21 (odd numbers) ....International Deck, Starboard side
Stations 15, 16, 17 &18 (please meet in) ....Checkers, International Deck
Stations 23 & 24 (please meet in)...........................Club Internationale, International Deck

4:30pm	**THE S/S NORWAY SAILS FOR ST. MAARTEN**

TRY A "BON VOYAGE" DRINK SPECIAL!!!
JOIN US AS THE S/S NORWAY PULLS AWAY FROM THE PIER!!!

4:30pm-6:30pm	Calypso Sailaway Music with NEW WAVE ....Pool Deck Aft
5:15pm-6:00pm	Musical Entertainment while enjoying cocktails.............Club Internationale, Int'l Deck

5:15pm	**Dive In Presentation**

See and hear about our Water Sports Program. This could be
a highlight of your cruise!
CHECKERS CABARET, INTERNATIONAL DECK

5:30pm- 7:00pm	**Open House in the Roman Spa** Come by for a demonstration of the treatments available. Dolphin Deck, Stair #3.

Good Evening
Evening Dress: Casual (No shorts after 6:00pm please)

6:00pm-Late	Casino opens for Live Gambling & Slot Machine Play.. Monte Carlo Room, Pool Deck
6:00pm-8:30pm	**Dive-In** Registration & Information available. Find out about this exciting program ....Int'l Deck, Forward, Starboard side
6:15pm	Caribbean Stud Poker Introduction. An Introduction to this exciting new Casino Game (Complementary Champagne to students)........ Monte Carlo Room, Pool Deck

7:30pm	**TOURS ASHORE**

Join your Shore Excursion Manager for information on all tours that are available for this cruise. (Rebroadcast on cabin T.V. Check schedule for times) Please bring the tour information sheet found in your cabin packet.
NORTH CAPE LOUNGE, POOL DECK

7:45pm-8:30pm	Dance Music and listening music with the **S/S Norway Trio** .... Club Internationale, Int'l Deck
7:45pm-8:30pm	Piano Music while sipping a cocktail .... Windjammer, Int'l Deck
7:45pm-8:30pm	45 & Over Singles Get Together.................................. Club Internationale, Int'l Deck
8:00pm	Tee-Up Welcome Aboard Social .... Le Rendezvous, Pool Deck Aft
8:00pm	Kids and Parents- Join our Youth Coordinators and get acquainted with the **Youth Program** onboard (please meet in) .... Trolland, International Deck
8:45pm-10:15pm	Dance to the Music of the **S/S Norway Showband** .... North Cape Lounge, Pool Deck
9:00pm-1:00am	Enjoy **CORPORATE JAM** & our duo **The Keys**............................Checkers Cabaret, Int'l Deck
9:30pm-1:00am	Dance to the **S/S Norway Quartet** .... Club Internationale, Int'l Deck
10:00pm	Teen Talk! (13-17 year olds) "Times a wastin'" ....Dazzles, Viking Deck Aft
10:00pm-2:00am	Piano Entertainment for your enjoyment .... Windjammer, Int'l Deck

---

10:15pm

North Cape Lounge, Pool Deck

CRUISE STAFF & SHIPMATE INTRODUCTIONS.
FUN & LAUGHS!! DON'T MISS IT!

We invite all passengers to join your Cruise Director, Charlie Oski and Cruise Staff. We will provide you with helpful information on shipboard activities, entertainment and all the fantastic ways you can really enjoy your cruise! We're looking forward to meeting you!

No Children at Tables Surrounding Stage Area Please

10:30pm-close	A Club called Dazzles opens with your **D.J. John**. No Children. Teens under the age of 18 years must leave the Disco by 11:30pm. Please carry I.D. Thank You!.......Viking Deck Aft
11:30pm	Singles Party! Join your **Cruise Staff**, for a party to "Break the Ice" Lots of fun & Prizes to be enjoyed...Dazzles, Viking Deck Aft
11:30pm-Midnight	Dance to the **S/S Norway Showband** .... North Cape Lounge, Pool Deck
Midnight-1:00am	"Ladies Night" Fuzzy Navels, Kamikazes & Sex on the Beach Drinks $2.00. Ladies Raffle for Prizes will be held at Midnight ....Dazzles, Viking Deck Aft

---

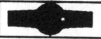 **PLEASE REMEMBER TO SET YOUR CLOCKS ONE HOUR AHEAD UPON RETIRING TONIGHT**

IMPORTANT INFORMATION

Purser's Office: The Purser's desk is located on International Deck, Port side, Forward and is open daily 8:00am-Midnight. Seasickness Tablets, Aspirin, Tylenol, Alka Seltzer and Band-Aids are available free of charge. Phone #101.

Wake Up Calls:-Phone #66

Public Rooms & Theatre: We kindly request guests not to reserve seats in the showrooms. No Smoking is allowed in the Saga Theatre.

Joggers: For jogging, Please use Olympic Deck Only. Available from 8:00am-8:00pm only. Note: Decks may be slippery when wet.

Note: Children are not permitted to use the elevators and are not permitted in the public rooms after 8:30pm without the supervision of an adult. Children under 18 years of age are not permitted in the Casino.

Win A World Cruise PLUS $10,000.00! Play The NORWAY's Lottery
Every Ticket is a Winner. Details available at the Lottery Terminals
"Pick 10" Lottery Tickets Available:

OUTSIDE BOTH DINING ROOMS	OUTSIDE NORTH CAPE
5:30-6:15pm & 8:00-8:45pm	10:00-10:15pm

Shipboard Information

Bar Hours

Sunspots Bar: Sky Deck Midships	1:00pm-6:00pm
Windjammer Lounge: International Deck Portside	5:00pm-2:00am
Checker's Cabaret: International Deck Midships	1:00-6:00pm & 9:00pm-??
Club Internationale: International Deck Aft	1:00pm-1:00am
Monte Carlo Bar: Pool Deck	5:30pm-???
North Cape Lounge: Pool Deck Aft	3:00pm-Midnight
Lido Bar: Pool Deck, Aft	12:30pm-7:00pm
Dazzles: Viking Deck, Aft	10:00pm-???

Drink of the Day:
Bon Voyage

Due to US Customs regulations , all of our lounges must close at 4:30pm for sailing. They will re-open once the ship is at sea.

Please do not bring personal liquor into public areas.

Meal Hours

Snacks & Sandwiches: Great Outdoor Restaurant	1:00pm-4:00pm
Bon Voyage Dinner: Both Dining Rooms	Main Seating: 6:00pm Late Seating: 8:30pm
Le Rendez-Vous Supper Club Reservations accepted beginning Sunday	Open Sunday-Friday For reservations please dial #106
Bon Voyage Buffet: Both Dining Rooms	Midnight-1:00am

Tickets for Sunday's, Monday's, Wednesday's & Thursday's Shows will be handed out during dinner this evening. Please carry these tickets with you for all shows as indicated in the Cruise News

Gift Shops	**Drug Store**	**Casino**	**Fitness Center**	**Ice Cream Parlor**
International Deck 6:00pm-10:00pm	Pool Deck 6:00-10:00pm	Pool Deck Slot Machines: 6:00pm-??? Live Tables: 6:00pm-???	Olympic Deck Aft 1:30pm-4:00pm (Open House Only	International Deck 4:00-9:00pm

Photo Gallery	**Tuxedo Rental**	**Beauty Salon**	**Roman Spa**
Pool Deck, Midships 8:30-11:00pm	The Islander 6:00-10:00pm	Viking Deck, Starboard Side 1:00-6:00pm For Appointments Phone #44420	Dolphin Deck, 1:00-7:00pm For Appointments Phone #44410

Information Desk	**Room Service**	**Medical Center**	**Onboard Credit**	**Cruise Consultant**
International Deck 12:30pm-Midnight Phone #101	24 Hours Blue Section Dial #104 Pink Section Dial #105	Viking Deck, 3:30-5:00pm	International Deck Opens Sunday	International Deck Future cruise Information & discounts Opens Sunday

☎ E m e r g e n c y   P h o n e   # 9 1 1

You can make Private, Satellite Telephone Calls directly from your cabin! This service is available 24 hours a day, everyday. Follow dialing instructions in your cabin.

Teen Cruiser

Special events for young adults ages 13 to 17
aboard THE BIG RED BOAT

Your Captain: P. Pantelarns
Youth Director: Julia Johansen

Saturday

Your Starcruise Director:
Jim Ward

Time		Activities	Location
7:30	- 10:00	Time to eat again! **Buffet Breakfast** is served.	Satellite Cafe
8:30		Join our Fitness Instructor for Morning Aerobics!	Starlight Cabaret
9:00		Splashdown Instruction.	Pool Side
9:00	- 12:00	Shops on board OPEN!	Lounge Deck
9:15		Perfume Seminar.	Mars Bar
★★★			
9:30	- 12:00	**Jammin '91 Teen Calypso Cruise Tickets** will be on sale all morning. Ask your teen counselor for assistance.	
9:30	- 10:00	**Wake Attack!** Yes it's especially when you are on vacation, to get up this early. Anyway, this is not a time to sleep! Come and meet your friends and find out what is happening today! Join your counselor for breakfast.	Sunrise Terrace
10:00	- 10:30	**Bridge Tour!**	
10:30	- 11:00	**Catch a Wave. It's Volleyball Time.** Come and have a real fun time as you splash your way to victory! If you're not swimming then join us at the pool to support your favorite side or come up and play games pool side.	Pool Side
11:00	- 11:30	**Ping Pong Tournament!**	Lounge Dk Veranda
11:30	- 12:00	**Nintendo.** Find a friend to challenge.	Teen Center
★★★			
2:00	- 5:00	Big Dipper Ice Cream Parlor is OPEN to create your own Sundae.	Pool Deck
4:00	- 5:00	English Afternoon Tea and Cakes.	Satellite Cafe
4:00		Movie Time *(See Schedule)*.	Hollywood Theater
★★★			
9:30	- 10:00	**Pop Trivia!** Test your pop knowledge.	Sunrise Terrace
10:00	- 10:30	**Games, Games, Games!**	Teen Center
10:00		All teens holding tickets for the **Jammin '91 Calypso Cruise** meet in the Sunrise Terrace where we will walk to the dock side and load the tender.	
10:15	- 12:00	**Jammin '91 Teen Calypso Cruise.** Games, Fun and Prizes. Dance to the Calypso band while we cruise around Marsh Harbor.	
10:45	- 11:30	Move and Groove to the latest hot sounds. Ask your counselor for a request to play as you **dance the night away**.	Broadway Showroom
11:30	- 12:00	Let's try **"Blind Leading the Blind"** and find our way around the ship.	
12:00	- 1:00	Midnight Fruit Buffet!	Satellite Cafe
★★★			

Today aboard **THE BIG RED BOAT**

PREMIER CRUISE LINES

Kids Call℠ Special activities for kids ages 5 t(

Your Captain: P. Pantelaras
Youth Director: Julia Johansen

Saturday

Youth Starcruise Director
Jim War(

Time			Activities	Location
			Pluto's Playhouse is open from 8:30 a.m.–10:00 p.m. *Baby-sitting 10:00 p.m.–1:30 a.m. on board the ship.*	
8:30	-	9:00	**"Cartoon Time."** See Mickey, Minnie, Donald and Pluto with their friends in action!	Pluto's Playhouse
9:00	-	9:15	Let's learn about the Star/Ship Oceanic and take **a video tour with Goofy!**	
9:15	-	9:45	**Tour the Star/Ship Oceanic's Bridge** and get your photo taken when you steer the ship! **Parents Please Note:** We leave the playhouse promptly at 9:15 am.	
9:45	-	10:15	**Mousercise!** Let's get fit the Goofy way!	Pluto's Playhouse
10:15	-	11:15	And now it's the highlight of the morning! Come with us to **an Unbirthday Party** and celebrate with our Disney Friends. Let's watch our **Amazing Magician** as he mysteriously surprises us with his Magic Tricks, Can you tell how he does them?	Starlight Cabaret
11:15	-	12:00	Let's all go swimming in our **"Splash Pool"** or maybe play on Snap City. It's Wet 'N Wild time on the Star/Ship Oceanic!	Pluto's Playhouse
12:00			**General pick up for Lunch.**	
12:00	-	7:00	The Kid's Room is OPEN for supervision only, to play, draw a picture or perhaps watch a film while doing a puzzle with your Oceanic Counselors. You'll always return for more!	Pluto's Playhouse

★★★

Time			Activities	Location
7:00	-	7:30	Everyone's favorite, **Play-Doh!** What shapes and characters can you make?	Pluto's Playhouse
7:30	-	8:00	Let's have some fun on the **Outside Playground!**	
8:00	-	8:30	Let's play some of your **favorite games** like "Duck, Duck, Goose", "Doggie, Doggie" and "In the River, On the Bank".	
8:30	-	9:00	**Hand Painting** is so much fun! Come and do a special kind of hand print for mom and dad to treasure forever.	
8:40	-	9:00	Learn all about **"The Living Seas"** starring Minnie Mouse.	
9:00	-	9:30	**Musical Games.** Musical Freeze or perhaps even Musical Chairs or maybe you could be your favorite animal.	
9:30	-	10:00	Let's have some fun in our Kitchen Corner with a **Bedtime Story** as we cool off with some lemonade.	

★★★

Saturday at Sea
Dress: Casual during the day, Formal during the evening

6:30 a.m.	Early Bird Coffee	Pastorale Cafe
8:00 a.m.	Pool & Whirlpools Open	Daphne/Boheme Deck
8:00 a.m.	Sports Deck Opens–Ping Pong, Basketball & Shuffleboard	Electra Deck Aft
8:00 a.m.	Invigorating Morning Walk (1 Mile)	Daphne Deck
9:00 a.m.	Cruisercise Program	Royal Fireworks Lounge
9:30 a.m. & 10:00 a.m.	Visit to the Ship's Bridge Meet outside the Royal Fireworks Lounge	
10:00 a.m.-Noon	Cruise Staff Hospitality Desk Opens Cards, Games & Books Available	Harmony Room
10:00 a.m.	Ping Pong Tournament	Electra Deck Aft
10:00 a.m.	Backgammon Tournament	Harmony Lounge
10:00 a.m.	Morning Movie	Intermezzo Theater
10:00 a.m.	Slot Machines Open	Carmen Deck
10:30 a.m.	Dance Class	Carmen Lounge
10:30 a.m.	Friends of Bill W Get Together	Royal Fireworks Lounge
11:00 a.m.	Horse Racing	Carmen Lounge
11:00 a.m.	Shuffleboard Tournament	Electra Deck Aft
12:00 noon-2:30 p.m.	Calypso Music on Deck	Pastorale Cafe
2:00 p.m.	Bridge Tournament	Harmony Room
2:00 p.m.-3:00 p.m.	Cruise Staff Hospitality Desk Opens Cards, Games and Books Available	Harmony Room
2:00 p.m.	Casino Opens	Carmen Deck Fwd
2:30 p.m.	Basketball Contest	Electra Deck Aft
3:00 p.m.	Final Jackpot Snowball Bingo The Pot Must Go Today!	Carmen Lounge
4:00 p.m.	Important Debarkation Talk Regarding Customs, Immigration & Baggage Handling	Carmen Lounge

---

	CAPTAIN'S FAREWELL PARTY	
1st Sitting	The Captain Cordially Invites	2nd Sitting
5:00 p.m.	All Passengers to his Farewell Cocktail Party Carmen Lounge	7:00 p.m.

6:00 p.m.	Early Evening Movie	Intermezzo Theater

	LET THE STARS COME OUT	
1st Sitting	* * * SHOWTIME * * *	2nd Sitting
8:30 p.m.	SPECTACULAR FAREWELL SHOW! Carmen Lounge	10:30 p.m.

7:30 p.m.-8:15 p.m.	Romantic Music for Dancing	Royal Fireworks Lounge
9:30 p.m.-1:30 a.m.	Music for your Dancing & Listening Pleasure	Royal Fireworks Lounge
9:30 p.m.-12:00 a.m.	Piano Bar Opens	Serenade Bar
10:00 p.m.-3:00 a.m.	Disco Opens	Disco
12:00 a.m.-1:00 a.m.	Farewell Buffet	Bacchanalia Restaurant

Operating Hours - Saturday

Purser's Office	8:00 a.m.-8:00 p.m.	Electra Deck Fwd
Credit Desk	Closed	
Doctor's Office	9:00 a.m.-11:00 a.m.	La Gioconda Deck
	4:30 p.m.-6:00 p.m.	Aft

(In case of emergency or outside office hrs. please dial "8")

Cruise & Tour Desk	Closed	
Radio Room	8:00 a.m.-Midnight	Aida Deck
Duty Free Shops	9:00 a.m.-12:30 p.m.	Carmen &
	2:30 p.m.-10:30 p.m.	Daphne Decks
Beauty Salon &	9:00 a.m.-12:00 noon	Fidelio Deck Fwd
Massage Therapy	2:00 p.m.-8:00 p.m.	
Casino		
Slot Machines	10:00 a.m.-2:00 a.m.	Carmen Deck Fwd
Tables	2:00 p.m.-2:00 a.m.	
Photo Gallery	10:30 a.m.-10:30 p.m.	Electra Deck Fwd
Swimming Pool	8:00 a.m.-Sunset	Daphne Deck Aft
Whirlpools	8:00 a.m.-10:00 p.m.	La Boheme Deck Aft
Video Arcade	Open 24 hours	Carmen Deck Fwd
Housekeeping	Open 24 hours	Electra Deck Fwd
Portraits	6:00 p.m.-10:30 p.m.	

(Outside Royal Fireworks Lounge)

Dining Today

(Dress for the evening: Formal)

7:00 a.m.-10:00 a.m.	Buffet Breakfast	Pastorale Cafe
7:30 a.m.-9:30 a.m.	Breakfast - Open Seating	Bacchanalia Restaurant
12:00 noon-2:30 p.m.	Buffet Lunch	Pastorale Cafe & Planets Counter
12:00 noon	Lunch - Early Sitting	Bacchanalia Restaurant
1:30 p.m.	Lunch - Late Sitting	Bacchanalia Restaurant
4:00 p.m.-5:00 p.m.	Coffee, Tea, Cookies *(Music with Caribbean Flavor)*	Pastorale Cafe
5:45 p.m.	Farewell Dinner Early Sitting	Bacchanalia Restaurant
8:00 p.m.	Farewell Dinner Late Sitting	Bacchanalia Restaurant
12:00 Midnight-1:00 a.m.	Farewell Buffet	Bacchanalia Restaurant

(Please note that the restaurant doors will be closed 15 minutes after commencement of meals.)

Sunday — Miami

Purser's Office	7:30 a.m. For Information Only	Electra Deck Fwd
Credit Desk	6:00 a.m.-9:00 a.m.	Electra Deck Aft
Photo Gallery	7:30 a.m.	Electra Deck Fwd
6:15 a.m.-10:00 a.m.	Coffee, Tea and Rolls	Pastorale Cafe
6:15 a.m.	Breakfast-Early Sitting	Bacchanalia Restaurant
7:30 a.m.	Breakfast-Late Sitting	Bacchanalia Restaurant

Gratuities

In response to many requests from passengers, the following is provided for guidance only:

Cabin Steward	$3.50 per person per day
Dining Room Waiter	$2.50 per person per day
Dining Room Busboy	$1.25 per person per day
Maitre d'	$4.00 per person per cruise

Important Debarkation Information

On-board Credit Accounts—Passengers who established their credit accounts with a major credit card will receive an itemized copy of their bill in their cabins Sunday morning. The credit card company will send the bill to your home at a later date. Passengers who established their accounts with a cash or travelers' cheque deposit, must come to the Credit Desk, located on Electra Deck Aft, on Sunday morning from 6:00 a.m. to 9:00 a.m. for final settlement.

Cabins—Baggage—All baggage securely locked and tagged, must be placed outside your cabin door by 3:00 a.m. Baggage not placed outside your cabin by this time must be carried off personally. Valuables, airline tickets and passports should be carried with you at all times.

Cabins—Please leave your cabin as soon as possible so that the cabin steward may prepare it for our arriving passengers. Remember to leave your cabin keys in the cabin.

Purser's Office—Please note that the purser's office will be open from 7:30 a.m. for information only. No monetary transactions can take place.

Comment Cards—In order to continue to improve our product and service to you, please fill out the comment card and deposit in the comment box in front of the Housekeeping Desk.

Disembarkation Procedures—Passengers will be allowed to disembark when all passengers baggage has been landed and Customs and Immigration formalities have been completed. As this procedure will take some time, you are kindly requested not to crowd the stairway areas. For your own comfort and convenience, we recommend you relax in the comfort of our public rooms until the ship has been cleared. Once you have left the ship, you will not be allowed to reembark. When you disembark you will find your luggage grouped by color code on the pier, ready for you to claim and take through customs, together with your your completed and duly signed customs' declaration form.

U.S. Agriculture—Forbids the entry of fruits, plants, meats and food items. Please do not remove from the ship.

Porters—Will be available in the terminal to assist you.

Immigration—As soon as the ship arrives in Miami, U.S. Immigration officials will board the ship. At that time all Non-U.S. Citizens, Aliens Residents and Canadian Citizens are requested to proceed immediately to the Serenade (Piano) Bar to clear with U.S. Immigration. The ship will not be cleared for passengers to go ashore until Immigration formalities have been completed.

U.S. Customs—A Customs Declaration Form will be delivered to your cabin tonight. This form must be completed by every passenger, or in the case of a family traveling together, by the head of the household. A member of the family must be present in the Royal Fireworks Lounge to check with U.S. Customs Inspector who will be in attendance after docking.

We wish you a safe trip back home and hope to see you soon on another cruise with us. We hope that we have fulfilled your expectation and we thank you for choosing Dolphin Cruise Line for your vacation.

QE2+

DAILY PROGRAMME

Captain: *ROBIN WOODALL*
Cruise Director: *LINDSAY FROST*
Deputy Cruise Director: *COLIN PARKER*
Social Director: *ANDREW GRAHAM*
Social Directress: *MAUREEN RYAN*

VOYAGE 792 No. 2
SATURDAY, 22nd June 1991
On Passage To: SOUTHAMPTON
Sunrise: 6.59am   Sunset: 9.30pm
Suggested Dress This Evening: FORMAL

"THE CAPTAIN'S TOAST" *Drawn by F. Barnard*

Our Special Highlights Today

At 11.00am in the Theatre
"EWEN, THE ROMANTIC"
an informal lecture by
RICHARD EWEN
Artist and Fine Arts Specialist

At 2.30pm in the Theatre
"WELCOME TO QE2"
Join Cruise Director,
LINDSAY FROST,
for an informal talk on this
famous ship and shipping line

FOR YOUR MORNING LEISURE

Throughout this voyage, the works of RICHARD EWEN, Artist and Fine Arts Specialist, will be on display in the Card Room.
The Artist will be present today from 9.30am to 11.30am and 4.00pm to 5.30pm

9.00	THE GOLDEN DOOR SPA AT SEA ORIENTATION An introduction to the SPA AT SEA PROGRAM	Queens Room
9.30	BRIDGE LECTURE with RAPHAEL and EDYTHE FRANKS	Theatre Bar
9.30	FINANCIAL PLANNING: "INVESTING IN THE 1990's: WHAT TO DO ABOUT LOWER INTEREST RATES" an informal lecture by HANK and DEANNA KATZ, Senior Vice President and Financial Consultants, Shearson Lehman Brothers	Theatre
9.30	SPELLING BEE: Put your thinking caps on!	Grand Lounge
10.00	HOW TO PUT ON YOUR LIFE JACKET A short video presentation	TV Channel 2
10.00	ATTENTION ALL YOUNG CRUISERS between the ages of 8 and 16! Meet KERRI-ANNE and JULIE ANN, your Youth Activities Directors, and find out what they have planned for you this voyage	Teen Centre
10.00	Today's BRAIN TEASER QUIZ is available	Outside Cruise Staff Centre
10.30	**PASSENGER EMERGENCY DRILL**—International Maritime Law requires that all passengers attend this important drill. Following the instructions in your cabin, please put on your life jacket and proceed to your emergency station for further information. Following this drill there will be a **CREW BOAT AND RAFT DRILL.** Whilst this drill in no way affects passengers directly, some ship's services may be curtailed. Thank you for your understanding.	
11.00	RICHARD EWEN (see front cover)	Theatre
11.00	COMPUTER LECTURE: "AN INTRODUCTION TO PERSONAL COMPUTERS" by QE2's Computer Expert HOWARD WEINSTEIN (repeated at 2.30pm and 4.00pm)	Computer Learning Centre
11.00	ASTROLOGY mini-readings by ELIZABETH GARRITY	Theatre Bar
11.00	SHIP'S MOBILE TOTE! Guess our mileage from sailing time yesterday to noon today. Cash prizes to be won! ($2.00 per bet).	Cruise Staff Centre and Public Rooms
11.15	COMPLIMENTARY DANCE CLASS with Dance Champions STEVE and DEBBIE McCORMICK	Queens Room
11.15	HAIRDRESSING AND BEAUTY DEMONSTRATION presented by STEINERS OF LONDON, the beauty salon on board	Grand Lounge

---

SAILING SOLO
At 12.00pm in the Theatre Bar
Cruise Director, LINDSAY FROST, and the Cruise Staff
invite all those passengers travelling alone for an informal get-together
Music by ATLANTIC AVENUE

FOR YOUR AFTERNOON LEISURE

12.00	QE2 HORSERACING Place bets on your favourite thoroughbred	Grand Lounge
2.00	PARTY and DUPLICATE BRIDGE with RAPHAEL and EDYTHE FRANKS	Queens Room
2.00	MEET THE CRUISE STAFF: Join Social Director, ANDREW GRAHAM, for an informal chat	Grand Lounge
2.30	"WELCOME TO QE2" (see front cover)	Theatre
2.30	HANDWRITING ANALYSIS: "The Write Stuff" an informal lecture by ALICE WALSH, Graphoanalyst	Theatre Bar
2.30	CASINO HAPPY HOUR Come play QE2's Super Slot Machines this afternoon and you could win a bottle of QE2 Malt Whiskey or a special bonus win as well as jackpots of up to $8,000.00. Full details are on display in the Casino	Players Club Casino
2.45	TANTALIZING TRIVIA QUIZ with a member of the Cruise Staff	Grand Lounge
3.00	Informal gathering of MASONIC BRETHREN	Midships Bar (inner area)
3.30	LADIES CLUB: SCARF TYING Join Social Directress, MAUREEN RYAN, and learn some new fashions. Don't forget to bring a scarf!	Grand Lounge

---

At 3.30pm in the Theatre
"HOW TO CURTAIL SEA AIR FROM SHRINKING YOUR CLOTHING"
an informal lecture by
HENRY BERK, M.D.

3.30	ELEMIS, IONITHERMIE and CATHIODERMIE presented by Steiners of London	Theatre Bar

---

At 4.00pm in the Grand Lounge
♪♪♪   **BONANZA BINGO**   ♪♪♪
Cash prizes to be won!

4.00	Teatime melodies with ATLANTIC AVENUE	Queens Room

CAPTAIN ROBIN WOODALL
Cordially invites all passengers dining in the Queens Grill, Princess Grills and Columbia Restaurant to join him and
his officers for cocktails this evening in the Queens Room from 7.00pm to 8.00pm
The Captain will receive his guests at the Forward Port side entrance by the Library.
A reception for passengers dining in the Mauretania Restaurant will be held tomorrow, Sunday, 23rd June

---

171

TONIGHT'S ENTERTAINMENT

At 10.00pm in the Theatre
A Special Recital featuring
BARBARA GEARY
Concert Pianist

THE GRAND LOUNGE
Showtime Tonight!

THE JEAN ANN RYAN SINGERS and DANCERS

present

"FOLLIES PARISIENNE"

with

THE MARK JOYCE SHOWBAND

Separate performances at 9.00pm and 11.00pm

(Please be advised that there is no reserving of seats prior to Showtime)

*To avoid overcrowding, we kindly request that passengers
dining later than 9.00pm attend the 11.00pm show*

(VIDEOS: Please note that in order to comply with copyright
laws, the use of video cameras during showtime is strictly prohibited)

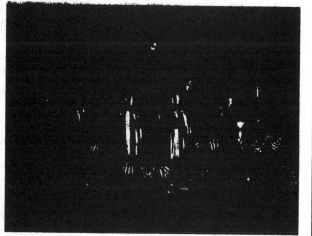

DANCE MUSIC THIS EVENING

THEATRE BAR
At 5.30pm GAZELLE
7.45pm and 10.30pm ATLANTIC AVENUE

QUEENS ROOM
At 10.00pm AFFIRMATION

GRAND LOUNGE
At 8.30pm and 10.30pm
THE MARK JOYCE SHOWBAND

PLAYERS CLUB CASINO

Opening Times: Change is available for the slot
machines from 10.00am
Tables: 2.30pm to 6.00pm and from 9.30pm onwards

*(Parents are respectfully reminded that children under age 18
are not permitted in the casino. The use of cameras or videos
is forbidden in the casino.)*

THE CLUB LIDO
Join us for a
GOLDEN OLDIES NIGHT
From 9.30pm join us for dancing with your QE2 DJ
SHAUN LOVELESS

At 9.30pm, join KERRI-ANNE

and JULIE ANN for a

COLLEGE CROWD GET-TOGETHER
At Midnight dance to the fantastic
sound of our resident disco band

GAZELLE

*(Parents are respectfully reminded that children under age 16
are not permitted in the Club Lido after 10.30pm)*

THE YACHT CLUB

(Aft of The Grand Lounge)
Entertainment at 7.30pm and 10.30pm with
GREG DIAKUN at the piano

DON'T FORGET TO ADJUST YOUR CLOCKS AND WATCHES BEFORE RETIRING TONIGHT!

CUNARD

SHIPBOARD INFORMATION

OPENING HOURS

THE CRUISE STAFF CENTRE: (Upper Deck E Stairway) is open today from 9.00am to 12.30pm and 2.30pm to 6.00pm for the borrowing of video tapes and games.

THE LIBRARY/OCEAN BOOKSHOP: (Quarter Deck, Port side) is open today from 9.00am to 1.00pm, 2.30pm to 6.00pm, and 9.30pm to 10.30pm.

TRAVEL and TOUR OFFICE: (Tel 3500. Aft of the Grand Lounge, Upper Deck Port side) will be open today from 9.00am to 12.00 Noon and from 2.00pm to 5.00pm for the sale of arrangements detailed in our "Welcome Aboard" Letter. For guests disembarking in Southampton, the final opportunity to book arrangements will be 5.00pm on Monday, 24th June.

Drink of the day:
"GOLDEN CADILLAC"
at a special price of $3.60

AFTER DINNER COFFEE: *FRENCH*
made with HINE BRANDY at a special price of $4.50.
Served in all restaurants and bars.

Bar Opening Hours:

YACHT CLUB BAR: 11.00am to 2.00am

THEATRE BAR: 11.00am to 2.00pm and 5.30pm to the Wee Small Hours

ONE DECK LIDO: 10.30am to 5.00pm (weather permitting)

CLUB LIDO: 10.30am to the Wee Small Hours

MIDSHIPS BAR: 11.00am to 2.00pm and 5.30pm to Midnight
(Please note that the Midships Bar is for First Class Passengers only)

Today's GOLDEN DOOR SPA AT SEA Schedule

(Spas are located on 6 Deck F Stairway and 7 Deck C Stairway)

Time	Activity	Location	Time	Activity	Location
7.30am	Deck Walk	Queens Room	3.00pm	Deck Walk	Boat Deck Aft
9.00am	Orientation	Queens Room	3.00pm	Intermediate Aerobics	6 Deck F Stairway
11.15am	Body Toning	6 Deck F Stairway	3.45pm	BODY AWARENESS/	6 Deck F Stairway
11.15am	Intro to Gym Equipment	7 Deck C Stairway		HEARTRATES	
12.00pm	Intro to Step Aerobics	6 Deck F Stairway	4.00pm - 6.00pm	Gym Guidance	7 Deck C Stairway
			5.00pm	Stretch and Relax	6 Deck F Stairway

SPORTS ON BOARD QE2 *with* MAUREEN OBERHAMMER

(All Sports activities are held on the Sports Area on Upper Deck unless otherwise indicated)

11.00am SPORTS ORIENTATION: Meet Maureen your Sports Director in the YACHT CLUB and learn about the activities scheduled for this voyage. Sign up for Putting, Paddle Tennis, Quoits, Shuffleboard and Mixed Couples SPORT-O-RAMA Tournaments. Improve your golf swing with a complimentary lesson.

12.00pm PADDLE TENNIS CLINIC: Learn How to Play the Game
3.00pm BASKETBALL: Court is open for three man games
3.00pm PADDLEBALL: Play the fast ball and wall game
3.15pm GOLF: Complimentary lessons
4.00pm VOLLEYBALL: Join in the fun with Mixed Open Games

COMING ATTRACTIONS

Monday, 24th June will be our
FANCY DRESS MASQUERADE COMPETITIONS
Materials for your costumes will be available from the Cruise Staff Centre from 10.00am to 12.00 noon and 3.00pm to 5.00pm on Sunday, 23rd June
Tuesday, 25th June will be our
PASSENGER TALENT SHOW
You may register your act up until 10.30am on the day of the show at the Cruise Staff Centre

MOVIES IN THE THEATRE

At 8.00pm and 11.00pm
"GREEN CARD"
(Comedy)
GERARD DEPARDIEU   ANDIE McDOWELL
Running Time: 1 hour 44 minutes
Cert: PG-13

Dining on Board QE2

A Light Continental Breakfast
is served in the Club Lido from 6.00am to 8.00am

Breakfast Buffet in The Lido
(Starboard side only)
8.00am to 10.00am

Breakfast in the Queens Grill, Princess Grill I, Princess Grill II, and Columbia Restaurant
8.00am to 10.00am

Breakfast Buffet in the Mauretania Restaurant
(for Mauretania passengers only)
A choice of buffet style or à la carte breakfast
is offered in an open seating.
7.30am to 10.00am

Luncheon in the Queens Grill, Princess Grill I, and Princess Grill II
1.00pm to 2.30pm

Luncheon in the Columbia Restaurant
12.30pm to 2.00pm

Luncheon in the Mauretania Restaurant
(for Mauretania passengers only)
A choice of buffet style luncheon as well as a luncheon
menu is offered in an open seating.

Luncheon Buffet in The Club Lido
(Starboard side)
12.00pm to 2.00pm

Hamburger Haven
On One Deck Lido
12.00 Noon to 2.30pm (weather permitting)
Light meals and salads available

Afternoon Teas
is served in the Queens Room, Club Lido,
and on the open decks (weather permitting)
4.00pm to 5.00pm

Children's Tea
will be served in the Columbia Restaurant at 5.30pm

Dinner in the Queens Grill, Princess Grill I, Princess Grill II and Columbia Restaurant
7.30pm to 9.00pm

Dinner in the Mauretania Restaurant
Main Sitting: 6.15pm (Last orders 6.45pm)
Late Sitting: 8.30pm

Midnight Snacks
in the Columbia from 12.00 midnight to 1.00am
(Wine and Beverage service)

Celebration

THE "FUN SHIPS" WELCOME ABOARD

CAPTAIN RENATO PIOVANO

SATURDAY, DAY 1
Sunset: 6:36 p.m.

Cruise Director
Steve Cassel

THE MASTER OF THE VESSEL WISHES TO EXTEND A PERSONAL WELCOME TO ALL PASSENGERS, HOPING THAT THIS CRUISE WILL BE A LONG REMEMBERED VACATION FOR ALL. ONCE AGAIN, WELCOME ABOARD!

Luggage will be delivered to your room as soon as possible. If you find any baggage in your cabin that doesn't belong to you, please notify the Purser or your Cabin Steward as soon as possible.

12:30–6:00 p.m.	Sail & Sign Credit Desk Opens	Promenade Desk
12:30–4:00 p.m.	Dining Room Reservations Made	Islands in the Sky Lounge
12:30–3:30 p.m.	Massage Appointment taken by Our Masseuse	Promenade Deck
1:30–4:00 p.m.	Video Diary Available, Underwater Camera and Snorkel Rentals	Main Deck
1:30–4:00 p.m.	Complimentary snacks served!	Wheelhouse Bar & Grill
2:00–4:00 p.m.	Beauty Salon opens for appointments only	Admiral Deck
2:00–4:00 p.m.	Our Calypso Band plays for your entertainment	Lido Deck Poolside
2:00–4:00 p.m.	Advance Tour tickets on sale	Shore Tours, Main Deck
2:00–4:00 p.m.	Disco opens for your enjoyment with DJ John	Promenade Deck
3:00–3:30 p.m.	Spa & Sports Talk	Astoria Lounge

4:00 p.m.	ms Celebration Sails for San Juan, Puerto Rico	

IMPORTANT:	Fire & Lifeboat Drill — The convention of Safety of Life at Sea and the U.S. Coast Guard makes this a command performance for all passengers. The drill will be held approximately 30 minutes after sailing. Please listen for the announcement. Thank you for your cooperation.

	After our Departure and Lifeboat Drill the Full Casino will open till 3:00 a.m. Featuring Dice Tables, Roulette, Blackjack, Wheel of Fortune, Slot Machines and Poker	Rainbow Club Casino
4:00–8:00 p.m.	Appointments for Massage	Beauty Salon, Admiral Deck
6:00 p.m.	Main Sitting Dinner	Vista & Horizon Dining Rooms
	*Please check the color of your Dining Room Seating Card: Vista Dining Room: Yellow for Main Seating Horizon Dining Room: Orange for Main Sitting	
7:00–8:00 p.m.	Shore tours on sale	Main Deck Lobby Area
7:15–8:00 p.m.	Complimentary Rum Swizzle Get Together. This is the perfect time to start meeting your fellow shipmates. Also enjoy our live Dixieland Band	Promenade Deck.
7:30–8:00 p.m.	Junior Cruiser Orientation Meeting. Bring your parents and meet your counselors.	Galax-Z Disco
8:00 p.m.	Late Sitting Dinner	Vista & Horizon Dining Rooms
	*Please check the color of your Dining Room Seating Card: Vista Dining Room: Blue for Late Seating Horizon Dining Room: Green for Late Sitting	Admiral Deck Forward Admiral Deck Aft
8:15–9:00 p.m.	Dance to the music of the "Celebration Orchestra"	Astoria Lounge
9:00 p.m.	JACKPOT BINGO — Join us and win some extra shopping cash. We play progressive bingo with jackpots reaching hundreds of dollars! Come early for a good seat to see the show that follows! Snowball Game $1500.00	Astoria Lounge
9:30 p.m.	"Singles Party"! Complimentary Rum Swizzles & Dancing, Fun & Games	Galax-Z Disco
9:30 p.m.–LATE	Enjoy music at the Trolley Bar	Promenade Deck
9:30 p.m.–LATE	Live Music for your Dancing pleasure	Endless Summer Lounge
9:30 p.m.–LATE	Live Music for Dancing into the Night	Islands in the Sky Lounge
10:00 p.m.–3:00 a.m.	Disco opens (16 years and under must be with parents)	Galax-Z Disco
10:30 p.m.	SHOWTIME IN THE ASTORIA LOUNGE — Introduction of Cruise Staff along with fun & games.	
MIDNIGHT–1:30 a.m.	Midnight Buffet is served	Horizon Dining Room
1:30–2:30 a.m.	Mini Buffet is served at the Trolley Coffee available 24 hours a day on Lido Deck	Promenade Deck

DRESS FOR THIS EVENING: Casual (Sunday evening will be our first formal night)

Movie: "The Fabulous Baker Boys" 1:00 p.m., 3:30, 6:00, 8:30, 11:00, 1:30 a.m. and 4:00

6:30 a.m.	Coffee for the early risers!	Wheelhouse Bar & Grill
7:45 a.m.	Main Sitting Breakfast	Vista & Horizon Dining Rooms

8:00–10:00 a.m.	Breakfast served on Deck	Wheelhouse Bar & Grill
8:00 a.m.	All Slot Machines open	Rainbow Club Casino
8:15 a.m.	Holy Mass/Interdenominational Service follows	Islands in the Sky
9:00 a.m.	Late Sitting Breakfast	Vista & Horizon Dining Rooms
9:00 a.m.–12:30 p.m.	Shops on board open	Admiral Deck
9:30–10:30 a.m.	Library opens	Admiral Deck
10:00–11:00 a.m.	Complimentary Bouillon is served	Wheelhouse Bar & Grill
10:00 a.m.–1:00 p.m.	Sail & Sign Bar Credit Desk open	Promenade Deck
10:00 a.m.	Travel Talk! An important take about U.S. Custom rules and regulations, upcoming ports and general ship information.	Astoria Lounge
11:00 a.m.	Nautica Spa Information	Nautica Spa, Verandah Deck
11:00 a.m.–3:00 p.m.	Tour Office Opens. Visa, MasterCard, American Express, Cash and Traveller's Checks accepted. The tours are limited so please book early!	Astoria Lounge
11:30 a.m.–2:30 p.m.	Light Lunch is served on the Deck	Wheelhouse Bar & Grill
12:00 NOON	Main Sitting Lunch is served	Vista & Horizon Dining Rooms
12:00 NOON–3:00 p.m.	Full Casino is open for your gaming pleasure	Rainbow Club Casino

1:00 p.m.	Trap Shooting for Beginners and Pros	Promenade Deck

1:00–5:00 p.m.	Enjoy Live Calypso Music	Lido Deck Poolside
1:00–2:00 p.m.	Library Opens — Sign up to meet Card, Bridge & Game Players	Admiral Deck
1:30 p.m.	Late Sitting Lunch	Vista & Horizon Dining Rooms
2:00 p.m.	Name that T. V. Tune	Lido Deck Poolside
2:30 p.m.	Jewelry Lecture & Perfume Talk	Endless Summer Lounge
3:00 p.m.	Complimentary Gambling Classes	Rainbow Club Casino

3:15 p.m.	Wine and Cheese Party! Enjoy all wines for only $2.50 Complimentary cheeses and fruits served	Galax-Z Disco
4:00–5:00 p.m.	Coffee, Tea, Ice Cream & Treats	Wheelhouse Bar & Grill
4:00–5:00 p.m.	Afternoon Tea is served	Red Hot Piano Bar
5:00 p.m.	Children's "Coketail" Party	Galax-Z Disco

Captain Renato Piovano cordially invites all passengers to his Gala Party

5:00 p.m.	Formal Party for all Main Sitting Passengers	Astoria Lounge
5:30–6:00 p.m.	Cocktail Music at the Piano Bar	Speak Easy Lounge
6:00 p.m.	Main Sitting Formal Dinner	Vista & Horizon Dining Rooms
7:00 p.m.	Formal Party for all Late Sitting Passengers	Astoria Lounge
7:30–8:00 p.m.	Cocktail Music at the Piano Bar	Speak Easy Lounge
8:00 p.m.	Late Sitting Formal Dinner	Vista & Horizon Dining Rooms
8:00 p.m.–LATE	Espresso's opens for specialty coffees and imported chocolates	Promenade Deck

8:30 p.m.	For Main Sitting	Leonard Miller Presents George Reich's	Astoria Lounge
10:30 p.m.	For Late Sitting	"Celebration'"	Astoria Lounge

Featuring the talented "Celebration Dancers"
and starring
Steve Cassel, Your Cruise Director
and from KC & the Sunshine Band, Vernon Maddox

9:30 p.m.–LATE	Piano Bar opens	Red Hot Piano Bar
9:30 p.m.–LATE	Great Music for your dancing pleasure	Islands in the Sky Lounge
9:30 p.m.–LATE	Live Music for your dancing pleasure	Endless Summer Lounge
10:00 p.m.–3:00 a.m.	Disco opens	Galax-Z Disco
10:00 p.m.	Couples & Lovers Party	Lido Deck Main Pool

12:00 MIDNIGHT	SPECIAL SHOW Adult Magic & Comedy with Rand Woodbury	Islands in the Sky Lounge
1:00 a.m.	Dance Contest	Galax-Z Disco

12:30–1:30 a.m.	Late Night Buffet served	Horizon Dining Room
1:30–2:30 a.m.	Mini Buffet served at Trolley	Promenade Deck

DRESS FOR THE EVENING: Formal (The next formal evening will be Thursday)

Movie: "Parenthood," 8:00 a.m., 10:30, 1:00 p.m. 3:30, 6:00, 8:30, 11:00, 1:30 a.m. and 4:00

PLEASE NOTE: The Port Side of the Astoria and Islands in the Sky Lounges are reserved for non-smoking passengers. Thank you for your cooperation in this special request.

6:00 a.m.	Coffee for the early risers!	Wheelhouse Bar & Grill
7:45 a.m.	Main Sitting Breakfast	Vista & Horizon Dining Rooms
8:00–10:00 a.m.	Breakfast served on the Deck	Wheelhouse Bar & Grill
8:00 a.m.	All Slot Machines open until San Juan arrival	Rainbow Club Casino
8:45 a.m.	Walk A Mile	Sport Deck
9:00 a.m.	Late Sitting Breakfast	Vista & Horizon Dining Rooms
9:30 a.m.	Horse Racing — Bet on your favorite horse. Cheer them across the finish line and win!	Astoria Lounge
9:45 a.m.	"Cardio Funk" Aerobics Class	Galax-Z Disco
10:00–11:00 a.m.	Soup and Bouillon are served	Wheelhouse Bar & Grill
10:00–11:00 a.m.	Library opens	Admiral Deck
10:00 a.m.–11:00 p.m.	Video Diary Reservations	Main Deck
10:30 a.m.	SHOPPING TALK — Learn where all the best buys are in San Juan, St. Thomas & St. Maarten and who offers specials for Celebration passengers	Astoria Lounge
11:30 a.m.–2:00 p.m.	Sandwiches are served	Lido Deck Poolside
11:30 a.m.–2:30 p.m.	Sun Lovers Lunch served	Wheelhouse Bar & Grill
12:00 NOON	Main Sitting Lunch	Vista & Horizon Dining Rooms
12:00 NOON–ARRIVAL	Full Casino opens	Promenade Deck
12:00 NOON–2:30 p.m.	Tour Office opens	Main Deck
1:00–5:00 p.m.	Enjoy Live Calypso Music	Lido Deck Poolside
1:00–2:00 p.m.	Library Opens	Admiral Deck
1:00 p.m.	Steiner's Skin Care Seminar-Workshop	Red Hot Piano Bar
1:00–2:00 p.m.	Trapshooting	Promenade Deck
1:30 p.m.	Late Sitting Lunch	Vista & Horizon Dining Rooms
2:15 p.m.	Grandmothers & Honeymoon Party — Complimentary champagne to all grandmothers, grandfathers, newlyweds or anniversary couples. Lots of surprises and laughs. Honeymooners get a complimentary picuture.	Astoria Lounge
2:45 p.m.	Balloon Bingo — Each Bingo winner gets to pick a balloon containing prizes ranging from souvenirs to a 14K gold Lucien Piccard watch! All in addition to BIG cash prizes! No prize under $100.00 Coverall Jackpot $1600.00	Astoria Lounge
3:00 p.m.	Pool Games	Lido Deck Poolside
4:00–5:00 p.m.	Afternoon Tea is served	Red Hot Piano Bar
4:00–5:00 p.m.	Ice Cream, Tea, Coffee & Treats.	Wheelhouse Bar & Grill
5:00 p.m.	Main Sitting Dinner	Vista & Horizon Dining Rooms
6:00 p.m.	The ms CELEBRATION arrives in San Juan, Puerto Rico. Remember to take your boarding pass with you when going ashore.	
7:00 p.m.	Late Sitting Dinner	Vista & Horizon Dining Rooms
10:30 p.m.–2:30 a.m.	Deck Party — Music, food, contests and prizes for everyone! Try our Bar Special Margarita for $2.25	Lido Deck
11:30 p.m.–1:00 a.m.	Mexican Buffet	Lido Deck

Movie: "Look Who's Talking" 8:00 a.m., 10:30, 1:00 p.m., 3:30, 6:00, 8:30, 11:00 and 4:00 a.m.

6:30 a.m.	Coffee for the early risers!	Wheelhouse Bar & Grill
6:30 a.m.	Main Sitting Breakfast	Vista & Horizon Dining Rooms
7:00–10:00 a.m.	Breakfast served on Deck	Wheelhouse Bar & Grill
7:45 a.m.	Late Sitting Breakfast	Vista & Horizon Dining Rooms
8:00 a.m.	ms Celebration arrives in St. Thomas, take your boarding pass with you when going ashore and be back to the ship no later than 5:00 p.m.	
8:00–9:00 a.m.	Tour Office opens for last minute tour purchases	Main Deck
10:00–11:00 a.m.	Bouillon is served	Wheelhouse Bar & Grill
11:30 a.m.–2:30 p.m.	Sun Lovers Lunch	Wheelhouse Bar & Grill
12:00 NOON–2:00 p.m.	Open Sitting Lunch	Horizon Dining Room
4:00–5:00 p.m.	Sandwiches are served at the Trolley	Trolley Bar
4:00–5:00 p.m.	Coffee, Tea, Ice Cream & Treats (Yummy!)	Wheelhouse Bar & Grill
4:00–5:30 p.m.	St. Thomas Deck Party	Lido Deck Poolside
5:00–6:00 p.m.	Cocktail Hour! Enjoy great music and our famous Guacamole & Chips with Salsa Dip!	Endless Summer Lounge
5:30 p.m.	ms Celebration sails for St. Maarten	
6:00 p.m.	Main Sitting Dinner	Vista & Horizon Dining Rooms
7:00–8:00 p.m.	Cocktail Hour! Enjoy great music and our famous Guacamole & Chips with Salsa Dip.	Endless Summer Lounge
7:00–10:00 p.m.	Shops open. Order your bottle of duty free liquor today!	Admiral Deck
8:00 p.m.	Late Sitting Dinner	Vista & Horizon Dining Rooms
8:00 p.m.	SHOWTIME! (Main Sitting) 10:30 (Late Sitting) Hilarious Comedy with Lewis Nixon The Magic and Mystery of Rand Woodbury Your Host and MC, Steve Cassel	Astoria Lounge
9:00 p.m.	SNOWBALL JACKPOT BINGO — Great Prizes	Astoria Lounge
9:30 p.m.–LATE	Music with "Chris" by the Trolley	Promenade Deck
9:30 p.m.–LATE	Music for Listening and Dancing	Islands in the Sky Lounge
9:30 p.m.–LATE	Dance Music with "Images"	Endless Summer Lounge
9:45 p.m.–LATE	Video Sing Along	Red Hot Piano Bar
10:00 p.m.	Disco opens with DJ 'John'	Galax-Z Disco
12:00 MIDNIGHT	SPECIAL SHOW — A Salute to the Music Greats with Suzanne Lukather	Islands in the Sky Lounge
12:30–1:30 a.m.	Late Night Dessert Buffet	Horizon Dining Room
1:30–2:30 a.m.	Mini Buffet at the Trolley	Promenade Deck

DRESS FOR THE EVENING: Casual

Movie: "Indiana Jones — The Last Crusade" 8:00 a.m., 10:30, 1:00 p.m., 3:30, 6:00, 8:30, 11:00, 1:30 a.m. and 4:00

IN CASE OF EMERGENCY ONLY CONTACT:
The West Indiana Company
West Indian Pier
St. Thomas, U.S. V.I.
Tel. (809) 774-1780

Tour Departure Times & Meeting Places

8:30–9:30 a.m.	St. Thomas Island & Coral World Tour	Departs from Deck 3 Gangway
8:30 a.m.	Morning Snorkel & Scuba Tours	Meet in the Disco
8:30 a.m.	St. John Island Tour	Meet on "A" Deck of Atlantis Lounge
12:30 p.m.	Afternoon Snorkel & Scuba Tours	Meet in the Disco
	(NOTE: Passengers on the Kon Tiki may pick up this tour in town by boarding the Kon Tiki Raft on the waterfront side of A.H. Rise Liquor Store at 1:45 p.m.	

6:30 a.m.	Coffee for early risers!	Wheelhouse Bar & Grill
6:30 a.m.	Main Sitting Breakfast	Vista & Horizon Dining Rooms

7:00 a.m.	ms Celebration arrives in St. Maarten. Please carry your boarding pass with you when you go ashore and be back to the ship no later than 4:30 p.m.

7:00–10:00 a.m.	Breakfast served on Deck	Wheelhouse Bar & Grill
7:45 a.m.	Late Sitting Breakfast	Vista & Horizon Dining Rooms
8:00–9:00 a.m.	Shore Tour Office opens	Main Deck Midship

10:00 a.m.	Volleyball Available	Verandah Deck
10:00–11:00 a.m.	Bouillon is served	Wheelhouse Bar & Grill

PLEASE NOTE:	All passengers on tours should meet at the designated areas listed at least 10 minutes early!

11:30 a.m.–2:30 p.m.	Sun Lovers Lunch is served on Deck	Wheelhouse Bar & Grill
12:00 NOON–2:00 p.m.	Open Sitting Buffet Lunch is served	Horizon Dining Rooms

4:00–5:30 p.m.	St. Maarten Deck Party	Lido Deck
4:00–5:00 p.m.	Coffee, Tea & Ice Cream	Wheelhouse Bar & Grill
4:00–5:00 p.m.	Sandwiches are served at the Trolley	Promenade Deck

4:00–6:00 p.m.	Music with Our Calypso Band	Lido Deck Poolside
4:30 p.m.	Volleyball Tournament — Join in!	Sport Deck
4:30 p.m.	TALENT SHOW SIGNUPS — Any passenger wishing to be in the Talent Show tonight must register at the Tour Office in the Main Lobby.	Main Deck

5:00 p.m.	ms Celebration sails for Miami, Florida. All passengers must be on board no later than 4:30 p.m.

5:00 p.m.	PASSENGER TALENT SHOW REHEARSAL & AUDITION. If you are going to be in the Talent Show this evening, you must attend this rehearsal! Please be on time. The Talent Show will be limited to 10 acts.	Astoria Lounge

5:00 p.m.–3:00 a.m.	Full Casino opens	Rainbow Club Casino

6:00 p.m.	Main Sitting Dinner	Vista & Horizon Dining Rooms
8:00 p.m.	Late Sitting Dinner	Vista & Horizon Dining Rooms

8:15–9:00 p.m.	Dance to the Music of the "Celebration Orchestra	Astoria Lounge
9:00 p.m.	JACKPOT BINGO — Chance at $1,800.00!	Astoria Lounge

9:30 p.m.–LATE	Relax with the song stylings of "Dan"	Red Hot Piano Bar
9:30 p.m.–LATE	Music by the Trolley with "Chris"	Promenade Deck
10:00 p.m.	Disco opens with DJ "John"	Galax-Z Disco

10:45 p.m.	PASSENGER TALENT SHOW	Astoria Lounge

12:00 MIDNIGHT	SPECIAL SHOW	Adult Rated — The Comedy of Lewis Nixon No Children Please	Islands in the Sky Lounge

12:30–1:30 a.m.	Late Night Buffet	Horizon Dining Room
1:30–2:30 a.m.	Mini Buffet at the Trolley	Promenade Deck

DRESS FOR THE EVENING: Casual

Movie: "Lethal Weapon II" 8:00 a.m., 10:30, 1:00 p.m., 3:30, 6:00, 8:30, 11:00, 1:30 a.m. and 4:00

IN CASE OF EMERGENCY ONLY CONTACT:
  St. Maarten Port Services
  Tel. (599) (5) 22304

6:30 a.m.	Coffee for early risers!	Wheelhouse Bar & Grill
7:45 a.m.	Main Sitting Breakfast	Vista & Horizon Dining Rooms
8:00–10:00 a.m.	Breakfast served on Deck	Wheelhouse Bar & Grill
8:00 a.m.	Slot Machines open until late	Rainbow Club Casino
9:00 a.m.	Late Sitting Breakfast	Vista & Horizon Dining Rooms
9:15 a.m.	Cardio Funk — Aerobics Classes	Galax-Z Disco
10:00–11:00 a.m.	Coffee, Tea & Bouillon served	Wheelhouse Bar & Grill
11:00 a.m.	Library Opens	Admiral Deck
9:30 a.m.	Horse Racing	Lido Deck
10:30 a.m.	Pig Racing	Lido Deck
10:45 a.m.	Frog Racing	Lido Deck
11:00 a.m.	Pillow Fighting — Try your luck on the slippery pole	Lido Deck
11:30 a.m.–2:30 p.m.	Sandwiches served on Deck	Lido Deck
11:30 a.m.–2:30 p.m.	Sun Lovers Lunch is served	Lido Deck
11:50 a.m.	Captain's Bulletin is announced from the Bridge	
12:00 NOON	Main Sitting Lunch	Vista & Horizon Dining Rooms
12:00 NOON	Full Casino Opens	Rainbow Club Casino
1:00–2:00 p.m.	Library Opens	Admiral Deck
1:00 p.m.	Ice Carving Demonstration	Lido Deck
1:00 p.m.	TRAPSHOOTING	Lido Deck
1:30 p.m.	Late Sitting Lunch	Vista & Horizon Dining Rooms
1:30 p.m.	The Calypso Band plays	Lido Deck
2:30 p.m.	PRO JACKPOT BINGO	Astoria Lounge
	Bring raffle tickets from the St. Thomas stores to Bingo today	
4:00 p.m.	Galley & Bridge Tours	Meet in the Astoria Lounge
4:00–5:00 p.m.	Tea Time	Red Hot Piano Bar
4:00 p.m.	Coffee, Tea, Ice Cream & Other Treats	Wheelhouse Bar & Grill
4:45–5:45 p.m.	Farewell Appreciation Get-Together (Main Sitting)	Islands in the Sky Lounge
	Music, Dancing & Complimentary Hors d'Oeuvres	
5:45 p.m.	Main Sitting Captain's Gala Dinner	Vista & Horizon Dining Rooms
7:00–8:00 p.m.	Farewell Appreciation Get-Together (Late Sitting)	Islands in the Sky Lounge
	Music, Dancing & Complimentary Hors d'Oeuvres	
8:00 p.m.	Late Sitting Captain's Gala Dinner	Vista & Horizon Dining Rooms
8:15 p.m.	SHOWTIME for Main Sitting 10:15 p.m. for Late Sitting	Astoria Lounge
	"Best of Broadway" featuring the "Celebration Dancers"	
	Your Cruise Director, Steve Cassel and Song Stylings of Suzanne Lukather	
9:30 p.m.–LATE	Sing Along with "Dan" at the Piano Bar	Red Hot Piano Bar
9:30 p.m.–LATE	Images Entertain You	Endless Summer Lounge
9:30 p.m.–1:00 a.m.	"Class Act" plays Dance Music	Islands in the Sky Lounge
10:00 p.m.	Disco opens with DJ — Lip Synch Contest at 1:00 a.m. — Register with DJ at Booth	Galax-Z Disco
11:30 p.m.–12:15 a.m.	The Horizon Dining Room opens for picture taking only	
	of the outstanding displays of the Grand Gala Buffet	
12:00 MIDNIGHT	SPECIAL SHOWTIME Direct from KC and the Sunshine Band	Islands in the Sky Lounge
	— Vernon Maddox	
12:30–1:30 a.m.	The Horizon Dining Room opens to partake of the sumptuous Gala Buffet	Horizon Dining Room
1:30–2:30 a.m.	Mini Buffet is served at the Trolley	Promenade Deck

DRESS FOR THE EVENING: Formal

Movie: "Family Business" 8:00 a.m., 10:30, 1:00 p.m., 3:30, 6:00, 8:30, 11:00, 1:30 a.m. and 4:00

GOOD MORNING
Sunrise: 6:44 a.m.

Time	Event	Location
6:30 a.m.	Coffee for all the early risers!	Wheelhouse Bar & Grill
7:45 a.m.	Main Sitting Breakfast	Vista & Horizon Dining Rooms
8:00 a.m.–LATE	Slot Machines open	Rainbow Club Casino
8:00–10:00 a.m.	Breakfast served on Deck	Wheelhouse Bar & Grill
9:00 a.m.	Late Sitting Breakfast	Vista & Horizon Dining Rooms
9:15 a.m.	Cardio Funk — Aerobics Classes	Galax-Z Disco
10:00–11:00 a.m.	Library is open for the return of all books	Admiral Deck
10:00–11:00 a.m.	Bouillon served	Wheelhouse Bar & Grill
10:00 a.m.	Ping Pong Tournament	Promenade Deck
10:30 a.m.	Men's Knobby Knees Competition	Astoria Lounge
11:00 a.m.	Debarkation Talk. It is very important that you attend this informative talk this morning, covering baggage handling, how to fill out custom forms, tips and gratuities, transportation, etc. This will make it much easier to disembark tomorrow in Miami	Astoria Lounge
11:30 a.m.–2:30 p.m.	Sun Lovers Lunch is served	Wheelhouse Bar & Grill
11:30 a.m.–2:30 p.m.	Sandwiches are served	Lido Deck
11:50 a.m.	Captain's Message from the Bridge	
12:00 NOON	Full Casino opens	Rainbow Club Casino
12:00 NOON	Main Sitting Lunch	Vista & Horizon Dining Rooms
1:00 p.m.	Trapshooting	Promenade Deck
1:00–2:00 p.m.	Masquerade Supplies available	Astoria Lounge
1:00–2:00 p.m.	Library is open for the return of all books and games Don't forget to pick up your deposits.	Admiral Deck
1:30 p.m.	Late Sitting Lunch	Vista & Horizon Dining Rooms
2:00 p.m.	Pie Eating Contest	Lido Deck
2:30 p.m.	The Newlywed Game & Not So Newlywed Game	Astoria Lounge
3:00 p.m.	MEGA BINGO — COVERALL $2000.00	Astoria Lounge
4:00 p.m.	Lotto-Fun Lottery Drawing	Astoria Lounge
4:00–5:00 p.m.	Coffee, Tea, Ice Cream & Other Treats	Wheelhouse Bar & Grill
4:15 p.m.	All Male Nightgown Contestants must register in the Galax-Z Disco. Please be in your outfit. Pick up your entry form at Cruise Director's Office window.	
Followed by:	The MALE NIGHTGOWN CONTEST	Astoria Lounge
4:30 p.m.	Tour of the Bridge	Meet on the Lido Deck
5:15 & 7:15 p.m.	"Fun Ship" Highlight Parties — Everyone is invited to enjoy some complimentary hors d'oeuvres, bar specials, live music and dancing.	Promenade Deck
6:00 p.m.	Main Sitting Dinner	Vista & Horizon Dining Rooms
8:00 p.m.	Late Sitting Dinner	Vista & Horizon Dining Rooms
8:15–9:00 p.m.	Dance to the "Celebration" Orchestra	Astoria Lounge
9:00 p.m.	BONANZA BINGO — Guaranteed payout of $2000.00	Astoria Lounge
9:30 p.m.–LATE	Enjoy Piano Music with "Dan"	Endless Summer Lounge
9:30 p.m.	Dance the night away with "Images"	Red Hot Piano Bar
10:00 p.m.	Disco opens with DJ "John"	Galax-Z Disco
10:30 p.m.	Registration for all masquerade contestants. Please be in your costume. Complimentary Champagne. Meet at the Red Hot Piano Bar	
11:00 p.m.	MASQUERADE PARADE	Astoria Lounge
12:30–1:30 a.m.	Late Night Buffet Served	Vista Dining Room
1:30–2:30 a.m.	Mini Buffet is served at the Trolley	Promenade Deck

DRESS FOR THE EVENING: Casual

Remember to please have your luggage outside your cabin door between 6:00 p.m. & 1:00 a.m.

Movie: "The War of the Roses" 8:00 a.m., 10:30, 1:00 p.m., 3:30, 6:00, 8:30, 11:00, 1:30 a.m. and 4:00

THANK YOUR FOR CRUISING ON THE "CELEBRATION! HAVE A SAFE TRIP HOME!

7/90

APPENDIX D

Fact Sheets

FACT SHEET

Ship:	– Britanis	Caledonian Star
Cruise Line:	– Fantasy Cruises	SeaQuest Cruises
Formerly:	– Monterey	North Star
Built:	– 1932	1966
Refurbished:	– 1986	1990
Registry:	– Panama	Bahamas
Tonnage:	– 26,000	3,095
Length:	– 638 feet	293 feet
Width:	– 82 feet	46 feet
Draft:	– ---	---
Stabilizers:	– ---	---
Bow Thrusters:	– ---	---
Speed:	– 20 knots	12.5 knots
Capacity:	– 1,100	134
Crew:	– International	International
Passenger Decks:	– Seven	Five
No. Staterooms:	– 565	68
		Outside Doubles – 63
		Outside Singles – 5

FACT SHEET

Ship:	– Americanis	Azur
Cruise Line:	– Fantasy Cruises	Fantasy Cruises
Formerly:	– Kenya Castle	---
Built:	– 1952	1971
Refurbished:	– 1987	1991
Registry:	– Panama	Panama
Tonnage:	– 20,000	15,000
Length:	– 576 feet	466 feet
Width:	– 74 feet	72 feet
Draft:	– ---	---
Stabilizers:	– ---	---
Bow Thrusters:	– ---	---
Speed:	– 16 knots	19 knots
Capacity:	– 610	660
Crew:	– International	International
Passenger Decks:	– Eight	Seven
No. Staterooms:	– 310	334
		Outside Doubles – 145
		Inside Doubles – 187
		Inside Singles – 2

182

Ship:	–	Caribe I
Cruise Line:	–	Commodore Cruise Line
Formerly:	–	Olympia
Built:	–	1953
Refurbished:	–	1989
Registry:	–	Panama
Tonnage:	–	23,000
Length:	–	612 feet
Width:	–	80 feet
Draft:	–	---
Stabilizers:	–	---
Bow Thrusters:	–	---
Speed:	–	17 knots
Capacity:	–	875
Crew:	–	345
	–	European Officers
		International Crew
Passenger Decks:	–	Eight
No. Staterooms:	–	440
		Suites – 18
		Outside Doubles – 197
		Inside Doubles – 225

Ship:	–	Carnivale
Cruise Line:	–	Carnivale Cruise Lines
Formerly:	–	Empress of Britain
Built:	–	1956
Refurbished:	–	1990
Registry:	–	The Bahamas
Tonnage:	–	27,250
Length:	–	640 feet
Width:	–	87 feet
Draft:	–	---
Stabilizers:	–	---
Bow Thrusters:	–	---
Speed:	–	21 knots
Capacity:	–	950
Crew:	–	550
	–	Italian Officers
		International Hotel Staff
Passenger Decks:	–	Nine
No. Staterooms:	–	482
		Outside Suites – 5
		Outside Deluxe – 8
		Outside w/2 Lowers – 168
		Outside Double Bed – 20
		Outside Upper/Lower – 15
		Outside Single – 1
		Inside w/2 Lowers – 143
		Inside Upper/Lower – 69
		Inside Singles – 12
		Inside Double Bed – 41

Ship:	–	Celebration
Cruise Line:	–	Carnival Cruise Lines
Formerly:	–	---
Built:	–	1987
Refurbished:	–	---
Registry:	–	Liberia
Tonnage:	–	48,000
Length:	–	733 feet
Width:	–	82 feet
Draft:	–	24 feet
Stabilizers:	–	Yes
Bow Thrusters:	–	Yes
Speed:	–	21 knots
Capacity:	–	1,896
	–	1,486 (Double Occupancy)
Crew:	–	670
	–	European Officers
		International Crew
Passenger Decks:	–	Ten
No. Staterooms:	–	743
		Outside Suites – 10
		Outside Twins – 435
		Outside Upper/Lowers – 8
		Inside Twins – 274
		Inside Upper/Lowers – 16

Ship:	–	Club Med I
Cruise Line:	–	Club Med Cruises
Formerly:	–	---
Built:	–	1990
Refurbished:	–	---
Registry:	–	Nassau, Bahamas
Tonnage:	–	10,000
Length:	–	617 feet
Width:	–	66 feet
Draft:	–	16 feet
Stabilizers:	–	---
Bow Thrusters:	–	---
Speed:	–	14 knots
Capacity:	–	386
Crew:	–	178
	–	32 French Officers
		146 International Crew
Passenger Decks:	–	Three
No. Staterooms:	–	193 (Outside)

	Constitution	CostaAllegra
Ship:	Constitution	CostaAllegra
Cruise Line:	American Hawaii Cruises	Costa Cruise Line
Formerly:	---	Alexandria
Built:	1951	1970
Refurbished:	1990	1992
Registry:	U.S.A.	Italy
Tonnage:	30,090	29,500
Length:	682 feet	615 feet
Width:	89 feet	84 feet
Draft:	26.5 feet	---
Stabilizers:	Yes	---
Bow Thrusters:	---	---
Speed:	23 knots	22 knots
Capacity:	798	800
Crew:	320 / American	European/International
Passenger Decks:	Nine	Eight
No. Staterooms:	396	405
	Outside Cabins - 177	Outside Cabins - 216
	Inside Cabins - 219	Inside Cabins - 189

	CostaClassica	CostaMarina
Ship:	CostaClassica	CostaMarina
Cruise Line:	Costa Cruise Line	Costa Cruise Line
Formerly:	---	Axel Johnson
Built:	1991	1969
Refurbished:	---	1990
Registry:	Italy	Italy
Tonnage:	50,000	25,000
Length:	718 feet	572 feet
Width:	98 feet	84 feet
Draft:	25 feet	---
Stabilizers:	---	---
Bow Thrusters:	---	---
Speed:	20.5 knots	22 knots
Capacity:	1,768 / 1,300 (Double Occupancy)	772
Crew:	650 / Italian Officers International staff	Italian
Passenger Decks:	Ten	Eight
No. Staterooms:	654	387
	Outside Cabins - 324	Outside Cabins - 184
	Inside Cabins - 210	Inside Cabins - 203

	Crown Monarch	Crown Odyssey
Ship:	Crown Monarch	Crown Odyssey
Cruise Line:	Crown Cruise Line	Royal Cruise Line
Formerly:	---	---
Built:	1990	1988
Refurbished:	---	---
Registry:	Panama	Bahamas
Tonnage:	15,270	34,250
Length:	494 feet	616 feet
Width:	69 feet	92 feet
Draft:	17.5 feet	---
Stabilizers:	Yes	---
Bow Thrusters:	Yes	---
Speed:	20 knots	22 knots
Capacity:	556	1,052
Crew:	French Officers Filipino Crew	470
Passenger Decks:	Seven	Ten
No. Staterooms:	265	526

Crown Monarch:
- Suites - 10
- Mini-suites - 23
- Outside Cabins - 202
- Inside Cabins - 30

Crown Odyssey:
- Apartments - 16
- Superior Deluxe - 20
- Junior Deluxes - 34
- Outside Cabins - 342
- Inside Cabins - 114

	CostaRiviera	Crown Jewel
Ship:	CostaRiviera	Crown Jewel
Cruise Line:	Costa Cruise Line	Crown Cruise Line
Formerly:	Marconi	---
Built:	1962	1992
Refurbished:	1988	---
Registry:	Italy	Bahamas
Tonnage:	31,500	20,000
Length:	700 feet	537 feet
Width:	94 feet	74 feet
Draft:	24 feet	18 feet
Stabilizers:	---	Yes
Bow Thrusters:	---	Yes
Speed:	20 knots	21.5 knots
Capacity:	500	900
Crew:	Italian Officers International staff	French Officers Filipino Crew
Passenger Decks:	Ten	Eight
No. Staterooms:	654	410

CostaRiviera:
- Outside Cabins - 324
- Inside Cabins - 210

Crown Jewel:
- Suites - 10
- Deluxe - 34
- Outside Cabins - 235
- Inside Cabins - 125
- Handicapped - 4

	Crown Princess	Crystal Harmony
Ship:	Crown Princess	Crystal Harmony
Cruise Line:	Princess Cruises	Crystal Cruises
Formerly:	---	---
Built:	1990	1990
Refurbished:	---	---
Registry:	British	Bahamas
Tonnage:	70,000	49,400
Length:	811 feet	791 feet
Width:	105 feet	97 feet
Draft:	---	24 feet
Stabilizers:	Yes	Fin Type Roll
Bow Thrusters:	Yes	Two transversal
Speed:	22.5 knots	23 knots
Capacity:	1,590	960
Crew:	Italian/International	505
Passenger Decks:	Twelve	Eight
No. Staterooms:	783	480

Crown Princess:
Outside Cabins - 624
Inside Cabins - 159

Crystal Harmony:
Crystal Penthouses - 4
Penthouse Suites - 26
Penthouses - 32
Outside Deluxe - 198
Inside Cabins - 19
Handicap-fitted - 4

	Cunard Countess	Cunard Princess
Ship:	Cunard Countess	Cunard Princess
Cruise Line:	Cunard Line	Cunard Line
Formerly:	---	---
Built:	1976	1977
Refurbished:	1986	1985
Registry:	Great Britain	Bahamas
Tonnage:	17,593	17,495
Length:	536 feet	536 feet
Width:	75 feet	74 feet
Draft:	---	18 feet
Stabilizers:	---	---
Bow Thrusters:	---	---
Speed:	18.5 knots	18.5 knots
Capacity:	790	802
Crew:	---	350
Passenger Decks:	Eight	Eight
No. Staterooms:	398	414

Cunard Countess:
Outside Cabins - 249
Inside Cabins - 149

Cunard Princess:
Outside Cabins - 255
Inside Cabins - 149

Ship:	- Daphne	Dawn Princess
Cruise Line:	- Costa Cruise Lines	Princess Cruises
Formerly:	- Port of Melbourne	Sylvania
Built:	- 1956	1958
Refurbished:	- 1988	1991
Registry:	- Liberia	Liberia
Tonnage:	- 16,000	25,000
Length:	- 532 feet	608 feet
Width:	- 74 feet	50 feet
Draft:	- ---	---
Stabilizers:	- ---	---
Bow Thrusters:	- ---	---
Speed:	- 21 knots	19.5 knots
Capacity:	- 420	890
Crew:	- ---	---
	Italian	Italian/Internatonal
Passenger Decks:	- Five	Eleven
No. Staterooms:	- 211	445
	Outside Cabins - 189	Outside Cabins - 228
	Inside Cabins - 22	Inside Cabins - 217

Ship:	- Delta Queen	Dolphin IV
Cruise Line:	- Delta Queen Steamboat Co.	Dolphin Cruise Line
Formerly:	- Port of Melbourne	Ithaca
Built:	- 1926	1956
Refurbished:	- 1984	1990
Registry:	- U.S.A.	Panama
Tonnage:	- 1,650	13,007
Length:	- 285 feet	501 feet
Width:	- 58 feet	65 feet
Draft:	- ---	---
Stabilizers:	- ---	---
Bow Thrusters:	- ---	---
Speed:	- 8 mph	17 knots
Capacity:	- 176	588
Crew:	- ---	---
	American	Internatonal
Passenger Decks:	- Four	Seven
No. Staterooms:	- 88	294
		Outside Cabins - 217
		Inside Cabins - 77

FACT SHEET

Ship:	Enchanted Isle	Enchanted Seas
Cruise Line:	Commodore Cruise Line	Commodore Cruise Line
Formerly:	Veendam/Ocean Monarch	Liberte/Queen of Bermuda
Built:	1957	1957
Refurbished:	1989	1990
Registry:	Panama	Panama
Tonnage:	23,395	23,500
Length:	617 feet	617 feet
Width:	84 feet	84 feet
Draft:	---	---
Stabilizers:	---	---
Bow Thrusters:	---	---
Speed:	18 knots	18 knots
Capacity:	731	736
Crew:	---	350
Passenger Decks:	Nine	Nine
No. Staterooms:	370	369
	Outside Cabins - 283	Outside Cabins - 290
	Outside Singles - 3	Inside Cabins - 79
	Inside Cabins - 84	

FACT SHEET

Ship:	Dreamward	Ecstasy
Cruise Line:	Norwegian Cruise Line	Carnival Cruise Lines
Formerly:	---	---
Built:	1992	1991
Refurbished:	---	---
Registry:	Bahamas	Liberia
Tonnage:	41,000	70,367
Length:	624 feet	855 feet
Width:	94 feet	104 feet
Draft:	---	25 feet
Stabilizers:	Yes	Yes
Bow Thrusters:	Yes	Yes
Speed:	21 knots	21 knots
Capacity:	1,246	2,634 / 2,044 (lower berths)
Crew:	---	920
Passenger Decks:	Ten	Ten
No. Staterooms:	621	1,022
	Outside Cabins - 529	Outside Suites - 28
	Inside Cabins - 92	Outside Demi-Suites - 26
		Outside Twins - 566
		Inside Twins - 393
		Inside Upper/Lowers - 19

Officers (Dreamward): International
Officers (Ecstasy): Italian Officers, International Staff

	Fair Princess	Fantasy
Ship:	Fair Princess	Fantasy
Cruise Line:	Princess Cruises	Carnival Cruise Lines
Formerly:	Carinthia	---
Built:	1956	1990
Refurbished:	1984	---
Registry:	Liberia	Liberia
Tonnage:	25,000	70,367
Length:	608 feet	855 feet
Width:	80 feet	104 feet
Draft:	---	25 feet
Stabilizers:	---	Yes
Bow Thrusters:	---	Yes
Speed:	19 knots	21 knots
Capacity:	890	2,634 / 2,044 (lower berths)
Crew:	---	920
	International	Italian Officers / International Staff
Passenger Decks:	Eleven	Ten
No. Staterooms:	445	1,022
	Outside Cabins - 228 Inside Cabins - 217	Outside Suites - 28 Outside Demi-Suites - 26 Outside Twins - 566 Inside Twins - 393 Inside Upper/Lowers - 19

	Frontier Spirit	Golden Odyssey
Ship:	Frontier Spirit	Golden Odyssey
Cruise Line:	SeaQuest Cruises	Royal Cruise Line
Formerly:	---	---
Built:	1990	1974
Refurbished:	---	1991
Registry:	Bahamas	Bahamas
Tonnage:	6,700	10,500
Length:	301 feet	427 feet
Width:	50 feet	63 feet
Draft:	15 feet	---
Stabilizers:	Yes	---
Bow Thrusters:	Yes	---
Speed:	---	22.5 knots
Capacity:	164	460
Crew:	---	200
		Greek
Passenger Decks:	Four	Seven
No. Staterooms:	82 (outside)	237
		Deluxe Suites - 8 Outside Deluxe - 181 Inside Deluxe - 46

FACT SHEET

	Holiday	Horizon	Independence	Island Princess
Ship:	Holiday	Horizon	Independence	Island Princess
Cruise Line:	Carnival Cruise Lines	Celebrity Cruises	American Hawaii Cruises	Princess Cruises
Formerly:	---	---	---	Island Venture
Built:	1985	1990	1951	1971
Refurbished:	---	---	1990	1992
Registry:	Bahamas	Liberia	U.S.A.	Great Britain
Tonnage:	46,052	46,811	30,090	20,000
Length:	727 feet	682 feet	682 feet	553 feet
Width:	92 feet	95 feet	79 feet	82 feet
Draft:	---	24 feet	26.5 feet	---
Stabilizers:	Yes	Yes	---	---
Bow Thrusters:	Yes	Yes	Yes	---
Speed:	21 knots	21.4 knots	23 knots	19 knots
Capacity:	1,760 / 1,452 (Double Occupancy)	1,352 (Lower Berths)	798	610
Crew:	---	642	320	---
Crew:	Italian Officers / International Crew	Greek Officers / American/European Staff / International Crew	American	British Officers / International Crew
Passenger Decks:	Nine	Nine	Nine	Seven
No. Staterooms:	726	677	396	305

Holiday:
Outside Cabins - 447
Inside Cabins - 279

Horizon:
Presidential Suites - 2
Suites - 18
Outside Double Bed - 40
Outside Twin Bed - 469
Inside Double Bed - 32
Inside Twin Bed - 112
Handicap-fitted - 4

Independence:
Outside Cabins - 177
Inside Cabins - 219

Island Princess:
Outside Cabins - 237
Outside Singles - 1
Inside Cabins - 67

FACT SHEET

	Ship 1	Ship 2
Ship:	Holiday	Horizon
Cruise Line:	Carnival Cruise Lines	Celebrity Cruises
Formerly:	---	---
Built:	1985	1990
Refurbished:	---	---
Registry:	Bahamas	Liberia
Tonnage:	46,052	46,811
Length:	727 feet	682 feet
Width:	92 feet	95 feet
Draft:	---	24 feet
Stabilizers:	Yes	Yes
Bow Thrusters:	Yes	Yes
Speed:	21 knots	21.4 knots
Capacity:	1,760 / 1,452 (Double Occupancy)	1,352 (Lower Berths)
Crew:	---	642
	Italian Officers / International Crew	Greek Officers / American/European Staff / International Crew
Passenger Decks:	Nine	Nine
No. Staterooms:	726	677

Holiday staterooms:
- Outside Cabins - 447
- Inside Cabins - 279

Horizon staterooms:
- Presidential Suites - 2
- Suites - 18
- Outside Double Bed - 40
- Outside Twin Bed - 469
- Inside Double Bed - 32
- Inside Twin Bed - 112
- Handicap-fitted - 4

FACT SHEET

	Ship 3	Ship 4
Ship:	Jubilee	Majesty of the Seas
Cruise Line:	Carnival Cruise Lines	Royal Caribbean Cruises
Formerly:	---	---
Built:	1986	1992
Refurbished:	---	---
Registry:	Liberia	Norway
Tonnage:	48,000	75,000
Length:	733 feet	880 feet
Width:	92 feet	106 feet
Draft:	24 feet 7 inches	25 feet
Stabilizers:	Yes	Yes
Bow Thrusters:	Yes	Yes
Speed:	21 knots	22 knots
Capacity:	1,896 / 1,486 (Double Occupancy)	2,766 / 2,354 (Double Occupancy)
Crew:	670	834
	Italian Officers / International Crew	Norwegian Officers / International Crew
Passenger Decks:	Ten	Fourteen
No. Staterooms:	743	1,177

Jubilee staterooms:
- Outside Suites - 10
- Outside Twins - 435
- Outside Uppers/Lowers - 8
- Inside Twins - 274
- Inside Uppers/Lowers - 16

Majesty of the Seas staterooms:
- Royal Suite - 1
- Owner's Suite - 3
- Suite - 8
- Deluxe w/Balcony - 50
- Larger - 84
- Standard - 586
- Handicap-fitted - 2
- Three-berth - 54
- Four-berth - 36
- Inside Standard - 445
- Inside Handicap - 2
- Inside Three-berth - 68
- Inside Four-berth - 76

FACT SHEET

	Mardi Gras	Meridian
Ship:	Mardi Gras	Meridian
Cruise Line:	Carnival Cruise Lines	Celebrity Cruises
Formerly:	Empress of Canada	---
Built:	1962	1991
Refurbished:	1985 - 1991	---
Registry:	The Bahamas	Bahamas
Tonnage:	27,250	30,440
Length:	650 feet	700 feet
Width:	87 feet	94 feet
Draft:	---	29 feet
Stabilizers:	---	Yes
Bow Thrusters:	---	Yes
Speed:	21 knots	24.5 knots
Capacity:	1,240 / 906 (Double Occupancy)	1,106
Crew:	550	580
	Italian Officers / International Crew	Greek Officers / International Crew / American/European Cruise Staff
Passenger Decks:	Nine	Eight
No. Staterooms:	457	553

Mardi Gras staterooms:

Outside Suites	6
Outside Deluxe	10
Outside Twin Beds	119
Outside Double Bed	33
Outside/Uppers/Lowers	9
Outside Singles	2
Convertible Sofa/Lower	14
Inside Twin Beds	154
Inside Upper/Lower	29
Inside Singles	6
Inside Double Bed	71
Inside King Bed	4

Meridian staterooms:

Suites	10
Deluxe Double Bed	20
Deluxe Twin	47
Outside Doubles	24
Outside Twins	190
Outside Upper/Lower	4
Inside Doubles	42
Inside Twins	194
Handicap-fitted	4
Inside Upper/Lower	24

FACT SHEET

	Mermoz	Mississippi Queen
Ship:	Mermoz	Mississippi Queen
Cruise Line:	Paquet French Cruises	Delta Queen Steamboat Co.
Formerly:	Jean Mermoz	---
Built:	1956	1976
Refurbished:	1984	1989
Registry:	The Bahamas	U.S.A.
Tonnage:	13,800	3,364
Length:	532 feet	382 feet
Width:	65 feet	78 feet
Draft:	---	---
Stabilizers:	---	---
Bow Thrusters:	---	---
Speed:	16 knots	8 mph
Capacity:	530	436
Crew:	---	---
	French/Indonesian	American
Passenger Decks:	Five	Seven
No. Staterooms:	292	202

Mermoz staterooms:

Outside Cabins	217
Outside Singles	17
Inside Doubles	58

Mississippi Queen staterooms:

Outside Cabins	135
Inside Cabins	67

	Nieuw Amsterdam	Noordam
Ship:	Nieuw Amsterdam	Noordam
Cruise Line:	Holland America Line	Holland America Line
Formerly:	---	---
Built:	1983	1984
Refurbished:	---	---
Registry:	Netherlands Antilles	Netherlands Antilles
Tonnage:	33,930	33,930
Length:	704 feet	704 feet
Width:	90 feet	90 feet
Draft:	---	---
Stabilizers:	Yes	Yes
Bow Thrusters:	---	---
Speed:	19 knots	19 Statute mph
Capacity:	1,214	1,214
Crew:	---	---
Decks:	Dutch/Indonesian/Filipino	Dutch/Indonesian/Filipino
Decks:	Ten	Ten
No. Staterooms:	605	605
	Outside Cabins - 411	Outside Cabins - 411
	Inside Cabins - 194	Inside Cabins - 194

	Monarch of the Seas	Nantucket Clipper
Ship:	Monarch of the Seas	Nantucket Clipper
Cruise Line:	Royal Caribbean Cruises	Clipper Cruise Line
Formerly:	---	---
Built:	1991	1984
Refurbished:	---	---
Registry:	Liberia	U.S.A.
Tonnage:	75,000	99.5
Length:	885 feet	207 feet
Width:	106 feet	37 feet
Draft:	---	8 feet
Stabilizers:	Yes	---
Bow Thrusters:	Yes	Yes
Speed:	22 knots	10 Statute mph
Capacity:	2,764	102
	2,354 (Double Occupancy)	
Crew:	827	28
	Norwegian Officers	American
	International Crew	
Decks:	Fourteen	Four
No. Staterooms:	1,177	51 (Outside)

Royal Suite	1
Owner Suites	3
Suites	8
Deluxe	50
Larger	84
Standard	586
Handicap-fitted	2
Three Berths	54
Four Berths	36
Inside Standard	445
Inside Handicap	2
Inside Four Berths	76

Ship:	- Norway	Ocean Pearl
Cruise Line:	- Norwegian Cruise Line	Pearl Cruises
Formerly:	- ss France	Pearl of Scandinavia
Built:	- 1960	1967
Refurbished:	- 1990	1988
Registry:	- Bahamas	Bahamas
Tonnage:	- 75,000	12,475
Length:	- 1,035 feet	517 feet
Width:	- 110 feet	66 feet
Draft:	- 34.5 feet	---
Stabilizers:	- Yes	---
Bow Thrusters:	- Yes	---
Speed:	- 18 knots	20 knots
Capacity:	- 2,044 (Double Occupancy)	480
Crew:	- 900	---
	Norwegian Officers	European/Filipino
	International Crew	
Decks:	- Eleven	Nine
No. Staterooms:	- 1,039	250
	Outside Cabins - 656	Outside Cabins - 193
	Inside Cabins - 383	Outside Singles - 5
		Inside Cabins - 46
		Inside Singles - 6

Ship:	- Nordic Empress	Nordic Prince
Cruise Line:	- Royal Caribberan Cruises	Royal Caribbean Cruises
Formerly:	- ---	---
Built:	- 1990	1990
Refurbished:	- ---	---
Registry:	- Liberia	Liberia
Tonnage:	- 44,300	48,563
Length:	- 692 feet	692 feet
Width:	- 100 feet	100 feet
Draft:	- ---	---
Stabilizers:	- Yes	---
Bow Thrusters:	- Yes	---
Speed:	- 19.5 knots	19.5 knots
Capacity:	- 2,000	1,602
	1,610 (Double Occupancy)	
Crew:	- 685	---
	International	International
Decks:	- Twelve	Twelve
No. Staterooms:	- 805	800
	Outside Cabins - 489	Outside Cabins - 485
	Inside Cabins - 316	Inside Cabins - 315

	Queen Elizabeth 2	Radisson Diamond
Ship:	Queen Elizabeth 2	Radisson Diamond
Cruise Line:	Cunard Line	Diamond Cruises
Formerly:	---	---
Built:	1969	1992
Refurbished:	1987	---
Registry:	Great Britain	Finland
Tonnage:	67,139	19,000
Length:	963 feet	415 feet
Width:	105 feet	105 feet
Draft:	32 feet	23 feet
Stabilizers:	Yes	Yes
Bow Thrusters:	Yes	Yes
Speed:	32.5 knots	---
Capacity:	1,850	354
Crew:	British Officers International Crew	170 Finnish/European/American
Decks:	Thirteen	Six
No. Staterooms:	932	177 Suites
	Outside Cabins - 662	
	Inside Cabins - 270	

	Ocean Princess	Pacific Princess
Ship:	Ocean Princess	Pacific Princess
Cruise Line:	Ocean Cruise Line	Princess Cruises
Formerly:	Italia	Sea Venture
Built:	1967	1971
Refurbished:	1984	1992
Registry:	Bahamas	United Kingdom
Tonnage:	12,200	20,000
Length:	492 feet	553 feet
Width:	71 feet	82 feet
Draft:	---	---
Stabilizers:	---	---
Bow Thrusters:	---	---
Speed:	20 knots	19 knots
Capacity:	520	610
	460 (Double Occupancy)	
Crew:	250	---
	European Officers European/Filipino Crew	British Officers International Crew
Decks:	Eight	Seven
No. Staterooms:	237	305
	Outside Cabins - 129	Outside Cabins - 238
	Inside Cabins - 108	Inside Cabins - 67

FACT SHEET

Ship:	- Regal Princess	Regent Sea
Cruise Line:	- Princess Cruises	Regency Cruises
Formerly:	- ---	Gripsholm
Built:	- 1991	1957
Refurbished:	- ---	1985
Registry:	- Liberia	Bahamas
Tonnage:	- 70,000	22,000
Length:	- 811 feet	631 feet
Width:	- 105 feet	83 feet
Draft:	- ---	---
Stabilizers:	- Yes	---
Bow Thrusters:	- Yes	---
Speed:	- 22.5 knots	19.5 knots
Capacity:	- 1,590	729
Crew:	- ---	---
	Italian Officers International Crew	European/International
Decks:	- Twelve	Eight
No. Staterooms:	- 795	
	Outside Cabins - 624	Outside Cabins - 338
	Inside Cabins - 171	Inside Cabins - 26
		Inside Singles - 1

FACT SHEET

Ship:	- Regent Star	Regent Sun
Cruise Line:	- Regency Cruises	Regency Cruises
Formerly:	- Statendam	Royal Odyssey
Built:	- 1957	1964
Refurbished:	- 1987	1982
Registry:	- Bahamas	Bahamas
Tonnage:	- 24,294	25,500
Length:	- 642 feet	627 feet
Width:	- 79 feet	81 feet
Draft:	- ---	---
Stabilizers:	- Yes	---
Bow Thrusters:	- ---	---
Speed:	- 19 knots	19 knots
Capacity:	- 950	836
Crew:	- ---	---
	European	European
Decks:	- Nine	Nine
No. Staterooms:	- 476	419'
	Outside Cabins - 293	Outside Cabins - 343
	Inside Cabins - 183	Inside Cabins - 76

Ship:	-	Renaissance I
Cruise Line:	-	Renaissance Cruises
Formerly:	-	---
Built:	-	1989
Refurbished:	-	---
Registry:	-	Italy
Tonnage:	-	4,500
Length:	-	297 feet
Width:	-	50 feet
Draft:	-	12 feet
Stabilizers:	-	Yes
Bow Thrusters:	-	Yes
Speed:	-	16 knots
Capacity:	-	100
Crew:	-	67
		European
Decks:	-	Five
No. Staterooms:	-	50
		Outside Cabins - 304
		Inside Cabins - 268

Ship:	-	Rotterdam
Cruise Line:	-	Holland America Line
Formerly:	-	---
Built:	-	1959
Refurbished:	-	1989
Registry:	-	Netherlands Antilles
Tonnage:	-	38,645
Length:	-	748 feet
Width:	-	94 feet
Draft:	-	---
Stabilizers:	-	Yes
Bow Thrusters:	-	---
Speed:	-	19 knots
Capacity:	-	1,075
Crew:	-	---
		Dutch/Indonesian/Filipino
Decks:	-	Ten
No. Staterooms:	-	672

Ship:	-	Royal Majesty
Cruise Line:	-	Majesty Cruise Line
Formerly:	-	---
Built:	-	1992
Refurbished:	-	---
Registry:	-	---
Tonnage:	-	32,400
Length:	-	568 feet
Width:	-	92 feet
Draft:	-	---
Stabilizers:	-	Yes
Bow Thrusters:	-	Yes
Speed:	-	---
Capacity:	-	1,056
Crew:	-	---
		Greek/International
Decks:	-	Nine
No. Staterooms:	-	544

Ship:	-	Royal Odyssey
Cruise Line:	-	Royal Cruise Line
Formerly:	-	Royal Viking Sea
Built:	-	1973
Refurbished:	-	1991
Registry:	-	Bahamas
Tonnage:	-	28,000
Length:	-	676 feet
Width:	-	83 feet
Draft:	-	---
Stabilizers:	-	Yes
Bow Thrusters:	-	---
Speed:	-	21.5 knots
Capacity:	-	765
Crew:	-	---
		Greek Officers and Crew
Decks:	-	Nine
No. Staterooms:	-	410
		Outside Cabins - 357
		Inside Cabins - 53

FACT SHEET

Ship:	Royal Princess	Royal Viking Queen
Cruise Line:	Princess Cruises	Royal Viking Line
Formerly:	---	---
Built:	1984	1992
Refurbished:	---	---
Registry:	British	Bahamas
Tonnage:	45,000	10,000
Length:	757 feet	438 feet
Width:	96 feet	62 feet
Draft:	---	17 feet
Stabilizers:	Yes	Yes
Bow Thrusters:	Yes	Yes
Speed:	22 knots	19.3 knots
Capacity:	1,200	212
Crew:	---	---
	British Officers International Crew	Scandinavian
Decks:	Nine	Six
No. Staterooms:	600	106 Outside Cabins

FACT SHEET

Ship:	Royal Viking Sun	Sagafjord
Cruise Line:	Royal Viking Line	Cunard Line
Formerly:	---	---
Built:	1988	1965
Refurbished:	---	1983
Registry:	Bahamas	Bahamas
Tonnage:	38,000	25,147
Length:	673 feet	620 feet
Width:	95 feet	82 feet
Draft:	23 feet	27 feet
Stabilizers:	Yes	Yes
Bow Thrusters:	Yes	---
Speed:	21.4 knots	20 knots
Capacity:	740	589
Crew:	---	352
	Scandinavian	
Decks:	Eight	Seven
No. Staterooms:	370	321

Royal Viking Sun:
- Penthouse Suites - 18
- Owner's Suite - 1
- Outside Deluxe - 126
- Outside Cabins - 206
- Inside Doubles - 19

Sagafjord:
- Luxury Suites - 25
- Doubles - 267
- Singles - 54

Ship:	SeaBreeze	Sea Goddess I
Cruise Line:	Dolphin Cruise Line	Cunard Sea Goddess
Formerly:	Royale	---
Built:	1958	1984
Refurbished:	1989	---
Registry:	Panama	Norway
Tonnage:	21,000	4,250
Length:	605 feet	350 feet
Width:	79 feet	47 feet
Draft:	29 feet	14 feet
Stabilizers:	---	Yes
Bow Thrusters:	---	Yes
Speed:	21 knots	17.5 knots
Capacity:	840 (Double Occupancy)	116
Crew:	400	89
	Greek Officers International Staff	European and American
Decks:	Nine	---
No. Staterooms:	421	58 Outside Suites
	Outside Cabins - 260	
	Inside Cabins - 161	

Ship:	Seabourn Pride	Seabourn Spirit
Cruise Line:	Seabourn Cruise Line	Seabourn Cruise Line
Formerly:	---	---
Built:	1988	1989
Refurbished:	---	1983
Registry:	Norway	Norway
Tonnage:	10,000	10,000
Length:	459 feet	459 feet
Width:	63 feet	63 feet
Draft:	---	---
Stabilizers:	Yes	Yes
Bow Thrusters:	Yes	Yes
Speed:	---	---
Capacity:	204	204
Crew:	140	140
	Norwegian Officers European Hotel Staff American/European Cruise Staff	Norwegian Officers European Hotel Staff American European Cruise Staff
Decks:	Six	Six
No. Staterooms:	90	96
	Regal Suites - 12	Regal Suites - 16
	Seabourn Suites - 88	Seabourn Suites - 80

	Sea Goddess II	Seaward
Ship:	Sea Goddess II	Seaward
Cruise Line:	Cunard Sea Goddess	Norwegian Cruise Line
Formerly:	---	---
Built:	1985	1988
Refurbished:	---	---
Registry:	Norway	Bahamas
Tonnage:	4,250	42,000
Length:	350 feet	700 feet
Width:	47 feet	96 feet
Draft:	14 feet	21 feet
Stabilizers:	Yes	Yes
Bow Thrusters:	Yes	Yes
Speed:	17.5 knots	20 knots
Capacity:	116	1,534
Crew:	89	630
	European and American	Norwegian Officers International Crew
Decks:	---	Nine
No. Staterooms:	58 Outside Suites	767 Outside Cabins - 486 Inside Cabins - 281

	Seawind Crown	Sir Francis Drake
Ship:	Seawind Crown	Sir Francis Drake
Cruise Line:	Seawind Cruise Line	Tall Ship Adventures
Formerly:	Vasco da Gama	---
Built:	1961	1917
Refurbished:	1989	1988
Registry:	Panama	Panama
Tonnage:	24,000	450
Length:	641 feet	165 feet
Width:	81 feet	28 feet
Draft:	---	9 feet
Stabilizers:	---	---
Bow Thrusters:	---	---
Speed:	21 knots	9 knots
Capacity:	656	64
Crew:	---	14
	International	
Decks:	Eight	---
No. Staterooms:	312 Outside Cabins - 209 Inside Cabins - 103	25

	Sky Princess	Skyward
Ship:	Sky Princess	Skyward
Cruise Line:	Princess Cruises	Norwegian Cruise Line
Formerly:	Fairsky	---
Built:	1984	1969
Refurbished:	---	1991
Registry:	Great Britain	Norway
Tonnage:	46,000	16,254
Length:	789 feet	525 feet
Width:	98 feet	78 feet
Draft:	---	22 feet
Stabilizers:	---	Yes
Bow Thrusters:	---	---
Speed:	22.6 knots	16 knots
Capacity:	1,200	730
Crew:	---	315
	British Officers International Crew	International
Decks:	Eleven	Eight
No. Staterooms:	600	364
	Outside Cabins - 385	Outside Cabins - 219
	Inside Cabins - 215	Inside Cabins - 145

	Seawind Crown	Sir Francis Drake
Ship:	Seawind Crown	Sir Francis Drake
Cruise Line:	Seawind Cruises	Tall Ship Adventures
Formerly:	---	---
Built:	1990	1917
Refurbished:	---	1988
Registry:	Greece	Panama
Tonnage:	24,000	450
Length:	641 feet	165 feet
Width:	81 feet	28 feet
Draft:	---	9 feet
Stabilizers:	---	---
Bow Thrusters:	---	---
Speed:	21 knots	9 knots
Capacity:	656	64
Crew:	---	14
	International	
Decks:	Eight	---
No. Staterooms:	327	25

FACT SHEET

Ship:	–	Song of America	Song of Flower
Cruise Line:	–	Royal Caribbean Cruises	Seven Seas Cruise Line
Formerly:	–	---	Explorer Starship
Built:	–	1982	1986
Refurbished:	–	---	1989
Registry:	–	Norwegian International	Oslo, Norway
Tonnage:	–	37,584	8,282
Length:	–	705 feet	409 feet
Width:	–	93 feet	52.5 feet
Draft:	–	22 feet	15.9 feet
Stabilizers:	–	Yes	---
Bow Thrusters:	–	Yes	---
Speed:	–	21 knots	17 knots
Capacity:	–	1,390	172
Crew:	–	500	---
		Norwegian Deck/Engine International Hotel	Norwegian Officers International Crew
Decks:	–	Eleven	Six
No. Staterooms:	–	695	107
		Outside Cabins – 395 Inside Cabins – 300	

FACT SHEET

Ship:	–	Song of Norway	Southward
Cruise Line:	–	Royal Caribbean Cruises	Norwegian Cruise Line
Formerly:	–	---	---
Built:	–	1970	1971
Refurbished:	–	1978	1990
Registry:	–	Norwegian International	Bahamas
Tonnage:	–	23,005	16,607
Length:	–	637 feet	536 feet
Width:	–	80 feet	75 feet
Draft:	–	22 feet	22 feet
Stabilizers:	–	Yes	Yes
Bow Thrusters:	–	Yes	Yes
Speed:	–	21 knots	16 knots
Capacity:	–	1,046 1,022 (Double Occupancy)	752
Crew:	–	400	320
		Norwegian Deck/Engine International Hotel	Norwegian Officers International Crew
Decks:	–	Eight	Seven
No. Staterooms:	–	511	375
		Outside Cabins – 328 Inside Cabins – 183	Outside Cabins – 263 Inside Cabins – 112

FACT SHEET

FACT SHEET

	Star Flyer	Star Princess
Ship:	Star Flyer	Star Princess
Cruise Line:	Clipper Ship Cruises	Princess Cruises
Formerly:	---	---
Built:	1991	1989
Refurbished:	---	---
Registry:	Luxembourg	Liberia
Tonnage:	3,025	63,500
Length:	360 feet	805 feet
Width:	50 feet	105 feet
Draft:	18.5 feet	---
Stabilizers:	Yes	---
Bow Thrusters:	Yes	---
Speed:	17 knots	22 knots
Capacity:	180	1,470
Crew:	60	---
	Belgian Officers European/West Indian Crew	International
Decks:	Four	Twelve
No. Staterooms:	90	735
		Outside Cabins - 570
		Inside Cabins - 165

FACT SHEET

	Sovereign of the Seas	Star Clipper
Ship:	Sovereign of the Seas	Star Clipper
Cruise Line:	Royal Caribbean Cruises	Clipper Ship Cruises
Formerly:	---	---
Built:	1988	1991
Refurbished:	---	---
Registry:	Norwegian International	Luxembourg
Tonnage:	73,219	3,025
Length:	880 feet	360 feet
Width:	106 feet	50 feet
Draft:	25 feet	18.5 feet
Stabilizers:	Yes	Yes
Bow Thrusters:	Yes	Yes
Speed:	21 knots	17 knots
Capacity:	2,690 / 2,282 (Double Occupancy)	180
Crew:	750	60
	Norwegian Deck/Engine International Hotel	Belgian Officers European/West Indian Crew
Decks:	Fourteen	Four
No. Staterooms:	1,141	90
	Outside Cabins - 722	
	Inside Cabins - 419	

FACT SHEET

	Starship Atlantic	Starship Majestic
Ship:	Starship Atlantic	Starship Majestic
Cruise Line:	Premier Cruise Lines	Premier Cruise Lines
Formerly:	Atlantic	Sun Princess
Built:	1982	1972
Refurbished:	1988	1989
Registry:	Liberia	Bahamas
Tonnage:	36,500	17,750
Length:	671 feet	545 feet
Width:	90 feet	81 feet
Draft:	25 feet	21 feet
Stabilizers:	Yes	Yes
Bow Thrusters:	Yes	Yes
Speed:	24 knots	21 knots
Capacity:	1,600	950 / 760 (Double Occupancy)
Crew:	500 / International	--- / International
Decks:	Eight	Seven
No. Staterooms:	549	373
	Outside Cabins - 371	Outside Cabins - 252
	Inside Cabins - 178	Inside Cabins - 121

FACT SHEET

	Starship Oceanic	Starward
Ship:	Starship Oceanic	Starward
Cruise Line:	Premier Cruise Lines	Norwegian Cruise Line
Formerly:	Oceanic	---
Built:	1965	1968
Refurbished:	1986	1987
Registry:	Panama	Bahamas
Tonnage:	40,000	16,107
Length:	782 feet	525 feet
Width:	96 feet	75 feet
Draft:	28 feet	22 feet
Stabilizers:	Yes	Yes
Bow Thrusters:	---	---
Speed:	26 knots	16 knots
Capacity:	1,138	758
Crew:	--- / International	315 / Norwegian Officers International Crew
Decks:	Eight	Seven
No. Staterooms:	569	394
	Outside Cabins - 246	Outside Cabins - 234
	Inside Cabins - 123	Inside Cabins - 160

Ship:	Statendam	Sun Viking
Cruise Line:	Holland America Line	Royal Caribbean Cruises
Formerly:	---	---
Built:	1992	1972
Refurbished:	---	---
Registry:	Panama	Norwegian International
Tonnage:	40,000	18,556
Length:	782 feet	563 feet
Width:	96 feet	90 feet
Draft:	28 feet	22 feet
Stabilizers:	Yes	Yes
Bow Thrusters:	---	---
Speed:	26 knots	21 knots
Capacity:	1,138	1,146 (Double Occupancy) 724
Crew:	---	320
	International	Norwegian Officers International Crew
Decks:	Eight	Eight
No. Staterooms:	569	380
	Outside Cabins - 246	Outside Cabins - 262
	Inside Cabins - 123	Inside Cabins - 118

Ship:	Sunward	Tropicale
Cruise Line:	Norwegian Cruise Line	Carnival Cruise Lines
Formerly:	Cunard Adventurer	---
Built:	1971	1982
Refurbished:	1989	1989
Registry:	Bahamas	Liberia
Tonnage:	14,100	36,674
Length:	485 feet	660 feet
Width:	70 feet	85 feet
Draft:	19 feet	23 feet
Stabilizers:	---	---
Bow Thrusters:	---	---
Speed:	16 knots	22 knots
Capacity:	676	1,400 1,022 (Double Occupancy)
Crew:	315	---
	Norwegian Officers International Crew	International
Decks:	Seven	Ten
No. Staterooms:	353	511
	Outside Cabins - 216	Outside Suites - 12
	Inside Cabins - 137	Outside Doubles - 307
		Outside Upper/Lower - 5
		Inside Doubles - 172
		Inside Upper/Lower - 15

	Viking Serenade	Vistafjord
Ship:	Viking Serenade	Vistafjord
Cruise Line:	Royal Caribbean Cruises	Cunard Line
Formerly:	---	---
Built:	1982	1973
Refurbished:	1991	1983
Registry:	Bahamas	Bahamas
Tonnage:	40,132	24,492
Length:	620 feet	628 feet
Width:	89 feet	82 feet
Draft:	22 feet	27 feet
Stabilizers:	---	Yes
Bow Thrusters:	---	---
Speed:	21 knots	21 knots
Capacity:	1,840 / 1,514 (Double Occupancy)	736
Crew:	610	379
	International	Norwegian Officers European Hotel Staff
Decks:	Eleven	Nine
No. Staterooms:	757	382
	Outside Cabins - 477	Outside Cabins - 325
	Inside Cabins - 280	Inside Cabins - 57

	Universe	Victoria
Ship:	Universe	Victoria
Cruise Line:	World Explorer Cruises	Fantasy Cruises
Formerly:	Atlantic	Dunnotter Castle
Built:	1953	1936
Refurbished:	1992	1991
Registry:	Liberia	Panama
Tonnage:	18,100	19,000
Length:	564 feet	573 feet
Width:	96 feet	72 feet
Draft:	---	---
Stabilizers:	---	---
Bow Thrusters:	---	---
Speed:	15 knots	16 knots
Capacity:	550	548
Crew:	---	---
	Chinese/American	International
Decks:	Five	Seven
No. Staterooms:	353	278
	Outside Cabins - 125	Outside Cabins - 205
	Outside Singles - 13	Outside Singles - 8
	Inside Cabins - 154	Inside Cabins - 65
	Inside Singles - 12	

FACT SHEET

Ship:	Westerdam	Westward
Cruise Line:	Holland America Line	Norwegian Cruise Line
Formerly:	Homeric	Royal Viking Star
Built:	1986	1972
Refurbished:	1990	1991
Registry:	Bahamas	---
Tonnage:	53,872	28,000
Length:	798 feet	674 feet
Width:	95 feet	83 feet
Draft:	---	24 feet
Stabilizers:	Yes	Yes
Bow Thrusters:	---	Yes
Speed:	22 knots	21 knots
Capacity:	1,494	790
Crew:	---	---
	Dutch/Indonesian/Filipino	Norwegian Officers International Crew
Decks:	Nine	Nine
No. Staterooms:	747	395
	Outside Cabins - 495	
	Inside Cabins - 252	

FACT SHEET

Ship:	Wind Song	Wind Spirit
Cruise Line:	Windstar Cruises	Windstar Cruises
Formerly:	---	---
Built:	1986	1986
Refurbished:	---	---
Registry:	Bahamas	Bahamas
Tonnage:	5,350	5,350
Length:	440 feet	440 feet
Width:	64 feet	64 feet
Draft:	13.5 feet	13.5 feet
Stabilizers:	Yes	Yes
Bow Thrusters:	Yes	Yes
Speed:	---	---
Capacity:	148	148
Crew:	91	91
	Norwegian Officers American/European Staff Indonesian/Filipino Crew	Norwegian Officers American/European Staff Indonesian/Filipino Crew
Decks:	Four	Four
No. Staterooms:	74	74

Ship:	-	Zenith
Cruise Line:	-	Celebrity Cruises
Formerly:	-	---
Built:	-	1991
Refurbished:	-	---
Registry:	-	Liberia
Tonnage:	-	47,500
Length:	-	682 feet
Width:	-	95 feet
Draft:	-	24 feet
Stabilizers:	-	Yes
Bow Thrusters:	-	Yes
Speed:	-	21.4 knots
Capacity:	-	1,374
Crew:	-	657
		Greek Officers
		American/European Staff
		International Crew
Decks:	-	Nine
No. Staterooms:	-	687
		Outside Cabins — 541
		Inside Cabins — 146

FACT SHEET

Ship:	-	Wind Star	Yorktown Clipper
Cruise Line:	-	Windstar Cruises	Clipper Cruise Line
Formerly:	-	---	---
Built:	-	1986	1988
Refurbished:	-	---	---
Registry:	-	Bahamas	U.S.A.
Tonnage:	-	5,350	99.5
Length:	-	440 feet	254 feet
Width:	-	64 feet	43 feet
Draft:	-	13.5 feet	8.5 feet
Stabilizers:	-	Yes	---
Bow Thrusters:	-	Yes	Yes
Speed:	-	---	12 statute mph
Capacity:	-	148	138
Crew:	-	91	37
		Norwegian Officers	American
		American/European Staff	
		Indonesian/Filipino Crew	
Decks:	-	Four	Four
No. Staterooms:	-	74	69

APPENDIX E

Staterooms, Deck Plans, and Fares

THE ZENITH

YOUR FIVE-STAR SHIP

Celebrity Cruises invites you to step aboard the newest addition to our world-class fleet: The mvZenith, continuing an acclaimed tradition of elegance at sea. From the smallest detail to our style of service, everything about the Zenith has been designed to make your cruise vacation a five-star experience.

❶ Whirlpools, Sun Deck; ❷ Olympic Health Club, Sun Deck; ❸ Meeting Room, Sun Deck; ❹ The "Grill", Marina Deck; ❺ Windsurf Bar and Cafe, Marina Deck; ❻ Swimming Pools, Marina Deck; ❼ Marina Bar, Marina Deck; ❽ Fleet Bar, Marina Deck; ❾ Rainbow Room, Fantasy Deck; ❿ Scorpio Disco, Fantasy Deck; ⓫ Galleria, Fantasy Deck; ⓬ Harry's Tavern, Fantasy Deck; ⓭ Mayfair Casino, Fantasy Deck; ⓮ Video Game Room, Fantasy Deck; ⓯ Caravelle Restaurant, Galaxy Deck; ⓰ Rendez-Vouz Lounge, Galaxy Deck; ⓱ Photo Gallery, Galaxy Deck; ⓲ Card Room, Galaxy Deck; ⓳ Library, Galaxy Deck; ⓴ Celebrity Show Lounge, Fantasy and Galaxy Decks; ● Lobby (not shown), Europa Deck; ● Beauty Parlor (not shown), Florida Deck; ● Children's Playroom (not shown), Europa Deck.

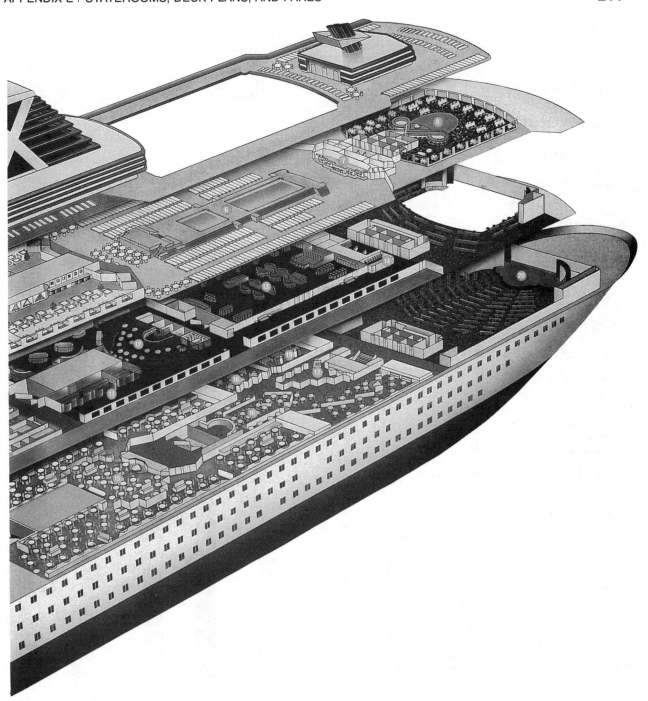

mv ZENITH

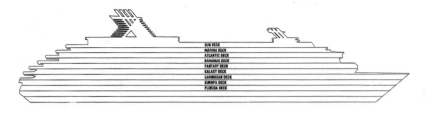

VITAL STATISTICS

Tonnage: 47,500

Length: 682 feet

Beam: 95 feet

Draught: 24 feet

Cruising
speed: 21.4 knots

Electric
current: 110 AC

Ship's
registry: Liberia

LEGEND

All cabins have
2 lower beds

- Convertible
  sofa bed

- Double bed

- Twin convertible
  to king size bed

.. Two upper berths

▴ Disabled equipped
  cabin with one
  upper berth

I Connecting cabins

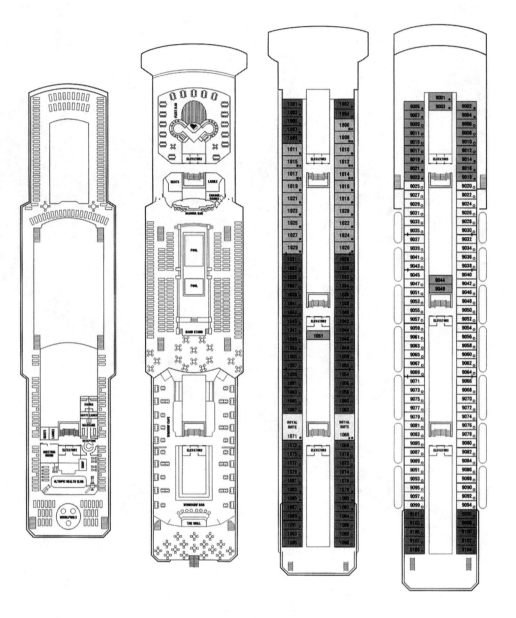

SUN DECK   MARINA DECK   ATLANTIC DECK   BAHAMAS DECK

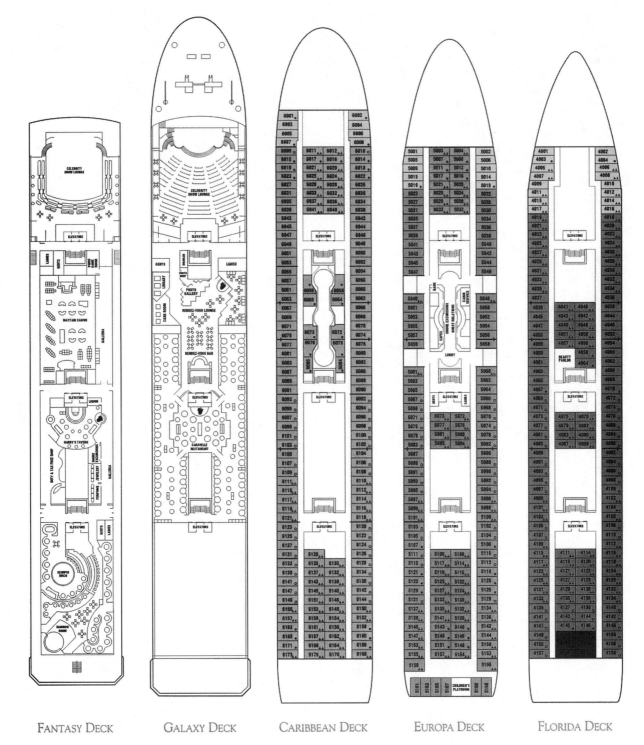

FANTASY DECK   GALAXY DECK   CARIBBEAN DECK   EUROPA DECK   FLORIDA DECK

MV ZENITH

Rates Per Person

Double occupancy.
Includes free air from
major U.S. cities.*

PEAK SEASON SAILINGS:
April 4–April 18;
June 20–August 22;
December 19, 26, 1992

VALUE SEASON SAILINGS:
April 25–June 13;
August 29–
December 12, 1992

PLAN AHEAD AND SAVE:
Save $300 per outside
cabin. Save $200 per
inside cabin. Make your
reservations early and
pocket the savings.

Reservations must be made 90 days
prior to sailing. Offer valid for cabin
categories 2–11. Holiday sailings
excluded. Savings based on double
occupancy and may not be combined
with any other promotional offer.

*For Air/Sea Gateway
cities and program specifics,
see inside back cover.

**Holiday Supplement for
Christmas Cruise,
December 19, 1992, $100,
and New Year's Cruise,
December 26, 1992,
$150 per person.

Cat.	Accommodations	Peak**	Value
1	ATLANTIC DECK: Outside. Royal suite, walk-in closet, bedroom with two lower beds or double bed, sitting room, windows and bath.	$3075	$2975
2	ATLANTIC DECK: Outside. Deluxe suite, with window, two lower beds or double bed, sitting area and bath.	2670	2570
3	ATLANTIC & BAHAMAS DECKS: Outside. Deluxe cabin with window, two lower beds or double bed.	2170	2070
4	BAHAMAS & CARIBBEAN DECKS: Outside. Cabin with window, two lower beds or double bed.	2050	1950
5	EUROPA DECK: Outside. Cabin with window, two lower beds or double bed.	2020	1920
6	FLORIDA DECK: Outside. Cabin with window, two lower beds or double bed.	1970	1870
7	BAHAMAS DECK: Outside. Cabin with window (obstructed view), two lower beds or double bed.	1870	1770
8	CARIBBEAN, EUROPA & FLORIDA DECKS: Outside. Two lower beds or double bed.	1780	1680
9	ATLANTIC, BAHAMAS & CARIBBEAN DECKS: Inside. Two lower beds or double bed.	1670	1570
10	EUROPA DECK: Inside. Two lower beds or double bed.	1570	1470
11	FLORIDA DECK: Inside. Two lower beds or double bed.	1470	1370
	FLORIDA DECK: Inside. Two lower beds or double bed.	1295	1195
	THIRD & FOURTH ADULTS IN CABIN:	795	795
	CHILDREN'S FARE: Under 12 sharing cabin with two full-paying adults. Under 2 years, free.	695	695

PORT/SERVICE CHARGES: $62.00 plus $3 Federal Excise Tax per person, including children and infants. Christmas Cruise, December 19, 1992 and New Year's Cruise, December 26, 1992, $67.00 plus $3 Federal Excise Tax per person, including children and infants. Cruise only air allowance, $250 per person.

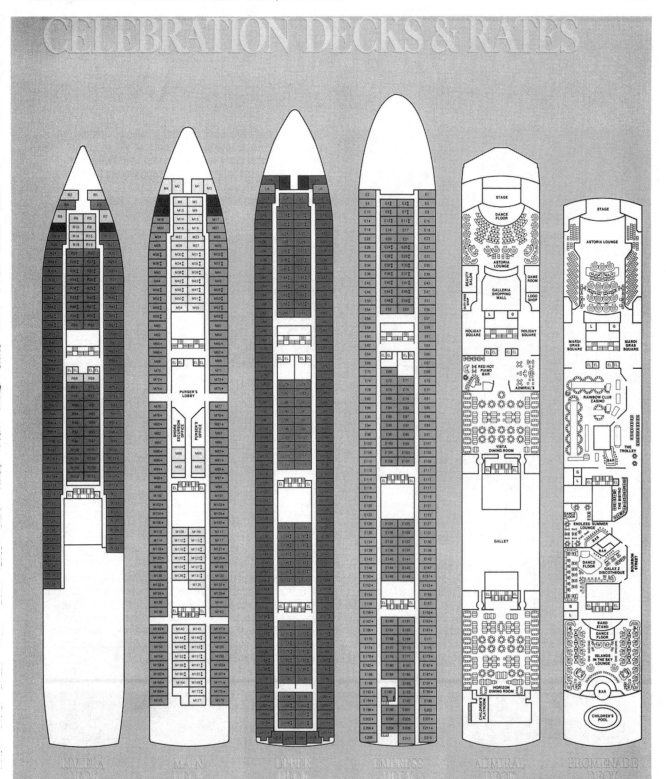

•• —2 Uppers   • —1 Upper   † —Twins/King and Double Convertible Sofa

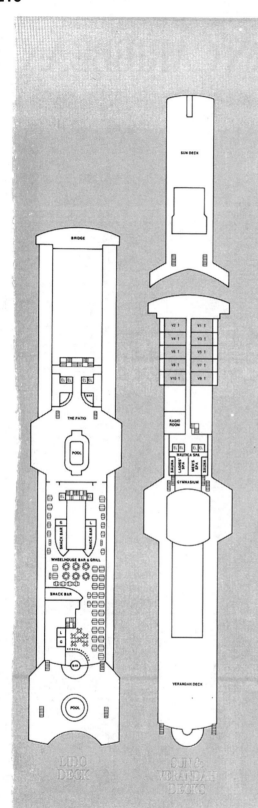

LIDO DECK

SUN & VERANDAH DECKS

CAT.	DECK	DESCRIPTION	VALUE	BASE	SEASON
12	Verandah	Verandah Suite, Twin/King	$2179	**$2239**	$2439
9	Empress	Outside, Twin/King	1629	**1689**	1759
8	Upper	Outside, Twin/King	1579	**1639**	1709
7	Main Empress	Outside, Twin/King Inside, Twin/King	1529	**1589**	1659
6	Upper Riviera	Inside, Twin/King Outside, Twin/King	1469	**1529**	1599
5	Main	Inside, Twin/King	1369	**1429**	1499
4	Riviera	Inside, Twin/King	1309	**1369**	1439
3	Upper	Outside, Upper & Lower	1209	**1269**	1339
2	Upper Main/Riviera	Inside, Upper & Lower Outside, Upper & Lower	1149	**1209**	1279
1	Riviera	Inside, Upper & Lower	999	**1099**	1199

Most twin-bedded cabins convert to king-sized beds.

Prices include round trip air fare from over 175 cities to Miami.
(See pages 58 and 59 for details and restrictions.)

SAILING DATES (COLOR OF DATE INDICATES APPLICABLE RATE)

January **4, 11,** 18, 25, 1992	October 3, 10, 17, 24, 31
February 1, 8, 15, 22, 29	November **7, 14, 21,** 28
March 7, 14, 21, 28	December 19, 26
April 4, 11, 18, **25**	January **2, 9,** 16, 23, 30, 1993
May 2, 9, **16, 23, 30**	February 6, 13, 20, 27
June **6,** 13, 20, 27	March 6, 13, 20, 27
July 4, 11, 18, 25	April 3, 10, **17, 24**
August 1, 8, 15, 22, **29**	May 1, 8, 15, **22,** 29
September 5, 12, 19, 26	June 5

All prices are per person, double occupancy plus port charges of $59 and international departure tax of $3 each. Prices are quoted in U.S. dollars.

Third and fourth person in stateroom with two full fare passengers, each pays flat rate of $399 (cruise only basis). On Fly Aweigh Air/Sea program third and fourth persons can enjoy the money saving all-inclusive Fly Aweigh rates listed on pages 58 and 59.

Single occupancy is available at 200% of fare. On some sailings, categories 1–3 are available at 150% of fare.

Single's Plan (Guaranteed Share Basis/4 in a stateroom): $650 per person; cruise only basis, plus port charges. (See page 61 for details.)

Christmas and New Year sailings: The Cruise Only Travel Allowance does not apply to the December 19 and 26 sailings. Add $100 per person to the season cruise rate for these sailings. Fly Aweigh passengers check page 58 for complete details.

CRUISE ONLY TRAVEL ALLOWANCE

Deduct $250 per person from the 7 day rates listed when buying the cruise not in conjunction with our Fly Aweigh or Rail/Sail programs.

THE BISTRO

S.S. CONSTITUTION

Created by the legendary designer Henry Dreyfuss and distinguished as the favorite cruise ship of Princess Grace of Monaco, the S.S. Constitution features fully-appointed staterooms and spacious cabins fashioned for uncompromising comfort.

Stateroom Color Key	Cruise Accommodations	1992 7 Day Cruise Only (per person)
O	Owner's Suite — *Exclusive Two-Room, Two-Bath Suite — Boat Deck*	On Request
IO	Inside Owner's Deluxe Stateroom — *Boat Deck*	On Request
AA	Deluxe Two-Room, Two-Bath Suite — *Sun Deck*	$3795
A	Outside Suite — *Sun/Upper Decks*	$2450
B	Deluxe Outside Stateroom — *Sun/Promenade/Upper/Main Decks*	$2250
C	Outside Stateroom — *Sun/Promenade/Upper/Main/Aloha Decks*	$2095
D	Outside Cabin — *Upper/Main/Aloha/Bali Decks*	$1950
DD	Outside Cabin — *Bali Deck*	$1825
	Deluxe Inside Stateroom — *Sun/Promenade/Upper/Main Decks*	$1895
F	Inside Stateroom — *Promenade/Upper/Main/Aloha Decks*	$1825
G	Inside Cabin — *Upper/Aloha Decks*	$1725
H	Economy Outside Cabin — *Upper/Bali Decks (Upper and Lower Berths)*	$1625
I	Economy Inside Cabin — *Bali/Coral Decks*	$1550
J	Budget Inside Cabin — *Coral Deck*	$1365
K	Thrifty Inside Cabin — *Upper/Aloha Decks (Upper and Lower Berths)*	$1125
	Third or Fourth Berth Guests — *Sharing room with two full-fare adults. Available in selected staterooms in categories AA through G and I.*	Adults AA $695 A-C $695 D-I $595 Children 16 and Under $425

Country of Registry: U.S.A.
Speed: 20 knots
Normal Crew: 320

Nationality of Crew: American
Displacement Tonnage: 30,090
Length: 682 ft.   Beam: 89 ft.
Cruise Capacity: 798

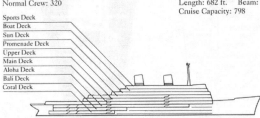

Sports Deck
Boat Deck
Sun Deck
Promenade Deck
Upper Deck
Main Deck
Aloha Deck
Bali Deck
Coral Deck

Port charges per passenger: $48.

U.S. cruise tax per passenger: $3.

All fares quoted in U.S. dollars, based on double occupancy.

For 7-day sailings add $150 per passenger surcharge for outside cabin space and $100 per passenger surcharge for inside cabin space on 12/19/92. Surcharge for 12/19/92 also applies to 3rds, 4ths; children are at 3rd and 4th rate.

Surcharge for exclusive (single) occupancy of stateroom: 100% additional for Owner's Suite, AA, and A. Additional 75% for categories B through K, and IO.

Some category C, G and J cabins are available as singles at no additional surcharge.

▽ Triple   ○ Quad

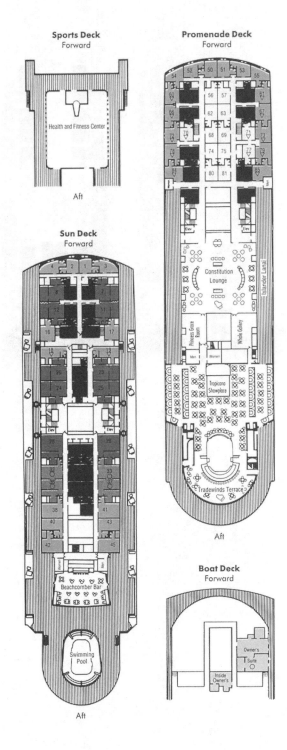

Sports Deck
Forward
Health and Fitness Center
Aft

Sun Deck
Forward
Beachcomber Bar
Swimming Pool
Aft

Promenade Deck
Forward
Constitution Lounge
Princess Grace Room
Whale Gallery
Islander Lanai
Tropicana Showplace
Tradewinds Terrace
Aft

Boat Deck
Forward
Owner's Suite
Inside Owner's

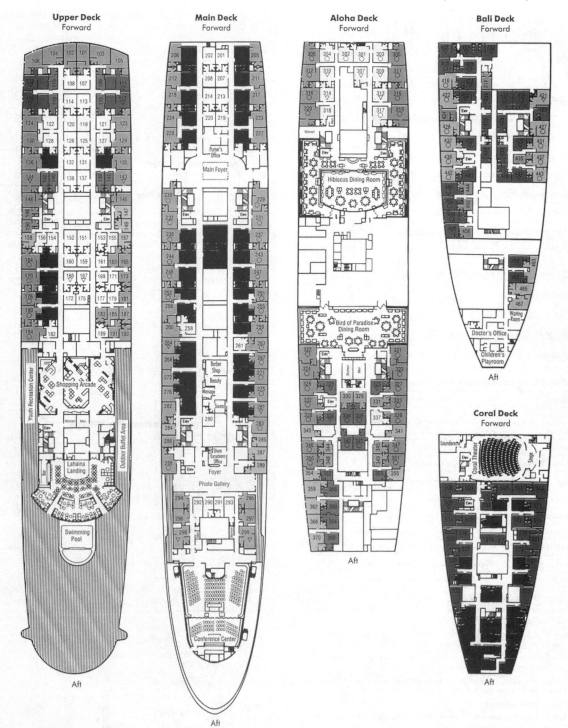

CostaClassica Facts And Figures

Country of registry: Italy. Cruise capacity: 1,300. Crew and staff: 650. Gross tonnage: 50,000. Length: 718.5 feet. Beam: 98.4 feet. Cruising speed: 20.5 knots. Electric current: 110v-60Hz. Air-conditioned and stabilized. Satellite communications system. Telephone, television, hair dryer and safe deposit boxes in every stateroom. Multiple meeting facilities. Beauty salon, barber, infirmary.

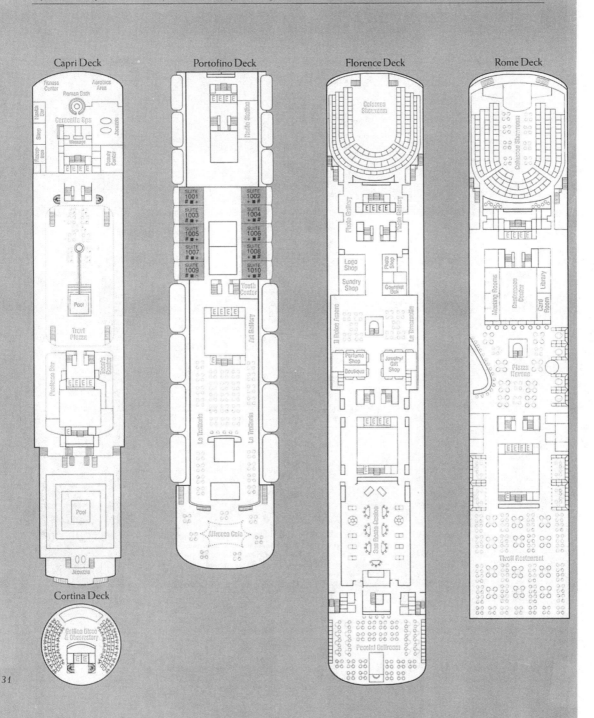

Capri Deck   Portofino Deck   Florence Deck   Rome Deck

Cortina Deck

31

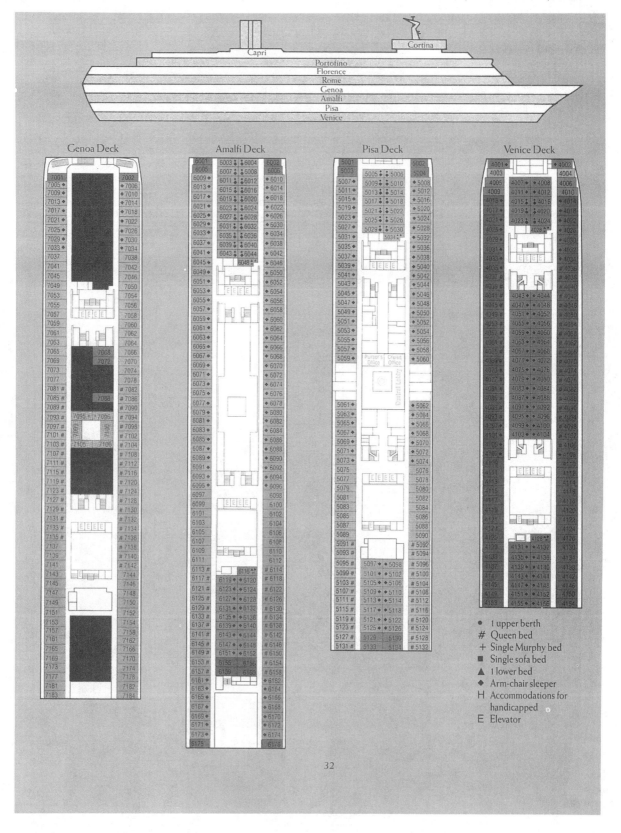

CROWN ODYSSEY DECK PLANS

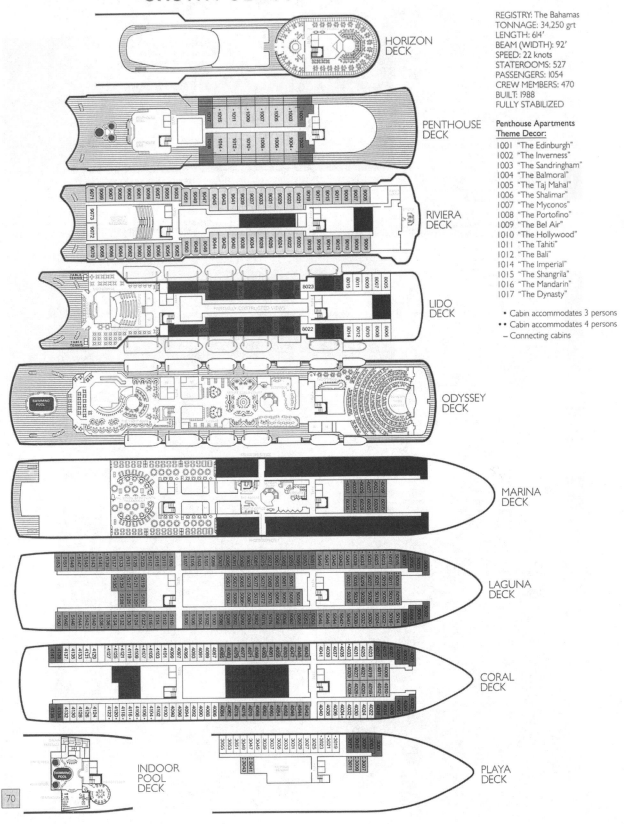

REGISTRY: The Bahamas
TONNAGE: 34,250 grt
LENGTH: 614'
BEAM (WIDTH): 92'
SPEED: 22 knots
STATEROOMS: 527
PASSENGERS: 1054
CREW MEMBERS: 470
BUILT: 1988
FULLY STABILIZED

Penthouse Apartments
Theme Decor:
1001 "The Edinburgh"
1002 "The Inverness"
1003 "The Sandringham"
1004 "The Balmoral"
1005 "The Taj Mahal"
1006 "The Shalimar"
1007 "The Myconos"
1008 "The Portofino"
1009 "The Bel Air"
1010 "The Hollywood"
1011 "The Tahiti"
1012 "The Bali"
1014 "The Imperial"
1015 "The Shangrila"
1016 "The Mandarin"
1017 "The Dynasty"

• Cabin accommodates 3 persons
•• Cabin accommodates 4 persons
– Connecting cabins

HORIZON DECK

PENTHOUSE DECK

RIVIERA DECK

LIDO DECK

ODYSSEY DECK

MARINA DECK

LAGUNA DECK

CORAL DECK

INDOOR POOL DECK

PLAYA DECK

		SEVEN-DAY		
		PEAK	VALUE	ECONOMY
1	STAR, INTERNATIONAL, NORWAY DECKS Grand deluxe suites. Living room, convertible double-bed sofa, picture windows, separate bedroom, two lower beds (may be arranged as a queen-size bed), TV, refrigerator, bathroom with tub and shower. Concierge service available.	$2995	$2895	$2845
2	NORWAY DECK Penthouse suites (some convert to two-room suite††). Floor-to-ceiling windows, private balcony. Sitting area, double bed or two lower beds (may be arranged as a queen-size bed), TV, refrigerator, bathroom with shower. Concierge service available.	2695	2595	2545
3	STAR, INTERNATIONAL, NORWAY DECKS Suites (some convert to two-room suite††). Sitting area, floor-to-ceiling windows, double bed or two lower beds (may be arranged as a queen-size bed), TV, refrigerator, bathroom with shower. Concierge service available.	2345	2245	2195
4	NORWAY DECK Outside staterooms. Sitting area, picture windows, two lower beds (may be arranged as a queen-size bed), TV, bathroom with shower.	2195	2095	2045
5	PROMENADE DECK Outside staterooms. Sitting area, picture windows, two lower beds (may be arranged as a queen-size bed), TV, bathroom with shower.	2125	2025	1975
6	ATLANTIC DECK Outside staterooms. Sitting area, most with picture windows, two lower beds (may be arranged as a queen-size bed), TV, bathroom with shower.	2025	1925	1875
7	BISCAYNE DECK Outside staterooms. Sitting area, some with picture windows, two lower beds (may be arranged as a queen-size bed), TV, bathroom with shower.	1945	1845	1795
8	CARIBBEAN DECK Outside staterooms. Sitting area, two lower beds (may be arranged as a queen-size bed), TV, bathroom with shower.	1875	1775	1725
9	STAR, INTERNATIONAL DECKS Superior inside staterooms. Two lower beds (some may be arranged as a queen-size bed), TV, bathroom with shower.	1625	1525	1475
10	NORWAY, PROMENADE, ATLANTIC, BISCAYNE, CARIBBEAN DECKS Inside staterooms. Two lower beds (most may be arranged as a queen-size bed), TV, bathroom with shower.	1425	1325	1275
	GUARANTEED SINGLES RATE Single occupancy of a stateroom will be assigned to the passenger. Assignment is at the sole discretion of the Company. Fare subject to availability. †Dreamward economy guaranteed singles rate $1645.	1895	1795	1675†
	THIRD/FOURTH PERSON Including infants and children sharing stateroom with two full-fare paying adults. — DREAMWARD	695	695	695
	WINDWARD	745	745	745

1992 SAILING DATES All cruises depart on Sunday. *Special Christmas and New Year's sailings. See notes for details.	DREAMWARD: Eastern	Dec 27*		Dec 13
	Western	Dec 20*		Dec 6
1993 SAILING DATES All cruises depart on Sunday. **Special repositioning cruises. See notes for details.	DREAMWARD: Eastern	Jan 24 Feb 7, 21 Mar 7, 21	Apr 4	Jan 10 Apr 18**
	Western	Jan 17, 31 Feb 14, 28 Mar 14, 28	Apr 11	Jan 3
	Bermuda	Jun 12, 19, 26 Jul 3, 10, 17, 24, 31	May 1, 8, 15, 22, 29 Jun 5	
	WINDWARD: Aruba		Jun 27 Jul 11, 25	May 30 Jun 13
	Barbados		Jun 20 Jul 4, 18	May 23 Jun 6

NOTES

Please Note: All prices quoted in U.S. dollars. Rates are per person based on double occupancy. Reservations subject to change in the event of full-ship charter.

Government Taxes And Fees: Dreamward: $3.00 per person, regardless of age. Windward: $6.00 per person, regardless of age. Additional charges may be assessed depending upon the originating Air/Sea gateway.

Port Charges: Per person, regardless of age: Caribbean cruises: $75; Bermuda cruises: $99.

Group And Charter Rates: Available on request.

Air/Sea Package Add-Ons: See pages 72-75.

Christmas And New Year's Sailings: The Dreamward will offer a special seven-day Christmas cruise departing Dec. 20, 1992. A seven-day New Year's cruise departs Dec. 27, 1992. For prices, add $150 to our regular cruise rates.

Special Sailings: On April 18, 1993, the Dreamward will offer a special 13-day cruise from Ft. Lauderdale to New York, with stops in Aruba, St. John, St. Thomas, San Juan, St. Maarten, Tortola/Virgin Gorda and Hamilton, Bermuda. On Oct. 16, 1993 the Dreamward will offer a 15-day cruise from New York to Ft. Lauderdale, with stops in Hamilton and St. George's, Bermuda, San Juan, St. Thomas, Aruba, Panama/Gatun Lake, Port Limon, Costa Rica and Grand Cayman. Call your travel agent for rates and details.

NCL Cruise Price Guarantee: While NCL guarantees the published rates once a deposit or full payment is received, NCL may assess surcharges due to increased costs, tariffs or taxes up to the date of sailing, despite full or partial payment.

Cruise-Only Travel Allowance: Passengers not requiring round-trip air transportation to New York may deduct $200 from the rates listed above. Passengers not requiring air transportation to Ft. Lauderdale or San Juan may deduct $250.

Standard Single Occupancy Fare: Passengers requesting single occupancy of a stateroom within a specific fare category will be charged 150-200% of the fare for the selected accommodation. Fare subject to availability.

SeaFare Discount Program: Book early and save 5-30% on the Dreamward and Windward. Rates are subject to availability. See pages 76-77 for more information.

†† If purchased together, can convert to a two-room suite: Star Deck—cabins 0001-0002, 0005-0006, 0007-0008, 0009-0010, 0200-0201, 0204-0205, 0206-0207, 0208-0209; International Deck—cabins 9000-9001, 9004-9005, 9006-9007, 9008-9009, 9010-9011, 9200-9201, 9204-9205, 9206-9207, 9208-9209, 9210-9211; Norway Deck—cabins 8000-8001, 8003-8004, 8005-8006, 8007-8008, 8009-8010, 8042-8043, 8044-8045, 8046-8047, 8048-8049, 8050-8051, 8052-8053, 8202-8203, 8204-8205, 8206-8207, 8208-8209, 8241-8242, 8243-8244, 8245-8246, 8247-8248, 8249-8250, 8251-8252.

DREAMWARD & WINDWARD

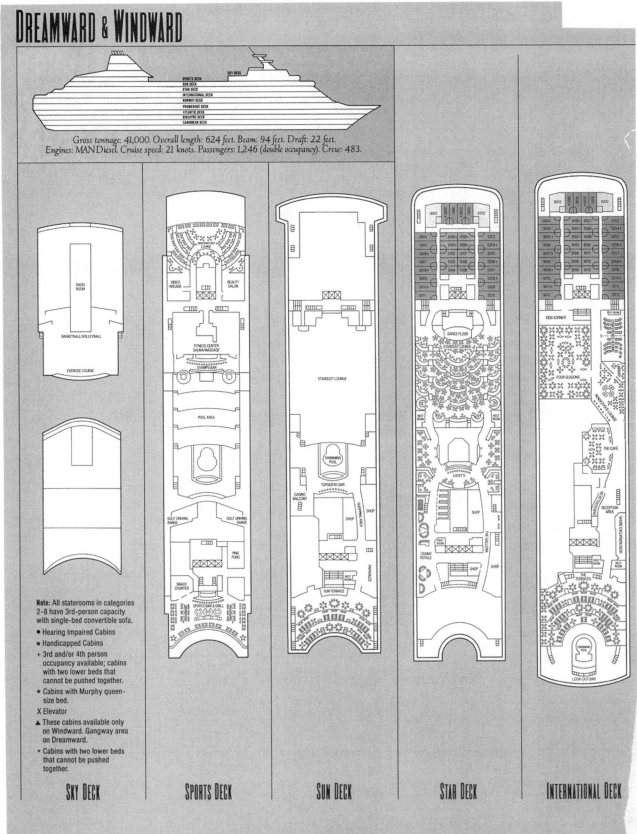

Gross tonnage: 41,000. Overall length: 624 feet. Beam: 94 feet. Draft: 22 feet.
Engines: MAN Diesel. Cruise speed: 21 knots. Passengers: 1,246 (double occupancy). Crew: 483.

Note: All staterooms in categories 2-8 have 3rd-person capacity with single-bed convertible sofa.

- Hearing Impaired Cabins
- Handicapped Cabins
- + 3rd and/or 4th person occupancy available; cabins with two lower beds that cannot be pushed together.
- ★ Cabins with Murphy queen-size bed.
- X Elevator
- ▲ These cabins available only on Windward. Gangway area on Dreamward.
- ★ Cabins with two lower beds that cannot be pushed together.

SKY DECK   SPORTS DECK   SUN DECK   STAR DECK   INTERNATIONAL DECK

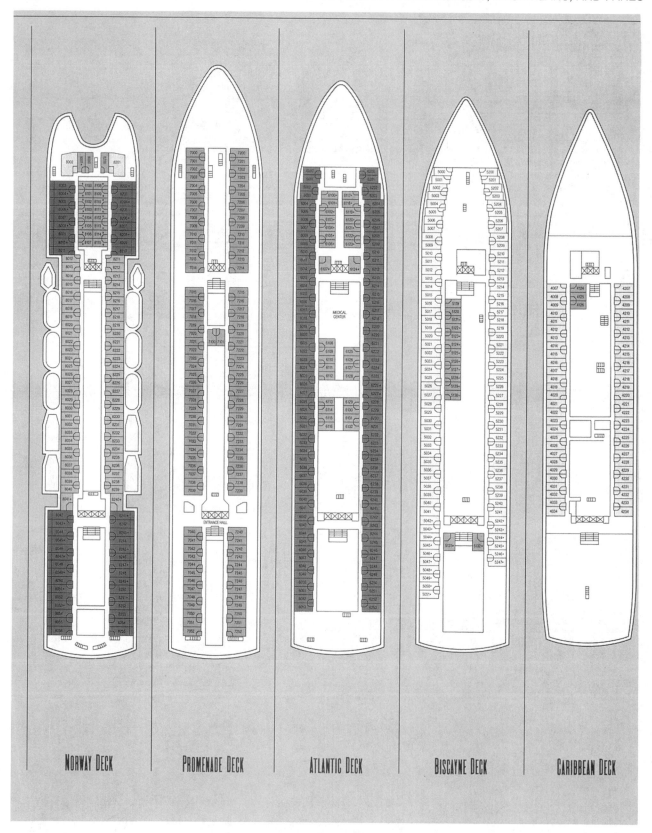

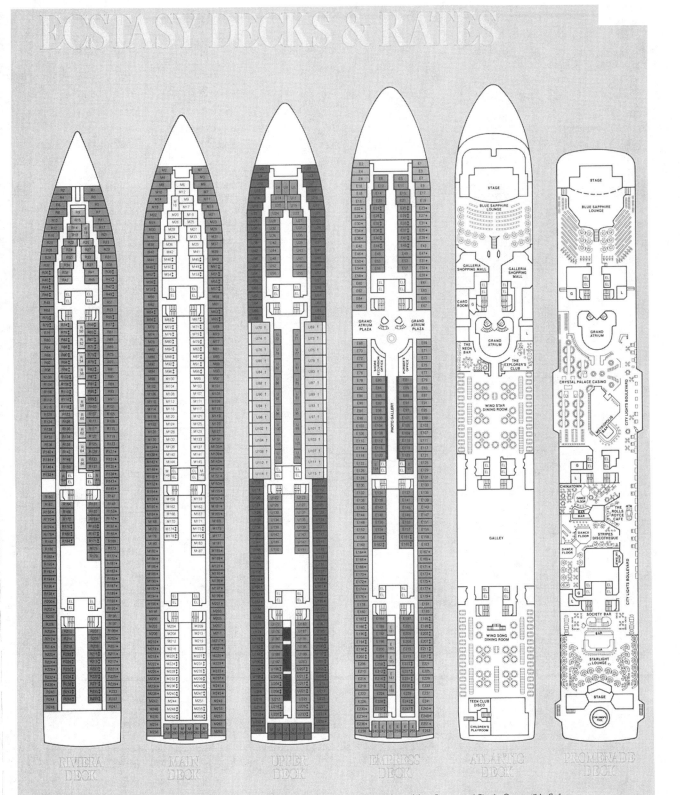

ECSTASY DECKS & RATES

RIVIERA DECK   MAIN DECK   UPPER DECK   EMPRESS DECK   ATLANTIC DECK   PROMENADE DECK

••—2 Uppers •—1 Upper †—Twins/King and Double Convertible Sofa ††—Queen and Single Convertible Sofa

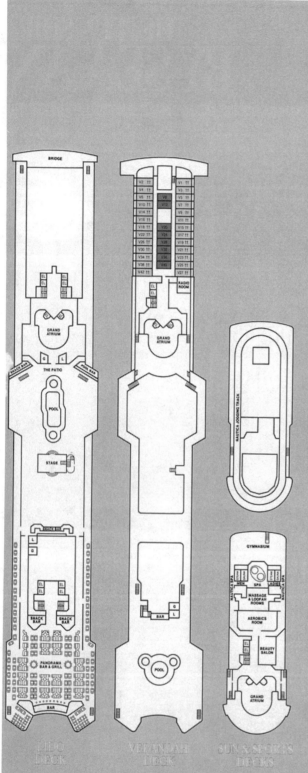

CAT.	DECK	DESCRIPTION	VALUE	BASE	SEASON
12	Upper	Verandah Suite, Twin/King	$2179	**$2239**	$2439
11	Verandah	Demi Suite, Queen	1979	2039	2239
9	Empress	Outside, Twin/King	1629	1689	1759
8	Upper	Outside, Twin/King	1579	1639	1709
7	Verandah Empress Main	Inside, Twin/King Inside, Twin/King Outside, Twin/King	1529	1589	1659
6	Upper Riviera	Inside, Twin/King Outside, Twin/King	1469	1529	1599
5	Main	Inside, Twin/King	1369	1429	1499
4	Riviera	Inside, Twin/King	1309	1369	1439
3	Empress	Inside, Upper & Lower	1209	1269	1339
2	Upper	Inside, Upper & Lower	1149	1209	1279
1	Riviera	Inside, Upper & Lower	999	1099	1199

Most twin-bedded cabins convert to king-sized beds.

Prices include round trip air fare from over 175 cities to Miami.
(See pages 58 and 59 for details and restrictions.)

SAILING DATES (COLOR OF DATE INDICATES APPLICABLE RATE)

Eastern Caribbean	Western Caribbean
January 12, 26, 1992	January 5, 19, 1992
February 9, 23	February 2, 16
March 8, 22	March 1, 15, 29
April 5, 19	April 12, 26
May 3, 31	May 24
June 14, 28	June 7, 21
July 12, 26	July 5, 19
August 9, 23	August 2, 16, 30
September 6, 20	September 13, 27
October 4, 18	October 11, 25
November 1, 15, 29	November 8, 22
December 13, 27	December 6, 20
January 10, 24 1993	January 3, 17, 24 1993
February 7, 21	February 14, 28
March 7, 21	March 14, 28
April 18	April 11, 25
May 2, 16, 30	May 9, 23
	June 6

All prices are per person, double occupancy plus port charges of $59 and international departure tax of $3 each. Prices are quoted in U.S. dollars.

Third and fourth person in stateroom with two full fare passengers, each pays flat rate of $399 (cruise only basis). On Fly Aweigh Air/Sea program third and fourth persons can enjoy the money saving all-inclusive Fly Aweigh rates listed on pages 58 and 59.

Single occupancy is available at 200% of fare. On some sailings, categories 1–3 are available at 150% of fare.

Single's Plan (Guaranteed Share Basis/4 in a stateroom): $650 per person; cruise only basis, plus port charges. (See page 61 for details.)

Christmas and New Year sailings: The Cruise Only Travel Allowance does not apply to the December 20 and 27 sailings. Add $100 per person to the season cruise rate for these sailings. Fly Aweigh passengers check page 58 for complete details.

CRUISE ONLY TRAVEL ALLOWANCE

Deduct $250 per person from the 7 day rates listed when buying the cruise not in conjunction with our Fly Aweigh or Rail/Sail programs.

14 day combination cruise savings: Fly Aweigh — deduct $250 per person, cruise only travel allowance; cruise only — deduct $500 per person, cruise only travel allowance. Savings apply to 14 day rate (200% of 7 day rate).

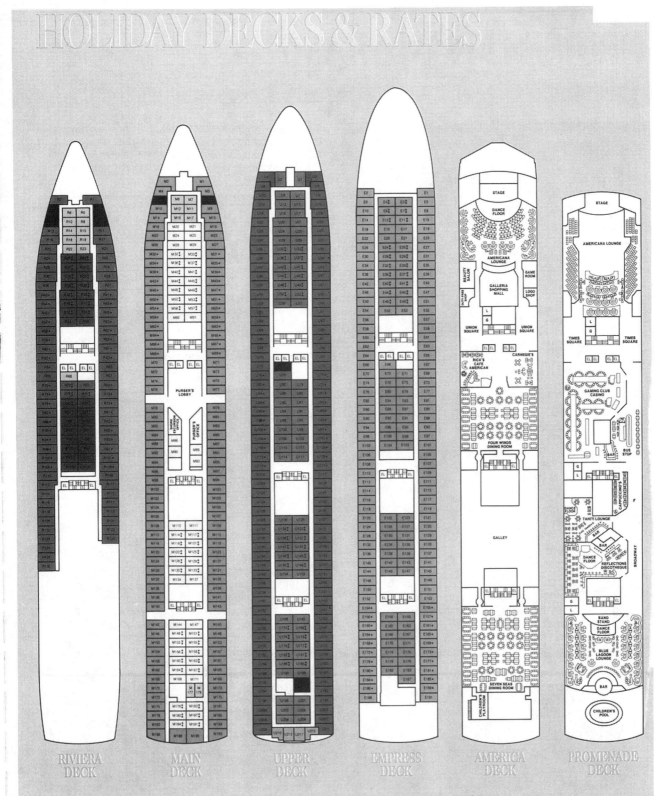

RIVIERA DECK   MAIN DECK   UPPER DECK   EMPRESS DECK   AMERICA DECK   PROMENADE DECK

●●—2 Uppers   ●—1 Upper   †—Twins/King and Double Convertible Sofa

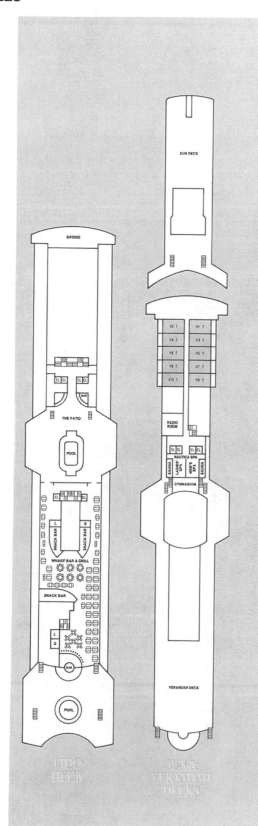

CAT.	DECK	DESCRIPTION	VALUE	BASE	SEASON
12	Verandah	Verandah Suite, Twin/King	$2179	$2239	$2439
9	Empress	Outside, Twin/King	1629	1689	1759
8	Upper	Outside, Twin/King	1579	1639	1709
7	Main Empress	Outside, Twin/King Inside, Twin/King	1529	1589	1659
6	Upper Riviera	Inside, Twin/King Outside, Twin/King	1469	1529	1599
5	Main	Inside, Twin/King	1369	1429	1499
4	Riviera	Inside, Twin/King	1309	1369	1439
3	Empress Upper	Inside, Upper & Lower Outside, Upper & Lower	1209	1269	1339
2	Upper Main/Riviera	Inside, Upper & Lower Outside, Upper & Lower	1149	1209	1279
1	Main/Riviera	Inside, Upper & Lower	999	1099	1199

Most twin-bedded cabins convert to king-sized beds.

Prices include round trip air fare from over 175 cities to Miami.
(See pages 58 and 59 for details and restrictions.)

SAILING DATES (COLOR OF DATE INDICATES APPLICABLE RATE)

January 4, 11, 18, 25, 1992
February 1, 8, 15, 22, 29
March 7, 14, 21, 28
April 4, 11, 18, 25
May 2, 9, 16, 23, 30
June 6, 13, 20, 27
July 4, 11, 18, 25
August 1, 8, 15, 22
September 12, 19, 26

October 3, 10, 17, 24, 31
November 7, 14, 21, 28
December 5, 12, 19, 26
January 2, 9, 16, 23, 30, 1993
February 6, 13, 20, 27
March 6, 13, 20, 27
April 3, 10, 17, 24
May 1, 8, 15, 22, 29
June 5

All prices are per person, double occupancy plus port charges of $59 and international departure tax of $3 each. Prices are quoted in U.S. dollars.

Third and fourth person in stateroom with two full fare passengers, each pays flat rate of $399 (cruise only basis). On Fly Aweigh Air/Sea program third and fourth persons can enjoy the money saving all-inclusive Fly Aweigh rates listed on pages 58 and 59.

Single occupancy is available at 200% of fare. On some sailings, categories 1–3 are available at 150% of fare.

Single's Plan (Guaranteed Share Basis/4 in a stateroom): $650 per person; cruise only basis, plus port charges. (See page 61 for details.)

Christmas and New Year sailings: The Cruise Only Travel Allowance does not apply to the December 19 and 26 sailings. Add $100 per person to the season cruise for these sailings. Fly Aweigh passengers check page 58 for complete details.

CRUISE ONLY TRAVEL ALLOWANCE

Deduct $250 per person from the 7 day rates listed when buying the cruise not in conjunction with our Fly Aweigh or Rail/Sail programs.

THE AMERICANA LOUNGE

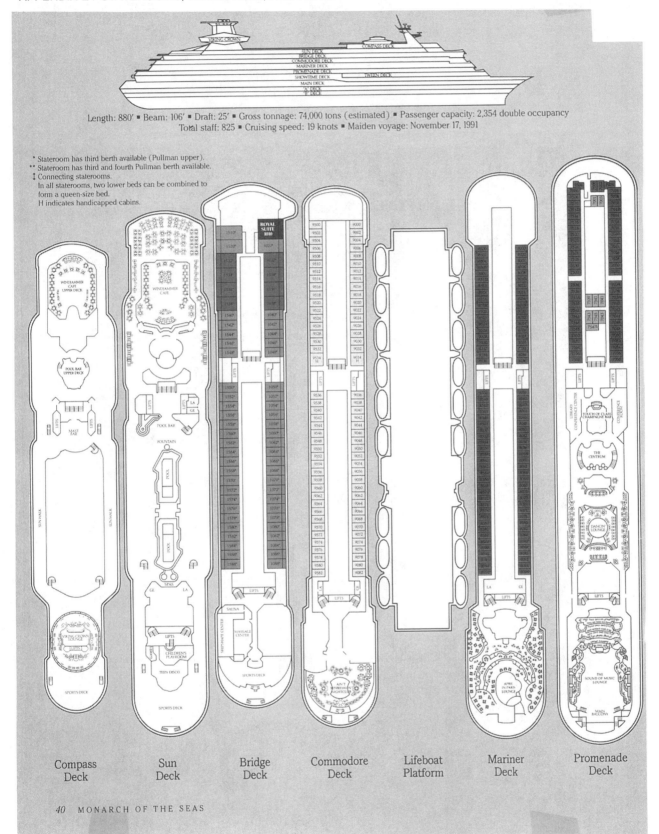

Length: 880′ ▪ Beam: 106′ ▪ Draft: 25′ ▪ Gross tonnage: 74,000 tons (estimated) ▪ Passenger capacity: 2,354 double occupancy
Total staff: 825 ▪ Cruising speed: 19 knots ▪ Maiden voyage: November 17, 1991

* Stateroom has third berth available (Pullman upper).
** Stateroom has third and fourth Pullman berth available.
‡ Connecting staterooms.
  In all staterooms, two lower beds can be combined to
  form a queen-size bed.
  H indicates handicapped cabins.

| Compass Deck | Sun Deck | Bridge Deck | Commodore Deck | Lifeboat Platform | Mariner Deck | Promenade Deck |

Monarch of the Seas

| Tween Deck | Showtime Deck | Main Deck | "A" Deck | "B" Deck |

The best vacation value in cruising.

Cabin Categories/Fares		7-Night Southern 1991			7-Night Southern 1992		
This chart lists the various accommodations and rates available to you, arranged by fare category and sailing date. Accommodations have also been color-coded to the deck plans at left. Fare categories R, A, B and C have bathtubs.		Peak Season*	Value Season*	Economy Season*	Peak Season*	Value Season*	Economy Season*
R	Royal Suite — private veranda.	$3330	$3260	$3195	$3380	$3310	$3245
A	Owner's Suite — private veranda.	2730	2660	2595	2780	2710	2645
B	Bridge Deck — deluxe outside suite, two lower beds, private veranda.	2480	2410	2345	2530	2460	2395
C	Bridge Deck — deluxe outside stateroom, two lower beds, balcony.	2305	2235	2170	2355	2285	2220
D	Commodore Deck — larger outside stateroom, two lower beds.	2170	2100	2035	2220	2150	2085
F	Mariner Deck/Promenade Deck/Tween Deck/Showtime Deck — outside stateroom, two lower beds.	1970	1900	1835	2020	1950	1885
G	Main Deck — outside stateroom, two lower beds.	1920	1850	1785	1970	1900	1835
H	"A" Deck — outside stateroom, two lower beds.	1865	1795	1730	1915	1845	1780
I	"B" Deck — outside stateroom, two lower beds.	1805	1735	1670	1855	1785	1720
K	Promenade Deck/Tween Deck/Showtime Deck — inside stateroom, two lower beds.	1795	1725	1660	1845	1775	1710
L	Main Deck — inside stateroom, two lower beds.	1745	1675	1610	1795	1725	1660
M	"A" Deck — inside stateroom, two lower beds.	1690	1620	1555	1740	1670	1605
N	"B" Deck — inside stateroom, two lower beds.	1630	1560	1495	1680	1610	1545
O	Main Deck — inside stateroom, two lower beds.	1530	1460	1395	1580	1510	1445
P	"A" Deck — inside stateroom, two lower beds.	1430	1360	1295	1480	1410	1345
Q	"B" Deck — inside stateroom, two lower beds.	1330	1260	1195	1380	1310	1245

UpFront Advance Purchase Discounts do not apply to Fare Categories O, P and Q.

UpFront: Book early and save	Sailing Dates					
Six month advance purchase discounts that help you save. You must book your cruise 180 days in advance of sailing to earn a discount off the appropriate cruise fare shown above. Discounts are available on all sailings. The discount level varies by sailing date. Use the guide below to determine program availability and your savings. Discounts do not apply to third/fourth person fares, or to air supplements as listed on pages 76-77. **Discounts do not apply to fare categories O, P, Q.**	Peak Season	Value Season	Economy Season	Peak Season	Value Season	Economy Season
	Nov. 17 †Dec. 22 †Dec. 29	Nov. 24	Dec. 1	Jan. 12 Jan. 19 Jan. 26 Feb. 2 Feb. 9 Feb. 16 Feb. 23 Mar. 1 Mar. 8 Mar. 15 Mar. 22 Mar. 29 Apr. 5 Apr. 12 †Dec. 20 †Dec. 27	Jan. 5 Apr. 19 June 14 June 21 June 28 July 5 July 12 July 19 July 26 Aug. 2 Aug. 9 Aug. 16 Oct. 11 Oct. 18 Oct. 25 Nov. 1 Nov. 8 Nov. 15 Nov. 22	May 3 May 10 May 17 May 24 May 31 June 7 Sept. 6 Sept. 13 Sept. 20 Sept. 27 Oct. 4 Nov. 29 Dec. 6 Dec. 13
Sailing dates in blue — Deduct 15% from applicable category in the column above the date selected.						
Sailing dates in green — Deduct 10% from applicable category in the column above the date selected.						
Sailing dates in purple — Deduct 5% from applicable category in the column above the date selected.						
Third/Fourth person, including infants and children, sharing stateroom with two full-fare paying adults.	$695	$695	$695	$745	$745	$745

INSIDE PASSAGE FARES

MS Nieuw Amsterdam & MS Noordam

	7-DAY CRUISES				ADVENTURE CRUISE	EXPLORER CRUISE*	TOUR SHIP UPGRADE SUPPLEMENTS	
	LOW SEASON	ECONOMY SEASON	VALUE SEASON	PEAK SEASON				
DOUBLE STATEROOMS	MAY 19, 21, 26 AND SEP 15, 17	MAY 28 JUN 2 SEP 8, 10	JUN 4-16 AUG 25, 27 SEP 1, 3	JUN 18 THROUGH AUG 20			TOURS 22, 23, 25	TOURS 32, 33
OUTSIDE					ADD-ON	ADD-ON		
A Staterooms Deluxe	$2,995	$3,095	$3,195	$3,295	$200	$275*	$ 720	$1,080
B Deluxe	2,475	2,575	2,675	2,775	200	275*	510	770
C Deluxe	2,295	2,395	2,495	2,595	200	275*	440	660
D Large	1,995	2,095	2,195	2,295	200	275*	320	480
E Large	1,910	2,010	2,110	2,210	200	275*	285	430
F Large	1,845	1,945	2,045	2,145	200	275*	260	390
G Standard	1,770	1,870	1,970	2,070	200	275*	230	345
INSIDE								
H Large	1,570	1,670	1,770	1,870	200	275*	150	225
I Large	1,495	1,595	1,695	1,795	200	275*	120	180
J Large	1,420	1,520	1,620	1,720	200	275*	90	135
K Standard	1,355	1,455	1,555	1,655	200	275*	65	95
L Standard	1,275	1,375	1,475	1,575	200	275*	30	50
M Standard	1,195	1,295	1,395	1,495	200	275*	Tour Base	Tour Base
3rd/4th Persons	600	650	700	750	200	275*		
Port Charges & Taxes	69	69	69	69				
Deposit Requirements	300	300	300	300				
Cancellation Fees Waiver	59	59	59	59				

MS Westerdam

	7-DAY CRUISES				ADVENTURE CRUISE	EXPLORER CRUISE*	TOUR SHIP UPGRADE SUPPLEMENTS	
	LOW SEASON	ECONOMY SEASON	VALUE SEASON	PEAK SEASON				
DOUBLE STATEROOMS	MAY 23 AND SEP 19	MAY 30 AND SEP 12	JUN 6, 13 AUG 29 SEP 5	JUN 20 THROUGH AUG 22			TOURS 22, 23, 25	TOURS 32, 33
OUTSIDE					ADD-ON	ADD-ON		
S Suites	$3,495	$3,595	$3,695	$3,795	$200	$275*	$ 920	$1,380
A Staterooms Deluxe	3,095	3,195	3,295	3,395	200	275*	760	1,140
B Deluxe	2,645	2,745	2,845	2,945	200	275*	570	860
C Deluxe	2,415	2,515	2,615	2,715	200	275*	490	730
D Large	2,115	2,215	2,315	2,415	200	275*	370	550
E Large	2,025	2,125	2,225	2,325	200	275*	330	500
F Large	1,950	2,050	2,150	2,250	200	275*	300	455
G Standard	1,870	1,970	2,070	2,170	200	275*	270	405
H Standard	1,770	1,870	1,970	2,070	200	275*	230	345
I Economy	1,550	1,650	1,750	1,850	200	275*	140	215
INSIDE								
J Standard	1,570	1,670	1,770	1,870	200	275*	150	225
K Standard	1,485	1,585	1,685	1,785	200	275*	115	175
L Standard	1,385	1,485	1,585	1,685	200	275*	75	115
M Standard	1,295	1,395	1,495	1,595	200	275*	40	60
N Standard	1,195	1,295	1,395	1,495	200	275*	Tour Base	Tour Base
3rd/4th Persons	600	650	700	750	200	275*		
Port Charges & Taxes	69	69	69	69				
Deposit Requirements	300	300	300	300				
Cancellation Fees Waiver	59	59	59	59				

- Single fares: 7-day Alaska Cruise fare is 150% of applicable cabin rate. Port Charges are additional.
- 4-day Alaska Cruises: 65% of 7-day Peak Season fare.
- 3-day Alaska Cruises: 45% of 7-day Peak Season fare. 3 and 4-day cruises are subject to availability.

*$10 fishing license must be purchased when in Alaska for Explorer Cruise.

Tour Ship Upgrade Supplements: Prices stated for tours on pages 26-29 are based upon the category M on the Nieuw Amsterdam and Noordam, and category N on the Westerdam identified as TOUR BASE. To upgrade to a superior stateroom category simply add the tour supplement amount, which corresponds to the category you desire, to the published tour price for that tour.

Guaranteed Share

A limited selection of double staterooms are available for non-smoking single guests willing to share as follows: Noordam and Nieuw Amsterdam— categories E and J. Westerdam— categories F and L. Guests pay the per person double occupancy published fare of the room category chosen. Holland America Line will assign a non-smoking person of the same sex to share with you.

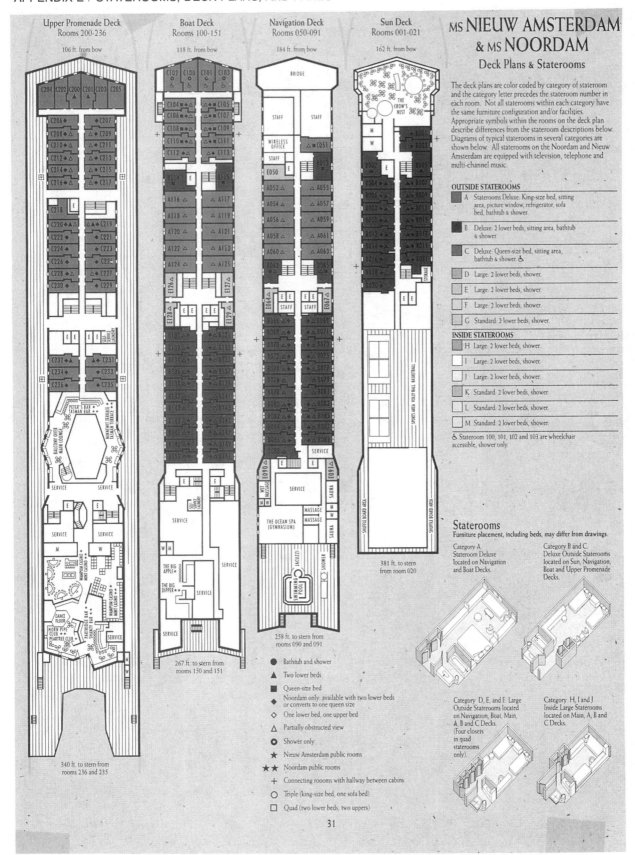

Upper Promenade Deck	Boat Deck	Navigation Deck	Sun Deck
Rooms 200-236	Rooms 100-151	Rooms 050-091	Rooms 001-021
106 ft. from bow	118 ft. from bow	184 ft. from bow	162 ft. from bow

MS NIEUW AMSTERDAM & MS NOORDAM

Deck Plans & Staterooms

The deck plans are color coded by category of stateroom and the category letter precedes the stateroom number in each room. Not all staterooms within each category have the same furniture configuration and/or facilities. Appropriate symbols within the rooms on the deck plan describe differences from the stateroom descriptions below. Diagrams of typical staterooms in several categories are shown below. All staterooms on the Noordam and Nieuw Amsterdam are equipped with television, telephone and multi-channel music.

OUTSIDE STATEROOMS

A Staterooms Deluxe: King-size bed, sitting area, picture window, refrigerator, sofa bed, bathtub & shower.

B Deluxe: 2 lower beds, sitting area, bathtub & shower.

C Deluxe: Queen-size bed, sitting area, bathtub & shower.

D Large: 2 lower beds, shower.

E Large: 2 lower beds, shower.

F Large: 2 lower beds, shower.

G Standard: 2 lower beds, shower.

INSIDE STATEROOMS

H Large: 2 lower beds, shower.

I Large: 2 lower beds, shower.

J Large: 2 lower beds, shower.

K Standard: 2 lower beds, shower.

L Standard: 2 lower beds, shower.

M Standard: 2 lower beds, shower.

Stateroom 100, 101, 102 and 103 are wheelchair accessible, shower only.

Staterooms

Furniture placement, including beds, may differ from drawings.

Category A
Stateroom Deluxe located on Navigation and Boat Decks.

Category B and C.
Deluxe Outside Staterooms located on Sun, Navigation, Boat and Upper Promenade Decks.

Category D, E, and F. Large Outside Staterooms located on Navigation, Boat, Main, A, B and C Decks. (Four closets in quad staterooms only).

Category H, I and J. Inside Large Staterooms located on Main, A, B and C Decks.

381 ft. to stern from room 020

258 ft. to stern from rooms 090 and 091

267 ft. to stern from rooms 150 and 151

340 ft. to stern from rooms 236 and 235

● Bathtub and shower
▲ Two lower beds
■ Queen-size bed
◆ Noordam only: available with two lower beds or converts to one queen size
◇ One lower bed, one upper bed
△ Partially obstructed view
◉ Shower only
★ Nieuw Amsterdam public rooms
★★ Noordam public rooms
+ Connecting rooms with hallway between cabins
○ Triple (king-size bed, one sofa bed)
□ Quad (two lower beds, two uppers)

31

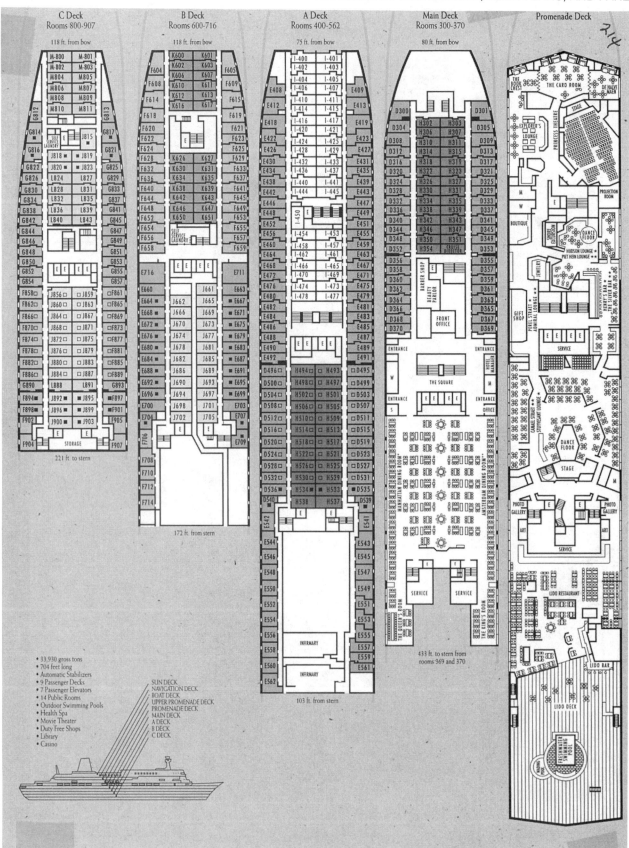

C Deck
Rooms 800-907

118 ft. from bow

221 ft. to stern

B Deck
Rooms 600-716

118 ft. from bow

172 ft. from stern

A Deck
Rooms 400-562

75 ft. from bow

103 ft. from stern

Main Deck
Rooms 300-370

80 ft. from bow

433 ft. to stern from rooms 369 and 370

Promenade Deck

- 33,930 gross tons
- 704 feet long
- Automatic Stabilizers
- 9 Passenger Decks
- 7 Passenger Elevators
- 14 Public Rooms
- Outdoor Swimming Pools
- Health Spa
- Movie Theater
- Duty Free Shops
- Library
- Casino

SUN DECK
NAVIGATION DECK
BOAT DECK
UPPER PROMENADE DECK
PROMENADE DECK
MAIN DECK
A DECK
B DECK
C DECK

		SEVEN-DAY		
		PEAK	VALUE	ECONOMY
OWS	**SUN DECK** Owner's suite. Living room, bedroom with king-size bed, dressing room. Floor-to-ceiling windows. Private wraparound balcony with patio table and chairs. TV, refrigerator. Bath with Roman tub and jacuzzi. Separate shower and powder room, double vanity. Concierge available.	$5645	$5400	$5235
1	**SKY DECK** Grand deluxe suites. Living room, bedroom with king-size bed, dressing room. Floor-to-ceiling windows. TV, refrigerator. Bath with Roman tub and jacuzzi. Separate shower and powder room, double vanity. Concierge available. **VIKING DECK** Grand deluxe suites. Living room, dining room, two bedrooms, king-size bed, TV, refrigerator, vanity, two full bathrooms. Concierge available.	5145	4900	4800
2A	**FJORD, SKY DECKS** Deluxe penthouse suites. Living room with sofa, two lower beds or king-size bed, vanity, floor-to-ceiling windows, private balcony, walk-in closet, TV, refrigerator, bathroom with tub and shower. Concierge available.	3600	3500	3400
2B	**FJORD, SUN, SKY, NORWAY DECKS** Penthouse suites. Floor-to-ceiling windows, private balconies (except Norway deck), living room with sofa, two lower beds, queen or king-size bed, vanity, walk-in closet, TV, refrigerator, bathroom with tub and shower. Concierge available.	3200	3100	3000
2C	**SUN, SKY DECKS** Junior penthouse suites. Floor-to-ceiling windows, private balcony, living room with sofa, two lower beds, queen or king-size bed, TV, refrigerator, bathroom with tub and shower. Concierge available.	2900	2800	2700
3A	**SKY DECK** Deluxe suites. Floor-to-ceiling windows, living room with sofa, two lower beds or king-size bed, vanity, TV, refrigerator, bathroom with tub and shower. Concierge available.	2625	2525	2425
3B	**SKY, POOL, FJORD DECKS** Junior suites. Floor-to-ceiling windows in Sky Deck suites. Sitting area with sofa, two lower beds, queen or king-size bed, vanity, TV, refrigerator, bathroom with tub and shower. Concierge available.	2435	2310	2260
4	**NORWAY, VIKING, FJORD DECKS** Deluxe outside staterooms. Two lower beds or double bed, TV, refrigerator, bathroom with tub and/or shower.	2310	2190	2140
5	**NORWAY, VIKING, POOL, INTERNATIONAL, OLYMPIC DECKS** Superior outside staterooms. Two lower beds, TV, refrigerator, bathroom with tub and/or shower.	2190	2090	2040
6	**NORWAY, VIKING, POOL, INTERNATIONAL, OLYMPIC DECKS** Outside staterooms. Two lower beds or double bed, TV, bathroom with tub and/or shower.	2095	1995	1945
7	**NORWAY, VIKING, FJORD DECKS** Superior inside staterooms. Two lower beds, TV, bathroom with tub and/or shower.	2010	1910	1860
8	**BISCAYNE, ATLANTIC DECKS** Outside staterooms. Two lower beds or double bed, TV, bathroom with tub and/or shower.	1955	1855	1805
9	**NORWAY, VIKING, POOL, INTERNATIONAL, FJORD DECKS** Inside staterooms. Two lower beds or double bed, TV, bathroom with tub and/or shower.	1875	1795	1725
10	**BISCAYNE, ATLANTIC DECKS** Inside staterooms. Two lower beds or double bed, TV, bathroom with tub and/or shower.	1780	1700	1630
S	**ATLANTIC, BISCAYNE, NORWAY, VIKING DECKS** Single occupancy cabins. Inside staterooms. Lower bed, TV, bathroom with shower.	1715	1595	1535
11	**VIKING, BISCAYNE, ATLANTIC, NORWAY DECKS** Outside staterooms. Upper and lower beds, TV, bathroom with shower.	1605	1505	1455
12	**VIKING, BISCAYNE, ATLANTIC, NORWAY, POOL, INTERNATIONAL DECKS** Inside staterooms. Upper and lower beds, TV, bathroom with shower.	1395	1295	1245
	GUARANTEED SINGLES RATE Single occupancy of a stateroom, other than a category S, will be assigned to the passenger. Assignment is at the sole discretion of the Company. Fare subject to availability.	1895	1645	1595
	THIRD/FOURTH PERSON Including infants and children sharing stateroom with two full-fare paying adults.	695	695	695

1992 SAILING DATES All cruises depart on Saturday. As of Dec. 5, 1992, The Norway will sail only the St. Maarten itinerary. *Christmas And New Year's Sailings: The Norway will offer a special seven-day Christmas cruise departing Dec. 19, 1992. A seven-day New Year's cruise departs Dec. 26, 1992. For prices, add $150 to our regular cruise rates.	Eastern Caribbean St. Maarten	Jan 18 Feb 1, 15, 29 Mar 14, 28 Dec 19*, 26*	Apr 11, 25 Jun 20 Jul 4, 18 Aug 1, 15 Oct 24	Jan 4 May 9, 23 Jun 6 Aug 29 Sep 12, 26 Oct 10 Nov 7, 21 Dec 5, 12
	Eastern Caribbean San Juan	Jan 25 Feb 8, 22 Mar 7, 21	Apr 4, 18 Jun 27 Jul 11, 25 Aug 8 Oct 31 Nov 28	Jan 11 May 2, 16, 30 Jun 13 Aug 22 Sep 5, 19 Oct 3, 17 Nov 14
1993 SAILING DATES All cruises depart on Saturday.	St. Maarten	Jan 16, 23, 30 Feb 6, 13, 20, 27 Mar 6, 13, 20, 27	Apr 3, 10, 17, 24 Jun 19, 26 Jul 3, 10, 17, 24, 31	Jan 2, 9 May 1, 8, 15, 22, 29 Jun 5, 12

NOTES

Please Note: All prices quoted in U.S. dollars. Rates are per person based on double occupancy. Reservations subject to change in the event of full-ship charter.

Government Taxes And Fees: $3.00 per person, regardless of age. Additional charges may be assessed depending upon the originating Air/Sea gateway.

Port Charges: All cruises $69 per person, regardless of age.

Group And Charter Rates: Available on request.

Air/Sea Package Add-Ons: See pages 72-75.

Cruise-Only Travel Allowance: Passengers not requiring round-trip air transportation to Miami may deduct $250 from the rates listed above.

Standard Single Occupancy Fare: Passengers requesting single occupancy of a stateroom within a specific fare category will be charged 150-200% of the fare for the selected accommodation. Fare subject to availability.

Special Quad Share Fare For Singles: All cruises $695. See pages 76-77 for details.

SeaFare Discount Program: Book early and save 5-32% on The Norway. Rates are subject to availability. See pages 76-77 for more information.

THE NORWAY

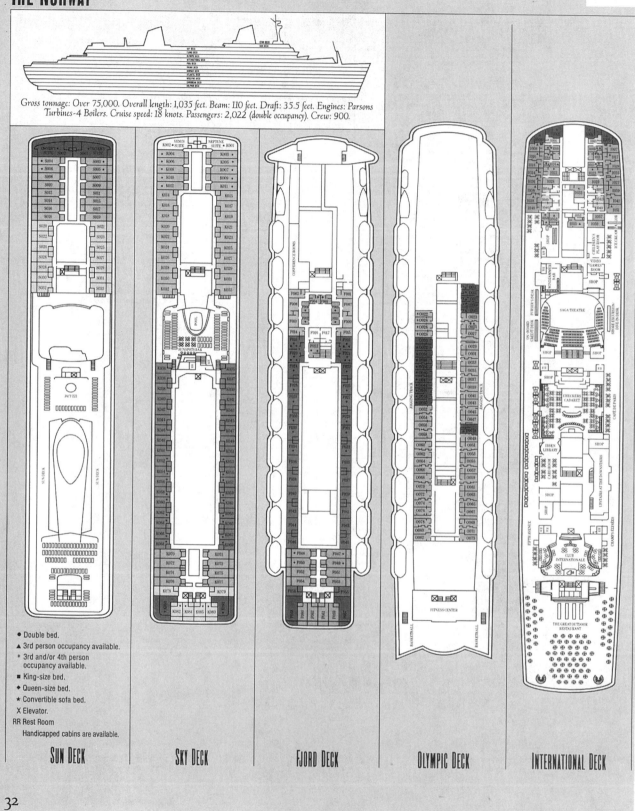

Gross tonnage: Over 75,000. Overall length: 1,035 feet. Beam: 110 feet. Draft: 35.5 feet. Engines: Parsons Turbines-4 Boilers. Cruise speed: 18 knots. Passengers: 2,022 (double occupancy). Crew: 900.

- ● Double bed.
- ▲ 3rd person occupancy available.
- * 3rd and/or 4th person occupancy available.
- ■ King-size bed.
- ◆ Queen-size bed.
- ★ Convertible sofa bed.
- X Elevator.
- RR Rest Room
  Handicapped cabins are available.

| SUN DECK | SKY DECK | FJORD DECK | OLYMPIC DECK | INTERNATIONAL DECK |

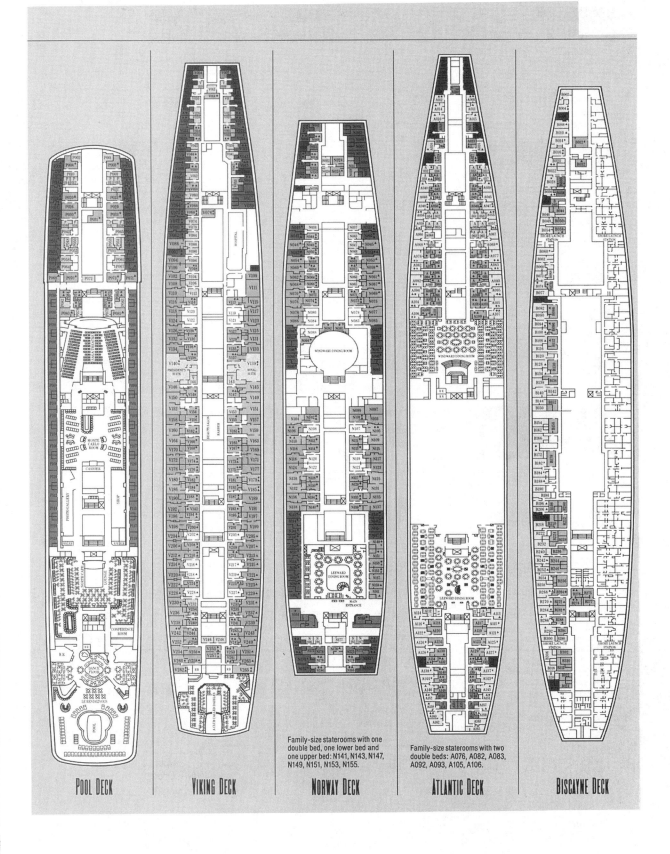

Family-size staterooms with one double bed, one lower bed and one upper bed: N141, N143, N147, N149, N151, N153, N155.

Family-size staterooms with two double beds: A076, A082, A083, A092, A093, A105, A106.

POOL DECK   **VIKING DECK**   **NORWAY DECK**   **ATLANTIC DECK**   **BISCAYNE DECK**

Queen Elizabeth 2 1992 transatlantic fares

Select your transatlantic voyage and find its fare season in the chart on page 41.
FARE A - QE2 one-way sea fare which includes FREE British Airways World Traveller Class (Economy) air transportation the other way.
FARE B - One leg of round-trip only *if* both ways are by sea. To calculate your complete round-trip fare, add applicable season's fare for each sailing.

Fares Per Person				Superthrift		Thrift		Value		Regular	
Cabin Category/Description	Restaurant	Class	Deck	A	B*	A	B*	A	B*	A	B*
Doubles											
A1 Luxury, outside w/ veranda, bath	Queens Grill	First	Signal	$7,890	$6,705	$8,840	$7,505	$9,815	$8,345	$10,315	$8,770
A2 Luxury, outside w/ veranda, bath	Queens Grill	First	Signal	6,725	5,715	7,520	6,395	8,345	7,095	8,765	7,445
A3 Luxury, outside w/ veranda, bath	Queens Grill	First	Signal	6,080	5,170	6,805	5,780	7,560	6,425	7,945	6,745
A4 Luxury, outside w/ veranda, bath	Queens Grill	First	Sports	5,725	4,870	6,420	5,455	7,115	6,055	7,490	6,360
B1 Ultra Deluxe, outside, 2 beds, bath	Queens Grill	First	1	5,620	4,780	6,295	5,345	7,000	5,950	7,330	6,240
B2 Ultra Deluxe, outside, 2 beds, bath	Queens Grill	First	2	5,235	4,450	5,855	4,975	6,495	5,525	6,815	5,795
C Ultra Deluxe, outside, 2 beds, bath	Queens Grill	First	Sports, Boat, 1, 2	4,650	3,950	5,205	4,420	5,740	4,880	6,025	5,115
D1 Ultra Deluxe, outside, 2 beds, bath	Princess Grill	First	1,2	4,320	3,675	4,745	4,035	5,240	4,445	5,500	4,680
D2 Ultra Deluxe, outside, 2 beds, bath	Princess Grill	First	3	4,000	3,400	4,475	3,810	4,975	4,235	5,210	4,430
E Deluxe, outside, 2 beds, bath	Columbia Restaurant	First	1,2	3,730	2,800	4,175	3,125	4,620	3,465	4,895	3,680
F Deluxe, outside, 2 beds, bath	Columbia Restaurant	First	2,3	3,595	2,695	4,030	3,020	4,470	3,350	4,710	3,530
G Outside, 2 beds, bath	Columbia Restaurant	First	3	3,450	2,590	3,865	2,900	4,295	3,220	4,500	3,380
H Outside, 2 beds, bath	Columbia Restaurant	First	1, 2, 3	3,285	2,465	3,675	2,765	4,090	3,075	4,290	3,210
I Outside, 2 beds, bath	Mauretania Restaurant	Transatlantic	4	2,655	1,990	2,980	2,245	3,250	2,430	3,380	2,540
J Outside, 2 beds	Mauretania Restaurant	Transatlantic	2, 3, 4, 5	2,290	1,720	2,565	1,930	2,840	2,130	2,980	2,245
K Outside, bed & upper	Mauretania Restaurant	Transatlantic	2, 3, 5	2,175	1,630	2,435	1,820	2,710	2,035	2,840	2,130
L Inside, 2 beds	Mauretania Restaurant	Transatlantic	1, 2, 3, 4, 5	2,065	1,545	2,310	1,735	2,565	1,930	2,710	2,035
M Inside, bed & upper	Mauretania Restaurant	Transatlantic	2, 4, 5	1,795	1,345	1,970	1,485	2,245	1,685	2,380	1,785
Suites**											
Queen Mary/Queen Elizabeth luxury duplex apartments	Queens Grill	First	Signal	27,940	23,750	31,290	26,570	34,750	29,540	36,520	31,030
Trafalgar/Queen Anne luxury duplex apartments	Queens Grill	First	Signal/ Sports	24,900	21,170	27,880	23,700	30,920	26,300	32,510	27,610
Singles											
UA Ultra Deluxe, outside, bed, bath	Queens Grill	First	Boat, 1, 2	5,950	5,055	6,645	5,655	7,380	6,280	7,745	6,590
UB Deluxe, outside, bed, bath	Columbia Restaurant	First	1, 2, 3	5,440	4,080	6,075	4,555	6,770	5,080	7,095	5,330
VC Inside, bed	Columbia Restaurant	First	1, 2, 3	3,595	2,695	4,030	3,020	4,490	3,370	4,715	3,535
WD Outside, bed	Mauretania Restaurant	Transatlantic	2, 3, 4	3,200	2,400	3,520	2,635	3,900	2,930	4,100	3,070
XE Inside, bed	Mauretania Restaurant	Transatlantic	2, 3, 4, 5	2,390	1,790	2,590	1,930	2,860	2,155	3,010	2,260
Port and Handling Charges Extra Per Person				$150	$150	$150	$150	$150	$150	$150	$150

All cabins on QE2 have shower and toilet. *See page 26 for air program conditions.
**Rate shown is for entire suite. Maximum 4 persons in Signal or Sports Deck.

Important fare notes for QE2:

1. All fares are quoted in U.S. dollars and are per person based on stated room capacity, except for luxury suites which are on a per suite basis.
2. The above published fares, and the additional port and handling charges may be subject to increase dependent on world conditions. Notice of fare changes will be given at least 30 days in advance of sailing date. Passengers have the option of accepting any such fare changes or additional charges, or terminating the Passage Contract. The latest fare at the time of sailing is applicable to all passengers on that voyage.
3. The above fares are for passage between New York and Southampton. See Transatlantic Sailing Schedule Notes on page 41 for more details. Fare supplements apply as noted.
4. Cunard reserves the right to refuse sale of accommodations at less than stated room capacity.
5. Single passengers occupying a double room in grades D1-M will pay 175% of the published fare. In grades A1-C, single passengers pay 200%.
6. 3rd/4th Person Rates: Many rooms can accommodate additional passengers. 3rd/4th persons pay half the fare for the least expensive cabin in their restaurant grade, and half the transatlantic air costs. Contact Cunard for details.

7. Dining Room Reservations: You may request a table size at the time of booking. Specific table confirmation will be given at embarkation.
8. Customs/Immigration fees are additional.
9. Port and handling charges are an additional per person charge.

If you are a member of the Cunard World Club, please be sure to advise us of your membership number when requesting a reservation, so that we can be sure you receive all the privileges of membership.

QE2 DECK PLANS*

Signal Deck, Sports Deck, Boat Deck, Upper Deck and Quarter Deck are not in scale.

UPPER DECK

BOAT DECK

SIGNAL DECK

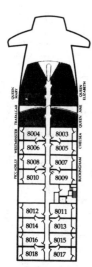

SPORTS DECK

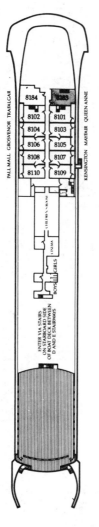

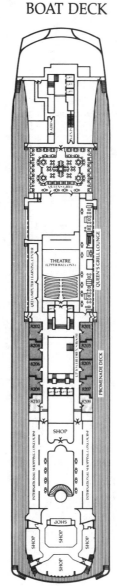

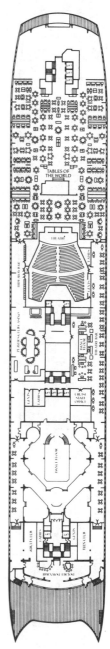

CABIN CATEGORY

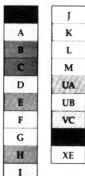

A	J
B	K
C	L
D	M
E	UA
F	UB
G	VC
H	XE
I	

QUARTER DECK

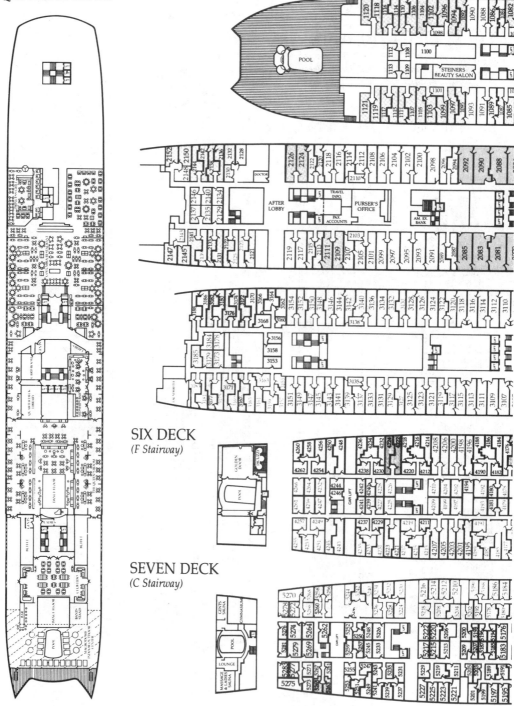

Courtesy of Cunard

SIX DECK
(F Stairway)

SEVEN DECK
(C Stairway)

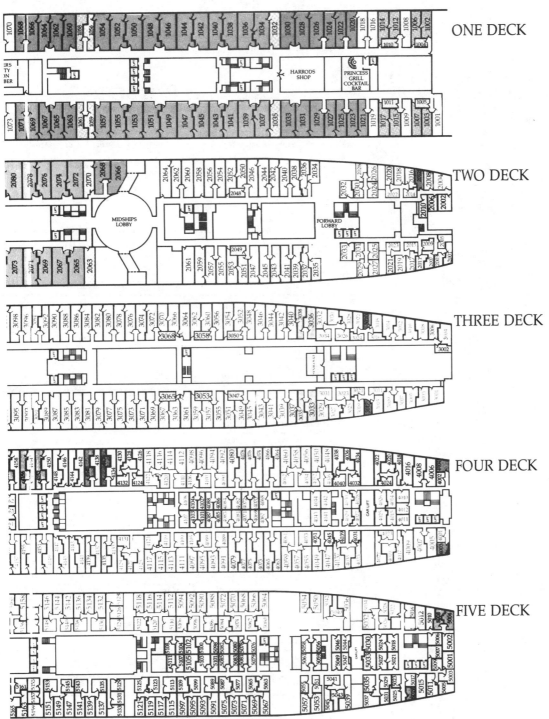

ONE DECK

TWO DECK

THREE DECK

FOUR DECK

FIVE DECK

These diagrams are for illustration only. Actual rooms may vary.

STATEROOM DIAGRAMS

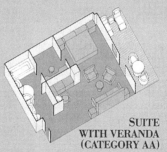

SUITE WITH VERANDA (CATEGORY AA)

Private bedroom with queen-sized bed. Sitting room area and private veranda for entertaining. TV. Refrigerator. Bath with tub and shower. Walk-in closet with dressing area.

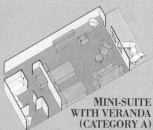

MINI-SUITE WITH VERANDA (CATEGORY A)

Private bedroom with twin beds, which make up into a comfortable queen-sized bed. Sitting room area and private veranda for entertaining. TV. Spacious closets. Refrigerator. Bath with tub and shower.

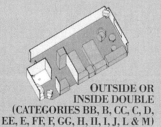

OUTSIDE OR INSIDE DOUBLE (CATEGORIES BB, B, CC, C, D, EE, E, FF, F, GG, H, II, I, J, L & M)

Outside staterooms have a picture window. Two lower beds, which make up into a comfortable queen-sized bed. Many staterooms with two upper berths. TV. Spacious closet. Refrigerator. Categories BB and B have a private balcony.

REGAL PRINCESS

1590 passengers. 70,000 gross tons. 811 feet in length. Pizzeria. Wine and caviar bar. Patisserie. Health and beauty center. Two pools, one with in-pool bar. Four whirlpool spas. Ultra-spacious staterooms, many with verandas and balconies. Domed observation lounge with entertainment complex and casino. Italian registered.

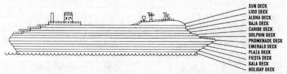

Stateroom Category	ACCOMMODATIONS	7-DAY CRUISE-ONLY FARES				
		Budget May 16, 23, Sept 19	Low May 30, Sept 12	Economy June 6, Sept 5	Value June 13, Aug 29	Peak June 20-Aug 22
		COLUMN 1	COLUMN 2	COLUMN 3	COLUMN 4	COLUMN 5
AA	Outside suite with veranda. ALOHA	$3,449	$3,549	$3,649	$3,749	$3,849
A	Outside mini-suite with veranda. ALOHA	$2,899	$2,999	$3,099	$3,199	$3,299
BB	Outside—two lower beds, with balcony. ALOHA	$2,549	$2,649	$2,749	$2,849	$2,949
B	Outside—two lower beds, with balcony. BAJA	$2,399	$2,499	$2,599	$2,699	$2,799
CC	Outside—two lower beds. ALOHA, BAJA	$2,199	$2,299	$2,399	$2,499	$2,599
C	Outside—two lower beds. CARIBE	$2,099	$2,199	$2,299	$2,399	$2,499
D	Outside—two lower beds. DOLPHIN	$2,049	$2,149	$2,249	$2,349	$2,449
EE	Outside—two lower beds. EMERALD	$1,949	$2,049	$2,149	$2,249	$2,349
E	Outside—two lower beds. PLAZA	$1,899	$1,999	$2,099	$2,199	$2,299
FF	Outside—two lower beds. PLAZA	$1,849	$1,949	$2,049	$2,149	$2,249
F	Outside—two lower beds (views obstructed). DOLPHIN	$1,799	$1,899	$1,999	$2,099	$2,199
GG	Outside—two lower beds. PLAZA	$1,699	$1,799	$1,899	$1,999	$2,099
G	Outside—one lower bed and one upper berth. FIESTA	$1,499	$1,599	$1,699	$1,799	$1,899
H	Inside—two lower beds. ALOHA	$1,599	$1,699	$1,799	$1,899	$1,999
II	Inside—two lower beds. BAJA, CARIBE	$1,549	$1,649	$1,749	$1,849	$1,949
I	Inside—two lower beds. DOLPHIN	$1,499	$1,599	$1,699	$1,799	$1,899
J	Inside—two lower beds. EMERALD	$1,399	$1,499	$1,599	$1,699	$1,799
L	Inside—two lower beds. PLAZA	$1,299	$1,399	$1,499	$1,599	$1,699
M	Inside—two lower beds. PLAZA	$1,199	$1,299	$1,399	$1,499	$1,599
	3rd/4th person in stateroom (adult/child)	$ 600	$ 650	$ 700	$ 750	$ 800
	Port Charges	$ 64	$ 64	$ 64	$ 64	$ 64

Cruise Fares (Columns 1-5) All fares are per person, U.S. dollars, based on double occupancy.

Single Occupancy Fares (Cruise only) For categories AA-B: 200% of full tariff. Category CC-M: 140% of full tariff (not eligible for Early Booking Discount).

REGAL PRINCESS DECK PLANS

Distances listed are from the bow or stern to the nearest stateroom.

° Designated stateroom will accommodate a third and fourth person.

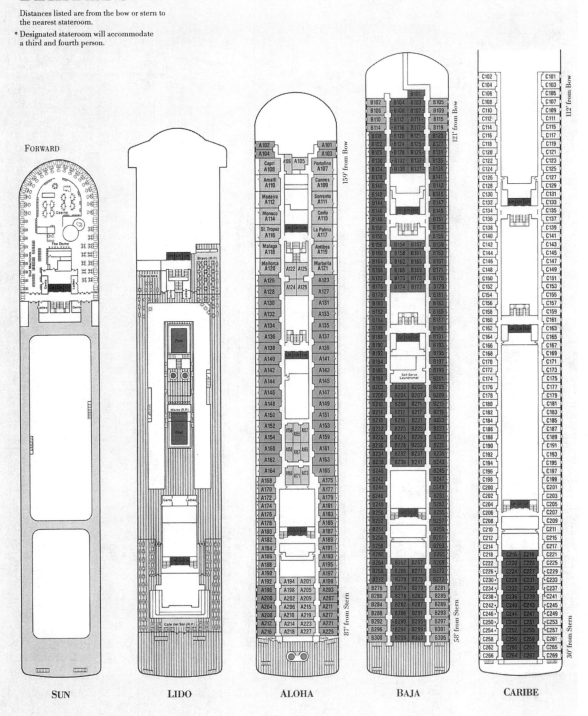

FORWARD

SUN   LIDO   ALOHA   BAJA   CARIBE

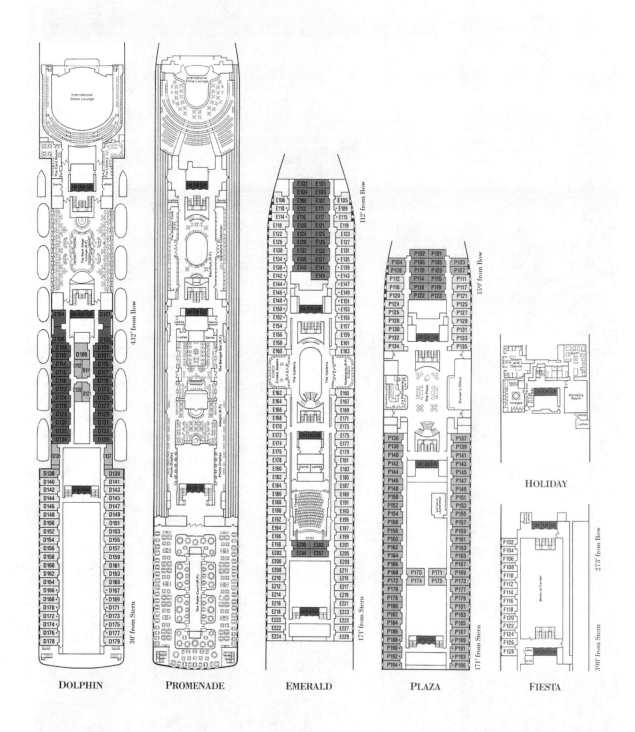

DOLPHIN

PROMENADE

EMERALD

PLAZA

HOLIDAY

FIESTA

ROYAL VIKING SUN

Historic Russia / Europe ROYAL VIKING SUN ✲

CRUISE DAYS	Copenhagen		FARE COLUMN #
14	To London (Tilbury)	2405	109

Hotel / Land Package

Extend your stay in Copenhagen or London with an optional 2-night pre- or post-cruise land package.

May 28	th	Copenhagen, Denmark; depart 6pm
May 29	f	cruise Baltic Sea
May 30	sa	Gdánsk (Gdynia), Poland; dock 8am, sail 6pm
May 31	su	cruise Gulf of Finland
Jun 1	m	Leningrad, USSR; dock 8am, overnight on board
Jun 2	tu	Leningrad, USSR; sail 6pm
Jun 3	w	Helsinki, Finland; dock 8am, sail 6pm
Jun 4	th	Stockholm, Sweden; dock 1pm, overnight on board
Jun 5	f	Stockholm, Sweden; sail 6pm
Jun 6	sa	Visby, Götland, Sweden; dock 8am, sail 6pm
Jun 7	su	cruise Baltic Sea
Jun 8	m	Oslo, Norway; dock 8am, sail 6pm
		cruise Oslofjord
Jun 9	tu	Arendal, Norway; dock 8am, sail 6pm
Jun 10	w	cruise North Sea
Jun 11	th	London (Tilbury), England; arrive 7am

RVT OPTION - Combine this cruise with a Royal Viking Tour. See page 63.

Historic Russia / Europe ROYAL VIKING SUN ✲

CRUISE DAYS	London (Tilbury)		FARE COLUMN #
14	To Copenhagen	2406	109

Hotel / Land Package

Extend your stay in London or Copenhagen with an optional 2-night pre- or post-cruise land package.

Jun 11	th	London (Tilbury), England; depart 6pm
Jun 12	f	cruise North Sea
Jun 13	sa	Hamburg, Germany; dock 8am, sail midnight
Jun 14	su	daylight transit of Kiel Canal
Jun 15	m	Rønne, Bornholm, Denmark; anchor 8am, sail 1pm
Jun 16	tu	Stockholm, Sweden; dock 9am, overnight on board
Jun 17	w	Stockholm, Sweden; sail 3pm
Jun 18	th	Helsinki, Finland; dock 8am, sail 6pm
Jun 19	f	Leningrad, USSR; dock 8am, overnight on board
Jun 20	sa	Leningrad, USSR; sail 6pm
Jun 21	su	cruise Gulf of Finland
Jun 22	m	Visby, Götland, Sweden; dock 8am, sail 6pm
Jun 23	tu	Gdánsk (Gdynia), Poland; dock 8am, sail 6pm
Jun 24	w	cruise Baltic Sea
Jun 25	th	Copenhagen, Denmark; arrive 7am

RVT OPTION - Combine this cruise with a Royal Viking Tour. See page 63.

Cruise & Air Fares

ROOM TYPE	109	ROOM TYPE	109	ROOM TYPE	109	ROOM TYPE	109
P	16,400	B1	8,000	E	7,440	F1	6,460
A	13,110	C	10,520	E1	7,090	J	6,040
B	8,560	D	7,720	F	6,740	J1	5,620

Air Add-Ons By Zone					
WEST	$400	CENTRAL	$300	EAST	FREE

Royal Viking Sun Owner's Suite available on request.

OWNER'S SUITE

OS

(Sky Deck) — This special suite includes two bathrooms, one with glassed-in whirlpool with ocean view, private veranda with floor to ceiling windows, bay window with seating area, living room, dining area, butler service, fully stocked bar at time of sailing, bedroom with twin beds that combine into king size bed.

PENTHOUSE

P

(Bridge, Sky Decks) Features include floor to ceiling windows with private veranda, living room and bedroom with retractable partition to allow ocean view from bedroom, spacious bathroom with tub, shower and extra vanity, fully stocked bar at time of sailing, butler service, a convertible sofa bed and twin beds that combine into king size bed.

DELUXES

A

(Discovery Deck) — Floor to ceiling windows with private veranda, sitting area with couch (some with sofa bed), bathroom with tub and shower, twin beds that combine into king size bed.

OUTSIDE DOUBLES/ SINGLES

B B1 C

(Scandinavia Deck) Floor to ceiling windows with private veranda (except B1, C staterooms), sitting area, bathroom with tub and shower (or shower only), twin beds that combine into king size bed. (C staterooms feature twin bed.)

OUTSIDE DOUBLES

D E E1 F F1

(Promenade, Atlantic, Pacific Decks) Sitting area, large windows (except forward E1 and F1 staterooms which have portholes), twin beds that combine into king size bed, bathroom with tub and shower (or shower only).

INSIDE DOUBLES

J J1

(Scandinavia, Promenade, Pacific Decks) — Two lower beds, bathroom with tub and shower (or shower only).

Deck Plans

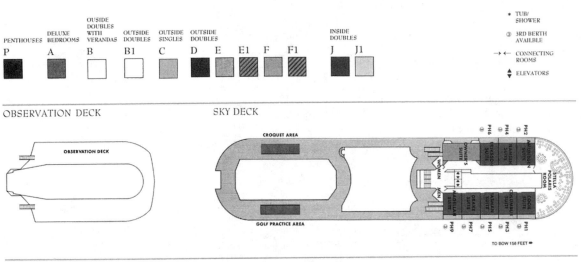

		OUTSIDE DOUBLES WITH	OUTSIDE	OUTSIDE	OUTSIDE					INSIDE	
PENTHOUSES	DELUXE BEDROOMS	VERANDAS	DOUBLES	SINGLES	DOUBLES					DOUBLES	
P	A	B	B1	C	D	E	E1	F	F1	J	J1

* TUB/SHOWER
③ 3RD BERTH AVAILBLE
→ ← CONNECTING ROOMS
▲ ELEVATORS

OBSERVATION DECK

OBSERVATION DECK

SKY DECK

BRIDGE DECK

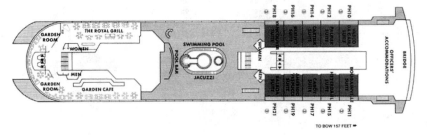

DISCOVERY DECK

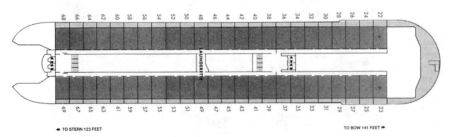

◄ TO STERN 123 FEET   TO BOW 141 FEET ►

SCANDINAVIA DECK

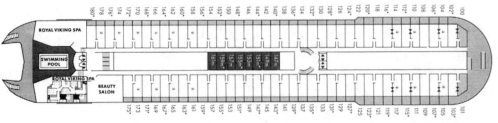

◄ TO STERN 123 FEET   TO BOW 96 FEET ►

80

Royal Viking Sun ✳

LENGTH - 673 FEET
BREADTH - 95 FEET
GROSS REGISTERED TONS - 36.000
BAHAMIAN REGISTRY

SKY DECK
OBSERVATION DECK
DISCOVERY
BRIDGE
NORWAY
SCANDINAVIA
ATLANTIC
PROMENADE
PACIFIC

STATEROOM FEATURES

WALK-IN CLOSET ◆ REFRIGERATOR ◆ COLOR TV ◆
VIDEO CASSETTE PLAYER ◆ TELEPHONE ◆
24-HOUR STEWARDESS CALL-BUTTON ◆ 110-220
ELECTRICAL CURRENT ◆ 3-CHANNEL RADIO ◆
SECURITY-LOCK DRAWER ◆ INDIVIDUAL
THERMOSTAT CONTROL ◆ FULL-LENGTH MIRROR

NORWAY DECK

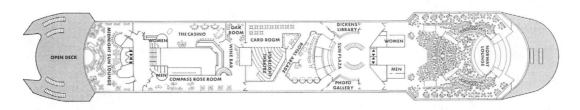

PROMENADE DECK

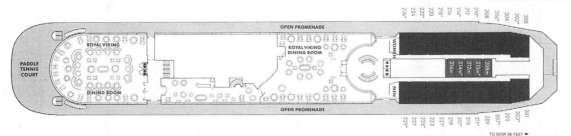

ATLANTIC DECK

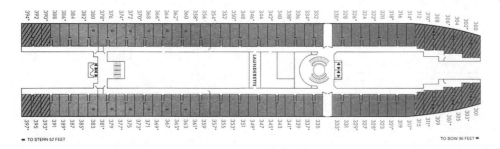

PACIFIC DECK

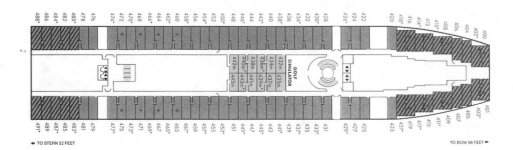

Sagafjord's 1992 cruise fares

All fares are per person and in U.S. dollars and include FREE air transportation.

CRUISE PROGRAM:	PANAMA CANAL				CARIBBEAN			
CRUISE STARTS:	January 6	April 8	May 15	September 6	April 22	October 25	December 6	December 20
FROM/ TO:	Ft. Lauderdale to Lima	Los Angeles to Ft. Lauderdale	Ft. Lauderdale to Los Angeles	Los Angeles to Ft. Lauderdale	Round-trip Ft. Lauderdale	Round-trip Ft. Lauderdale	Round-trip Ft. Lauderdale	Round-trip Ft. Lauderdale
LENGTH:	9 Days	14 Days	14 Days	14 Days	11 Days	14 Days	14 Days	16 Days
GRADES: DOUBLE ROOMS								
AA	$6,570	$8,010	$7,320	$7,520	$5,050	$6,360	$6,010	$10,470
A	6,110	7,030	6,400	6,600	4,510	5,670	5,350	9,290
B	5,450	6,320	5,740	5,940	4,070	5,110	4,830	8,350
C	4,540	5,620	5,100	5,280	3,630	4,550	4,300	7,400
D	4,340	5,380	4,860	5,060	3,490	4,360	4,130	7,080
E	4,180	5,150	4,640	4,840	3,340	4,170	3,900	6,770
F	4,010	4,950	4,420	4,620	3,140	3,910	3,700	6,450
G	3,780	4,670	4,110	4,310	2,940	3,650	3,460	6,010
H	3,590	4,250	3,850	4,050	2,730	3,390	3,210	5,550
I	3,420	4,000	3,510	3,710	2,540	3,130	2,970	5,120
J	3,190	3,740	3,170	3,370	2,380	2,940	2,790	4,690
GRADES: LUXURY SUITES								
X	$10,170	$13,300	$11,940	$12,140	$7,970	$10,120	$9,540	$17,920
Y	9,250	12,020	10,770	10,970	7,250	9,200	8,670	16,250
Z	6,800	8,890	8,140	8,340	5,600	7,080	6,680	11,860
GRADES: SINGLES PLUS THIRD/FOURTH IN ROOM, AND PORT AND HANDLING CHARGES								
KA	$6,630	$8,010	$7,170	$7,370	$5,050	$6,360	$6,010	$10,210
LB	5,450	6,320	5,600	5,800	4,070	5,110	4,830	8,660
MC	4,960	5,620	5,080	5,280	3,660	4,590	4,340	7,710
ND	4,500	4,680	4,190	4,390	3,050	3,800	3,600	6,770
OE	4,210	3,740	3,270	3,470	2,380	2,940	2,790	6,010
3rd/4th Person	2,045	2,350	1,970	2,170	1,530	1,850	1,760	2,550
Port & Handling	$ 135	$ 200	$ 200	$ 200	$ 125	$ 135	$ 135	$ 155
PRE/POST CRUISE HOTEL AND SIGHTSEEING PROGRAM FARES								
Pre/Post	$150/—	$350/150	$150/350	$350/150	$150/150	$150/150	$150/150	$150/150
AIR TRANSPORTATION PROGRAM FARES								
East	FREE	FREE	FREE	FREE	FREE	FREE	FREE	FREE
Central	FREE	FREE	FREE	FREE	FREE	FREE	FREE	FREE
West	FREE	FREE	FREE	FREE	FREE	FREE	FREE	FREE
***CREDITS FOR NON-USE OF COMPLIMENTARY AIR PROGRAM**								
Air Credit	$600	$275	$275	$275	$275	$275	$275	$275

*Deduct the amounts in this section from your cruise fare if you choose not to take advantage of Cunard's complimentary air program.

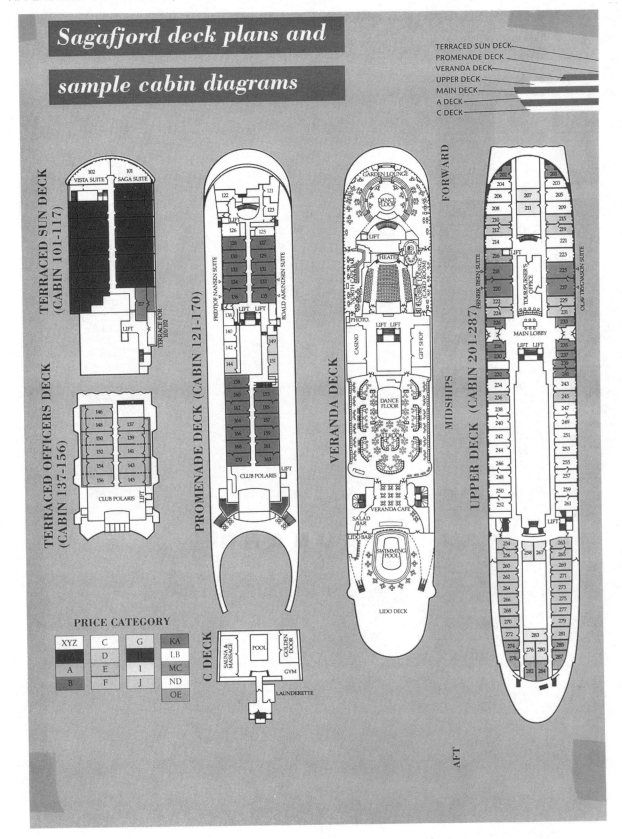

Sagafjord deck plans and sample cabin diagrams

TERRACED SUN DECK
PROMENADE DECK
VERANDA DECK
UPPER DECK
MAIN DECK
A DECK
C DECK

TERRACED SUN DECK (CABIN 101-117)

TERRACED OFFICERS DECK (CABIN 137-156)

PROMENADE DECK (CABIN 121-170)

VERANDA DECK

UPPER DECK (CABIN 201-287)

FORWARD

MIDSHIPS

AFT

PRICE CATEGORY

XYZ	C	G	KA
	D	H	LB
A	E	I	MC
B	F	J	ND
			OE

C DECK

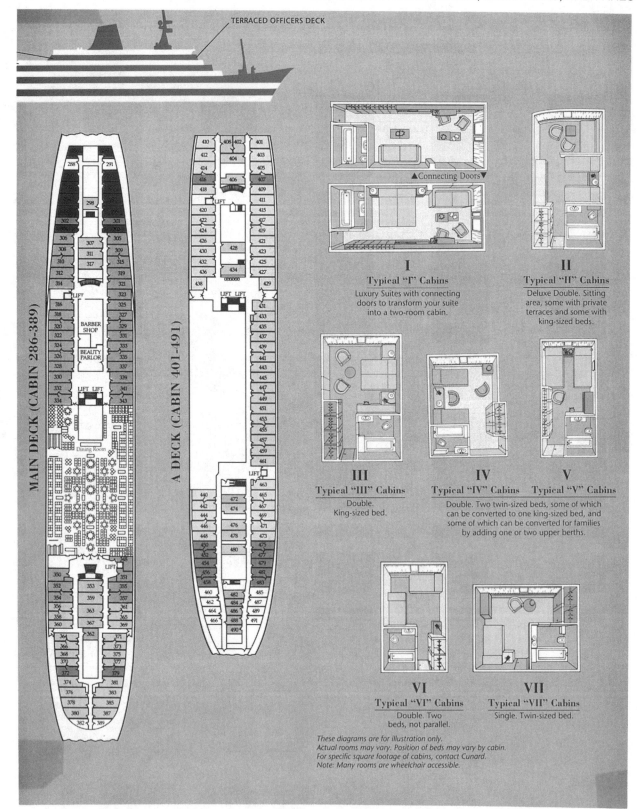

TERRACED OFFICERS DECK

MAIN DECK (CABIN 286–389)

A DECK (CABIN 401–491)

BARBER SHOP

BEAUTY PARLOR

Dining Room

▲Connecting Doors▼

I
Typical "I" Cabins
Luxury Suites with connecting
doors to transform your suite
into a two-room cabin.

II
Typical "II" Cabins
Deluxe Double. Sitting
area, some with private
terraces and some with
king-sized beds.

III
Typical "III" Cabins
Double.
King-sized bed.

IV
Typical "IV" Cabins

V
Typical "V" Cabins
Double. Two twin-sized beds, some of which
can be converted to one king-sized bed, and
some of which can be converted for families
by adding one or two upper berths.

VI
Typical "VI" Cabins
Double. Two
beds, not parallel.

VII
Typical "VII" Cabins
Single. Twin-sized bed.

*These diagrams are for illustration only.
Actual rooms may vary. Position of beds may vary by cabin.
For specific square footage of cabins, contact Cunard.
Note: Many rooms are wheelchair accessible.*

October 1991 through May 1993

Date/Cruise Name	Length	Ports of Call	Air Program	Pre/Post Tours	Land Excursion	Lecture Series	Connoisseur Series	Suite-Room Fares** Cruise Fare	Combination Add-On	Suite Fares** Cruise Fare	Combination Add-On
April 3-14, 1992 Indonesia/Thailand	11 Days	**Bali,** Palopa, Ujung Pandang, Semarang, Pulau Pelangi, Singapore, Kuala Lumpur, Pulau Pangkor, **Phuket**	✈	☀	🌴	🏛		$8,000	$4,000	$12,000	$6,000
April 14-24, 1992 Thailand/India	10 Days	**Phuket,** Male, Goa, **Bombay**				🏛		$4,900	$2,500	$7,400	$3,700
April 24-May 7, 1992 India/Suez	13 Days	**Bombay,** Hodeidah, Aqaba, Sharm-El-Sheik, Hurghada, Transit Suez Canal, **Alexandria**				🏛		$5,100	$2,600	$7,700	$3,900
May 7-November 1, 1992 Europe		Sea Goddess II will be sailing in Europe. Please refer to pages 10-11 for information.									
November 1-15, 1992 Suez/India	14 Days	**Haifa,** Port Said, Transit Suez Canal, Hurghada, Aqaba, Djibouti, **Bombay**				🏛		$5,600	$2,800	$8,400	$4,200
November 15-28, 1992 India/Malaysia	13 Days	**Bombay,** Goa, Male, Phuket, Pulau Pangkor, Kuala Lumpur, **Singapore**				🏛		$7,800	$3,900	$11,700	$5,900
November 28-December 8, 1992 Malaysia/Indonesia	10 Days	**Singapore,** Pulau Pelangi, Semarang, Ujung Pandang, Bau Bau, Palopa, Lombok, **Bali**	✈		🌴	🏛		$8,100	$4,100	$12,200	$6,100
December 8-22, 1992 Indonesia/Australia	14 Days	**Bali,** Komodo, Larantuka, Darwin, Seven Spirit Bay, Thursday Island, Cape York, Lizard Island, Cooktown, Low Isles, Townsville, Whitsunday Island, Hayman Island, Orpheus Island, **Cairns**	✈		🌴	🏛	🌙	$10,500	$5,300	$15,800	$7,900
December 22, 1992-January 5, 1993 Australia/Papua New Guinea Christmas/New Year's	14 Days	**Cairns,** Cooktown, Lizard Island, Deboyne Lagoon, Rabaul, Lae, Trobriand Island, Herald Cay, Whitsunday Island, Hayman Island, Townsville, **Cairns**	✈		🌴	🏛		$11,900	$6,000	$17,900	$9,000
January 5-19, 1993 Australia/Indonesia	14 Days	**Cairns,** Orpheus Island, Whitsunday Island, Hayman Island, Townsville, Low Isles, Cooktown, Lizard Island, Flinders Island, Cape York, Thursday Island, Seven Spirit Bay, Darwin, Larantuka, Komodo, **Bali**	✈		🌴	🏛		$10,500	$5,300	$15,800	$7,900
January 19-30, 1993 Indonesia/Malaysia	11 Days	**Bali,** Lombok, Komodo, Palopa, Ujung Pandang, Semarang, Pulau Pelangi, **Singapore**	✈		🌴	🏛		$8,800	$4,400	$13,200	$6,600
January 30-February 10, 1993 Indonesia/Malaysia	11 Days	**Singapore,** Pulau Pelangi, Semarang, Ujung Pandang, Bau Bau, Palopa, Komodo, Lombok, **Bali**	✈		🌴	🏛		$8,800	$4,400	$13,200	$6,600
February 10-20, 1993 Indonesia/Malaysia	10 Days	**Bali,** Komodo, Palopa, Ujung Pandang, Semarang, Pulau Pelangi, **Singapore**	✈		🌴	🏛		$8,100	$4,100	$12,200	$6,100
February 20-March 3, 1993 Malaysia/Thailand	11 Days	**Singapore,** Pulau Pangkor, Phuket, Penang, Kuala Lumpur, Malacca, Pulau Tioman, Ko Samui, **Bangkok**	✈		🌴	🏛		$8,800	$4,400	$13,200	$6,600
March 3-13, 1993 Thailand/Malaysia	10 Days	**Bangkok,** Ko Samui, Pulau Tioman, Malacca, Kuala Lumpur, Penang, Phuket, Pulau Pangkor, **Singapore**	✈		🌴	🏛		$8,100	$4,100	$12,200	$6,100
March 13-27, 1993 Malaysia/China	14 Days	**Singapore,** Kuantan, Pulau Tioman, Sanya, Zhanjiang, Hong Kong, Xiamen, Shanghai, Zhenjiang, **Nanjing**	✈		🌴	🏛		$10,500	$5,300	$15,800	$7,900
March 27-April 10, 1993 China/Malaysia	14 Days	**Nanjing,** Zhenjiang, Shanghai, Xiamen, Hong Kong, Zhanjiang, Sanya, Pulau Tioman, Kuantan, **Singapore**	✈		🌴	🏛		$10,500	$5,300	$15,800	$7,900
April 10-23, 1993 Malaysia/India	13 Days	**Singapore,** Kuala Lumpur, Pulau Pangkor, Phuket, Male, Goa, **Bombay**				🏛		$7,800	$3,900	$11,700	$5,900
April 23-May 6, 1993 India/Suez	13 Days	**Bombay,** Hodeidah, Aqaba, Sharm-El-Sheik, Hurghada, Transit Suez Canal, **Alexandria**				🏛		$5,600	$2,800	$8,400	$4,200

Sea Goddess Orient Cruises Air Program

All guests sailing on Orient, Java Seas, and Australia cruises will receive complimentary round-trip Economy Class air transportation between the port of embarkation and disembarkation, and one of the 24 U.S. gateways listed at right. Passengers who do not wish to take advantage of this complimentary air program will receive an air credit of $1,000 per person. First Class and Business Class upgrade arrangements are available at a supplementary cost. Complimentary transfers between the airport and the pier are available on the days of embarkation and disembarkation.

Gateway Cities

Atlanta	Houston	Pittsburgh
Boston	Los Angeles	Sacramento
Chicago	Miami/Fort Lauderdale	St. Louis
Cleveland	Minneapolis	San Diego
Dallas	Newark	San Francisco
Denver	New York	Seattle
Detroit	Philadelphia	Tampa
Hartford	Phoenix	Washington, D.C.

Accommodations

SUITE-ROOMS
Each suite-room is equipped
with separate sitting room,
bar, mini-refrigerator and
home entertainment center
with radio, remote control
color television and VCR.

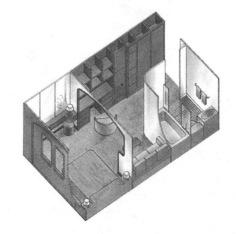

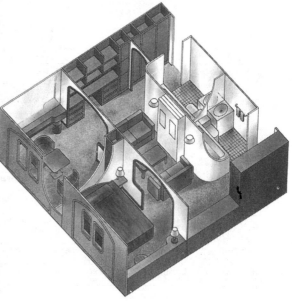

SUITE
A retractable sliding door
transforms two suite-rooms
into a lavish suite with twice
the living area and two
separate baths.

Deck Plans

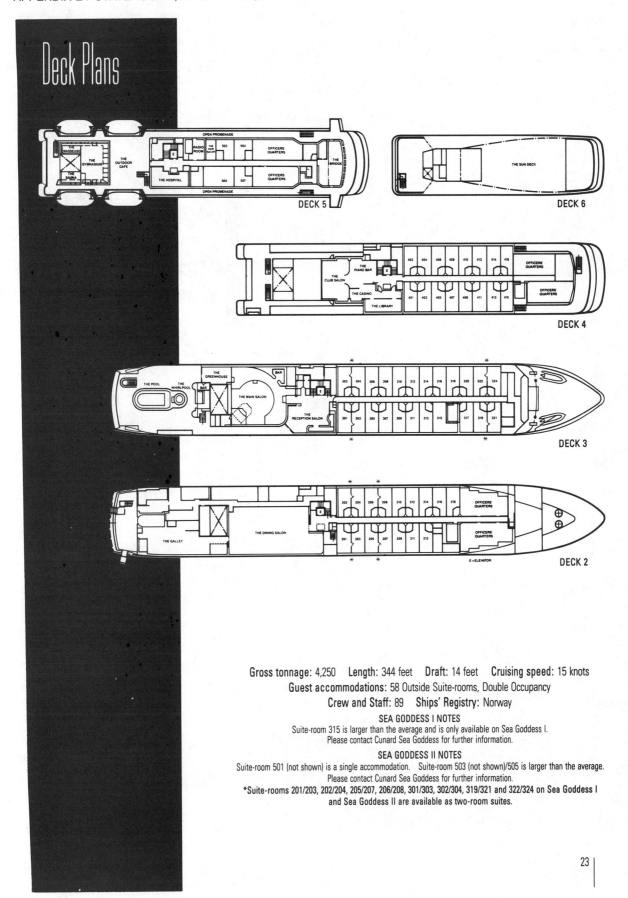

DECK 5

DECK 6

DECK 4

DECK 3

DECK 2

E = ELEVATOR

Gross tonnage: 4,250   Length: 344 feet   Draft: 14 feet   Cruising speed: 15 knots
Guest accommodations: 58 Outside Suite-rooms, Double Occupancy
Crew and Staff: 89   Ships' Registry: Norway

SEA GODDESS I NOTES
Suite-room 315 is larger than the average and is only available on Sea Goddess I.
Please contact Cunard Sea Goddess for further information.

SEA GODDESS II NOTES
Suite-room 501 (not shown) is a single accommodation.   Suite-room 503 (not shown)/505 is larger than the average.
Please contact Cunard Sea Goddess for further information.
*Suite-rooms 201/203, 202/204, 205/207, 206/208, 301/303, 302/304, 319/321 and 322/324 on Sea Goddess I
and Sea Goddess II are available as two-room suites.

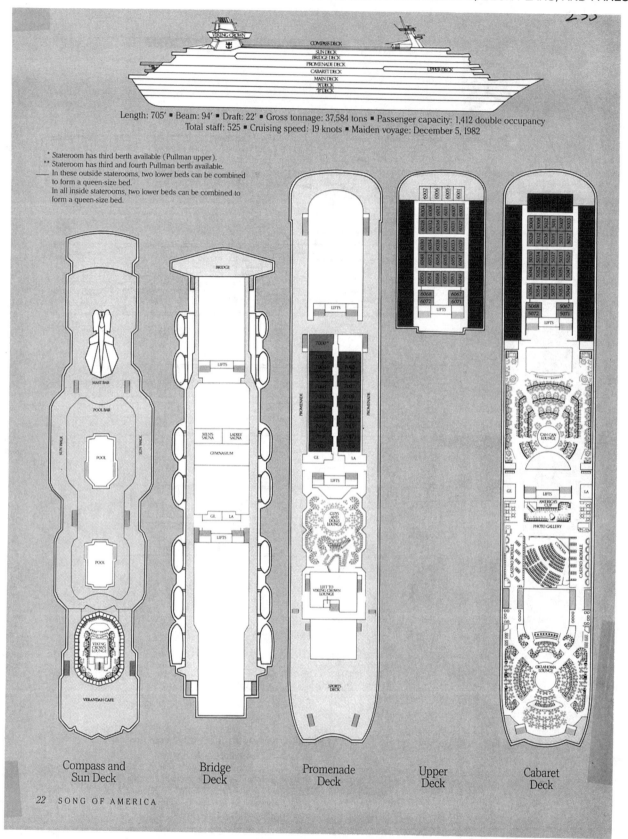

Length: 705' ■ Beam: 94' ■ Draft: 22' ■ Gross tonnage: 37,584 tons ■ Passenger capacity: 1,412 double occupancy
Total staff: 525 ■ Cruising speed: 19 knots ■ Maiden voyage: December 5, 1982

* Stateroom has third berth available (Pullman upper).
** Stateroom has third and fourth Pullman berth available.
— In these outside staterooms, two lower beds can be combined to form a queen-size bed.
In all inside staterooms, two lower beds can be combined to form a queen-size bed.

Compass and Sun Deck

Bridge Deck

Promenade Deck

Upper Deck

Cabaret Deck

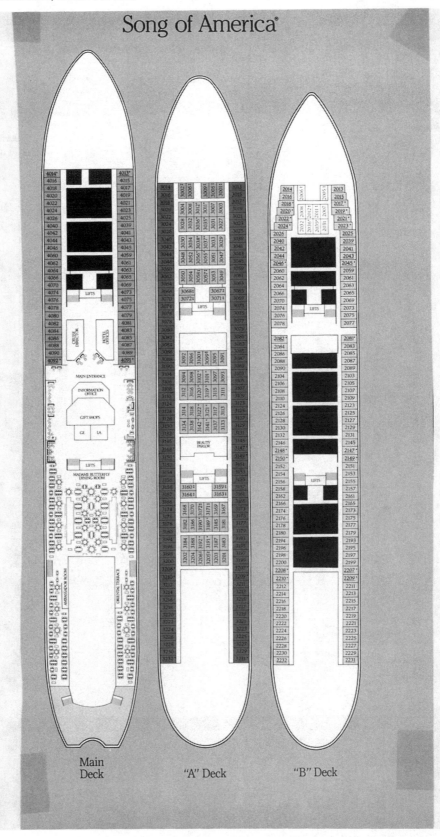

Song of America®

Main Deck

"A" Deck

"B" Deck

STAR PRINCESS DECK PLANS

1494 passengers. 63,500 gross tons. 804 ft. in length. Pizzeria, wine and caviar bar. Patisserie. Health and beauty center. Three pools, one with in-pool bar. Four whirlpool spas. Ultra spacious staterooms. 270° observation lounge. Casino. Three-story atrium lobby with shopping arcade. Liberian registered.

237

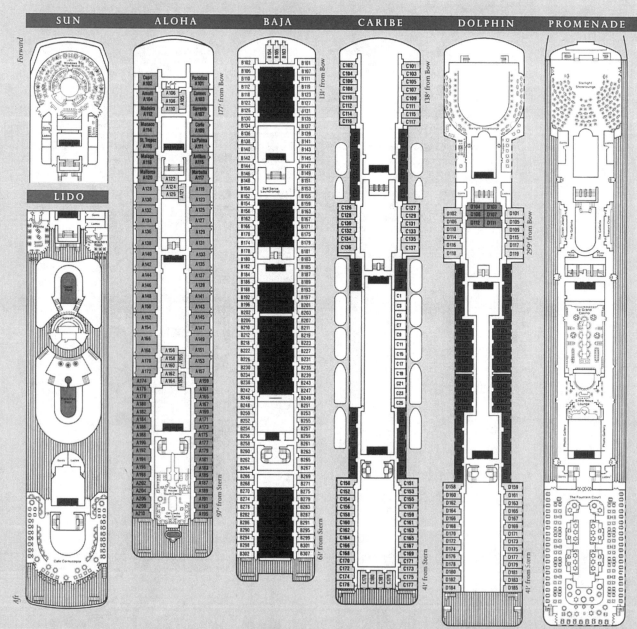

| SUN | ALOHA | BAJA | CARIBE | DOLPHIN | PROMENADE |

LIDO

STATEROOM DIAGRAMS

SUITE WITH VERANDA
(CATEGORY AA)

Private bedroom with queen-sized bed. Sitting room area and private veranda for entertaining. TV. Refrigerator. Bath with tub and shower. Walk-in closet with dressing area.

MINI-SUITE WITH VERANDA
(CATEGORY A)

Private bedroom with twin beds, which make up into a comfortable queen-sized bed. Sitting room area and private veranda for entertaining. TV. Spacious closets. Refrigerator. Bath with tub and shower.

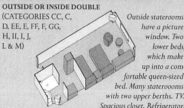

OUTSIDE OR INSIDE DOUBLE
(CATEGORIES CC, C, D, EE, E, FF, F, GG, H, II, I, J, L & M)

Outside staterooms have a picture window. Two lower beds, which make up into a comfortable queen-sized bed. Many staterooms with two upper berths. TV. Spacious closet. Refrigerator.

26

EMERALD — PLAZA — HOLIDAY — FIESTA

Distances listed are from the bow or stern to the nearest stateroom.

STAR PRINCESS FARES

FARES INCLUDE FREE AIR TRANSPORTATION*

238

FARE COLUMN	5	6	7	8	9	10
	9-DAY	12-DAY	12-DAY	12-DAY	14-DAY	12-DAY
	4/5	4/14-4/26, 10/11-10/23	5/8-5/20, 9/29	6/1-6/25	7/7-9/15	11/4
EARLY BOOKING DISCOUNT	$250	$250	$250	$250	$250	$250
ROOM CODES						
AA	$6,590	$9,190	$9,290	$9,440	$10,790	$7,790
A	5,190	7,440	7,540	7,690	8,740	5,990
CC	3,790	5,090	5,190	5,340	5,890	4,390
C	3,690	4,990	5,090	5,240	5,790	4,290
D	3,590	4,890	4,990	5,140	5,690	4,190
EE	3,490	4,790	4,890	5,040	5,590	4,090
E	3,390	4,690	4,790	4,940	5,490	3,990
FF	3,290	4,590	4,690	4,840	5,390	3,890
F	3,190	4,490	4,590	4,740	5,290	3,790
GG	3,090	4,390	4,490	4,640	5,190	3,690
G	2,990	4,290	4,390	4,540	5,090	3,590
H	2,890	4,140	4,240	4,390	4,940	3,490
■	2,790	4,040	4,140	4,290	4,840	3,390
I	2,690	3,940	4,040	4,190	4,740	3,290
J	2,590	3,840	3,940	4,090	4,640	3,190
L	2,490	3,740	3,840	3,990	4,540	3,090
M	2,390	3,640	3,740	3,890	4,440	2,990
3RD AND 4TH BERTH- ADULTS AND CHILDREN	1,195	1,820	1,870	1,945	2,220	1,495
TRAVEL ALLOWANCE	600	800	800	800	800†	600

EARLY BOOKING DISCOUNT Passengers can deduct $250 per person when booked and under deposit by February 14, 1992. Early Booking Discounts do not apply to 3rd or 4th berth passengers or singles in categories CC-M.

TRAVEL ALLOWANCE Passengers (including those in 3rd and 4th berths) not using Princess' Seabird Air program can deduct the amounts shown from their cruise fare.

CRUISE FARES All fares are for each adult in U.S. dollars based on double occupancy.

SINGLE OCCUPANCY FARES For categories AA-A: 200% of full tariff; CC-M: 140% of full tariff.

PORT CHARGES Passenger port charges, including taxes, are additional and range from $89 to $163 depending on the ship's itinerary.

*Special air program applies for residents of Canada. An air add-on of $300 applies from Honolulu and Anchorage.

†For the 8/18 and 9/1 sailings, the Travel Allowance is $700.

STATEROOM DESCRIPTIONS

ROOM CODES	DECKS	STATEROOM DESCRIPTION	ROOM CODES	DECKS	STATEROOM DESCRIPTION
AA	ALOHA	Outside Suite w/ Veranda	GG	FIESTA	Outside—Two Lower Beds (portholes only)
A	ALOHA	Outside Mini-Suite w/ Veranda	G	CARIBE (Mid)	Outside—Two Lower Beds (partial view obstruction)
CC	ALOHA	Outside— Two Lower Beds	H	ALOHA	Inside— Two Lower Beds
C	BAJA	Outside— Two Lower Beds	■	BAJA	Inside— Two Lower Beds
D	CARIBE, DOLPHIN	Outside— Two Lower Beds	I	DOLPHIN	Inside— Two Lower Beds
EE	EMERALD	Outside— Two Lower Beds	J	EMERALD	Inside— Two Lower Beds
E	PLAZA (Mid)	Outside— Two Lower Beds	L	PLAZA	Inside— Two Lower Beds
FF	PLAZA (Fore)	Outside— Two Lower Beds	M	PLAZA (Fore)	Inside— Two Lower Beds
F	CARIBE, DOLPHIN	Outside—Two Lower Beds (views obstructed)			

27

Premier's Orlando Sun Vacation

Premier's magical Orlando Sun Vacation includes:

🐭 Your choice of Stateroom categories 1-9.

🐭 Accommodations at an Orlando-area hotel based on stateroom category.

🐭 Four-day Walt Disney World Passport for unlimited admission to the Magic Kingdom Park, EPCOT Center, and the Disney-MGM Studios Theme Park, and your choice of River Country or Pleasure Island.

🐭 The world famous Disney characters aboard the Big Red Boat.

🐭 Guided tour of Spaceport USA or the United States Astronaut Hall of Fame.

🐭 Economy rental car with unlimited mileage for 2 guests; 3 or more guests receive an intermediate car.

🐭 Round-trip coach airfare. (Some cities require an air supplement. See pages 40-41.)

Ask about extended days, hotel and car upgrades and drive/air allowances.

Note: See page 52 for 1992 sailing and seasonality dates. Rates are per person, double occupancy. Port charges are an additional $41 per person.

7-Day Cruise & Disney Vacation Rates*

Stateroom Category		Hotel	Super Value	Value	Season
1	Inside Cabins: Upper/Lower Beds. Outside Cabins (Atlantic Only).	Rodeway Inn, Best Western Plaza International or similar.	$ 780	$ 819	$ 859
2	Outside Cabins: Double Bed, 2 Lowers, or Upper/Lower Beds. Inside Cabins (Atlantic Only).	Rodeway Inn, Best Western Plaza International or similar.	$ 890	$ 929	$ 969
3	Inside Cabins: 2 Lower Beds or Double Bed.	Rodeway Inn, Best Western Plaza International or similar.	$ 1010	$ 1049	$ 1089
4	Inside Cabins: 2 Lower Beds or Double Bed.	Rodeway Inn, Best Western Plaza International or similar.	$ 1110	$ 1149	$ 1189
5	Outside Cabins: 2 Lower Beds, Queen Bed, or Double Bed.	Howard Johnson Park Square, Star Quality Resort, The Floridian of Orlando or similar.	$ 1180	$ 1219	$ 1259
6	Outside Cabins: 2 Lower Beds, Queen Bed, or Double Bed.	Howard Johnson Park Square, Star Quality Resort, The Floridian of Orlando or similar.	$ 1250	$ 1289	$ 1329
7	Deluxe Outside Cabins: 2 Lower Beds or Queen Bed.	Howard Johnson Park Square, Star Quality Resort, The Floridian of Orlando or similar.	$ 1310	$ 1349	$ 1389
8	Suites: 2 Lower Beds, Queen Bed or Double Bed.	Sonesta Village or similar.	$ 1360	$ 1399	$ 1439
9	Apartment Suites: King and Queen (Atlantic & Oceanic Only) Private Veranda (Oceanic Only).	Sonesta Village or similar.	$ 1520	$ 1559	$ 1599
	3rd, 4th, & 5th guest air-inclusive rate when sharing a cabin and hotel accommodations with 1st & 2nd guests.		$ 620	$ 659	$ 699

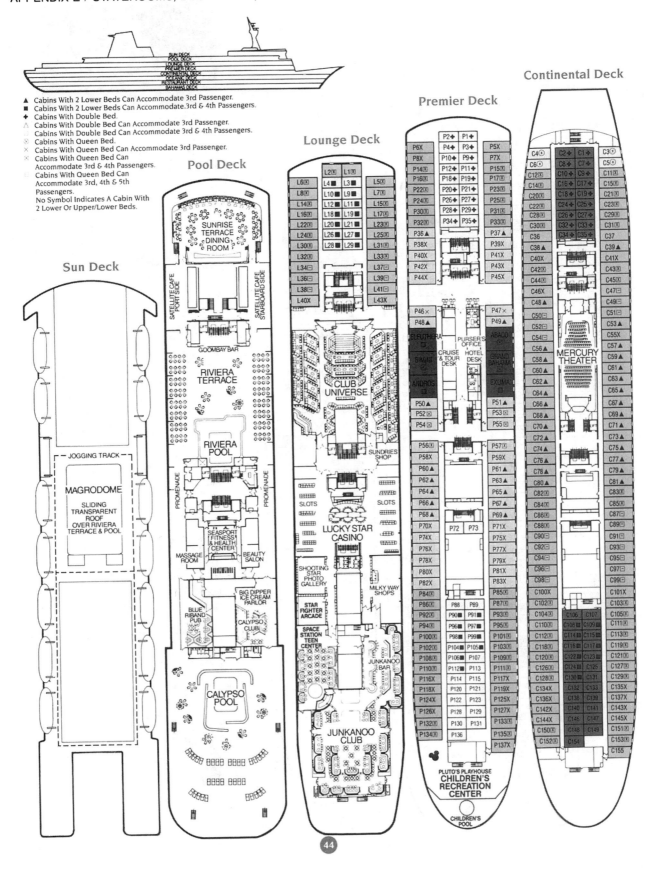

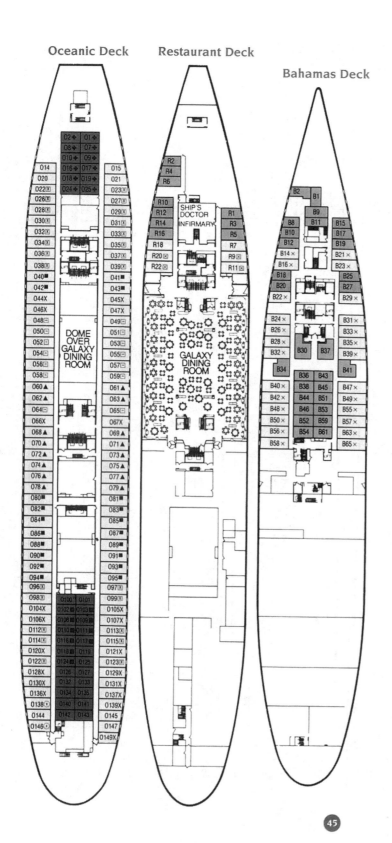

Oceanic Deck   Restaurant Deck

Bahamas Deck

3-DAY Leaves Every Friday From Terminal 4

DAY	PORT	ARRIVE	DEPART
Fri	Port Canaveral		4:30pm
Sat	Nassau	1:30pm	
Sun	Nassau/Out Island		5:00pm
Mon	Port Canaveral	9:00am	

4-DAY Leaves Every Monday From Terminal 4

DAY	PORT	ARRIVE	DEPART
Mon	Port Canaveral		4:30pm
Tues	Nassau	1:30pm	
Wed	Nassau/Out Island		5:00pm
Thu	At Sea		
Fri	Port Canaveral	8:00am	

Gross Tonnage:	36,500
Overall Length:	671 Feet
Beam:	90 Feet
Draft:	25 Feet
Cruise Speed:	24 Knots
Crew:	500

1	Inside or Outside Cabins: Upper/Lower Beds.
2	Inside or Outside Cabins: Double Bed, 2 Lowers, or Upper/Lower Beds.
3	Inside Cabins: 2 Lower Beds or Double Bed.
4	Inside Cabins: 2 Lower Beds or Double Bed.
5	Outside Cabins: 2 Lower Beds or Queen Bed.
6	Outside Cabins: 2 Lower Beds or Queen Bed.
7	Deluxe Outside Cabins: Queen Bed.
8	Suites: 2 Lower Beds or Queen Bed.
9	Apartment Suites: 2 Lower Beds or Queen Bed.

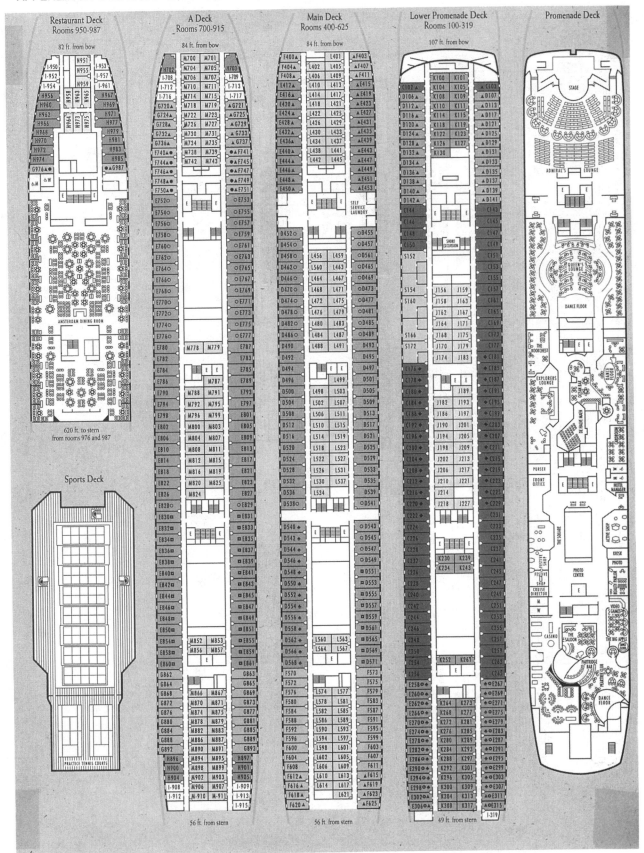

Restaurant Deck
Rooms 950-987

82 ft. from bow

AMSTERDAM DINING ROOM

620 ft. to stern
from rooms 976 and 987

Sports Deck

PRACTICE TENNIS COURTS

A Deck
Rooms 700-915

84 ft. from bow

56 ft. from stern

Main Deck
Rooms 400-625

84 ft. from bow

SELF SERVICE LAUNDRY

56 ft. from stern

Lower Promenade Deck
Rooms 100-319

107 ft. from bow

SHORE EXCURSION

49 ft. from stern

Promenade Deck

STAGE

ADMIRAL'S LOUNGE

QUEEN'S LOUNGE

DANCE FLOOR

THE BOOKCHEST

EXPLORERS LOUNGE

DE HAUTE MAKER

PURSER

FRONT OFFICE

HOTEL MANAGER

THE SQUARE

ACTIVE SHOP

KIOSK

PHOTO

FESTIVE SHOP

PHOTO CENTER

CRUISE DIRECTOR

VIDEO GAMES

CASINO

THE SALOON

THE BIG APPLE

PARTRIDGE BAR

DANCE FLOOR

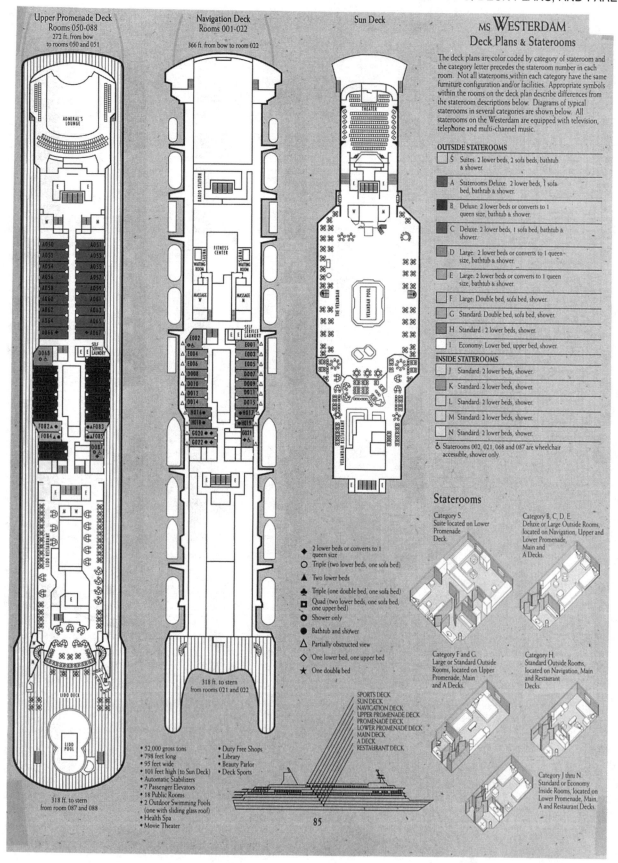

Upper Promenade Deck
Rooms 050-088
272 ft. from bow
to rooms 050 and 051

Navigation Deck
Rooms 001-022
366 ft. from bow to room 022

Sun Deck

MS WESTERDAM
Deck Plans & Staterooms

The deck plans are color coded by category of stateroom and the category letter precedes the stateroom number in each room. Not all staterooms within each category have the same furniture configuration and/or facilities. Appropriate symbols within the rooms on the deck plan describe differences from the stateroom descriptions below. Diagrams of typical staterooms in several categories are shown below. All staterooms on the Westerdam are equipped with television, telephone and multi-channel music.

OUTSIDE STATEROOMS

S Suites: 2 lower beds, 2 sofa beds, bathtub & shower.

A Staterooms Deluxe: 2 lower beds, 1 sofa bed, bathtub & shower.

B Deluxe: 2 lower beds or converts to 1 queen size, bathtub & shower.

C Deluxe: 2 lower beds, 1 sofa bed, bathtub & shower.

D Large: 2 lower beds or converts to 1 queen size, bathtub & shower.

E Large: 2 lower beds or converts to 1 queen size, bathtub & shower.

F Large: Double bed, sofa bed, shower.

G Standard: Double bed, sofa bed, shower.

H Standard: 2 lower beds, shower.

I Economy: Lower bed, upper bed, shower.

INSIDE STATEROOMS

J Standard: 2 lower beds, shower.

K Standard: 2 lower beds, shower.

L Standard: 2 lower beds, shower.

M Standard: 2 lower beds, shower.

N Standard: 2 lower beds, shower.

♿ Staterooms 002, 021, 068 and 087 are wheelchair accessible, shower only.

Staterooms

Category S.
Suite located on Lower Promenade Deck.

Category B, C, D, E.
Deluxe or Large Outside Rooms, located on Navigation, Upper and Lower Promenade, Main and A Decks.

Category F and G.
Large or Standard Outside Rooms, located on Upper Promenade, Main and A Decks.

Category H.
Standard Outside Rooms, located on Navigation, Main and Restaurant Decks.

Category J thru N.
Standard or Economy Inside Rooms, located on Lower Promenade, Main, A and Restaurant Decks.

♦ 2 lower beds or converts to 1 queen size
○ Triple (two lower beds, one sofa bed)
▲ Two lower beds
♣ Triple (one double bed, one sofa bed)
▣ Quad (two lower beds, one sofa bed, one upper bed)
⊘ Shower only
● Bathtub and shower
△ Partially obstructed view
◇ One lower bed, one upper bed
★ One double bed

SPORTS DECK
SUN DECK
NAVIGATION DECK
UPPER PROMENADE DECK
PROMENADE DECK
LOWER PROMENADE DECK
MAIN DECK
A DECK
RESTAURANT DECK

• 52,000 gross tons
• 798 feet long
• 95 feet wide
• 101 feet high (to Sun Deck)
• Automatic Stabilizers
• 7 Passenger Elevators
• 18 Public Rooms
• 2 Outdoor Swimming Pools (one with sliding glass roof)
• Health Spa
• Movie Theater

• Duty Free Shops
• Library
• Beauty Parlor
• Deck Sports

318 ft. to stern
from rooms 021 and 022

318 ft. to stern
from room 087 and 088

85

APPENDIX F

A Cruise Brochure

Holland America Line
A TRADITION OF EXCELLENCE

1993
EUROPEAN CRUISES

Introducing the
ms Statendam

EUROPE

A TIMELESS ADVENTURE

Enduring, enveloping Europe. The very mention conjures up visions of grand palaces and centuries-old castles once defended by gallant knights. Of magnificent concert halls filled with the music of Mozart, Chopin, Strauss.

Of galleries studded with treasures by Michelangelo, Da Vinci, Monet. And Mediterranean shores unchanged since the days of the Roman Empire. Europe is a living museum. Vibrant, exciting and overflowing with thrilling places to visit and things to do. And now that the Wall and the Iron Curtain have been torn down in Germany and Eastern Europe, there's even more of it to savor. A reborn St. Petersburg. A reunited Berlin. A revolutionary new Europe! There's never been a better time to visit the Continent. Or a more luxurious way to experience it than aboard the newest ship to cruise its fjords and rivieras...Holland America Line's magnificent new ms Statendam (dazzling details on pages 4-5). Her twelve inaugural European cruises promise to be the events of the 1993 cruise season. 12-and 13-day cruises that let you discover the treasures of the Baltic, the splendor of Europe's great western cities, the magic of the Mediterranean. Plus one very fabulous 35-day Grand Europe Cruise that includes it all. Come, discover the new Europe — on the new ms Statendam.

Bernini's peerless baroque colonnades mark the way through St. Peter's Basilica in Rome.

CONTENTS

SET SAIL WITH A

TRADITION *of* EXCELLENCE

Breakfast in the dining room, the Lido or in bed . . . whatever is best for you.

"Welkom aan boord!" You turn to see an attractive young woman dressed in the traditional Dutch costume. Prim apron. Starched white cap. Her arms overflowing with long stem Apeldoorn tulips. Her friendly greeting coming straight from the heart. You both smile big smiles for the camera. You immediately feel the difference. Traditional little touches that set Holland America Line worlds apart from the others. Traditions that have prompted many to call us the world's best cruise line.

Your smile is our reward. Because we sail under a "tipping not required" policy.

Reputations for excellence are not built overnight. It's an art that takes years to perfect. Few cruise lines have such a long seafaring record as Holland America Line. None has such a distinguished one. We've been helping people discover new worlds for over 119 years. Actually, way before then, starting back in the 16th century when bold and skillful Dutch sea captains sailed out to explore new worlds and

made the Netherlands the foremost maritime power on the globe.

By the 19th century, when sail gave way to steam, Dutch ships were in the forefront bringing the Old World and the New closer together — with regular monthly service between The Netherlands and New York. By the time the Twenties roared around,

famed transAtlantic luxury liners such as Holland America's Rotterdam abandoned the rigors of the wintertime North Atlantic and instead headed for the sunshine of the Mediterranean. Itineraries became increasingly diverse: trips to the North Cape and Spitzbergen, the Baltic and Black Seas, and the

Orient; voyages around South America and Africa; and four- and five-month circumnavigations of the globe. Every voyage was as great an adventure as the destination. With Holland America Line, it still is.

Today, as we commission the Statendam (newest member of our fine fleet) to Europe, we remind you of our rich maritime history. We also remind you that it is our people, the soul of our ships, that have given us our reputation for excellence.

You'll experience it in the warm hospitality of our Dutch captain and his officers, famed as much for their expert seamanship as for the care and thoroughness in everything they do.

In our Indonesian and Filipino crew, wonderfully gracious people who come from a heritage where providing service is an art, an honor. People who have it in their souls to be gentle and respectful and friendly. It's their approach to each other, to life, to you. And it comes straight from the heart in the countless little ways in which they are dedicated to seeing that your cruise is as perfect as can be. Like your waiter remembering your preferences from the first time you mention them to the end of your voyage. The maitre d'hotel accommodating your special dietary needs. Your room steward, always at your beck and call, turning down your bed at night, leaving a sweet dreams chocolate on your pillow.

It's the kind of service you won't find on any other cruise line. Only Holland America. Welkom aan boord! 🕸

A toast from your charming Dutch officers.

3

A GRAND NEW

A GRAND

Long and sleek and sparkling new, Holland America's ms Statendam sets sail with a century-old tradition of excellence.

Statendam. It's one of the best known names in ocean liner history…and one of the proudest names in Holland America Line's 119-year history. Four ships — circa 1898, 1916, 1927 and 1957 — have borne the Statendam name. Some were flagships of our fleet, all were favorites of our guests. And now, the ms Statendam of 1993 — with her added features and classic design— will carry Holland America's time-honored tradition of excellence well into the future.

4

ADVENTURE · ON
NEW SHIP

The ms Statendam is a beautiful ship. A triumph of the architects, designers and shipbuilder's art. They can be very proud. The moment you step on board, you realize that you are on a very special ship. A fine collection of European art. A three-story atrium with shops and cafes and promenades all around. Is this a luxury liner, or is this the greatest way to travel? Actually, the Statendam is both. For though the Statendam will carry you to Europe's most

Our tables are set with Rosenthal china and fine silver, but it is our dining room staff that is the real celebration, always attentive, always near, but never intrusive.

A dancing fountain at the heart of a three story atrium.

glamorous cities, she's a destination all her own. Wherever she is…she's the perfect place to be…every bit as exciting as the European ports she'll visit.

On board are all the amenities you would expect of a grand luxury ship. And many you wouldn't. Imagine sipping espresso in a cafe reminiscent of one on the Champs-Elysees. Ordering lunch on the Lido deck from a pasta bar that rivals those of Naples. Or dining in a restaurant with a sweeping view of Venice, or wherever the Statendam happens to be.

(We've thoughtfully located the two-tiered Rotterdam Dining Room at the stern of the ship, providing unsurpassed views on three sides.)

There are spacious teak decks dotted with swimming pools and whirlpool spas. And an Ocean Spa that looks like it belongs on the French Riviera — saunas, steam rooms, Swedish massage, views of Europe while you're working out.

Between shopping sprees in Paris, Rome and London, there's the Statendam's glittering arcade. Duty-free with names that please…Dior,

Chanel, Waterford. There's a mini Monte Carlo in the casino. Big-name entertainment in the Van Gogh Show Lounge. The Late Night Buffet in the wonderful Lido Restaurant, hallmark of every Holland America Line ship, with its charming bar on one side, a swimming pool on the other, and the ocean all around.

The dazzling new Statendam. She is a ship with a Continental flair. An affinity for elegance. A respect for tradition. Come, be among the first to experience her many charms as she cruises the scenic rivieras of Europe. ❧

5

EUROPEAN ODYSSEY

Multi-million dollar yachts in the harbor, a debonair crowd in the casino . . . the Monaco of legend.

The adventure begins conveniently in *New York,* the vibrant city that has welcomed so many Holland America Line ships through history. You board, feeling somewhat smug in the fact that, although you are traveling to Europe during the peak season, you will manage to elude the crowds. With the Statendam as your home base, there will be no crowded train depots or hectic city traffic to contend with. No hotels to check in and out of. No sense of racing from city to city trying to fit it all in.

Instead, your European holiday will be relaxed, leisurely, enjoyed one exciting port at a time. It

OUR GRAND EUROPE CRUISE

Imagine: 35 glorious days to and within Europe. Rolling the dice in Monte Carlo one day. Sipping wine in an elegant French chateau the next. All the while enjoying the uncommon luxuries of one of the most sensational ships ever to cruise the Continent —Holland America Line's grand new ms Statendam.

will be a holiday that is, in some way, perhaps even life changing.

You settle into the Statendam's spacious Mondriaan Lounge topside, your window to the world. To port, Manhattan. To starboard, the famed Statue of Liberty. Ahead, a European encounter of the most wonderful kind. Although barely an hour at sea, you're already in another world, navigating by your own special sense of time. Gradually, all that once seemed important gives way to the gentle rhythm of the sea. You discover that you don't need cash — for the beverage you're having in

Welcome to Bordeaux," the region of fine wines and fine dining."

the lounge, for souvenirs and gifts from the duty-free shopping arcade, for shore excursions or anything else. You are now living in Holland America Line's famous cashless society. Just sign for anything you want.

You also discover that a transAtlantic cruise is the most luxurious way to travel between North America and Europe. First, a perfectly timed spring-time stop in sunny *Hamilton, Bermuda* to explore scenic flower-bordered roads and pink sand beaches. Then it's five carefree days to unwind. Playing on magnificent teak decks. Dancing in chandeliered ballrooms. Sipping champagne from sparkling goblets. Anticipating the excitement that lies ahead. Meeting new friends with whom you may share the experience.

Suddenly, there's *Horta*

Famous in Pisa, the tower by Pisano.

EUROPEAN ODYSSEY

in the Azores, a group of unspoiled mountainous islands that seem to appear from out of the blue. Step ashore. There's Caldeira, a crater created by a now-extinct volcano, to contemplate, a spectacular coast road to drive, distinctive lace made of agave thread to buy.

Enjoy the remarkable sculpture of the cathedral and baptistry of Florence.

You arrive on the Continent — on Spain's famed Costa del Sol, no less — relaxed, refreshed and ready to sightsee.

From *Malaga,* travel to *Granada,* site of the fantastic Alhambra Moorish palace, stunningly beautiful with its pinkish walls, delicately carved columns and luxuriant fountains — the closest you may come to an "Arabian Nights" setting.

In the heart of France's fabled Cote d'Azur is Monaco, the tiny jeweled principality of the rich and famous. *Monte Carlo's* elegant 120-year-old casino, resplendent in red velvet, crystal chandeliers and gilded ceilings. Here Richard regaled Liz with the huge diamond. Mata Hari shot a Russian spy. And the Englishman Charles Deville Wells broke the bank repeatedly and turned 10,000 gold francs into a million. You can try your own luck.

Your arrival in *Livorno* means an optional shore excursion to see *Pisa's* world-famous Leaning Tower, tilting 14 feet out of perpendicular. And to *Florence,* epicenter of the Italian Renaissance.

Everywhere, find prime examples of that glorious age. Michelangelo's *David* at the Academia. Works by da Vinci, Botticelli and Raphael at the extraordinary Uffizi Gallery. Brunelleschi's fabulous Duomo. Ghiberti's Gates of Paradise!

When in *Rome* for two full days and overnight, do as the Romans do. Pause for a cappuccino in a charming sidewalk cafe. Shop little boutiques

of high fashion on the trendy Via Condotti. Do the monuments: the Colosseum, Forum and Pantheon, the Spanish Steps, the Vatican where you will find the serene beauty of the Sistine Chapel. Bella Roma, no? Bella Roma, Si!

Completing her grand sweep through the Mediterranean, the Statendam visits *Palma de Mallorca,* on the largest of Spain's Balearic Islands. Shop for

famous Mallorcan pearls. Explore the Caves of Drach with their fantastic underground lakes and forests of stalagmites and stalactites. Travel to nearby Valldemosa to hear the story of Chopin's and George Sands' romantic winter of 1838.

Rounding the Rock of Gibraltar, *Lisbon* is next. You'll have from noon 'til noon to experience everything from the imposing Moorish castle

The canals of Amsterdam flow into a countryside dotted with picturesque windmills.

of Sao Jorge to Lisbon's after-dark charm…a carafe of red wine, *cabrito assado,* the haunting medley of the Portuguese *fado* songs.

From the port of La Coruna, make your pilgrimage to *Santiago di Compostela,* one of the three holy cities of the Middle Ages. As many as two million pilgrims a year "took up the cockleshell" — the sign of St. James the Apostle — and made the journey to the grandiose cathedral built over his tomb.

One of the many joys of the Statendam is the impressive wine list featuring the specialties of some countries you'll visit… Italian Chianti, French Bordeaux. Appropriately, the Statendam pauses in *Bordeaux, France,* gateway to the elegant chateau wineries that produce the region's world-famous wines. Tastings included, of course. Salut!

In *Zeebrugge, Belgium,* optional excursions are possible to *Brugge,* the Venice of the North with its romantic canals, weeping willows and graceful swans. And to *Brussels,* cockpit of the western world, seat of the European Economic Community and NATO.

Next is delightful *Amsterdam,* where you may cruise its famed canals and visit museums housing masterpieces by Rembrandt and Van Gogh.

Then into the Baltic for a sampling of Scandinavia. In *Copenhagen,* once upon a time is right now – in the home of Hans Christian Andersen, the Tivoli Gardens, the Little Mermaid. In historic *Kalmar,* explore its imposing seaside castle, defender of Sweden for over 800 years. From *Warnemünde,* travel to a reunited Berlin. And in *Oslo,* visit museums devoted to the Vikings and their ships.

Finally, there is *Tilbury* on the Thames, gateway to an extended holiday in London. (See Page 24.) ❧

Taste the fruit of the vine at Bordeaux's towered and turreted Chateau La Riviere.

10

GRAND EUROPE CRUISE

35 DAYS   FROM $7,250

SAILING DATE FROM NEW YORK TO LONDON   May 7, 1993

DAY	DATE	PORT	ARRIVE	DEPART
FRI	MAY 7	NEW YORK, NEW YORK		4:30PM
SAT	MAY 8	At sea (Atlantic Ocean)		
SUN	MAY 9	Hamilton, Bermuda	8:00AM	4:00PM
MON-THU	MAY 10-13	At sea		
FRI	MAY 14	Horta, Azores	7:00AM	1:00PM
SAT-SUN	MAY 15-16	At sea (Atlantic Ocean)		
MON	MAY 17	Malaga/Granada, Spain	8:00AM	5:00PM
TUE	MAY 18	At sea (Balearic Sea)		
WED	MAY 19	Monte Carlo, Monaco	9:00AM	11:00PM
THU	MAY 20	Livorno/Florence/Pisa, Italy	8:00AM	11:00PM
FRI	MAY 21	Civitavecchia/Rome, Italy	8:00AM	
SAT	MAY 22	Civitavecchia		11:45PM
SUN	MAY 23	Scenic cruising by Sardinia and Corsica		
MON	MAY 24	Palma de Mallorca, Balearic Islands, Spain	8:00AM	5:00PM
TUE	MAY 25	At sea (Mediterranean Sea)		
WED	MAY 26	Lisbon, Portugal	NOON	
THU	MAY 27	Lisbon		NOON
FRI	MAY 28	La Coruna/Santiago di Compostela, Spain	8:00AM	11:00PM
SAT	MAY 29	At sea (Bay of Biscay)		
SUN	MAY 30	Bordeaux, France	7:00AM	6:00PM
MON	MAY 31	At sea (English Channel)		
TUE	JUN 1	Zeebrugge/Brugge/Brussels, Belgium	8:00AM	11:00PM
WED	JUN 2	Amsterdam, The Netherlands	8:00AM	11:00PM
THU	JUN 3	At sea (North Sea)		
FRI	JUN 4	Copenhagen, Denmark	9:00AM	
SAT	JUN 5	Copenhagen		1:00AM
SUN	JUN 6	Kalmar, Sweden	7:00AM	5:00PM
MON	JUN 7	Warnemünde/Berlin, Germany	7:00AM	11:00PM
TUE	JUN 8	At sea (Kattegat)		
WED	JUN 9	Oslo, Norway	8:00AM	6:00PM
THU	JUN 10	At sea (North Sea)		
FRI	JUN 11	TILBURY/LONDON, ENGLAND	8:00AM	

OUTSIDE STATEROOMS		GRAND EUROPE CRUISE
☐ PS Penthouse Suite		US $28,105
☐ S Suites		19,115
☐ A Deluxe		15,415
☐ B Deluxe		14,135
☐ C Standard		12,365
☐ D Standard		11,275
☐ E Standard		10,490
☐ F Standard		10,040
☐ G Standard		9,600
☐ H Standard		9,170

INSIDE STATEROOMS		
☐ I Standard		9,170
☐ J Standard		8,710
☐ K Standard		8,215
☐ L Standard		7,725
☐ M Standard		7,475
☐ N Standard		7,250
Each Guest Sharing Stateroom with Two Full-Fare Guests		3,625
Children Under Two Years Old Accompanied by Two Full-Fare Adults		250
Cruise Only Credit		300
Port Charges and Taxes		245
1st Deposit Requirement At Time Of Booking		1,000
2nd Deposit Requirement By November 4, 1992		2,000
Balance of payment due by January 4, 1993		
Cancellation Fees Waiver		300

Refer to deck plans on pages 26 and 27 for specific facilities in each stateroom.

B O O K   E A R L Y   A N D   S A V E

Grand Europe Cruise guests who have made reservations and deposit by **October 1, 1992**, save 10% on applicable fares. Does not apply to 3rd/4th guests.

Please refer to page 25 for our convenient Home City Air Program.

An evening cruise on the River Thames takes you under the Tower Bridge.

B·A·L·T
Treasures

ST. PETERSBURG, SCANDINAVIA, BERLIN WITHOUT WALLS

Summer. It's the perfect time to head for Northern Europe. To Scandinavia, Land of the Midnight Sun—Oslo, Stockholm, Helsinki, Copenhagen. To Russia and its great cities of St. Petersburg and Moscow, where world events have changed our lives. And to Berlin, a great metropolis reveling in the excitement of its new-found freedom. Our 13-night Baltic Cruises include it all. Plus London and Amsterdam.

Copenhagen's endearing landmark — the Little Mermaid.

Ah, the Fjords of Norway. So majestic, so breathtaking they defy explanation in mere words. Norway's most celebrated composer, Edvard Grieg, knew (as he gazed through the window of his fjord-side home) that only the crescendos of a full orchestra could offer just description. One, the Oslofjord, leads straight to the heart of *Oslo*, where many cultural attractions are devoted to the Vikings. Learn all about them at the wonderful Viking Ship Museum and the neighboring Norwegian Folk Museum.

Stockholm is a city whose natural beauty and national treasures have been jealously guarded by the city fathers. In Galma Stan (Old Town), 700-year-old buildings house 20th century boutiques and restaurants. Nearby is the huge Royal Palace, where you can watch the guard change, oogle the Crown Jewels and see the lovely State Rooms. And just outside Stockholm, lovely Drottningholm, the country home of the Swedish royal family and site of Europe's oldest continually operating theater, its original sets, stage machinery and props still in perfect working order.

Helsinki is a stroller's city, tidy and compact. Within a few blocks you'll find all the major sights: the colorful open-air market with its delicious summer bounty; the showrooms of famous

names in fabric, china and crystal...Marimekko, Arabia, Iittala; lovely Senate Square with its historic buildings and striking cathedral.

For a storybook adventure, *Copenhagen* calls. Everywhere, the fairy tale unfolds. In the harborside statue of Hans Christian Andersen's "Little Mermaid." In the gaily painted row houses on the quay.

In the thousands of twinkling lights illuminating the summer sky over the fantasyland that is Tivoli. Even the Stroget, Copenhagen's pedestrian-only shopping street, is a dream come true...famed Danish silver, glassware, arts and crafts.

Across the Baltic Sea lies Germany, whole again after nearly half a century. On November 9, 1989

Berlin's divisive Wall came tumbling down. On an optional shore excursion, relive the excitement and energy of that famous day as you stroll along Unter den Linden and through the Brandenburg Gate. On the other side, jewels hidden away for decades: Humboldt University, alma mater of Marx and Engels. The German

Berlin's Brandenburg Gate once again ushers visitors onto bustling Unter den Linden.

German State Opera House, built by Frederick the Great in 1743. A bevy of museums, including the Pergamon with its monumental altar. A charming outdoor cafe on the Spree Canal, the perfect spot to contemplate the significance of it all. ⁂

B·A·L·T·I·C *Treasures*

RUSSIA: THE CLASSIC & THE REBORN

Glorious Leningrad. Once Peter's. Once Lenin's. Today, with the Soviet Union reconstructed, suddenly Peter's again. Reborn, renamed St. Petersburg. Still Russia's great "Window on Europe." And, without doubt, the highlight of each of our 13-night Baltic Cruises.

Built on the shores of the Baltic, St. Petersburg is Peter the Great's vision, a city very nearly perfectly planned, its great beauty lying in the unsurpassed blend of Russian and Western European architecture. Isn't it wonderful how the colorful facades of the buildings are in striking contrast to the Northern skies. There's St. Isaac's Cathedral, aglow with malachite and other precious stones. Catherine the Great's magnificent blue and gold palace. And the primary destination for most visitors, the Hermitage, one of the largest, oldest and most expansive museums in the world. The name originally applied to a royal retreat Catherine built next to the Winter Palace. It now describes the entire museum — all five buildings, six major sections,

353 rooms. So much great art is packed into the rooms—8 Titians, 25 Rembrandts, 40 Rubens and many works by Monet — for example, that it is easy to miss a major masterpiece such as Raphael's *Madonna Connestabile* (Room 229). Or Picasso's various periods... Blue,

Pink and Cubist, Rooms 346 and 347.

Tonight, aboard the Statendam, Sevruga caviar in the Rotterdam Dining Room, a White Russian in the Explorer's Lounge.

Catherine the Great's Palace, regal curator of the world's great art.

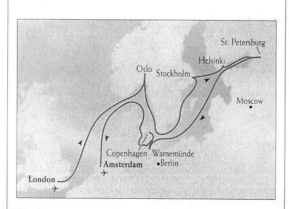

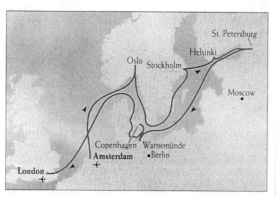

London to Amsterdam Cruise

13 DAYS   FROM $4,260

SAILING DATES FROM LONDON		June 11, July 7, August 2

DAY	PORT	ARRIVE	DEPART
0	TILBURY/LONDON, ENGLAND		5:00PM
1	At sea		
2	Oslo, Norway, Scenic Cruising Oslofjord	8:00AM	2:00PM
3	At sea (Baltic Sea)		
4	Stockholm, Sweden	NOON	6:00PM
5	Helsinki, Finland	10:00AM	6:00PM
6	St. Petersburg (Leningrad)/Moscow, Russia	7:00AM	
7	St. Petersburg		3:00PM
8	At sea (Baltic Sea)		
9	Warnemünde/Berlin, Germany	7:00AM	11:00PM
10	Copenhagen, Denmark	1:00PM	11:00PM
11	At sea (North Sea)		
12	Amsterdam, The Netherlands	9:00AM	
13	AMSTERDAM, disembark	8:00AM	

B O O K   E A R L Y   A N D   S A V E

Baltic Cruise guests save $250 if reservations and deposit are made by **March 1, 1993**. Does not apply to 3rd/4th guests.

Please refer to page 25 for our convenient Home City Air Program.

Amsterdam to London Cruise

13 DAYS   FROM $4,260

SAILING DATES FROM AMSTERDAM		June 24, July 20, August 15

DAY	PORT	ARRIVE	DEPART
0	AMSTERDAM, THE NETHERLANDS, embark		3:00PM
1	Amsterdam		12:45AM
2	Oslo, Norway, Scenic Cruising Oslofjord	7:00AM	2:00PM
3	At sea (Baltic Sea)		
4	Stockholm, Sweden	NOON	6:00PM
5	Helsinki, Finland	10:00AM	6:00PM
6	St. Petersburg (Leningrad)/Moscow, Russia	7:00AM	
7	St. Petersburg		3:00PM
8	At sea (Baltic Sea)		
9	Warnemünde/Berlin, Germany	7:00AM	11:00PM
10	Copenhagen, Denmark	1:00PM	7:00PM
11	At sea (North Sea)		
12	Tilbury/London, England	10:00AM	
13	TILBURY/LONDON, disembark	8:00AM	

OUTSIDE STATEROOMS		LONDON TO AMSTERDAM CRUISE	AMSTERDAM TO LONDON CRUISE
PS	Penthouse Suite	US $16,230	US $16,230
S	Suites	11,075	11,075
A	Deluxe	8,950	8,950
B	Deluxe	8,215	8,215
C	Standard	7,195	7,195
D	Standard	6,570	6,570
E	Standard	6,120	6,120
F	Standard	5,860	5,860
G	Standard	5,610	5,610
H	Standard	5,365	5,365
INSIDE STATEROOMS			
I	Standard	5,365	5,365
J	Standard	5,100	5,100
K	Standard	4,800	4,800
L	Standard	4,535	4,535
M	Standard	4,395	4,395
N	Standard	4,260	4,260
Each Guest Sharing Stateroom with Two Full-Fare Guests		2,130	2,130
Children Under Two Years Old Accompanied by Two Full-Fare Adults		250	250
Cruise Only Credit		600	600
Port Charges and Taxes		90	90
Deposit Requirement		650	650
Cancellation Fees Waiver		159	159

Refer to deck plans on pages 26 and 27 for specific facilities in each stateroom.

GLORIOUS CITIES, GLITTERING ISLANDS, GLAMOROUS RIVIERAS

To sail the Mediterranean is to take a journey through time. Past centuries of civilizations and remnants of eras gone by. When great kings and caesars ruled from splendid palaces. And bold sea captains ventured across the deep blue waters of the Mediterranean in search of new worlds. Today, millions travel to the Mediterranean… to bask in warm, golden sunshine, to throw the dice in ornate casinos, to wander through towns unchanged since medieval days. It is the perfect setting for a cruise vacation. And no one offers more excitement, more variety in a Mediterranean cruise than Holland America Line.

MEDITERRANE MAGIC

Four 12-day cruises. Each one unique. Each one featuring a very special part of Europe and Mediterranean.

◆ August 28 *European Capitals Cruise*–London to Rome, with opportunities to visit six of Western Europe's great capital cities.

◆ September 9 *Eastern Mediterranean Cruise*–round trip from Rome, featuring Venice, Athens and the Greek Islands.

◆ September 21 *Western Mediterranean Cruise*–round trip from Rome, featuring the French, Italian and Spanish Rivieras.

◆ October 3 *Rome to Lisbon Cruise*–featuring Florence, Monaco, Grenada and Gibraltar.

Which will it be? A question with no wrong answers, but wonderful choices to have.

AUGUST 28 EUROPEAN CAPITALS CRUISE

There is nothing like a city. It is man's ultimate artifact, the object in which his genius is most comprehensively, most intensely displayed. Nowhere will you find that energy better displayed than in the glorious capital cities of Europe. And nowhere will you find

Behold, the Eiffel Tower at evening, every girder lit in glorious detail.

a more thoroughly enjoyable way to visit them than on Holland America Line's European Capitals cruise. With the Statendam as your floating hotel, you'll visit each city, with no concern about where to go or what to see. Because our guest lecturers and knowledgeable cruise staff will have already filled you in; and you will have already planned each landing from a wide choice of optional shore excursions.

The excitement begins in *London*, home of the

Inside Rome's Colosseum, there are ghosts of gladiators to discover.

the casbah-like streets of the Alfama.

From Cadiz it is a short drive to *Seville* in the heart of storybook Andalusia. It's all here, everything you've ever dreamed of Spain. The drama of the opera…Don Giovanni, Carmen, the Barber of Seville. The thrill of the bullfight. The flair of flamenco. The quintessential Spanish community… white-washed stucco houses with lacy wrought iron balconies and cascades of scarlet geraniums. Si. Seville!

After whirling the roulette wheel in the Statendam's casino (and a gambling lesson from the cruise staff) you arrive in *Monte Carlo* ready to take on all bets.

Finally, there is *Civitavecchia*, your portal to *Rome*, the Eternal City where the moment is everything. Especially to visitors with a passion for all things Italian — Gucci, Armani, fettaccine at Alfredo's. A post-cruise vacation will give you the opportunity to experience it all.

SEPTEMBER 9 EASTERN MEDITERRANEAN CRUISE
Have you ever dreamed of riding a gondola down the

Queen. (Come early and take advantage of a pre-cruise package and you'll have time to watch the changing of the guard at her royal palace.)

Amsterdam is next, a full day to enjoy its many Dutch treats: the Museum Quarter with its Van Goghs and Rembrandts, the flower market bursting with color, the diamond houses, sparkling with "Amsterdam cuts." Tonight, a Dutch treat from Holland America: the first of many glittering stage revues in the fabulous Van

Gogh Show Lounge.

Zeebrugge, Belgium, is your gateway to *Brugges*, lovely city in Flanders fields; and *Brussels*, the city that aspires to become the "capital of Europe." Both the perfect place to sample a famous Belgium waffle, and to buy a yard of lace.

Ah, then there is romantic *Paris*, easily reached from the port of *La Havre*. What will be your pleasure madame, monsieur? A leisurely stroll along the Champs-Elysees to view the fabulous Arc de Triomphe? A trip to the

top of the Eiffel Tower? A browse through the new Louvre? Tonight, in the Rotterdam dining room, enjoy cuisine as fine as you'll find in any Parisian restaurant. Escargots bourguignonne. Consomme Francaise. Caesar Salad. Duckling a L'Orange. Crepes Suzette, flamed to perfection.

In *Lisbon* it is the Moors who left their mark. In the imposing castle of Sao Jorge, its ancient walls enclosing lovely gardens, streams, and strutting white peacocks. And in

MEDITERRANEAN MAGIC

Dazzling white chapels on the Island of Mykonos.

graceful canals of Venice, past palaces from which the Doges once ruled? Sipping metaxa in the glow of a Greek Island sunset? Strolling through Imperial Rome, past the Colosseum, the Pantheon, the memories of Caesar and Cicero? Then come along, as the Statendam makes her appearance in some of the most alluring, sight-filled ports in the Mediterranean, Adriatic and Aegean seas.

First, a leisurely day cruising to the famous resort, *Taormina*, the pride of Sicily since Roman times. Next, *Valletta*, the capital of Malta, its lengthy list of conquerors reading like a "who's who" of Mediterranean history. Will you step ashore to explore the Grand Master's Palace, legacy of the heroic Knights of the Order of St. John? Or will you remain on board seeking conquests of your own…at bridge, backgammon, jackpot bingo!

And now, *Venezia!* As you sip your morning coffee in the ambiance of the Rotterdam Dining Room, the vistas of the city embrace you from three sides – a panoramic view of Venice right from your breakfast table. With that preview, you're off to see the sights: St. Mark's Cathedral, the Doge's Palace, the Bridge of Sigh's.

In *Athens*, center of the classical world, stand in the shadow of Athena's Parthenon one moment, shop the flea market for shaggy flokati rugs the next. Then answer the call of the Oracle on an optional excursion to Delphi, Greece's magical archeological site.

Then on to the glorious Greek island of *Mykonos*. Can you find your way out of its maze of narrow, twisting alleyways lined with chic boutiques, galleries, tavernas? Or do you want to?

On *Corfu*, there are groves of ancient olive trees to stroll. The beautiful beaches of Paleokastritsa to explore. Tales of Odysseus to hear.

As you cruise through Italy's *Lipari Islands*, you find a comfortable deck chair on the Lido (close to the pool and pasta bar) and watch as the tiny islands parade by. Right past the smoldering islet of *Stromboli*.

Returning to Rome, you have the full day for further exploration and the Statendam is your home for the night.

SEPTEMBER 21 WESTERN MEDITERRANEAN CRUISE

Who among us hasn't dreamed of perfect summer days on the Italian and French Rivieras? Joining the jet setters at the gaming tables of Monte Carlo one day, sipping cappuccino in a Portofino cafe the next. The experience can be yours on our Western Mediterranean Cruise.

As the Statendam sails from Rome, you settle into your luxurious stateroom, home for the next 12 days. A flyer is slipped under your door announcing shore excursions tomorrow in *Naples*. Which will it be? The ruins of Pompeii? The heart-stopping vistas of Amalfi Drive? The beautiful Isle of Capri and its enchanting Blue Grotto?

After a cruise by smouldering Stromboli and visits to *Messina* and *Malta*, all things Spanish are next. A calypso lesson in the Queen's Lounge. A cool Sangria poolside on the Lido. The isle of *Mallorca*, famous for its pearls. And *Barcelona*, where you'll find the "Modernismo" fantasies of architect Antonio Gaudi, including his Church of Sacred Family, its intriguing open-work spires dominating the city.

From Sete, France, travel to *Carcassonne*, a fortified medieval town alive with boutiques and quaint cafes specializing in the city's famous *cassoulet*.

The Statendam will spend the full day and evening in *Monte Carlo*. If you leave the casino shortly before sailing, breakfast in bed in the morning will be welcome… hot coffee, croissants, fruit yogurt… just as you ordered it the day before.

After the excitement of Monte Carlo, you'll love *Portofino*. Quaint. Quiet. Picturesque with its cobbled piazza and row of brightly-painted quayside houses.

The lovely charm of a Spanish Senorita!

Then on to *Ajaccio*, Corsica's main town and port. There's Napoleon's birthplace to visit, robust wine to sample, the fresh, spicy scent of lavendar, thyme and rosemary to breath in.

OCTOBER 3 ROME TO LISBON CRUISE

The French, Italian and Spanish Rivieras. This cruise has it all, plus Madiera and the Canary Islands.

Sailing from *Rome*, it doesn't take long to adapt to the dolce vita lifestyle. There's cappucino in the Java Cafe. A pasta bar and a whirlpool on the Lido Deck! And all kinds of touring possibilities on the Italian Riviera: *Florence*, birthplace of the Italian Renaissance; *Pisa*, home of the famous Leaning Tower. *Milan*, home of the world-famous La Scala opera house, lavish in red velvet, forever reveling in the performances of Caruso and Pavarotti.

In the heart of France's fabled Cote d'Azur is *Villefranche*, your portal to the delights of the French Riviera. To the east is the postage-stamp Principality of Monaco with its famed casino of *Monte Carlo*. To the west, *Nice*, Queen of the Riviera. And all around, the dazzling Mediterranean light that enchanted Picasso, Matisse and Chagall.

Next, a rare treat. From Sete, travel to the walled city of *Carcassonne*, an agglomeration of fortifications dating back to the 1st century Roman Empire. In this city of winding streets, stone and half-timbered houses, time stands still. Listen very carefully and you may hear the knights gallop through the gates.

On the Spanish Riviera, call at Malaga, gateway to *Granada* and the enchanted world of the Alhambra Palace.

Next, *Gibraltar*. A bit of Britain clinging tenaciously to a cliff between Spain and the sea. Among the attractions here: the mischievous Barbary Apes; St. Michael's Cave; any friendly pub along Main Street.

A leisurely loop into the Atlantic takes you to *Las Palmas* on Grand Canary; and to lovely *Madeira*, an island that's as soft and sweet as her wine.

En route to *Lisbon*, the breeze is fresh. The sea, azure. In the splendor of a Mediterranean sunset you share a cocktail with friends. Perhaps in the lively Ocean Bar. Perhaps on the private verandah of your elegant suite. A silver moon rises out of a purple sky. This is dolce vita. This is Holland America's Mediterranean.

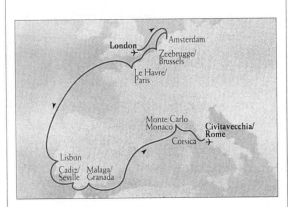

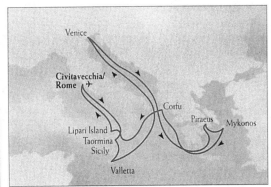

European Capitals Cruise

12 DAYS			FROM $3,750	

SAILING DATE FROM LONDON				August 28

DAY	DATE	PORT	ARRIVE	DEPART
SAT	AUG 28	TILBURY/LONDON, ENGLAND		5:00PM
SUN	AUG 29	Amsterdam, The Netherlands	9:00AM	11:00PM
MON	AUG 30	Zeebrugge/Brussels, Belgium	9:00AM	7:00PM
TUE	AUG 31	Le Havre/Paris, France	7:00AM	
WED	SEP 1	Le Havre		1:00AM
THU	SEP 2	At sea (Atlantic Ocean)		
FRI	SEP 3	Lisbon, Portugal	7:00AM	6:00PM
SAT	SEP 4	Cadiz/Seville, Spain	9:00AM	11:00PM
SUN	SEP 5	Malaga/Granada, Spain	8:00AM	5:00PM
MON	SEP 6	At sea (Mediterranean)		
TUE	SEP 7	Monte Carlo, Monaco	9:00AM	
WED	SEP 8	Monte Carlo		1:00PM
		Scenic cruising by Corsica		
THU	SEP 9	CIVITAVECCHIA/ROME, ITALY	7:00AM	

OUTSIDE STATEROOMS		EUROPEAN CAPITALS CRUISE	EASTERN MEDITERRANEAN CRUISE
PS	Penthouse Suite	US $14,240	US $14,240
S	Suites	9,720	9,720
A	Deluxe	7,860	7,860
B	Deluxe	7,210	7,210
C	Standard	6,325	6,325
D	Standard	5,780	5,780
E	Standard	5,380	5,380
F	Standard	5,155	5,155
G	Standard	4,930	4,930
H	Standard	4,715	4,715

INSIDE STATEROOMS			
I	Standard	4,715	4,715
J	Standard	4,485	4,485
K	Standard	4,230	4,230
L	Standard	3,995	3,995
M	Standard	3,870	3,870
N	Standard	3,750	3,750
Each Guest Sharing Stateroom with Two Full-Fare Guests		1,875	1,875
Children Under Two Years Old Accompanied by Two Full-Fare Adults		250	250
Cruise Only Credit		600	600
Port Charges and Taxes		100	90
Deposit Requirement		600	600
Cancellation Fees Waiver		159	159

Refer to deck plans on pages 26 and 27 for specific facilities in each stateroom.

Eastern Mediterranean Cruise

12 DAYS			FROM $3,750	

SAILING DATE FROM ROME				September 9

DAY	DATE	PORT	ARRIVE	DEPART
THU	SEP 9	CIVITAVECCHIA/ROME, ITALY		5:00PM
FRI	SEP 10	Scenic daylight cruising the Strait of Messina		
		Taormina, Sicily, Italy	NOON	6:00PM
SAT	SEP 11	Valletta, Malta	8:00AM	3:00PM
SUN	SEP 12	At sea (Adriatic Sea)		
MON	SEP 13	Venice, Italy	8:00AM	
TUE	SEP 14	Venice		2:00AM
WED	SEP 15	At sea		
THU	SEP 16	Piraeus/Athens, Greece	8:00AM	11:00PM
FRI	SEP 17	Mykonos, Greece	7:30AM	1:00PM
SAT	SEP 18	Corfu, Greece	12:30PM	6:30PM
SUN	SEP 19	Scenic cruising by Stromboli Volcano		
		Lipari Island, Italy	NOON	6:00PM
MON	SEP 20	Civitavecchia/Rome, Italy	9:00AM	
TUE	SEP 21	CIVITAVECCHIA/ROME disembark	7:00AM	

Athens' Parthenon, still breathtaking despite the ravages of time.

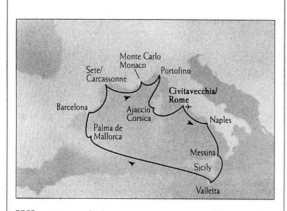

WESTERN MEDITERRANEAN CRUISE

12 DAYS   FROM **$3,750**

SAILING DATE FROM ROME				September 21
DAY	DATE	PORT	ARRIVE	DEPART
TUE	SEP 21	CIVITAVECCHIA/ROME, ITALY		5:00PM
WED	SEP 22	Naples, Italy	7:00AM	11:00PM
THU	SEP 23	Scenic cruising by Stromboli Volcano	8:00AM	10:00AM
		Messina, Sicily, Italy	1:00PM	7:00PM
		Cruising the Strait of Messina		
FRI	SEP 24	Valletta, Malta	8:00AM	5:00PM
SAT	SEP 25	At sea (Mediterranean Sea)		
SUN	SEP 26	Palma de Mallorca,		
		Balearic Islands, Spain	8:00AM	5:00PM
MON	SEP 27	Barcelona, Spain	8:00AM	11:00PM
TUE	SEP 28	Sete/Carcassonne, France	8:00AM	6:00PM
WED	SEP 29	Monte Carlo, Monaco	8:00AM	
THU	SEP 30	Monte Carlo		1:00AM
		Portofino, Italy	8:00AM	5:00PM
FRI	OCT 1	Ajaccio, Corsica, France	8:00AM	5:00PM
SAT	OCT 2	Scenic cruising by Corsica		
		and Sardinia, cruising the		
		Strait of Bonifacio		
SUN	OCT 3	CIVITAVECCHIA/ROME, ITALY	7:00AM	

B O O K   E A R L Y   A N D   S A V E

European Capitals, Eastern and Western Mediterranean and Rome to Lisbon Cruise guests save $250 if reservations and deposit are made by **May 1, 1993**. Does not apply to 3rd/4th guests.

Please refer to page 25 for our convenient Home City Air Program.

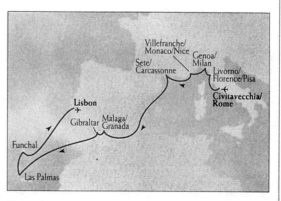

ROME TO LISBON CRUISE

12 DAYS   FROM **$3,750**

SAILING DATE FROM ROME				October 3
DAY	DATE	PORT	ARRIVE	DEPART
SUN	OCT 3	CIVITAVECCHIA/ROME, ITALY		5:00PM
MON	OCT 4	Livorno/Florence/Pisa, Italy	7:00AM	11:00PM
TUE	OCT 5	Genoa/Milan, Italy	7:00AM	11:00PM
WED	OCT 6	Villefranche/Nice, France, Monaco	7:00AM	6:00PM
THU	OCT 7	Sete/Carcassonne, France	7:00AM	6:00PM
FRI	OCT 8	At sea (Balearic Sea)		
SAT	OCT 9	Malaga/Granada, Spain	7:00AM	11:00PM
SUN	OCT 10	Scenic cruising the Bay of Gibraltar		
		Gibraltar	10:00AM	5:00PM
MON	OCT 11	At sea (Atlantic Ocean)		
TUE	OCT 12	Las Palmas, Canary Islands	8:00AM	5:00PM
WED	OCT 13	Funchal, Madeira Islands	9:00AM	6:00PM
THU	OCT 14	At sea (Atlantic Ocean)		
FRI	OCT 15	LISBON, PORTUGAL	7:00AM	

OUTSIDE STATEROOMS		WESTERN MEDITERRANEAN CRUISE	ROME TO LISBON CRUISE
PS	Penthouse Suite	US $14,240	US $14,240
S	Suites	9,720	9,720
A	Deluxe	7,860	7,860
B	Deluxe	7,210	7,210
C	Standard	6,325	6,325
D	Standard	5,780	5,780
E	Standard	5,380	5,380
F	Standard	5,155	5,155
G	Standard	4,930	4,930
H	Standard	4,715	4,715
INSIDE STATEROOMS			
I	Standard	4,715	4,715
J	Standard	4,485	4,485
K	Standard	4,230	4,230
L	Standard	3,995	3,995
M	Standard	3,870	3,870
N	Standard	3,750	3,750
Each Guest Sharing Stateroom with Two Full-Fare Guests		1,875	1,875
Children Under Two Years Old Accompanied by Two Full-Fare Adults		250	250
Cruise Only Credit		600	600
Port Charges and Taxes		110	125
Deposit Requirement		600	600
Cancellation Fees Waiver		159	159

Refer to deck plans on pages 26 and 27 for specific facilities in each stateroom.

Portuguese fishermen mending their nets.

T H E   E S S E N C E   O f   R E L A X A T I O N

The Classic Atlantic

Have you ever dreamed of a grand and glorious cruise? Of leaving routine behind for days that flow by as sweetly as a dream? Of sailing aboard a ship that ·brings back the glamour, romance and service of those early-day TransAtlantic crossings?

Well, your dreams have been fulfilled. In the fall of 1993, the ms Statendam — the newest addition to our fleet — will make a momentous 10-night voyage, charting a course from Lisbon, Portugal to Ft. Lauderdale, Florida.

One day out of Lisbon and there's still Portugal — the *Azores*, legendary islands of the lost Continent of Atlantis. Step ashore in *Ponta Delgada* to explore the island of Sao Miguel. Then it's five glorious days at sea — lounging on teak decks, dining on exquisite cuisine, being entertained till the wee hours. Doing everything, or nothing at all. Because that's what this cruise is all about: doing what you please, when you please, without a thought to tomorrow.

All too soon, you're on the other side of the ocean, in *Hamilton, Bermuda*, where beaches gleam pink in the noon-day sun and helmeted "bobbies" in Bermuda shorts direct traffic from a "Birdcage." Then there's Ft. Lauderdale, not the end of a wonderful cruise, but the beginning of a lifetime of memories. ༄

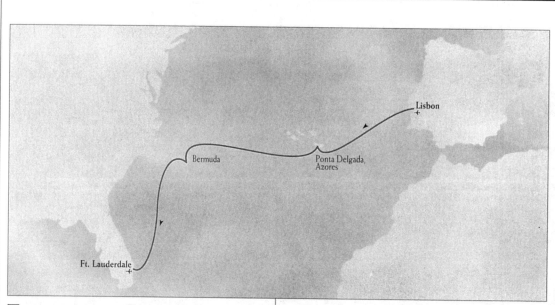

TRANSATLANTIC CRUISE

10 DAYS   FROM $2,495

SAILING DATE FROM LISBON				October 22
DAY	DATE	PORT	ARRIVE	DEPART
FRI	OCT 22	LISBON, PORTUGAL		5:00PM
SAT	OCT 23	At sea (Atlantic Ocean)		
SUN	OCT 24	Ponta Delgada, Azores	NOON	6:00PM
MON-THU	OCT 25-28	At sea (Atlantic Ocean)		
FRI	OCT 29	Hamilton, Bermuda	8:00AM	4:00PM
SAT-SUN	OCT 30-31	At sea (Atlantic Ocean)		
MON	NOV 1	FT. LAUDERDALE, FLORIDA	8:00AM	

Blue sky, warm sun, sandy beaches. Bermuda has everything you'd want in a tropical isle.

OUTSIDE STATEROOMS		TRANSATLANTIC CRUISE
PS	Penthouse Suite	US $9,675
S	Suites	6,580
A	Deluxe	5,305
B	Deluxe	4,865
C	Standard	4,255
D	Standard	3,880
E	Standard	3,610
F	Standard	3,460
G	Standard	3,305
H	Standard	3,155
INSIDE STATEROOMS		
I	Standard	3,155
J	Standard	3,000
K	Standard	2,830
L	Standard	2,655
M	Standard	2,570
N	Standard	2,495
Each Guest Sharing Stateroom with Two Full-Fare Guests		1,250
Children Under Two Years Old Accompanied by Two Full-Fare Adults		250
Cruise Only Credit		300
Port Charges and Taxes		175
Deposit Requirements		400
Cancellation Fees Waiver		74

Refer to deck plans on pages 26 and 27 for specific facilities in each stateroom.

B O O K   E A R L Y   A N D   S A V E

Transatlantic Cruise guests save $250 if reservations and deposit are made by **June 1, 1993**. Does not apply to 3rd/4th guests.

Please refer to page 25 for our convenient Home City Air Program.

PRE-AND POST-CRUISE VACATION PACKAGES

You'll be embarking and disembarking in some of the most exciting cities in the world. London. Amsterdam. Rome. Lisbon. As long as you're here, why not see the sights with our special pre-and post-cruise packages.

Don't miss the Queen's Guards!

LONDON

Samuel Johnson wrote, "When a man is tired of London he is tired of life." There are the grand buildings: the Tower of London and St. Paul's Cathedral, Westminster Abbey and the Houses of Parliament. Buckingham Palace, where the "Changing of the Guard" occurs daily at 11:30 a.m. The shopping treasures of Harrod's on Knightsbridge. Afternoon tea at three.
Package includes:
• Transfer between airport or ship and hotel.
• Two nights at the Grosvenor House hotel and baggage handling.
• Full English breakfast daily.
• 3-1/2 hour West End Sightseeing Tour.
• Transfer between hotel and ship or airport.

Single	US $640
Double	$415
3rd/4th Person*	$200

AMSTERDAM

"Welkom" to Europe's most fun-loving city. It even looks like fun, with its flower-bedecked gabled houses and maze of canals - more than even Venice. In the colorful markets, cheeses transcend gouda and edam. On the Rokin, diamond houses glitter with millions of "Amsterdam cuts." And splendid art museums house the works of native sons Van Gogh and Rembrandt. Equally stirring is a visit to the Anne Frank Huis, where the young Jewish girl and her family hid from the Nazis.
Package includes:
• Transfer between airport or ship and hotel.
• 2 nights at the Amsterdam Marriott Hotel and baggage handling.
• 3 hour city sightseeing tour.
• Transfer between hotel and airport or ship.

Single	US $475
Double	$265
3rd/4th Person*	$155

ROME

Roma non basta una vita - "For Rome, one life is not enough." Plan your time here carefully, as the Eternal City's sights are endless - and awe-inspiring. You'll head instinctively for the Vatican and its splendid Sistine Chapel. The Roman Forum, where Caesar once ruled. The Colosseum, theatre of the gladiators. The magnificent domed Pantheon, built by Agrippa in 27 B.C. The Spanish Steps and the Piazza de Spagna, ideal for people

Visit the Forum in Rome.

Among Holland's gifts to the world: Apeldoorn tulips and gouda cheese.

watching. Whatever you do, don't forget to toss a coin into the Trevi Fountain, to guarantee your return.
Package includes:
• Transfer between airport or ship and hotel.
• 2 nights at the Hotel Majestic Roma and baggage handling.
• American breakfast daily.
• 3 hour city sightseeing tour.
• Transfer between hotel and ship or airport.

Single	US $760
Double	$560
3rd/4th Person*	$320

LISBON

It was from this great city, in the Portuguese Age of Discovery, that Vasco de Gama navigated the Cape of Good Hope, Magellan, the world. Now it's your turn for discovery as you explore Lisbon's wide boulevards and cobblestone streets. There's the Alfama, the old Moorish quarter where you'll find the magnificent ruins of Castelo de Sao Jorge, its ancient walls enclosing lovely garden, streams, and strutting white peacocks. The Chiado, Lisbon's chic shopping district, brimming with art nouveau coffeehouses and Old World charm. And on the outskirts of the city, Belem, famous for its exquisite examples of Manueline architecture.

Lisbon is alive with theatre, dance and colorful costumes.

Package includes:
• Transfers between airport or ship and hotel.
• 2 nights at the Le Meridien hotel with baggage handling.
• American buffet breakfast daily.
• 3 hour city sightseeing tour.
• Transfer between hotel and airport or ship.

Single	US $635
Double	$395
3rd/4th Person*	$235

*3rd/4th persons will be accommodated in rooms with 2 double beds.

All of the above rates are per person in US dollars and subject to change without notice. Similar hotels may be substituted when necessary.

Fly Cruise Plan

ms Statendam European cruises are made very affordable with Holland America's Fly Cruise Plan. Depending on your Home City, you either fly free or at substantially reduced fares to and from the cruise of your choice. Check the air gateways listed on this page for the applicable fare from your home city. If the airport nearest yours is not on the our Home City Gateway list, you can still take advantage of this money-saving program. Just fly or drive to any of our Home City gateways listed and join the Holland America program from there.

Our Fly Cruise Plan also applies to third and fourth guests sharing a stateroom with two full-fare guests. Transfers to and from the airport and pier are included on days of (dis)embarkation.

Guests not requiring our Fly Cruise Plan to or from the ports of (dis)embarkation can deduct the Cruise Only Credit listed in the fare column for the cruise of your choice.

Special Assignment/ Special Requests

We regret that seat assignments/special requests cannot be confirmed. Your travel agent may assist with these arrangements within 30 days of flight departure. Air reservations do not include special assistance nor medical requests.

Overnight Hotel Accommodations

Due to airline schedules, overnight hotel accommodations may be required at the port of (dis)embarkation. Scheduling of flights and hotels used will be determined by Holland America.

The hotel accommodations, transfers between airport/hotel and hotel/pier as well as bellman gratuities are included in your cruise fare.

Guests not using the flights determined by Holland America, have the option of reserving hotel space at the hotels and at the rates listed in the next column.

New York, New York
New York Marriott Marquis Hotel

Single	US $310
Double	$190
3rd/4th Person*	$115

London, England
Grosvenor House Hotel

Single	US $315
Double	$205
3rd/4th Person*	$100

Amsterdam, Holland
Amsterdam Marriott Hotel

Single	US $235
Double	$130
3rd/4th Person*	$75

Rome, Italy
Hotel Majestic Roma

Single	US $395
Double	$295
3rd/4th Person*	$175

Lisbon, Portugal
Le Meridien Portugal Hotel

Single	US $315
Double	$195
3rd/4th Person*	$115

*3rd/4th persons will be accommodated in rooms with two double beds.

All of the above rates are per person, per night and include taxes, transfers between airport/hotel and hotel/pier as well as bellman gratuities, service charge and taxes. Breakfast included daily in London, Rome and Lisbon hotel rates. All rates are in U.S. dollars and subject to change without notice. Similar hotels of equal standard may be substituted when necessary.

General Air Information

Fly Cruise Plan reservations will be on a request only basis within thirty days of sailing. Within 15 days of sailing, Cruise Only reservations are available for sale.

Holland America reserves the right to change or alter flights as required by airline schedule changes or other factors beyond our control. If tickets are already in possession of the travel agent, the travel agent will be asked to re-validate or re-issue such tickets whenever possible.

Any change made by the guest in the air routing/fare basis of the airline ticket supplied in conjunction with Holland America's air program will be charged to the guest.

At the time of ticketing, Holland America will provide a roundtrip air ticket using the carriers, routing and structure of our choice. Most eastbound schedules will include an overnight flight across the Atlantic.

We will use applicable airfares in effect at the time of departure (subject to airline tariff rules and regulations). The airfares are based on capacity controlled, as well as promotional and group fares.

Stopovers will not be permitted.

A final flight itinerary will be sent with your travel documents.

The maximum refund for unused flight coupons shall be equal to the air add-on amount paid to Holland America, if any.

Home City Air Gateways

U.S. Gateways		1993 Europe Cruises	
FROM		FROM	
Akron/Canton, OH	US $300	Milwaukee, WI	US $300
Albany, NY	FREE	Minneapolis/St. Paul, MN	300
Albuquerque, NM	300	Nashville, TN	300
Allentown, PA	FREE	New Orleans, LA	300
Anchorage, AK	400	New York, NY	FREE
Atlanta, GA	FREE	Norfolk, VA	FREE
Austin, TX	300	Oakland, CA	400
Baltimore, MD	FREE	Oklahoma City, OK	300
Bangor, ME	FREE	Omaha, NE	300
Boston, MA	FREE	Orlando, FL	FREE
Buffalo, NY	FREE	Philadelphia, PA	FREE
Cedar Rapids, IA	300	Phoenix, AZ	400
Charlotte, NC	FREE	Pittsburgh, PA	FREE
Chicago, IL	300	Portland, ME	FREE
Cincinnati, OH	FREE	Portland, OR	400
Cleveland, OH	FREE	Providence, RI	FREE
Colorado Springs, CO	300	Raleigh/Durham, NC	FREE
Dallas/Ft. Worth, TX	300	Reno, NV	400
Dayton, OH	300	Richmond, VA	FREE
Denver, CO	300	Rochester, NY	FREE
Des Moines, IA	300	Sacramento, CA	400
Detroit, MI	300	St. Louis, MO	300
Ft. Lauderdale, FL	FREE	Salt Lake City, UT	400
Ft. Myers, FL	FREE	San Antonio, TX	300
Fresno, CA	400	San Diego, CA	400
Grand Rapids, MI	300	San Francisco, CA	400
Harrisburg, PA	FREE	San Jose, CA	400
Hartford, CT	FREE	Sarasota, FL	FREE
Honolulu, HI	400	Seattle/Tacoma, WA	400
Houston, TX	300	Spokane, WA	400
Indianapolis, IN	300	Syracuse, NY	FREE
Kansas City, MO	300	Tampa, FL	FREE
Las Vegas, NV	400	Tucson, AZ	400
Los Angeles, CA	400	Tulsa, OK	300
Louisville, KY	300	Washington, DC	FREE
Memphis, TN	300	West Palm Beach, FL	FREE
Miami, FL	FREE	Wichita, KS	300

Canadian Gateways			
FROM		FROM	
Calgary, AB	US $400	Toronto, ON	US $300
Edmonton, AB	400	Vancouver, BC	400
Montreal, PQ	300	Victoria, BC	400
Ottawa, ON	300	Winnipeg, MB	400

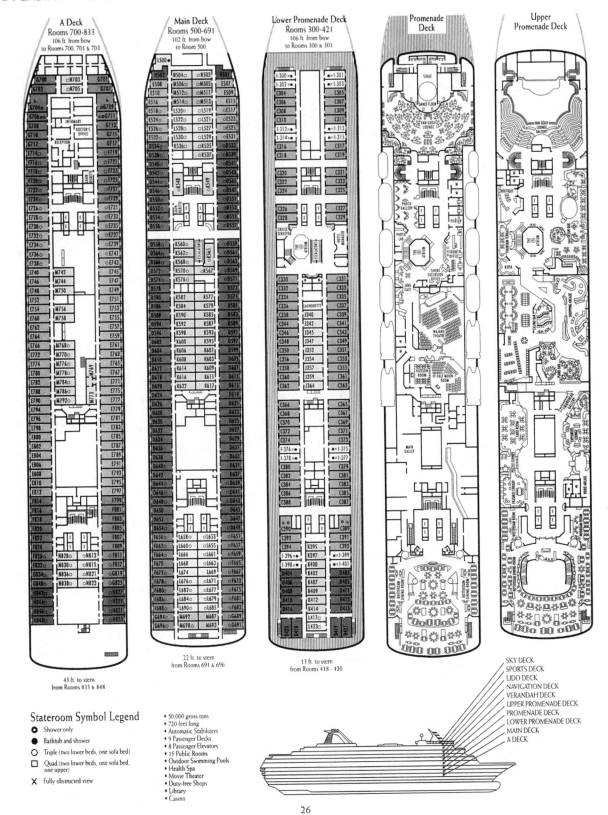

Stateroom Symbol Legend

- ● Shower only
- ● Bathtub and shower
- ○ Triple (two lower beds, one sofa bed)
- □ Quad (two lower beds, one sofa bed, one upper)
- X Fully obstructed view

- 50,000 gross tons
- 720 feet long
- Automatic Stabilizers
- 9 Passenger Decks
- 8 Passenger Elevators
- 15 Public Rooms
- Outdoor Swimming Pools
- Health Spa
- Movie Theater
- Duty-free Shops
- Library
- Casino

26

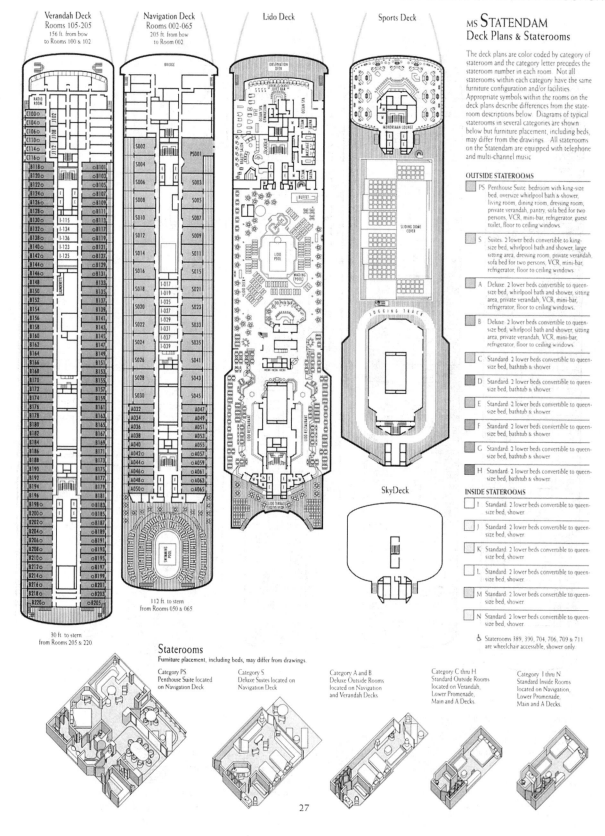

Verandah Deck
Rooms 105-205
156 ft. from bow
to Rooms 100 & 102

Navigation Deck
Rooms 002-065
205 ft. from bow
to Room 002

Lido Deck

Sports Deck

SkyDeck

30 ft. to stern
from Rooms 205 & 220

112 ft. to stern
from Rooms 050 & 065

ms STATENDAM
Deck Plans & Staterooms

The deck plans are color coded by category of stateroom and the category letter precedes the stateroom number in each room. Not all staterooms within each category have the same furniture configuration and/or facilities. Appropriate symbols within the rooms on the deck plans describe differences from the stateroom descriptions below. Diagrams of typical staterooms in several categories are shown below but furniture placement, including beds, may differ from the drawings. All staterooms on the Statendam are equipped with telephone and multi-channel music.

OUTSIDE STATEROOMS

PS Penthouse Suite: bedroom with king-size bed, oversize whirlpool bath & shower, living room, dining room, dressing room, private verandah, pantry, sofa bed for two persons, VCR, mini-bar, refrigerator, guest toilet, floor to ceiling windows.

S Suites: 2 lower beds convertible to king-size bed, whirlpool bath and shower, large sitting area, dressing room, private verandah, sofa bed for two persons, VCR, mini-bar, refrigerator, floor to ceiling windows.

A Deluxe: 2 lower beds convertible to queen-size bed, whirlpool bath and shower, sitting area, private verandah, VCR, mini-bar, refrigerator, floor to ceiling windows.

B Deluxe: 2 lower beds convertible to queen-size bed, whirlpool bath and shower, sitting area, private verandah, VCR, mini-bar, refrigerator, floor to ceiling windows.

C Standard: 2 lower beds convertible to queen-size bed, bathtub & shower.

D Standard: 2 lower beds convertible to queen-size bed, bathtub & shower.

E Standard: 2 lower beds convertible to queen-size bed, bathtub & shower.

F Standard: 2 lower beds convertible to queen-size bed, bathtub & shower.

G Standard: 2 lower beds convertible to queen-size bed, bathtub & shower.

H Standard: 2 lower beds convertible to queen-size bed, bathtub & shower.

INSIDE STATEROOMS

I Standard: 2 lower beds convertible to queen-size bed, shower.

J Standard: 2 lower beds convertible to queen-size bed, shower.

K Standard: 2 lower beds convertible to queen-size bed, shower.

L Standard: 2 lower beds convertible to queen-size bed, shower.

M Standard: 2 lower beds convertible to queen-size bed, shower.

N Standard: 2 lower beds convertible to queen-size bed, shower.

♿ Staterooms 389, 390, 704, 706, 709 & 711 are wheelchair accessible, shower only.

Staterooms
Furniture placement, including beds, may differ from drawings.

Category PS
Penthouse Suite located on Navigation Deck

Category S
Deluxe Suites located on Navigation Deck

Category A and B
Deluxe Outside Rooms located on Navigation and Verandah Decks.

Category C thru H
Standard Outside Rooms located on Verandah, Lower Promenade, Main and A Decks.

Category I thru N
Standard Inside Rooms located on Navigation, Lower Promenade, Main and A Decks.

27

MS STATENDAM STATEROOMS

The moment you step into your Statendam stateroom you'll gladly claim it as your "home away from home." For it is truly spacious. Comfortable too. There's room to kick off your shoes, relax and entertain. With room to spare for all your belongings. Full-length double closets and extra-deep chests of drawers.

Explore a little further and you'll find all the comforts of home. A direct dial phone, air conditioning that you control. French-milled soaps and fragrant shampoos. A closed-circuit TV to watch movies, shipboard activities and cruising previews in relaxed privacy. The stateroom descriptions below describe other amenities in the different categories of rooms. Pictured below are stateroom mockups constructed by the shipyard.

PS PENTHOUSE SUITE

The Statendam Penthouse Suite affords its occupants approximately 937 square feet of the ultimate in luxury and a 189 square foot private balcony adjoins the living area. Living room, dining room, private bedroom with king-size bed, extra large bathroom with over-size whirlpool bath and separate shower; dressing room, guest toilet. Even a pantry for exclusive room service. And, of course, a VCR, mini-bar and refrigerator. Floor to ceiling windows offer an unrestricted wide ocean view.

Approx. 1,126 sq. ft.
(incl. verandah)

S SUITES

Grand, gracious, elegant accommodations. Aside from the penthouse suite, our largest staterooms have a comfortable bedroom with two lower beds convertible to king-size bed, whirlpool bath and shower, large sitting area, dressing room, private verandah, sofa bed for two persons, VCR, mini-bar, refrigerator, floor to ceiling windows.

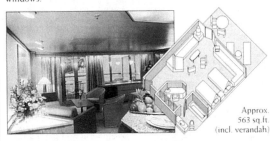

Approx.
563 sq. ft.
(incl. verandah)

A & B DELUXE OUTSIDE DOUBLE ROOMS

Luxuriously large and extremely desirable. These spacious staterooms give you two lower beds convertible to queen-size, whirlpool bath and shower, sitting area, private verandah, VCR, mini-bar, refrigerator and floor to ceiling windows.

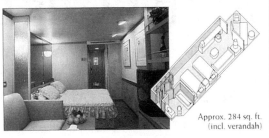

Approx. 284 sq. ft.
(incl. verandah)

C – H LARGE OUTSIDE DOUBLE ROOMS

These delightful large window staterooms are furnished with two lower beds convertible to queen-size bed, bathtub and shower.

Approx. 190 sq. ft.

I – N STANDARD INSIDE DOUBLE ROOMS

These comfortable rooms are furnished with two lower beds convertible to queen-size bed, shower and small sitting area.

Approx. 187 sq. ft.

WHAT YOU NEED TO KNOW BEFORE YOU GO

Perhaps you're a first time visitor to Europe. Or maybe this is your first Holland America cruise. In either case, you probably have lots of questions about traveling to and within those storied lands— and about life aboard a Holland America Line ship. To help you prepare for the trip and to anticipate any special needs, we've compiled the answers to some of the travel questions you might have.

How Do I Make Dining Room Reservations?

We recommend making your dining room requests in advance through your travel agent. You may select First or Second Sitting, Smoking or Non-smoking areas, tables for two, four, six or eight. We'll do everything we can to honor your requests. Dining Room Reservations will be confirmed by the maitre d' only on the day of sailing and you'll find a confirmation card in your stateroom. Normal meal hours in the dining room are:

Breakfast	Open seating	8:00 am
Lunch	Open seating	12:30 pm
(Time subject to change)		
Dinner	First Sitting	6:15 pm
	Second Sitting	8:15pm

Are There Other Restaurants Besides The Formal Dining Room?

Yes. For informal breakfasts and luncheons, you're going to love the casual atmosphere of the Lido, the hallmark of every Holland America cruise ship.

The charming restaurant presents cornucopian buffets, and an ice cream bar plus a choice of hamburgers or a taco bar on deck. The Lido is also the scene of our popular Late Night Buffet.

What's The Dress Code Aboard Ship?

There is no rigid dress code on Holland America ships. For daytime wear, the emphasis should be on comfort, and don't forget your bathing suit for use of the ship's pools. The program for the day delivered each evening to your room will announce the suggested evening dress, either casual, informal or formal. For informal evenings, dresses or pantsuits for ladies and lightweight jackets for men. For formal evenings, cocktail dresses or gowns for ladies and a lightweight suit, or even tuxedo (always your option) for men.

While ashore, appropriate dress will depend somewhat on the area you are visiting. We respectfully suggest you do not over-pack. There are many shopping opportunities both aboard ship and ashore.

We're Visiting So Many Different Countries. What About Currency?

U.S. dollars are readily accepted as are travelers checks and major credit cards. If you choose to use U.S. dollars, carry smaller denominations—ones, fives, tens, twenties. This way, you'll be sure of getting change back in like kind. Money is easily exchanged at local banks. (Sorry, the Front Office does *not* handle foreign currency exchange.)

When May I Embark The Ship?

Embarkation generally begins 3 hours prior to departure, however, hours will vary depending on sailing times.

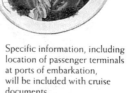

Specific information, including location of passenger terminals at ports of embarkation, will be included with cruise documents.

May I Invite Guests Aboard Prior To Sailing?

Holland America, upon evaluation of customer concerns, has implemented a "no visitor" policy, and regrets any inconvenience this may cause. However, friends may easily arrange to send a bon voyage gift directly to your stateroom. Or you may throw a party of your own for fellow guests. Champagne, canapes, mixers, etc., may be ordered by using the Gift Order List enclosed in your documentation packet.

WHAT YOU NEED TO KNOW *BEFORE YOU GO*

WILL MY HAIR DRYER/ ELECTRIC SHAVER WORK ABOARD SHIP?

Each stateroom is equipped with 110-volt, alternating current. So most hair dryers, electric shavers and other small appliances not exceeding 500 watts (110 volts) may be used in the stateroom outlets. No converters are necessary. (For safety reasons, please respect the ship's rule of *no ironing* in your stateroom. Ironing rooms are available.)

ARE SHORE EXCURSIONS AVAILABLE?

Yes. And there are many choices in each port. To help you plan yor activities ashore, a Shore Excursion booklet will be provided in your stateroom; and several port lectures will be held during the course of your cruise.

WHAT ABOUT "FORMAL" NIGHTS?

Contrary to popular belief, you don't need to bring a lot of fancy clothes. There are special occasions during your cruise when formal attire is suggested. Dark business suits or tuxedo, if you wish, are appropriate for men. For the ladies, tea-length dresses or long gowns. If you

enjoy dressing for those special evenings, here's your chance. But remember, the choice is always yours.

WE'RE ACTIVE PEOPLE. WON'T WE GET BORED ON A CRUISE?

Not on a Holland America cruise! We have more than enough activities to keep you occupied from sunup to sundown. Each evening before you retire, your room steward will deliver a program of all the things you can do—or not do—the next day. Chances are you'll have a hard time choosing, since many different activities are offered each hour. Just look at a few of the choices offered on one typical day:

6:30-8:00 a.m. Rise and shine for early morning coffee in the Lido Restaurant, a brisk walk or jog around the Promenade Deck, an eye-opening breakfast. Or sleep in.

9:30 a.m. What will it be? Aerobics class, a workout in the gym, get your Passport to Fitness stamped, trapshooting off the aft deck?

10:30 a.m. Play games, golf putting, tennis, backgammon, checkers, ping pong. Enter the Mileage Pool.

11:30 a.m. Rehearse for the Talent Show. Attend a craft class. Join the ship's Hostess for coffee. Win at Morning Cash Bingo.

Youngsters are simply enchanted by shipboard life.

12:00 Noon. Break for lunch. Al fresco on the Lido, or full service in the dining room.

1:30 p.m. Learn a new dance step. Tour the Bridge. Go to the horse races.

2:30 p.m. Attend a yoga class. Play Trivial Pursuit. Take an art and history tour of the ship. See a movie.

3:30 p.m. Time for more Cash Bingo. A port lecture. A photography class. Royal Dutch Tea.

4:30 p.m. Join the pool games. Have a massage or sauna. Get ready for what's next.

5:30 p.m. Meet friends for cocktails and dancing. Head for dinner.

7:30 p.m. to whenever. Dance to a mellow combo or the spirited sounds of swing. See a lively Broadway revue, a world-class singer, an illusionist or comedian. Bet on a good time in the casino. See a movie. Head for the disco, where the beat goes on long after you've sampled the Lido's late night buffet.

Holland America Line

Farewell Dinner

MS STATENDAM
Captain W.H. Eulderink, Commander
Dirk Zeller, Hotel Manager
Europe Cruise

APPETIZERS

Pearls of the Ocean
Sevruga caviar with the classical trimmings of chopped egg white, egg yolk, parsley and onion, served with toast points.

Norwegian Smoked Salmon
Thinly sliced smoked salmon on Boston lettuce with onion rings, capers, crushed peppercorns and toast points.

Pate au Poivre Vert
A coarse textured pate dotted with peppercorns on a mirror of cumberland sauce.

Fruit Cup
Sections of fresh fruit with a dash of Benedictine.

Crudite
Fresh garden vegetables with paprika dip.

HOT APPETIZERS

Tempura Shrimp
Lightly battered shrimp with hoisin sauce.

SOUPS

Cream of Asparagus
Fresh green asparagus tips are blended with beef broth, cream and herbs.

Clear Ox-Tail
Brought to taste with Madeira wine and served with a cheese stick.

SALADS

Caesar Salad
Torn romaine with Parmesan cheese, garlic croutons and tossed with our special anchovy dressing.

Tossed Greens
With sections of tomato, avocado and hearts of palm.
Choice of dressing: Italian, Dill with Lemon, Caesar, Thousand Island or our Low Calorie Dressing.

INTRODUCING HOLLAND AMERICA'S PASSPORT TO FITNESS

A most rewarding way to cruise. Holland America has one of the most exciting activity programs at sea, the Passport to Fitness.

Register on board ship, and we'll issue a passport in your name. Then you're off to join the fun, earning a stamp for each program activity you participate in. You can earn a beautiful Passport to Fitness T-shirt, sun visor, a handsome shoulder bag or a wind breaker.

And it's so easy, because there are so many different ways to earn stamps. Walk a mile. Join an aerobics class. Play paddle tennis, shuffleboard or volleyball. (Win a tournament and you'll earn two stamps!) You can even earn stamps by indulging in a pampering massage. In the dining room, earn stamps by choosing selections from the "Perfect Balance" portion of our menus.

Look for the flyer in your stateroom and arrange for your

Entrées

Broiled Lobster Tail
This delicacy of the ocean is served with garlic butter, sugar snap peas and saffron rice. You may also order it as a Surf and Turf if you desire by combining half a lobster tail with a petite filet of beef.

Poached Russian Halibut Steak "Veronique"
Topped with seedless grapes and Hollandaise sauce, served with pureed potatoes, carrots and a half moon cake.

Mixed Grill
A charcoal petite filet mignon, noisette of veal and a lamb chop, presented with fresh julienne of vegetables and a stuffed half potato.

Your Farewell Turkey
The traditional way to celebrate your Holland America Line Cruise, comes from Vermont and is accompanied by Giblet Gravy, corn bread staffing made of sage, chestnuts, celery and apply, served with glazed yams, Brussel sprouts and orange-cranberry compote.

The Spa Cuisine
In accordance with the American Heart Association, Holland America Line is proud to serve

Stirfried Vegetable Plate
Broccoli, carrots, onions, snowpeas, peppers, mushrooms and tofu are stirfried with fresh herbs in sunflower oil and served on a bed of pasta. Approximately 200 calories.

A Baked Idaho Potato
With sour cream and bacon bits will be served upon request with any entree.

Imported Cheeses And Fruit
Our international selection of cheeses from the silver tray with Dutch rusks, crackers, pumpernickel and crisp bread. Selection of fresh fruits, calimyrna figs, dates or stemginger in syrup.

Desserts

The Baked Alaska
This traditional desert of the High Seas is marched into the dining room by your Indonesian Stewards in a sparkling festive ceremony.

Tonight Our Late Buffet Will Feature
A Dessert Extravaganza

Presented by
our Executive Chef
Wolfgang Wasshausen
and his Kitchen Brigade.

Beverages
Coffee, tea, milk and freshly brewed decaffesnated coffee. Please ask your Diningroom Steward for our selection of herbal teas.

Passport to Fitness. You'll agree: there has never been a more fun, or more rewarding way to cruise.

We'll Be Celebrating An Anniversary/ Birthday. Can Special Arrangements Be Made?

Of course. Just make your request known to your travel agent and confirm with the maitre d' upon boarding. Usually a festive cake will be provided, compliments of the line. But your wish is our command—just ask us.

Can The Dining Room Accommodate Special Diets?

Salt-free, kosher or any other special dietary meals can be easily arranged in advance and requested by your travel agent at the time of booking. Please reconfirm this request with the maitre d' when you come aboard.

What If I Forget My Toothbrush?

Holland America's tradition of excellence means providing guests with every convenience, evidenced in the wonderful gift and luxury items in our duty-free shops. And if you forget to pack something, our on board shops are well stocked with all the essentials—from suntan lotion and toiletries to books, magazines and film. All purchases on board are assessed in U.S. dollars.

Who Should I Tip And How Much?

Among Holland America's longstanding traditions of excellence is a "tipping not required" policy. Our Indonesian and Filipino crew comes from a culture where rendering generous, attentive service is an honor. So they expect no reward beyond the knowledge that you are pleased. You are free, however, to extend monetary recognition if you wish; it's entirely up to you. (Company policy prohibits us from suggesting how much.)

How Do I Pay For Shipboard Purchases?

As for money on board ship, you can forget about carrying it. Because Holland America ships sail with the tradition of a "cashless society." Simply sign a receipt for each of your purchases just as you would at a fine hotel on land, then settle your account with one convenient transaction at the end of the cruise—with VISA, American Express or MasterCard; or with cash, traveler's check or a personal check.

What About My Laundry?

Complete laundry, pressing and dry cleaning facilities are available on board. And ironing rooms, coin-operated washing machines and dryers are available on board for your use.

What If I Need To Call Home?

If you need to contact friends, relatives or business associates during the cruise, you may do so by using our radio ship-to-shore telephone. Similarly, others may contact you in the same way. Your documentation packet will contain more specific information, including the phone number for your ship during its specific location.

Will I Get Seasick?

All Holland America ships are equipped with stabilizing "fins" that counteract more than 80 percent of the roll of a ship, and motion sickness, which used to be a problem on the high seas, is now relatively uncommon. However, medications are available if needed.

May We Have More Than Two In A Stateroom?

To help you share the excitement of your cruise and Europe with your family and friends, we offer considerably reduced fares for each guest sharing a stateroom with two full-fare guests. However, staterooms with appropriate accommodations are limited so act on these savings early.

What If I Prefer A Single Stateroom Accommodation?

A limited selection of double staterooms is available for single occupancy in the following categories at the percentage indicated of the double occupancy fare.

Grand Europe Cruise

Categories PS, S, A & B	200% less $300.
Categories C – H	150%
Categories I – N	125%

Baltic, European Capitals, Mediterranean/Western Europe and Transatlantic Cruises

Category PS	195%
Categories S, A & B	190%
Categories C – N	150%

Can I Share A Stateroom?

A limited selection of double staterooms in categories F & K are available on a guaranteed basis for single, non-smoking guests willing to share. Guests pay the per person double occupancy published fare. Holland America will assign a person of the same sex to share with you.

How Much Time Should I Allow For Airline And Ship Connections?

For arrivals and departures in all (dis)embarkation ports, it is recommended that, for those guests not requiring our Home City air program, a minimum of three hours in U.S. cities and 4-5 hours in European cities be allowed to ensure adequate time for transfer between the airport and pier, customs inspections and airport security checks.

General Information

Reservations

Travel agencies provide valuable service and counseling to prospective travelers. We encourage you to make your Holland America reservations with a travel agent who understands your individual needs. Since accommodations are limited by the number of staterooms, reservations should be made as early as possible. Travel agencies are not owned or controlled by Holland America. Your deposits and payments are to be paid to the travel agency with whom you made your reservations. Travel documents will be issued only if and when full payment has been received by Holland America from the travel agency. Refunds for cancelled or unused services will normally be made to the same travel agency on the basis of the amount actually received by Holland America less any applicable cancellation fees and charges. You are responsible for obtaining from your travel agency monies either retained by the agency or received by the agency from Holland America.

Deposit and Final Payment Requirements

The per person, per cruise deposit requirements to secure reservations and Cancellation Fees Waiver amounts are listed with the cruise fares and must be received within 10 days after reservation date. Cancellation Fees Waiver, if desired, must be paid at the time of first deposit; see Cancellation Fees Waiver and Additional Baggage Protection for details.

Final payment for Grand Europe Cruise is due no later than January 4, 1993 and 75 days prior to departure on all other cruises.

In most cases, we are able to provide you with travel documents, including your Cruise Contract, at approximately 30 days prior to departure. Travel documents, however, are only issued after final payment has been received by Holland America Line.

Travel agents should make checks payable and send to:
Holland America Line
P.O. Box C34013
Seattle, WA 98124-1013 USA
For faster processing, please include a confirmation number on your check. Travel agents, please note that MCO's and credit cards will not be accepted.

Cruise Fares

Traveling with Holland America Line is one of the best vacation values around. Your cruise fare includes night after glorious night aboard the elegant ms Statendam, all meals and entertainment onboard ship, a gala welcome aboard reception and, where applicable, air transportation and transfers between airport, hotel and ship. Not included, however, are items of a personal nature or optional programs or activities, such as alcoholic beverages, soft drinks, laundry and dry cleaning, shore excursions or optional on-board activities such as trap shooting. All fares and prices in this brochure are in U.S. dollars, per person.

Change Charges

Changing your itinerary after reservations have been made can result in loss of advantages gained by early planning. In addition, the results of last-minute changes may be disappointing. To cover administrative costs, a charge of up to $50 per person will be made if you request a change in your travel arrangements less than 60 days prior to commencement of travel. Change charges are not assessed for stateroom upgrades or for the addition of services, unless air reservations are altered and/or travel documents must be reissued.

Cancellation Policy

A full refund (except for amounts paid for Cancellation Fees Waiver) will be made for written cancellations of the 35-day Grand Europe cruise received by Holland America at least 121 days prior to the date on which you are to commence travel (by air, rail, sea or otherwise). Guests who cancel after that date for any reason, including medical reasons, are subject to the following cancellation fees:

◆ 120-75 days prior to commencing travel   50% of gross fare
◆ up to 74 days prior to commencing travel   100% of gross fare

For the other Europe and Transatlantic cruises outlined in this brochure, a full refund (except for amounts paid for Cancellation Fees Waiver) will be made for written cancellations received by Holland America at least 91 days prior to the date on which you are to commence travel (by air, rail, sea or otherwise). Guests who cancel after that date for any reason, including medical reasons, are subject to the following cancellation fees:

◆ 90-60 days prior to commencing travel $200
◆ 59-30 days prior to commencing travel $300
◆ 29-15 days prior to commencing travel   50% of gross fare
◆ up to 14 days prior to commencing travel   100% of gross fare

Given that the resale of cancelled space will likely result in a lost opportunity to sell other space, these fees are due regardless of resale.

Name changes require the prior approval of Holland America, and may not always be possible. Cruise contracts are non-transferable. Name changes are considered reservation cancellations and are subject to cancellation fees.

Cancellation Fees Waiver and Additional Baggage Protection

Cancellation Fees Waiver (CFW) protection allows you, for any reason, to provide written cancellation up to 24 hours prior to commencement of travel without being subject to cancellation fees. CFW is optional, must be paid at time of first deposit, and is not refundable. The per person, per cruise costs are listed with the cruise fares.

In addition, Holland America assumes an additional $500 of liability for lost, damaged or delayed baggage of passengers who purchase CFW. The baggage policies of Holland America are explained in detail below.

CFW is not insurance, it provides no rights other than those explained above. For example, it does not protect double-triple-quad occupancy rates should any one or more members of your party cancel nor does it cover expenses or unused services due to trip interruption.

Travel Insurance

We suggest you discuss with your travel agent the various travel insurance programs that are available from insurance companies. Policies can be purchased that provide protection in the event of trip cancellation, trip interruption, personal injury or damage to property. Holland America Line does not endorse any particular type of policy or insurer nor do we receive any economic benefit from your purchase of these policies.

Early Reservation Savings Plan

The following savings are available to those guests who book and submit deposits early.

For Grand Europe cruise guests, deposit by October 1, 1992 and save 10% of applicable fare. For Baltic Cruise guests, deposit by March 1, 1993 and save $250. For European Capitals, Eastern and Western Mediterranean and Rome to Lisbon cruise guests, deposit by May 1, 1993 and save $250. For Transatlantic Cruise guests, deposit by June 1, 1993 and save $250.

The Early Reservations Savings Plan does not apply to 3rd/4th guests, pre/post cruise hotels or packages or shore excursions.

Dining Room Seating

Your travel agent will accept your dining room reservation request.

We'll do everything we can to honor your requests. Dining Room Reservations will be confirmed by the maitre d' only on the day of sailing and will be placed in your stateroom upon boarding. Normal meal hours in the dining room:

Breakfast	Open seating	8:00 am
Lunch	Open seating	12:30pm
Dinner	First sitting	6:15 pm
	Second sitting	8:15 pm

(Breakfast and lunch times may vary depending upon port times.)

Special Diets

Salt-free, kosher or any other special dietary meals require 30 days advance arrangements and may be arranged through your travel agent at the time of booking. Reconfirm this request with the maitre d' when you come aboard.

Electricity

The same personal grooming appliances you use at home will work in your stateroom. Our current is 110 AC.

Laundry & Pressing

Laundry, pressing and dry cleaning facilities are available on board. Coin operated washing machines and dryers are available on board for your use.

"Cashless Society"

You won't need large amounts of cash. On board, you simply sign for purchases and services provided. At the end of your cruise, settle your itemized bill at the Front Office.

Cash, personal checks, traveler's checks, American Express, VISA, or MasterCard are accepted. All charges on board are assessed in U.S. dollars.

Tips

We sail under a "tipping not required" policy. That means the company policies expressly forbids any form of solicitation. Of course, staff members may accept gratuities when they are voluntarily offered for exceptional and outstanding service.

Embarkation

Embarkation generally begins 3 hours prior to departure, however, hours will vary depending on sailing times. Specific information, including location of passenger terminals at ports of embarkation, will be included with cruise documents.

SHORE EXCURSIONS

All shore excursions are optional at an additional charge. For 35-day Grand Europe Cruise guests, a number of the extended overland tours have very limited membership because of restrictions on hotel accommodations and/or transportation facilities in some of the travel areas. A fully detailed brochure will be available and mailed to Grand Europe Cruise guests in advance of departure. For all cruise guests there are many choices in each port. To help you plan your activities ashore, a Shore Excursion Booklet will be provided in your stateroom; and several port lectures will be held during the course of your cruise. Due to the popularity of these excursions, we suggest you contact the Shore Excursion Office early in the cruise.

Holland America Line-Westours Inc., or tour operators may change or cancel any excursion and may decline to permit guest(s) to take, or remain on an excursion, all without notice or liability whatsoever to Holland America Line-Westours Inc., the ship, the Shipowner, any subsidiaries or affiliated companies, employees, officers, crew and/or underwriters.

PETS

Animals or pets are not allowed with the exception of service animals for disabled passengers. Please notify your travel agent at time of booking if you intend to board a service animal.

REGISTRATION OF VALUABLES

In order to avoid problems when reentering the United States, we strongly recommend that U.S. residents register their valuables with U.S. Customs before departure. You must do this at a Customs office near your home. Items that should be registered generally include those not manufactured in the United States. Customs pays particular attention to cameras (including special lenses and video equipment), binoculars, radios, foreign-made watches and appliances.

VISITORS

Holland America Line, upon evaluation of customer concerns, has implemented a "no visitor" policy and regrets any inconvenience this may cause.

UPGRADE POLICY

Holland America Line reserves the right to upgrade a guest or guests to more expensive category accommodations at no additional cost.

MEDICAL SERVICES

The Statendam is equipped with limited medical facilities that are staffed by a physician and registered nurses. The physician is an independent contractor. If you become ill during the voyage and the physician

is unable to care for your needs on board, you will be transfered to medical facilities on shore. If your condition will require that you have special medical apparatus or assistance on board, we must be made aware of that at time of booking in order to determine whether we can accommodate your needs. If you are using prescription drugs, please bring an adequate supply with you and keep them in your carry-on luggage.

IMMIGRATION

All guests must carry a valid passport for the duration of the cruise. Check with your travel agent or Holland America for Visa requirements.

Non-U.S. citizens who have previously been admitted to the United States for permanent residence and who will be returning to the United States must carry your passport and Alien Registration Receipt Card form I-151. Resident aliens not in possession of this form should obtain one at the nearest office of the U.S. Immigration Service.

It may be necessary for guests to have valid vaccination certificates as required by the countries visited. Complete health information will be furnished in ample time before sailing.

PASSENGERS WITH DISABILITIES/PREGNANCY

Holland America Line does not discriminate against persons on the basis of disability. We seek, to the extent feasible, to accommodate the needs of persons with disabilities so they are able to enjoy our ships and other facilities in the same manner and to the same extent as persons who do not have disabilities. Holland America has a limited number of staterooms designed for handicap access. In addition, service animals are permitted onboard ships if prior arrangements have been made at time of booking. In limited situations where an individual with a disability would be unable to satisfy certain specified safety and other criteria, even when provided with appropriate auxiliary aids and services, we may find it necessary to ask the individual to make alternative travel arrangements. It is essential that we be notified of any special medical, physical or other requirements of passengers at the time of booking. Due to the limited medical facilities on the ships, we will not accept reservations for women who will be

30 or more weeks pregnant as of the time their travel with Holland America concludes.

UNACCOMPANIED BAGGAGE

For the convenience of Grand Europe Cruise guests, unaccompanied baggage will be accepted in New York in advance of sailing date. No arrangements are available for forwarding unaccompanied baggage from London. Complete information will be provided with cruise documents.

BAGGAGE POLICY

Holland America will carry as baggage only your personal effects for your wearing, comfort or convenience during your travel with Holland America. Your baggage needs to be placed in securely constructed and locked suitcases or trunks. During your travel, you should not leave money, jewelry or other valuables left lying about the ship, in your stateroom, in hotels, on buses or elsewhere. Holland America Line ships provide, at no extra charge, either safe-deposit boxes in the ship's Front Office or stateroom safes. Certain hotels may also provide similar facilities. Your use of safe-deposit boxes, stateroom safes or similar facilities will not increase Holland America's liability as described below.

Holland America cannot be responsible for any loss or damage that occurs before baggage comes into Holland America's actual custody when you begin your travel with us or after baggage leaves Holland America's actual custody at the end of your travel with us. In particular, please note that we assume no responsibility for loss, damage or delay while baggage is in the custody of airlines. Holland America also does not assume any responsibility for loss or of damage to perishable items, medicine, liquor, cash, jewelry, film, videotape, video equipment, cameras, or similar valuables, securities or other financial instruments.

If Holland America, due to any cause whatsoever, is liable for loss of, damage to, or delay of, your property, the amount of Holland America's liability will not exceed $100 ($600 for guests who have purchased Cancellation Fees Waiver) unless you have specified to Holland America in writing the true value of your property and paid to Holland America before departure 1% of the value in excess of $100 or $600, as applicable. In that event, Holland America's liability will be limited to the amount so specified.

RESPONSIBILITY

The ms Statendam is owned by Wind Surf Limited, which is an affiliate of Holland America Line-Westours Inc. Transportation aboard the ship is provided solely by the Shipowner and pursuant to the Cruise Contract that you will receive prior to embarkation. Please read the Cruise Contract carefully and as soon as you receive it.

Off-Ship Services (such as airlines and other off-ship transportation carriers, shore excursions, meals,

accommodations, air ambulance and shoreside physicians) are generally performed by independent contractors. Those Off-Ship Services which are performed by independent contractors are solely at your risk and subject to the terms or arrangements made by you or on your behalf with the independent contractor furnishing the Off-Ship Service. Holland America Line assumes no responsibility with respect to these Off-Ship Services (including for delay, injury, death or damage to property) even though it may collect monies or make arrangements for the services.

Situations may arise which, in the opinion of Holland America Line, make it necessary for Holland America to cancel, advance or postpone a scheduled departure, change itineraries or make substitutions involving hotels, restaurants, ports of call, other travel components, vessels or other modes of transportation. If this should occur, Holland America does not assume responsibility or liability for any losses, inconvenience or expenses incurred by guests as a result. Your full cruise fare will be refunded, however, if the cruise is cancelled prior to initial embarkation. Holland America is not required to make refunds once travel commences regardless of the reason for a guest being unable to complete his/her travel.

INCREASES IN FARES, PORT CHARGES OR TAXES

Fares quoted in this brochure are those in effect at the time of printing. If cost factors, including airline costs, dictate the need for fare increases, Holland America Line may do so at any time prior to departure. Guests can cancel (without paying a cancellation fee) rather than accept a fare increase. If a governmental authority increases port charges, fees or taxes, Holland America reserves the right to pass on these increases.

SHIP'S REGISTRY

The ms Statendam is registered in the Bahamas.

Holland America Line has registered trademarks in the United States and various foreign countries for the names and phrases "Holland America," "Holland America Line," "Westours," and "A Tradition of Excellence," as well as for the modern and antique ship design logo.

Should you need to contact Holland America prior to sailing, please use this address:
Holland America Line-Westours Inc.
300 Elliott Avenue West
Seattle, Washington 98119
U.S.A.

Welcome To The World Of Holland America

Come escape to the world of Holland America Line. There are tranquil seas to voyage, exotic lands to explore, and day after day to let the real world pass you by. Ask your travel agent for our brochures and just look at the possibilities

GRAND WORLD CRUISE

The Rotterdam's 1993 Grand World Cruise is 77 to 99 days of total adventure. It is also the sum of many wonderful parts. 14 exciting segments, ranging from 12 to 44 days. Choose any segment, or a combination of two or three. As it has been said, there is no trip in the world like the one around it and there is no better way than aboard the Rotterdam, the grande dame of the seas.

GRAND CIRCLE ORIENT/ SOUTH PACIFIC CRUISE

In the Fall of 1993, the Rotterdam sets sail to lands of pure enchantment—from Seattle and Vancouver, B.C. to Japan, the Soviet Far East, China, Hong Kong, Australia, New Zealand and through the South Pacific returning to Los Angeles. 14 exotic ports, 57 memorable days.

CARIBBEAN CRUISES

There's nothing like a sun-drenched beach or the beat of a steel drum to give you a new lease on life. And nobody offers more inspiring ways through the Caribbean than Holland America Line. Pack your suntan lotion and join us, fall through spring.

ALASKA-CANADA'S YUKON-CANADIAN ROCKIES

Step ashore with Holland America Westours—the leader in Alaska touring—to explore Gold Rush Country, Denali National Park, Land of the Midnight Sun, and more. Over 30 exciting cruisetours, spring through fall.

ALASKA CRUISES

Experience one of the last great frontiers on earth, wrapped in the warmth of Holland America Line hospitality. Featuring 7-day Inside Passage Glacier Bay and Glacier Route cruises.

PANAMA CANAL

Without a doubt, to transit the Panama Canal is a memorable vacation. Especially when that cruise is made aboard one of the magnificent ships of Holland America Line, the World's Best. Reserve this epic voyage in the spring or fall.

HAWAII CRUISES

Blessed by the sun, lapped by the sea, Hawaii is everybody's favorite destination. Especially when experienced aboard the ss Rotterdam, Holland America's proud flagship. Go for 8, 10 or 16 days, in September 1992 and April 1993.

INDEX